ARCHITECTURE NOW!
HOUSES

3

IMPRINT

PROJECT MANAGEMENT
Florian Kobler, Cologne

COLLABORATION
Harriet Graham, Turin
Inga Hallsson, Cologne

PRODUCTION
Ute Wachendorf, Cologne

DESIGN
Sense/Net Art Direction
Andy Disl and
Birgit Eichwede, Cologne
www.sense-net.de

GERMAN TRANSLATION
Kristina Brigitta Köper, Berlin

FRENCH TRANSLATION
Jacques Bosser, Montesquiou

© VG BILD-KUNST
Bonn 2013, for the works
of Ben van Berkel, Carsten
Höller, and Marcel Odenbach

PRINTED IN ITALY
ISBN 978–3–8365–3591–5

© 2013 TASCHEN GMBH
Hohenzollernring 53
D–50672 Cologne
www.taschen.com

ARCHITECTURE NOW!
HOUSES

HÄUSER / MAISONS

Philip Jodidio

3

TASCHEN

CONTENTS

INTRODUCTION

LIVING IN THE NETWORK

Times are hard, or at least they are for some people. One might think that contemporary architecture would suffer, or even that creativity would be blunted by the brute forces of practicality and good economics. Private houses are something of a microcosm of the architecture world, reflecting the ups and downs of the rest of the profession, in a somewhat rarified or amplified way. Indeed, it is rarely if ever the "middle class" that calls on a qualified architect for the design of a new house. This is a privilege usually reserved to the well off. Times of crisis have not abated the trend seen at least over the past 30 years or more that allows, to put it bluntly, the rich to get richer. In the United States, for example, 64% of income growth in the period before the recent crisis (1979–2007) went to the top 10% of earners.[1] An even more pronounced gap exists for the very wealthy, the top 0.01% of earners in the US who currently claim a greater share of income in the country than at any time on record.[2] The truth is thus that these are no lean times for the wealthy and that, as a result, luxurious homes are still being built, all over the world, for the rich. The selection of projects made for this book has willfully looked elsewhere, beyond the "palaces" that have sprung up from Sri Lanka to Toronto, to interesting efforts to design very small but practical residences, as often is the case in Japan, for example. The Japanese acceptance of family homes that are well under 100 square meters in size is, of course, due to historical, cultural, and demographic factors. The population density and land cost in cities such as Tokyo makes big houses almost impossible. This tendency to natural modesty, as it were, is perhaps compensated by a willingness of clients in Japan to call on young, innovative architects. Though there is no reason that a vast home cannot be an architectural marvel, it seems clear that real innovation can come with the forces of constraint that mean budgets are limited, or that land is in short supply.

THE WAVE AND THE TREES

Some architects have also concentrated their talents on areas of need. Shigeru Ban from Tokyo is an example in this sector, proposing new disaster relief architecture almost every time there is a major earthquake or tsunami—again with the so-called Tohoku earthquake and tsunami that struck northeastern Japan on March 11, 2011. Tadao Ando, author of two of the more spectacular homes in this volume, located in Monterrey, Mexico, and in Sri Lanka was a member of the panel created by the Japanese government to guide the reconstruction efforts after the 2011 earthquake. Beyond considerations related to the immediate need to rebuild, however, Ando took a decidedly long view of the issues raised: "I think Japan needs to rethink its connection to family, love for one's country, role in Asia and the responsibilities as an individual living on this planet. Japan has forgotten about this over the last 30 years," he told the *Wall Street Journal*. Tadao Ando has previously been involved in efforts to plant trees in large numbers, in the Seto Inland Sea of Japan for example. In the case of the Tohoku earthquake, he stated: "As a way to restart Japan's spirit I came up with an idea of a 'Forest of Repose.' I think it would be good to build a people's forest in each of the devastated prefectures—Miyagi, Iwate, and Fukushima—and this has been authorized in the Diet." Ando suggested that the care required to maintain the trees, "which would also act as a natural barrier between sea and the towns that would be rebuilt farther inland, and watching them grow would remind residents of what occurred there in 2011. He said this kind of living memorial with 'natural shape' is more appropriate than erecting a building," according to the *Wall Street Journal*.[3] In the United States, where the scars opened by Hurricane Katrina

1
Li Xiaodong, Water House, Yuhu
Village, Lijiang, China, 2006–09

have healed with great difficulty, the ongoing project started by actor Brad Pitt, called Make It Right, has yielded interesting results. The Float House (New Orleans, Louisiana, USA, 2008–09, page 284), designed by the Pritzker Prize winner Thom Mayne and Morphosis, seeks to find ways to make homes not only affordable, but ready for predictable natural disasters. Attached to steel masts anchored in 13.7-meter-deep concrete piles, this residence is able to float on flood waters, rising as much as 3.65 meters above its usual setting without any damage, returning to its original location as waters recede. As Morphosis states: "Global climate change is triggering ever-harsher floods and natural disasters. Nearly 200 million people worldwide live in high-risk coastal flooding zones, and, in the US alone, over 36 million people currently face the threat of flooding. The Float House prototype proposes a sustainable way of living that adapts to this uncertain reality."

THE GOOD, THE BAD, AND THE UGLY

The idea behind the *Architecture Now!* series of books is that no specific geographic area or architectural style is privileged. The only limits on the contents of *Architecture Now! Houses 3* may have to do with the breadth of knowledge of the author, but since these books have quite literally been best sellers for more than 10 years, there is no shortage of proposals and offers of information. The result, in the best case, is that *Architecture Now! Houses 3* might be considered a broad overview of the different types of residences that have been built in the past three or four years all over the world. What determines the content in this case would be the best of what has been done anywhere in the world. The word "best" of course is a subjective one and readers who may disagree with the choice made here are asked for their indulgence. That said, a book like *Architecture Now! Houses 3* offers advantages that are related directly to its "subjective" choice of the best new residences in the world considered from an architectural point of view. Internet sites that claim to provide an overview of just about everything happening in contemporary architecture surely exist—but, curiously, they mostly tend to have the same photos and the same texts (at the same time). They also tend to make few distinctions between what we might flippantly call "the good, the bad, and the ugly." The book is not dead quite yet.

FROM CHINA TO CHILE

A message that this particular volume most probably conveys is that "good" architecture can now be found almost anywhere on the planet where the means and the will to build more than a simple shelter can be found. There are houses in Chile, Paraguay, Mexico, Peru, and Brazil in this book. There are houses in the United States and Canada, in France, the Netherlands, Germany, Switzerland, Portugal, and Spain. There are houses in New Zealand, Japan, Korea, and China, or even Sri Lanka and Ghana. Of course this list is not exhaustive, and vast areas are not represented, but on the whole great homes are springing up almost everywhere on earth and there is something profoundly new in this trend to geographic expansion. A few years ago, it would have been unheard of to see a splendid 1200-square-meter private residence in China. Today, a 48-year-old Chinese architect called Wang Shu has won the Pritzker Prize, the most prestigious award of the profession. Here and now, a house built in Korea has been designed by an American architect (Daeyang Gallery and House, Seoul, South Korea, 2010–12, page 214), and another house in Pasadena is the work of a noted Chinese architect (Glen Oaks Residence, Pasadena, California, USA,

2

2
*Antón García-Abril, La Trufa
(The Truffle), Costa da Morte,
Spain, 2010*

2009–11, page 262). Frontiers, barriers, and distance fall in the face of communication on a planetary scale. Architecture can no longer thrive in circumstances of isolation and unfettered nationalism. Travel and the Internet make everything everywhere instantly available.

Nor is this book in any respect conceived with the intention of promoting a style or a type of house. Rather, as is the case in the broader, more inclusive world of contemporary architecture, the most diverse styles coexist here. References to the past, to the history of architecture have entered, indeed permeated, the new houses seen here. This is no longer the superficial pastiche of now very "ancient" Post-Modernism, it is the fruit of a very real process of thought and inclusion that ultimately represents the complete rejection of the *tabula rasa* so famously declared by Walter Gropius and others early in the 20th century. The "modern" is very much with us, though Modernism has evolved so considerably as to be almost unrecognizable, even when architects like John Pawson or David Chipperfield are concerned. "Modern" means "of or relating to recent times or the present." Architecture, like other creative disciplines, has always relied heavily on the past—the art of building could not be ignored even in the heyday of the International Style. The sea change in attitudes toward the past may indeed have come with the emergence of Post-Modernism in the late 1960s and with Robert Venturi's manifesto *Complexity and Contradiction in Architecture* (1966). In 1972, Venturi returned with a second short book called *A Significance for A&P Parking Lots, or Learning from Las Vegas*. In its better known form, this book was revised and published in 1977 under the title *Learning from Las Vegas: the Forgotten Symbolism of Architectural Form*. In a way, the titles of these books say it all, but the sometimes extravagant forms that emerged from the offices of Michael Graves, Robert A. M. Stern, or Venturi himself had more to do with properly embalming the corpse of Modernism than with giving birth to new life in architecture.

IT'S IN THE DNA

That new life exists today because architects have rediscovered their own DNA, the generations and centuries of the art of building that preceded and enriched their own capacity to create. It is enough to look at the Water House by Li Xiaodong (Yuhu Village, Lijiang, China, 2006–09, page 7) and ask if the past and the present have not engendered real modernity here. Even those who are not familiar with the history of China can surely feel the weight of these stones and the presence of water all through the house. What makes this kind of project different from earlier Post-Modernism or "contextualism" is the realization in architectural circles that the past is not merely a question of façade—it is a real continuity that concerns materials and forms, but also functions.

Houses in Japan published in this volume, including House NA by Sou Fujimoto (Tokyo, Japan, 2010, page 186), are moving into new territory in a different way, redefining living space at the same time as they experiment with a radical openness that is at the limit of obviating the usual requirements for private space. Again, this is due to Japanese tradition where *shoji* screens or sliding panels have permitted "flexible space" for centuries, but it is also a testimony to the extreme density of populations, in particular along the eastern corridor between Tokyo and Osaka. Tradition in these instances is omnipresent as the background and underlying force behind innovation. That may be the simplest way to define the real changes that have come about since Venturi praised the A&P Parking Lot. His earlier title *Complexity and Contradiction* may be closer to the substance of what is happening today. Rather than a clean slate and a sharp grid, architects nearly all over the world have accepted, or even amplified, the inherent presence of ambiguity in any building. This does not mean that functionality is in anyway set aside, but, particularly in private houses, flexibility has become the watchword. Families may recompose; spaces may need to be used for other purposes. Rather than the postwar American suburban model that called for distinct dining, living, and kitchen spaces, architects today and their clients distinguish between "public" and "private" areas in a house. A living space, just as often as not, is the open conjugation of living, dining, cooking, and even entertainment. Bedrooms and bathrooms remain "private" for obvious reasons, but where climate permits, even here, the formerly strict limits between inside and outside are blurred by full glazing or sliding surfaces.

LOOKING FOR THE GARDEN

The most ambitious and costly of the homes published here almost inevitably create a fruitful dialogue with their natural setting, on a seashore, in a forest, or above a lake. There is a relation here to Modern architecture (with an upper case "M") where glazing, as in the Farnsworth House by Mies van der Rohe (Plano, Illinois, USA, 1951), set the example for much of today's residential design, or integration into a natural setting, as in Wright's Fallingwater (Mill Run, Pennsylvania, USA, 1935). It is as though the purest expression of privilege for the wealthy house owner might be the rediscovery of nature in a fully protected and contemporary environment—a search for the lost "Garden" that in truth animates much of the history of architecture in general. Where nature is too far, as in urban Japan, architects and clients seek it nonetheless, in the form of potted plants or views of the sky.

Those familiar with the *Architecture Now!* books will have noted that the work of artists is sometimes included, where there is a clear relation between art and architecture. In this book, there is one house for an artist (Jean-Pierre Raynaud) but also several houses designed by architects for themselves. Tradition (or humor) would have it that architects are often poorly lodged in their own creations, but perhaps the architects' houses here are an exception to the rule. The Spanish architect Antón García-Abril, for example, has not hesitated to experiment in his tiny (25 m²) shelter called La Trufa (The Truffle, Costa da Morte, Spain, 2010, page 8). "The Truffle is a piece of nature built with earth, full of air," he says. A space within a stone that sits on the ground and blends with the territory. It camouflages, by emulating the processes of mineral formation in its structure, and integrates with the natural environment, complying with its laws. Aside from the way he conceived the structure, made of concrete with 50 cubic meters of hay as the only formwork, Antón García refers here explicitly to the "Cabanon" of Le Corbusier (Roquebrune, Cap Martin, France, 1951), the small log cabin where the Swiss architect spent his last night before drowning nearby in 1965.

PURPLE, ORGANIC, AND ALIEN

A much more extensive architect's residence is Ma Qingyun's Glen Oaks Residence. This 340-square-meter addition to a mid-20th-century house is described by the current Dean of the School of Architecture at the University of Southern California (USC) as "purple, organic, and alien." Ma Qingyun is the founder of MADA s.p.a.m., one of the first major firms to emerge from the liberalization of Chinese law that allowed individual architects to begin to sign their own work as opposed to participating only in large "institutes." Including a double-height semipublic gallery, kitchen, study, and third-floor dance studio for Ma's wife Shouning Li, the structure has circular windows and is clad in "shotcrete" that gives it a continuous, relatively rough "skin." The ramped circulation of the addition, connecting to the old house, represents the Chinese architect's take on American suburban house design and proposes ways to give new functionality to a residence designed for another era. With his professional background, Ma Qingyun is fully aware of American architectural traditions and typology. The fact that he dares to challenge and reinvent as fundamental an "icon" as the American postwar family house might be considered a sign of the times. California may be the place where Rudolf Schindler, Richard Neutra, John Lautner, and Frank Gehry thrived, each designing groundbreaking houses in their time, but Ma Qingyun's addition to his own house deals in an even more fundamental way with the changes in lifestyle that directly influence the architecture of the home, in America and elsewhere.

Susanne Nobis, born in Munich in 1963 worked in the offices of Renzo Piano and Herzog & de Meuron before creating her own office in Berg in 2000. It is not far from her office that she designed a house for herself, on the very pleasant banks of Lake Starnberg (Toward Landscape, Lake Starnberg, Berg, Germany, 2006–10, page 296). Inspiring herself by the form of traditional boathouses seen along the lake, she created two volumes, one with an open gallery and another designated as the "bedroom house." She has used a titanium skin "folded" over a timber structure to create spaces that are both warm and modern. Both volumes open, with fully glazed façades, toward the lake. Seeing this house, which breaks down many of the barriers between different building types (the boathouse and the residence) one might almost feel that being an architect is a wonderful thing—especially if one can live in such a home.

A TURTLE AND A FLOWERPOT

Pasadena could hardly be considered an "exotic" location for an innovative house, but Cape Coast (Ghana), 165 kilometers west of Accra on the Gulf of Guinea might seem to be one of the points further on earth from the contemporary art scene in Europe. And yet, this, more precisely in the town of Biriwa, is where the noted German artist Carsten Höller and Marcel Odenbach, a well-known video artist, decided to build a vacation house (House Turtle, 1999–2009, page 220). As Höller writes, it "was designed with the following considerations: a) to have a maximum of air flow through and under the house to avoid the necessity of air conditioning; b) to make the construction unattractive for mosquitoes and keep other animals, including snakes, at bay; c) to favor 87 or 93° angles over 90° angles, in order to increase/decrease the perception of distance and straightness; d) to collect rainwater from the roof and the terraces underground; e) to make the house look 'unfinished.'" Set up on thin columns overlooking the ocean, the house has a most singular presence. It is quite literally alone above the beach, a place to escape from another world, or to find a new one, at the ends of the earth as we know it.

3
MADA s.p.a.m., Glen Oaks Residence,
Pasadena, California, USA, 2009–11

3

Jean-Pierre Raynaud, born in 1939, is a noted French artist who has sought in his own way in the past to isolate himself from the events and noise of Paris, for example, for a time by living underground in a house essentially of his own design (Le Mastaba, built in collaboration with the architect Jean Dedieu, 1986) in La Garenne Colombes, just 10 kilometers from the city center. At La Garenne Colombes, Raynaud created and exhibited his own works, ranging from giant flowerpots coated in gold leaf to foreign flags made into works of art by his intervention. More recently, seeking the assistance of his friend, the architect and interior designer Jean-Michel Wilmotte, Raynaud created a new place to work in Barbizon (France, 2009, page 406). Fifty-eight kilometers from Paris, Barbizon is known as the home of a school of painting of the same name that included such significant 19th-century painters as Théodore Rousseau and Jean-François Millet. Stripping an old house called the Clos d'Hortense of later additions, the architect added a generous glass-covered space where Raynaud exhibits many of his works. This *verrière* also opens the house toward its wooded setting and the artist's own 4000-square-meter garden, where Raynaud has worked in collaboration with the landscape designer Neveux Rouyer to create the kind of unity between art, architecture, and nature that he is fond of. "More than a problem of architecture, it is a matter of space that is involved," states Jean-Pierre Raynaud. "As is the case with works of art, it is inside a surface that everything happens, whence the importance in past centuries of a frame that delineated the territory of the work of art. In the past 50 years, painting has freed itself of this barrier in order to see an osmosis between the project of the artist and life. This is obvious in the *Water Lilies* of Monet, in the works of Jackson Pollock, or in the monochromes of Yves Klein. Space has always been a part of thinking for me—space where everything is possible." Indeed, Jean-Pierre Raynaud has long worked at the frontier between architecture and art, making his own house in La Celle Saint Cloud, also near Paris, beginning in 1969, until its demolition 24 years later. With the rubble from the demolition, Raynaud organized a noted 1993 exhibition at the CAPC in Bordeaux. In this exceptional case, the architecture of the artist's atelier can be considered a part of his work in art—here in close collaboration with Jean-Michel Wilmotte. Jean-Pierre Raynaud concludes: "I am incapable of being a consumer in the conventional sense. My spaces were never built to encounter daily life, but just so that they can exist."[4]

ON A CLIFF, ABOVE THE SEA

A location almost as surprising for a major work of contemporary residential architecture as the Gulf of Guinea is the southernmost tip of Sri Lanka, facing the Indian Ocean. And yet the neighboring localities of Mirissa and Weligama have recently seen the construction of two houses by important architects, both of them Japanese. As it happens the clients for these homes are a Belgian father and son, directors of a successful local tire company. The first to be completed is the House in Sri Lanka (Mirissa, Sri Lanka, 2006–09, page 54) by Tadao Ando. Measuring no less than 2577 square meters, this substantial edifice was delayed by the events of December 2004, when a tsunami devastated the region. First consulted by Pierre Pringiers earlier in that year, Ando completed the commission only five years later. Specialists were brought from Japan to assure that Ando's trademark concrete would be up to his usual standards, but the basic design is fully faithful to the Pritzker Prize winner's geometric vocabulary and skillful alternation of opaque and transparent effects. A rather spectacular horizon pool reaches out from the second level of the house to the vast ocean, a gesture requested by the client in this instance.

4
Pezo von Ellrichshausen, Arco House, Concepción, Chile, 2011

4

The story of the tsunami also has a direct bearing on the second house, Villa Vista (Weligama, Sri Lanka, 2007–10, page 68), an 825-square-meter house built for Koenraad Pringiers. Shigeru Ban had been involved in the design of post-tsunami rehabilitation houses in the locality of Hambantota, up the coast from Weligama. The earthquake of December 26, 2004, which unleashed the catastrophic tsunami, killed an estimated 38 000 people in Sri Lanka. A one-million-dollar charity program was initiated by the real-estate group Colliers International to rebuild the area after the earthquake, and Shigeru Ban Architects donated their time and efforts to this project. Made of compressed-earth blocks and wood, a total of 50 houses, of which 36 had been completed by April 30, 2006, were planned. The area of each house is 71 square meters and their approximate cost was $13 000. Intended to be environmentally friendly and sizeable enough to be comfortable, the houses made of natural materials stay cool within even when outside temperatures are very high. Furniture units made of local rubber tree wood are also part of the designs. Villa Vista might seem a world away from this type of disaster relief effort, and yet, since the same architect is involved, the link in time and space can, indeed, be made. Set like his parents' residence on a hilltop site, this home seeks to frame the view of the ocean. Shigeru Ban uses solid wood, light cement boards, and woven coconut leaves that permit it to "blend into the local ambiance." The architect designed a woven "wickerwork" pattern for the ceiling of the residence with bands of teak 80 millimeters wide and 3 millimeters thick. Clearly, Shigeru Ban sought more actively than Tadao Ando to "blend" into local structural traditions. This is actually a trait that is inscribed in the nature of his architecture, which appears to vary considerably according to its location. Ban has also made frequent use of materials that are ecologically sustainable, such as structural paper tubes (not employed here). This is not to say that Tadao Ando is insensitive to the location of the Sri Lanka House. On the contrary, his great strength has always been his ability to place a building in its natural setting and to make the most of the location. The approaches of the two Japanese architects are naturally different.

HALFWAY TO PARADISE

The Brazilian architects Thiago Bernardes and Paulo Jacobsen are familiar with clients who seek to build very large and luxurious homes. The Joá House (Rio de Janeiro, Brazil, 2010–11, page 116), which has an area of no less than 3500 square meters, is no exception. It is set on a generous 16 000-square-meter plateau, with spectacular views of São Conrado, Barra da Tijuca, where most of the events for the 2016 Olympic Games will be held, and the famous 840-meter-high monolith of the Pedra da Gávea that looms above the residence. In this climate, architects have the freedom to create a real continuity between exterior and interior spaces. The most evident materials are brick, wood, and glazing and these easily make the transition from inside to outside, reinforcing the impression of uninterrupted space. Inserted into a tropical garden atmosphere, the sheer size of the house is rarely evident in the photos published in this volume, and yet, this is in some sense an expression of the ultimate luxury—a very large private house in an idyllic setting. Here, the residents can actually live in a metropolis while enjoying the views and environment of a resort. Though curves are not really a part of the plans of the Joá House, the residence can bring to mind the much smaller house that Oscar Niemeyer designed for himself on the Estrada das Canoas above the São Conrado area of Rio (1952–53). At the time, it was not considered fashionable for the wealthy or powerful to live above the city—that being the more usual location of the *favelas* in Rio. Tradition has a way of changing though, especially when architects like Oscar Niemeyer lead the way.

5
SANAA, Shakujii Apartment, Tokyo,
Japan, 2009–10

LIVING WITHIN A TREE

Although it is in many respects a country of deep traditions, Japan also seems to be the country in the world that most easily accepts radical experimentation in architecture, including in the domain of the home. This acceptance is surely related to the fact that architects tie their challenges to the usual order with arguments and realities that also have a connection to the past. One of the most unusual residences published here is House NA by Sou Fujimoto. Born in 1971, Fujimoto is already well known in architectural circles for his innovative approach, at the limit of what some might consider conceivable. In this instance, he has designed a house that is almost entirely open to the street environment; with its white steel structure and shifted floor plates, the architect compares this house to a tree. In a fascinating play on the connections that can be made between the past, present, and future of architecture, Sou Fujimoto refers at once to "living within a tree" as some of our most distant ancestors surely did, and to "a platform for a network type of communication in space." Though the actual practicality of this arrangement is difficult to discern, there is obviously a will to accommodate a young attitude, built more on Internet than on the machine-driven world of the past.

Another Tokyo realization, this time by the noted Pritzker Prize winning firm SANAA, also relies on shifted floor plates or "slabs that exist on various levels." Here, as in House NA, the idea is not to create a two-dimensional flexible space, but, indeed, to engender flexibility in three dimensions. Contact with nature, the sky, wind, or even potted plants is consistent in the case of the Shakujii Apartment (Tokyo, Japan, 2009–10, page 360) with Japanese urban culture. Radical in their conception, these apartments are nonetheless carefully integrated to the scale of the street environment where they are located. While some early Modernist scheme willfully broke with their immediate surroundings to create "unique" objects, this is obviously not the goal of SANAA. This is architecture that is different, new, and yet corresponds in many respects to very old cultural needs and requirements. Where flexibility on a single plane has often been touted as a new way to build homes, these architects have quite literally taken the argument to an entirely different level.

A NEST IN THE FOREST

Keisuke Maeda, born in 1974, is even younger than Sou Fujimoto. He is also not from the usual Tokyo or Osaka environment, but, rather, is a native of Hiroshima, where he opened his own office, UID architects, in 2003. His Nest house (Onomichi, Hiroshima, Japan, 2010, page 378) explores connections to nature in a more overt way than the Tokyo houses presented here. "It is like a principle that expands from a nest in a forest, to a forest, then to the earth, and ultimately to the universe," says the architect. The 121-square-meter residence is, indeed, like a stylized wooden nest, but here, with large openings and an obvious relation to its forested site. Also influenced by a natural setting, the Pilotis in a Forest house (Kita-Karuizawa, Gunma, Japan, 2010, page 198) by Go Hasegawa (born in 1977) seems at first glance to have more to do with tree houses than with the traditional residence that is anchored in the earth. Hasegawa explains: "I used the forest as the building's walls." He compares the suspended living area to a "small attic-like space" where a 1.8-meter ceiling and a low dining table sitting on a glass floor seek to "convey the sense that the natural environment outside is larger and closer." Though the architect does not specifically emphasize the ecological credentials of this structure, he clearly sought to preserve mature trees, and to bring the clients closer to nature. "In good weather, you can relax under the pilotis in the middle of the forest," he says, "and after the sun goes down, sleep outside among the towering trees." This is a weekend residence, and the owners, like most Japanese, probably spend more time in a dense urban environment than they might in a forest, especially one that they can actually live and sleep in. With a floor area of just 77 square meters, the Pilotis in a Forest, like Fujimoto's House NA, seeks out instincts that existed before history, the feeling of living in the trees.

AMERICA IS STILL THERE

Though radical experimentation with residential typology seems less frequent in North America these days than when Frank Gehry was playing with materials in an artistic way as he did in the Norton House (Venice, California, 1983), some very beautiful houses are still rising, often in rural or natural settings. A case in point is Rick Joy's Woodstock Farm Estate (Woodstock, Vermont, USA, 2007–09, page 236) located in the Green Mountains. The "elongated stone-ended gable" house owes more in its exterior appearance to farm structures than it does to modern architecture, as does the neighboring two-story barn that is part of the complex. The interiors are faithful to the relative austerity of the exterior design, but clearly provide for the kind of comfort and modernity to which today's clients in the market for an "architect's" house are accustomed. The Canadian architects Shim-Sutcliffe designed a vacation house for Museum of Modern Art Director Glenn Lowry (House on Henry's Meadow, Vale Perkins, Canada, 2008–09, page 372). Located on the western shore of Lake Memphremagog, near the border between Quebec and Vermont, this residence is designed making use of local tradition that sees stacks of firewood surrounding farms. The stacked-wood effect and the use of such materials as local white pine boards for the interior cladding do relate the house to structures that are farm-oriented, while providing the views and comfort that go with contemporary life.

Shim-Sutcliffe are also the authors of a residence that Glenn Lowry has called "one of the most important private houses in North America." The Integral House (Toronto, Canada, 2005–09, page 366) gets back into the category of the "mansion" with its 1394 square meters of floor area. Located in a wooded Toronto ravine, the house includes space for music and a performance area that can seat 150 people. The complex, curving patterns of the plan of the house have to do with the client's life as the author of best-selling mathematics textbooks. Full-height glazing inserted between the "syncopated oak fins" that make up the most visible interior and exterior feature of the house allow for generous views of the wooded site, giving the impression of being immersed in nature, and even open to it, despite a climate that is rigorous in winter. The client asked only for "curves and a performance space" but was willing, according to the Toronto *Star* newspaper, to buy an existing house on the site for $5.4 million and tear it down to make way for his new masterpiece. "From the street," explains the newspaper, "only two stories are visible. The main living space was built one floor below street level so it feels like you're descending into the ravine. The back half of the house is glass mixed with oak fins. The house has minimal interior decoration—the trees outside are the real focal point. They are visible from all five floors. 'The aspiration is that the project feels timeless,' architect Brigitte Shim said."[5] Reference to cost is often a "taboo" when it comes to very large homes, but this is a part of their story as well. Indeed, it is one of the privileges of private house design

6
Jakob van Ringen, Wilderness House,
Wilderness, South Africa, 2010

6

when a client has the means and is willing to put them to use to create an exceptional residence. This was clearly the case of James Stewart, the client for the Integral House.

EVERYTHING IS POSSIBLE

In a way, the work of one office presented in this book might give an idea of the importance and scope of residential architecture. Christian Pottgiesser, born in 1965 in Germany, is based in Paris and created his firm architecturespossibles in 2005 in Paris. The name of his office is meant to imply that at the beginning of a project, any form of architecture is possible. His L House (Yvelines, France, 2007–11, page 328) seems to prove his point, because its configuration is far from being ordinary. Rather than a single "building," Pottgiesser suggested five towers for a client with four children—one for each child and one for the parents, on a garden site near an 18th-century "Orangerie." The towers are set in a 47-meter-long "amoeboid" base. Existing house typology might never have suggested such a solution, and yet it was not only within the realm of the possible, but actually appears to meet the needs of the client quite well. Though the priorities here, in Yvelines, are clearly quite different than those of an architect working in Tokyo, the project here, in many respects confirms the idea that at the outset, any form can be imagined where a house is concerned. Pottgiesser sought a relation to the 18th-century remnants of a French chateau for the L House, while anchoring the residence in a decidedly contemporary form: architects like Sou Fujimoto are searching for ways to actually reinvent the house, putting aside decades, and sometimes centuries, of preconceptions of the functions and spaces of a house. The network referred to by Fujimoto is very much in the spirit of these times, and there is no apparent reason that a house might not resemble a web of spaces to be navigated in a vast number of ways, no longer imposing "its" logic on inhabitants. Imagine architecture that is no longer as rigid as the materials that make up walls and roofs, imagine *Architecture Now!*

[1] Ezra Klein, "The Rich Get Richer in One Chart," *The Washington Post*, September 9, 2010, http://voices.washingtonpost.com/ezra-klein/2010/09/the_rich_getting_richer_in_one.html. Accessed on April 23, 2012.

[2] Gus Lubin, "23 Mind-Blowing Facts About Income Inequality In America," *Business Insider*, November 7, 2011, http://www.businessinsider.com/new-charts-about-inequality-2011-11#the-top-001-the-super-elite-claim-a-greater-share-of-the-income-than-any-time-on-record-3. Accessed on April 23, 2012.

[3] Yoree Koh, "Building Anew Out of Tsunami's Rubble," *The Wall Street Journal*, Asia, June 6, 2011. http://online.wsj.com/article/SB10001424052702304906004576366643979766836.html. Accessed on April 23, 2012.

[4] Jean-Pierre Raynaud, e-mail to the author, April 28, 2012.

[5] Katie Daubs, "The House that Math Built," *Toronto Star*, February 4, 2011. http://www.thestar.com/news/article/933017--the-house-that-math-built. Accessed on April 23, 2012.

EINLEITUNG

WOHNEN IM NETZ(WERK)

Es sind schwere Zeiten – zumindest für manche. Muss man also davon ausgehen, dass auch die zeitgenössische Architektur zu kämpfen hat? Oder wenigstens die Kreativität unter dem Diktat von Zweckmäßigkeit und Wirtschaftlichkeit leidet? Private Wohnbauten sind so etwas wie der Mikrokosmos der Architektur – Spiegel einer Branche mit ihren Höhen und Tiefen. Dabei ist es selten der Mittelstand, der sein Eigenheim von qualifizierten Architekten planen lässt; tatsächlich ist dies meist ein Privileg der finanziell Bessergestellten. Die Entwicklung der letzten 30 Jahre, die dazu geführt hat, dass die Reichen immer reicher werden, hat sich auch durch die jüngsten Krisen nicht abgeschwächt. In den Vereinigten Staaten entfielen 64 % des Einkommenszuwachses 1979 bis 2007, also vor der letzten Krise, auf die landesweit bestverdienenden 10 % der Bevölkerung.[1] Noch größer ist die Schere im Hinblick auf die wirklich begüterten 0,01 % Topverdiener der USA, die gegenwärtig einen größeren Anteil am Einkommen haben als je zuvor.[2] Tatsache ist: Für Bessergestellte sind die fetten Zeiten längst nicht vorbei, weshalb in aller Welt nach wie vor luxuriöse Eigenheime entstehen. Die Projektauswahl für diesen Band hat jedoch ganz bewusst einen anderen Fokus und konzentriert sich nicht in erster Linie auf „Wohnpaläste", die von Sri Lanka bis Toronto aus dem Boden schießen, sondern vielmehr auf interessante Versuche, kleine und doch praktische Wohnbauten zu planen, wie dies etwa in Japan oft der Fall ist. Dass in Japan Eigenheime mit weit unter 100 m² Wohnfläche weithin Zuspruch finden, hat natürlich historische, kulturelle und demografische Gründe. Bevölkerungsdichte und Grundstückspreise machen große Wohnbauten in Städten wie Tokio nahezu unmöglich. Diese Bescheidenheit, wenn man so will, wird in gewisser Weise durch die Bereitschaft japanischer Bauherren wettgemacht, junge, innovative Architekten zu engagieren. Obwohl es natürlich keinerlei Grund gibt, warum ein weitläufiges Anwesen kein architektonisches Highlight sein sollte, leuchtet doch ein, dass echte Innovation gerade durch Einschränkungen gefördert wird – sei es, dass Budgets knapp oder Grundstücke schwer zu haben sind.

DIE WELLE UND DIE BÄUME

Einige Architekten stellen ihre Fähigkeiten auch in den Dienst von Hilfsprogrammen. Shigeru Ban aus Tokio ist ein Beispiel hierfür: Nach fast allen größeren Erdbeben und Tsunamis der letzten Jahre entwickelte er Notunterkünfte – in jüngster Zeit nach dem großen Tohoku-Seebeben und dem nachfolgenden Tsunami, der Nordjapan am 11. März 2011 überrollte. Tadao Ando, Architekt zwei spektakulärer Wohnbauten in diesem Band (in Monterrey, Mexiko, und Sri Lanka) war Mitglied einer Wiederaufbaukommission, die die japanische Regierung nach dem Tohoku-Beben 2011 ins Leben gerufen hatte. Ando warf deutlich langfristigere Fragen auf, die über den unmittelbaren Wiederaufbau hinausgingen: „Ich glaube, dass Japan sein Verhältnis zur Familie, seine Liebe zum eigenen Land, seine Rolle in Asien und die Verantwortung des Einzelnen auf diesem Planeten überdenken muss. Dies ist in Japan im Lauf der vergangenen 30 Jahre in Vergessenheit geraten", so Ando im *Wall Street Journal.* Schon früher hatte sich Tadao Ando für groß angelegte Baumpflanzungsaktionen engagiert, etwa an der Seto-Inlandsee. Nach dem Tohoku-Beben äußerte er: „Als Beitrag zur Stärkung der japanischen Moral kam mir der Gedanke, einen ‚Wald der Ruhe' zu pflanzen. Ich halte es für sinnvoll, in sämtlichen verwüsteten Präfekturen – Miyagi, Iwate und Fukushima – einen Bürgerwald zu pflanzen; ein Vorschlag, der inzwischen auch vom japanischen Parlament verabschiedet wurde." Ando geht davon aus, dass die Menschen durch die Pflege der Bäume, „die zugleich als natürlicher Schutzwall zwischen dem Meer und den Städten dienen (die weiter landeinwärts wieder aufzubauen

7
Morphosis, Float House,
New Orleans, Louisiana,
USA, 2008–09

wären), ebenso wie durch das Wachstum der Bäume, daran erinnert werden könnten, was 2011 geschehen ist". Er hält ein solches „lebendiges Mahnmal in ‚natürlicher Form' für angemessener als den Bau eines Gebäudes", so der Architekt zum *Wall Street Journal.*[3]

In den Vereinigten Staaten, wo die Wunden nur langsam heilen, die der Hurrikan Katrina schlug, hat das von Brad Pitt initiierte Projekt *Make It Right* einige interessante Entwürfe hervorgebracht. Das Float House (New Orleans, Louisiana, 2008–09, Seite 284), ein Entwurf des Pritzker-Preisträgers Thom Mayne und seines Büros Morphosis, soll nicht nur Eigenheime erschwinglich machen, sondern auch vor vorhersehbaren Naturkatastrophen schützen. Dank Stahlstützen, die in 13,7 m tiefen Betonpfählen verankert sind, kann das Haus bei Hochwasser unbeschadet bis zu 3,65 m hoch über den Boden erhoben und nach Flutrückgang auf sein ursprüngliches Niveau abgesenkt werden. Morphosis erläutert: „Der globale Klimawandel führt zu immer dramatischeren Überflutungen und Naturkatastrophen. Weltweit leben fast 200 Millionen Menschen in stark hochwassergefährdeten Zonen; allein in den USA sind derzeit über 36 Millionen Menschen von Hochwasser bedroht. Der Prototyp des Float House steht modellhaft für einen nachhaltigen Lebensstil, der dieser realen Unsicherheit Rechnung trägt."

DAS GUTE, DAS SCHLECHTE UND DAS HÄSSLICHE
Zum Konzept der Reihe *Architektur heute!* gehört es u. a., weder eine geografische Region noch bestimmte Architekturstile zu bevorzugen. Die einzigen Grenzen beim Inhalt von *Architektur heute! Häuser 3* resultieren aus dem Kenntnisstand des Autors – doch da sich die Reihe seit über zehn Jahren als veritabler Bestseller erweist, gibt es durchaus keinen Mangel an Projektvorschlägen oder Hinweisen. Im besten Fall bietet *Architektur heute! Häuser 3* ein breit gefächertes Spektrum an Wohnbauten, die in den letzten drei bis vier Jahren weltweit realisiert wurden. Vorgegeben wird der Inhalt des Bandes von den besten international gebauten Projekten. Natürlich ist subjektiv, was hier das „Beste" ist, und so werden die Leser, die mit der getroffenen Auswahl hier und da nicht einverstanden sind, um Nachsicht gebeten. Dennoch bietet ein Buch wie *Architektur heute! Häuser 3* auch Vorteile, gerade aufgrund der „subjektiven" Auswahl der aus architektonischer Sicht besten Wohnhäuser. Natürlich gibt es Onlineportale mit dem Anspruch, einen Gesamtüberblick über alles zu bieten, was derzeit in der zeitgenössischen Architektur geschieht – doch interessanterweise finden sich auf fast allen Portalen (zeitgleich) dieselben Fotografien und Texte. Hinzu kommt, dass sie kaum zwischen Gutem, Schlechtem und Hässlichem unterscheiden. Das Buch ist also noch längst nicht tot.

VON CHINA BIS NACH CHILE
Eines belegt dieser Band ohne Frage: „Gute" Architektur ist inzwischen überall auf diesem Planeten zu finden, wo es finanzielle Mittel und die Absicht gibt, mehr zu bauen als ein einfaches Dach über dem Kopf. In diesem Buch finden sich Häuser aus Chile, Paraguay, Mexiko, Peru und Brasilien; Häuser aus den USA und Kanada, Frankreich, den Niederlanden, Deutschland, der Schweiz, Portugal und Spanien; aus Neuseeland, Japan, Korea und China, selbst Sri Lanka oder Ghana. Diese Liste ist natürlich nicht vollständig, weite Bereiche sind in diesem Band nicht repräsentiert – und doch lässt sich prinzipiell sagen, dass großartige Wohnbauten fast überall zu finden sind: Dieser Trend zunehmender geografischer Verbreitung ist etwas fundamental Neues. Noch vor wenigen Jahren hätte man in China kaum ein luxuriöses, 1200 m²

8

*8
Sebastián Irarrázaval,
Container House 1, Santiago,
Chile, 2010*

großes Privatanwesen vermutet. Heute gewinnt Wang Shu, ein 48-jähriger Chinese, den Pritzker-Preis, die renommierteste Auszeichnung der Branche. Heute entwirft ein amerikanischer Architekt ein Haus in Korea (Haus mit Galerie Daeyang, Seoul, Südkorea, 2010–12, Seite 214), plant ein chinesischer Architekt ein Haus in Pasadena (Glen Oaks Residence, Pasadena, Kalifornien, USA, 2009–11, Seite 262). Grenzen fallen, Entfernungen haben angesichts weltweiter Kommunikation immer weniger Bedeutung. Architektur kann heute nicht mehr im Windschatten von Isolation und zügellosem Nationalismus gedeihen. Internet und Reisen machen alles überall sofort verfügbar.

Dieser Band will keinem bestimmten Stil oder Haustypus das Wort reden. Stattdessen finden sich hier nebeneinander – wie in der bunten Welt der zeitgenössischen Architektur auch – die verschiedenartigsten Stile. Historische Rückbezüge auf die Architekturgeschichte fließen in die hier vorgestellten Neubauten ein, ja ziehen sich wie ein roter Faden durch die Entwürfe. Dies ist kein oberflächliches Pasticcio, wie man es aus der inzwischen überalterten Postmoderne kennt, hier zeigt sich echte Auseinandersetzung und Umsetzung – eine kategorische Absage an die berühmte, Anfang des 20. Jahrhunderts von Walter Gropius erklärte Tabula rasa. Dennoch ist die Moderne noch deutlich spürbar, wenn auch in stark veränderter, mitunter fast unkenntlicher Form, selbst bei Architekten wie John Pawson oder David Chipperfield. „Modern" will heißen: „den Bezug zur jüngeren Vergangenheit oder der Gegenwart suchend". Die Architektur hat, wie andere kreative Disziplinen auch, immer stark aus der Vergangenheit geschöpft – selbst auf dem Höhepunkt des International Style kam man nicht ohne die Tradition der Baukunst aus. Der Wendepunkt im Verhältnis zur Vergangenheit wurde möglicherweise tatsächlich durch das Aufkommen der Postmoderne in den späten 1960er-Jahren und das Erscheinen von Robert Venturis Manifest *Komplexität und Widerspruch in der Architektur* (1966, dt. 1978) herbeigeführt. 1972 meldete Venturi sich mit einem zweiten, kürzeren Buch zurück, *A Significance for A&P Parking Lots, or Learning from Las Vegas*. Besser bekannt wurde die Publikation in überarbeiteter Form, erschienen 1977 (dt. 1979) unter dem Titel *Lernen von Las Vegas: zur Ikonografie und Architektursymbolik der Geschäftsstadt*. Die Titel dieser Bücher mögen einiges auf den Punkt bringen, doch letztendlich ist die Postmoderne mit den oft extravaganten Formen, die Michael Graves, Robert A. M. Stern oder Venturi entwarfen, eher der Versuch, den Leichnam der Moderne fein säuberlich einzubalsamieren, als Geburtshelfer einer neuen Architektur zu sein.

DAS GEHEIMNIS LIEGT IN DER DNA

Dass heute neue Architektur existiert, hat auch damit zu tun, dass Architekten ihre eigene DNA wiederentdecken: jene generationen- und jahrhundertealten Bautraditionen, die ihnen vorausgegangen sind und ihr kreatives Potenzial beflügeln. Ein Blick auf das Water House von Li Xiaodong (Dorf Yuhu, Lijiang, China, 2006–09, Seite 7) genügt, um zu sehen, dass hier aus Vergangenheit und Gegenwart eine echte Moderne entstanden ist. Selbst wer nicht mit der chinesischen Geschichte vertraut ist, spürt unmittelbar, welch eindrucksvolle Präsenz die Steine und das Wasser im ganzen Haus besitzen. Was solche Projekte von Postmoderne oder „Kontextualismus" unterscheidet, ist das zunehmende Bewusstsein in Architektenkreisen, dass Vergangenheit keine Frage der Fassade ist – vielmehr geht es um echte Kontinuität, die sich in Material und Form spiegelt, ebenso wie in der Funktion.

Die in diesem Band vertretenen japanischen Häuser, darunter auch das Haus NA von Sou Fujimoto (Tokio, 2010, Seite 186), erobern auf ganz andere Weise Neuland und definieren nicht nur den Wohnraum als Typus neu, sondern experimentieren zugleich mit einer radikalen Offenheit, die bisweilen soweit geht, die üblichen Vorstellungen von Privatsphäre zu unterlaufen. Auch dies ist wiederum vor dem Hintergrund japanischer Tradition zu sehen, in der *shoji*-Wandschirme oder -Schiebetüren „flexible" Räume definierten. Doch natürlich hat dies auch mit der extremen Bevölkerungsdichte des Landes zu tun, gerade im östlichen Korridor zwischen Tokio und Osaka. In solchen Fällen ist „Tradition" allgegenwärtig als Hintergrund und grundlegender Antrieb für Innovation. Es lässt sich wohl kaum anschaulicher machen, welch fundamentaler Wandel stattgefunden hat, seit Venturi sein Loblied auf die Parkplätze von Las Vegas gesungen hat. Venturis ältere Publikation *Komplexität und Widerspruch in der Architektur* beschreibt eher, was heute geschieht. Statt mit spitzem Bleistift bei null anzufangen, sind sich Architekten fast überall auf der Welt bewusst, dass jedes Bauwerk Vieldeutigkeiten birgt – und betonen dies oft. Dies bedeutet keineswegs, dass Funktionalität keine Rolle mehr spielt, allerdings ist Flexibilität besonders bei privaten Wohnbauten zum Schlüsselwort avanciert. Familien verändern sich; Räume werden im Lauf der Zeit anders genutzt. Statt klar definierter Räume für Essen, Wohnen und Kochen, wie sie das typische amerikanische Vorstadthaus typologisch noch vorsah, unterscheiden Architekten und Bauherren heute zwischen „öffentlichen" und „privaten" Arealen. In den Wohnbereichen fließen in den meisten Fällen Wohnen, Essen, Kochen und Unterhaltung ineinander. Schlafzimmer und Bäder bleiben aus offensichtlichen Gründen „privat", doch wo es das Klima erlaubt, verschwimmen die Grenzen zwischen Innen- und Außenraum durch geschosshohe Verglasung oder Schiebeelemente immer stärker.

SUCHE NACH DEM GARTEN

Die ambitioniertesten und kostspieligsten Wohnbauten in diesem Band sind ausnahmslos Entwürfe, die einen echten Dialog mit der umgebenden Landschaft führen, ob nun an der Küste, im Wald oder an einem See. Hier zeichnet sich ein Bezug zur klassischen Moderne ab: Deren Einsatz großflächiger Verglasung – wie beim Farnsworth House von Mies van der Rohe (Plano, Illinois, USA, 1951) –, deren Einbettung in den landschaftlichen Kontext – wie bei Wrights Fallingwater (Mill Run, Pennsylvania, USA, 1935) – sind noch heute leuchtende Vorbilder für einen Großteil aktueller Wohnbauarchitektur. Fast scheint es, als wäre die Wiederentdeckung der Natur in einem geschützten und zeitgenössischen Umfeld der kompromissloseste Ausdruck von Privilegiertheit für wohlhabende Hausbesitzer. Es ist die Suche nach dem verlorenen „Garten", die sich wie ein roter Faden durch die Architekturgeschichte zieht. Auch dort, wo die Natur außer Reichweite liegt, etwa im urbanen Japan, suchen Architekten und Bauherren unermüdlich nach ihr – in Form von Kübelpflanzen oder dem Blick in den Himmel.

Wer die Reihe *Architektur heute!* kennt, weiß, dass immer wieder auch Arbeiten von Künstlern vorgestellt werden, sofern sich ein klarer Bezug zwischen Kunst und Architektur ausmachen lässt. In diesem Band vertreten ist ein Haus für den Künstler Jean-Pierre Raynaud, aber auch verschiedene Häuser, die Architekten für sich persönlich entworfen haben. Zwar heißt es traditioneller- oder humorvollerweise, Architekten seien mit ihren eigenen Entwürfen eher schlecht bedient, doch unsere Beispiele sind vielleicht die Ausnahme von der Regel. Der spanische Architekt Antón García-Abril etwa hat bei seinem kleinen, 25 m² großen Feriendomizil La Trufa (Die Trüffel, Costa da Morte, Spanien,

2010, Seite 8) keine Experimente gescheut. „La Trufa ist ein Stück Natur, gebaut aus Lehm und luftig dazu", so der Architekt. Der aus einem Stein ausgehöhlte Raum ruht auf der Erde und verschmilzt mit seinem Umfeld. Er tarnt sich, ahmt mit seiner Struktur die Prozesse der Mineralbildung nach und fügt sich in den landschaftlichen Kontext und dessen Regeln. Antón García, der seinen Bau aus Beton plante, mit 50 m³ Heu als einzigem Schalungsmittel, bezieht sich hier explizit auf Le Corbusiers Cabanon (Roquebrune, Cap Martin, Frankreich, 1951) – jenes kleine Blockhaus, in dem der Schweizer Architekt seine letzte Nacht verbachte, bevor er 1965 ganz in der Nähe ertrank.

VIOLETT, ORGANISCH UND FREMDARTIG

Ein weitaus größeres Architektendomizil ist die Glen Oaks Residence von Ma Qingyun. Der Dekan der Architekturfakultät der University of Southern California (USC) beschrieb die 340 m² große Erweiterung eines Altbaus aus den 1950er-Jahren als „violett, organisch und fremdartig". Ma Qingyun gründete MADA s.p.a.m., eines der ersten großen chinesischen Architekturbüros, die seit der Liberalisierung der Gesetzgebung namentlich für ihre Entwürfe zeichnen dürfen, statt für übergeordnete „Institute" zu arbeiten. Zum Haus in Pasadena gehören eine halböffentliche Galerie mit doppelter Geschosshöhe, Küche, Arbeitszimmer sowie ein Tanzstudio für Mas Ehefrau Shouning Li. Der Bau hat runde Fenster und ist mit Spritzbeton verschalt – wodurch eine durchgehende, relativ raue Gebäudehülle entsteht. Die geschwungene Auffahrt, die den Altbau mit der Erweiterung verbindet, illustriert wie der chinesische Architekt amerikanische Vorstadtarchitektur interpretiert, wie er neue Wege sucht, Wohnbauten einer vergangenen Ära eine neue Funktionalität zu geben. Durch seinen beruflichen Hintergrund ist Ma Qingyun bestens mit amerikanischen Bautraditionen und -typologien vertraut. Dass er es wagt, eine so klassische „Ikone" wie das amerikanische Eigenheim der Nachkriegsära zu hinterfragen und neu zu interpretieren, ist vielleicht ein Zeichen der Zeit. Kalifornien mag zwar der Ort sein, an dem Architekten wie Rudolf Schindler, Richard Neutra, John Lautner oder Frank Gehry in ihrer Zeit mit bahnbrechenden Entwürfen große Erfolge feierten, doch Ma Qingyuns Erweiterungsbau setzt sich fundamentaler mit den Veränderungen des Lebensstils auseinander, die Einfluss auf die Architektur von Wohnhäusern haben – in Amerika wie anderswo.

Susanne Nobis, 1963 in München geboren, arbeitete für Renzo Piano und Herzog & de Meuron, ehe sie 2000 ihr eigenes Büro in Berg gründete. In der Nähe ihres Büros entwarf sie ihr Wohnhaus am landschaftlich reizvollen Starnberger See (Toward Landscape, Berg, 2006 bis 2010, Seite 296). In Anlehnung an die traditionellen Bootshäuser am Starnberger See entwarf die Architektin zwei Baukörper, einen mit offener Galerie, den anderen als „Schlafzimmerhaus". Für die Gebäudehülle wählte die Architektin eine Titanblechschicht, die um eine Holzkonstruktion „gefaltet" wurde – so entstanden ebenso warme wie moderne Räume. Beide Baukörper öffnen sich mit ihren vollständig verglasten Fassaden zum See. Sieht man ein Haus wie dieses, das sich über typologische Grenzen (Bootshaus und Wohnbau) hinwegsetzt, fragt man sich, wie wunderbar es sein muss, Architekt zu sein – zumal, wenn man in einem solchen Haus wohnen kann.

9
Carsten Höller and Marcel Odenbach,
House Turtle, Cape Coast,
Ghana, 1999–2009

SCHILDKRÖTE UND BLUMENTOPF

Pasadena mag kein besonders „exotischer" Standort für innovatives Bauen sein, anders als Cape Coast (Ghana), 165 km westlich von Accra am Golf von Guinea, das ungleich weiter von der zeitgenössischen Kunstszene Europas entfernt zu sein scheint. Dennoch ist es gerade die Stadt Biriwa, in der sich der renommierte deutsche Künstler Carsten Höller und Marcel Odenbach, ein bekannter Videokünstler, ihr Ferienhaus bauten (House Turtle, 1999–2009, Seite 220). Höller schreibt, dieses „Schildkrötenhaus" „wurde unter Berücksichtigung folgender Kriterien geplant: a) maximale Luftzirkulation durch und unter dem Haus, um auf Klimatisierung verzichten zu können, b) Maßnahmen zum Schutz gegen Moskitos und andere Tiere wie Schlangen, c) Einsatz von 87°- oder 93°-Winkeln statt üblicher 90°-Winkel, um den Eindruck von Entfernung und geraden Winkeln zu verstärken/verringern, d) Sammeln von Regenwasser über das Dach und unterhalb der Terrassen, e) das Haus ‚unfertig' erscheinen zu lassen." Der aufgeständerte Bau mit Blick auf's Meer ist von ungewöhnlicher Präsenz. Er schwebt einsam über dem Strand, ist ein Ort, um vor einer anderen Welt zu flüchten oder eine neue zu finden – am Ende der uns bekannten Welt.

Der renommierte französische Künstler Jean-Pierre Raynaud, Jahrgang 1939, zog sich früher zeitweise in sein weitgehend selbst entworfenes, unterirdisches Haus Le Mastaba (Kooperation mit dem Architekten Jean Dedieu, 1986) in La Garenne Colombes, 10 km vom Stadtzentrum zurück, um dem Pariser Lärm und Trubel zu entfliehen. Raynaud arbeitete in La Garenne Colombes und stellte dort auch seine Werke aus: übergroße Blumentöpfe, z.T. mit Blattvergoldung, oder Länderflaggen, die er in Kunstwerke verwandelte. Vor einiger Zeit wandte sich Raynaud an seinen Freund, den Architekten und Innenarchitekten Jean-Michel Wilmotte, um eine neues Atelier in Barbizon zu realisieren (2009, Seite 406). Barbizon, 58 km vor Paris, wurde als Heimat der gleichnamigen Schule in der französischen Malerei bekannt, der im 19. Jahrhundert Künstler wie Théodore Rousseau und Jean-François Millet angehörten. Dort ließ der Architekt spätere Anbauten an das Anwesen Clos d'Hortense entfernen und ergänzte den Bau um einen großzügigen verglasten Raum, in dem Raynaud seine Werke präsentiert. Diese *verrière* öffnet das Haus auch zur waldigen Umgebung und zum 4000 m² großen Garten. Hier kooperierte Raynaud mit dem Landschaftsarchitekten Neveux Rouyer, um ein für ihn typisches Gesamtkunstwerk aus Kunst, Architektur und Natur zu realisieren. Raynaud erklärt: „Hier geht es weniger um ein architektonisches Problem, als um den Raum. Wie bei den meisten Kunstwerken spielt sich alles innerhalb einer bestimmten Fläche ab, weshalb in den vergangenen Jahrhunderten auch besonderer Wert auf den Rahmen gelegt wurde, der gewissermaßen das Territorium des Kunstwerks markierte. In den letzten 50 Jahren hat sich die Malerei von solchen Grenzen befreit; für die Künstler kam es zu einer völligen Durchdringung von Leben und Werk. Das zeigt sich etwa bei Monets *Seerosen*, im Werk Jackson Pollocks oder den monochromen Gemälden eines Yves Klein. In meinem Denken hat der Raum immer eine große Rolle gespielt – ein Raum, in dem alles möglich ist." Raynaud setzt sich tatsächlich schon lange mit den Grenzen zwischen Architektur und Kunst auseinander. So baute er ab 1969 sein Haus La Celle Saint Cloud unweit von Paris, das er 24 Jahre später abreißen ließ. Mit dem Schutt organisierte Raynaud 1993 seine berühmte Ausstellung am CAPC in Bordeaux. Bei dem hier vorgestellten Projekt darf die Architektur des Ateliers tatsächlich als Teil des künstlerischen Oeuvres gelten – realisiert in enger Zusammenarbeit mit Jean-Michel Wilmotte. Raynaud bringt es auf den Punkt: „Ich bin unfähig, Konsument im üblichen Sinn zu sein. Die Räume, die ich gebaut habe, waren nie für den Alltag bestimmt; sie wurden gebaut um zu sein."[4]

10

10
Tadao Ando, House in Sri Lanka,
Mirissa, Sri Lanka, 2006–09

AUF EINEM HÜGEL, ÜBER DEM MEER

Die Südspitze Sri Lankas mit Blick auf den Indischen Ozean ist ein ebenso überraschender Standort für einen architektonisch anspruchsvollen, zeitgenössischen Wohnbau wie der Golf von Guinea. Und doch wurden hier in jüngster Zeit zwei Häuser in den nahegelegenen Orten Mirissa und Weligama realisiert, beide von bedeutenden japanischen Architekten. Bauherren der beiden Häuser sind Vater und Sohn aus Belgien, Direktoren einer erfolgreichen ortsansässigen Reifenfabrik. Der zuerst fertiggestellte Bau, ein Entwurf Tadao Andos, ist das Haus in Mirissa (Sri Lanka, 2006–09, Seite 54). Der Bau des nicht weniger als 2577 m² großen Anwesens verzögerte sich durch die Ereignisse im Dezember 2004, als ein Tsunami die Region verwüstete. Nachdem Bauherr Pierre Pringiers im selben Jahr erstmals Kontakt zu Ando aufgenommen hatte, konnte der Architekt den Auftrag erst fünf Jahre später abschließen. Spezialisten aus Japan wurden hinzugezogen, um sicherzustellen, dass der für Ando typische Beton seinen Ansprüchen entsprach; im Entwurf selbst zeigt sich das vertraute geometrische Vokabular und kunstvolle Wechselspiel opaker und transparenter Flächen des Pritzker-Preisträgers. Ein spektakulärer sog. Infinity Pool erstreckt sich auf der oberen Ebene des Anwesens bis zum weiten Ozean – eine eigens von den Bauherren gewünschte bauliche Geste.

Der Tsunami betraf im weitesten Sinn auch den zweiten Bau, die Villa Vista (Weligama, Sri Lanka, 2007–10, Seite 68), ein 825 m² großes Domizil für Koenraad Pringiers. Shigeru Ban hatte zuvor Unterkünfte für den Wiederaufbau in Hambantota entworfen, einen Küstenort nördlich von Weligama. Das Erdbeben vom 26. Dezember 2004, das den katastrophalen Tsunami ausgelöst hatte, forderte in Sri Lanka etwa 38 000 Menschenleben. Nachdem die Immobilienfirma Colliers International ein Hilfsprogramm für 1 Million Dollar ins Leben gerufen hatte, engagierte sich Shigeru Ban mit seinem Büro für dieses Projekt. Insgesamt 50 Häuser aus Stampflehmziegeln und Holz wurden geplant, von denen 36 bis zum 30. April 2006 realisiert werden konnten. Jedes Haus verfügt über 71 m² Nutzfläche und kostet rund 13 000 Dollar. Die umweltfreundlich und in annehmbarer Größe geplanten Wohnbauten wurden mit natürlichen Baustoffen realisiert und bleiben selbst bei hohen Temperaturen kühl. Zum Entwurf gehört auch Mobiliar aus regionalem Gummibaumholz. Selbst wenn die Villa Vista auf den ersten Blick nicht viel mit diesem Hilfsprogramm gemein hat, ist es doch derselbe Architekt, dieselbe Zeit und dieselbe Region, die sie verbindet. Die Villa für Koenraad Pringiers liegt wie das Anwesen seiner Eltern auf einem Hügel und rahmt den Blick aufs Meer. Shigeru Ban arbeitete mit Massivholz, Zementleichtbauplatten und Kokospalmblättern, durch die sich der Bau „in das lokale Ambiente fügt". Für die Decken im Haus entwarf der Architekt ein Flechtwerk aus 80 mm breiten und 3 mm starken Teakholzbändern. Offenkundig ging es Ban stärker als Tadao Ando um eine Anbindung an lokale Bautraditionen. Tatsächlich ist dies ein Wesensmerkmal seiner Architektur, die je nach Standort erheblich variiert. Ban arbeitet außerdem häufig mit ökologisch nachhaltigen Baumaterialien, etwa mit tragenden Pappröhren (die hier jedoch nicht zum Einsatz kamen). Seine große Stärke ist seine Fähigkeit, Bauten in ihre landschaftliche Umgebung zu integrieren und das Potenzial des jeweiligen Standorts optimal zu nutzen. Die Philosophie dieser beiden japanischen Architekten ist sichtlich sehr verschieden.

AUF HALBEM WEG INS PARADIES

Die brasilianischen Architekten Thiago Bernardes und Paulo Jacobsen haben Erfahrung mit Bauherren, die ungewöhnlich große und luxuriöse Häuser wünschen. Das Haus Joá (Rio de Janeiro, 2010–11, Seite 116) mit seiner Nutzfläche von nicht weniger als 3500 m² ist hier
keine Ausnahme. Das Anwesen liegt auf einem großzügigen 16 000 m² großen Plateau mit spektakulärer Aussicht auf die Stadtteile São Conrado und Barra da Tijuca, wo ein Großteil der Olympischen Sommerspiele 2016 stattfinden wird, und bietet den Blick auf den berühmten,
840 m hohen Granitfelsen Pedra da Gávea, der über der Villa aufragt. Klimazonen wie diese erlauben den Architekten, ein echtes Raumkontinuum zwischen außen und innen zu gestalten. Prominente Baumaterialien sind hier Backstein, Holz und Glas, was zum fließenden Übergang
von Innen- und Außenraum beiträgt und den Eindruck eines fließenden Kontinuums unterstreicht. Durch die Einbindung des Baus in die tro-
pische Gartenlandschaft wird seine beeindruckende Größe auf den Aufnahmen in diesem Band nur bedingt deutlich – und doch ist dies in
gewisser Weise ein Ausdruck für ultimativen Luxus: ein außergewöhnlich großes Privatanwesen in idyllischer Lage. Hier kann man in einer
Metropole wie Rio leben und zugleich die Ausblicke und die Annehmlichkeiten eines Hotelresorts genießen. Auch wenn geschwungene Linien
beim Haus Joá sichtlich keine Rolle spielen, darf man sich an das ungleich kleinere Privatanwesen erinnert fühlen, das Oscar Niemeyer an der
Estrada das Canoas oberhalb des São-Conrado-Viertels von Rio baute (1952–53). Damals galt es unter den Wohlhabenden und Mächtigen
durchaus nicht als schick, oberhalb der Stadt zu wohnen – wo viele Favelas von Rio liegen. Doch auch Traditionen ändern sich, umso mehr,
wenn Architekten wie Oscar Niemeyer den Weg weisen.

WOHNEN IM BAUM

Obwohl Japan in vielerlei Hinsicht zutiefst traditionell ist, scheint es dennoch eines jener Länder zu sein, in denen man sich am ehesten
auf radikale Experimente in der Architektur einlässt – dies gilt auch für Wohnbauten. Diese Bereitschaft hat sicherlich auch damit zu tun, dass
Architekten dort überkommene Formen infrage stellen, indem sie wiederum Bezüge zur Geschichte suchen. Einer der ungewöhnlichsten hier
vorgestellten Wohnbauten ist das Haus NA von Sou Fujimoto. Fujimoto, Jahrgang 1971, in Architekturkreisen längst für seinen innovativen
Ansatz bekannt, geht oft an die Grenzen des Vorstellbaren. Hier entwarf er ein Haus, das straßenseitig fast vollständig transparent ist: Der Architekt vergleicht den Bau wegen seiner weißen Stahlkonstruktion und den gegeneinander versetzten Bodenplatten mit einem Baum. Fouji-
moto spielt auf faszinierende Weise mit Vergangenheit, Gegenwart und Zukunft der Architektur und spricht vom „Wohnen im Baum" – was
unsere Vorfahren zweifellos taten – ebenso wie von einer „Plattform für vernetzte Kommunikation im Raum". Auch wenn man Zweifel an der
Praktikabilität eines solchen Wohnkonzepts haben mag, spiegelt sich hier doch unverkennbar eine junge Perspektive, die stärker auf das Internet setzt als auf die maschinelle Dominanz früherer Zeiten.

Ein anderes Tokioter Projekt, allerdings vom Pritzker-Preisträger SANAA, zeichnet sich ebenfalls durch gegeneinander versetzte Bodenplatten aus: „Platten auf verschiedenen Ebenen". Wie schon beim Haus NA geht es nicht darum, einen Raum zu planen, der nur in der zweidimensionalen Fläche flexibel ist, sondern Flexibilität dreidimensional zu realisieren. Typisch für die urbane Kultur Japans ist die Suche nach

Kontakt zur Natur, dem Himmel, dem Wind, wenn auch nur in Form von einfachen Topfpflanzen – was sich in dem Shakujii Apartment (Tokio, 2009–10, Seite 360) spiegelt. Radikal in ihrer Konzeption wurden die Wohnungen von der Größe her sensibel in das Straßenumfeld integriert. Während manche Vertreter der frühen Moderne bewusst den Bruch mit dem unmittelbaren Umfeld suchten, um „Solitäre" zu schaffen, ist dies für SANAA offenkundig nicht das Ziel. Diese Architektur ist anders, neu, und knüpft doch in vielerlei Hinsicht an sehr alte kulturelle Bedürfnisse an. Während Flexibilität in der zweidimensionalen Ebene oft als neue Strategie des Wohnbaus gepriesen wurde, gelingt es diesen Architekten, dieses Credo buchstäblich auf gänzlich neue Ebenen zu heben.

EIN NEST IM WALD

Keisuke Maeda, Jahrgang 1974, ist etwas jünger als Sou Fujimoto. Er stammt nicht, wie so viele, aus Tokio oder Osaka, sondern aus Hiroshima, wo er 2003 sein Büro UID architects gründete. Sein Entwurf, das Haus Nest (Onomichi, Hiroshima, 2010, Seite 378), sucht nach ungleich direkterer Integration in die Natur als die hier vorgestellten Wohnbauten in Tokio. Der Architekt beschreibt sein Konzept als „Prinzip, das den Bogen schlägt vom Nest zum Wald, zur Erde und hinaus ins Universum". Der 121 m² große Bau wirkt tatsächlich wie ein stilisiertes Nest aus Holz, öffnet sich mit seinen großzügigen Fassadenöffnungen jedoch zum waldnahen Standort. Auch das Projekt Pilotis in a Forest (Kita-Karuizawa, Gunma, Japan, 2010, Seite 198), ein Entwurf von Go Hasegawa (Jahrgang 1977), zeugt von der Auseinandersetzung mit der unmittelbaren Umgebung der Architektur und scheint auf den ersten Blick mehr mit einem Baumhaus als mit einem traditionellen, erdgebundenen Wohnbau gemein zu haben. Hasegawa führt aus: „Ich habe den Wald als Wand interpretiert." Den darüber schwebenden Wohnbereich beschreibt er als „kleinen Raum, wie einen Dachboden". Die 1,8 m hohen Decken und ein niedriger Esstisch über einem gläsernen Bodeneinsatz „lassen den landschaftlichen Außenraum größer wirken und näher rücken". Obwohl der Architekt die ökologischen Aspekte seines Entwurfs nicht gesondert hervorhebt, bemühte er sich offenkundig, ältere Bäume zu erhalten und den Bauherren größere Nähe zur Natur zu ermöglichen. „Bei gutem Wetter kann man zwischen den Piloten mitten im Wald entspannen", so der Architekt, „und nach Sonnenuntergang draußen unter den mächtigen Bäumen schlafen." Der Bau ist ein Wochenendhaus, dessen Eigentümer, wie die meisten Japaner, mehr Zeit in einem dichtbesiedelten urbanen Umfeld verbringen, als in einem Wald – geschweige denn in einem Wald, in dem sie wohnen und schlafen können. Mit einer Nutzfläche von 77 m² folgt der Bau ebenso wie Fujimotos Haus NA einem Instinkt, der bis in graue Vorzeit zurückreicht: dem Impuls, in Bäumen zu wohnen.

MIT AMERIKA IST NOCH ZU RECHNEN

Auch wenn radikale Experimente im Wohnbau in Nordamerika heute wesentlich seltener sind als zu Zeiten, in denen Frank Gehry künstlerisch mit Materialien spielte wie beim Norton House (Venice, Kalifornien, 1983), entstehen nach wie vor außergewöhnliche Häuser, oft in ländlicher Lage oder landschaftlicher Umgebung. Ein Beispiel hierfür ist der Woodstock Farm Estate (Woodstock, Vermont, 2007–09, Seite 236) in den Green Mountains, ein Entwurf von Rick Joy. Das „gestreckte Giebelhaus mit gemauerter Stirnseite" scheint äußerlich stärker der ländlichen als der zeitgenössischen Architektur verpflichtet; dasselbe gilt für die angrenzende zweistöckige Scheune auf dem Gelände. Innen

11
Go Hasegawa, Pilotis in a Forest,
Kita-Karuizawa, Gunma, Japan, 2010

hält der Bau, was die eher strenge Fassade verspricht, bietet dabei jedoch jenen Komfort, den Bauherren heutzutage von einem „Architekten-haus" erwarten. Das kanadische Architekturbüro Shim-Sutcliffe wiederum entwarf ein Ferienhaus für den Direktor des Museum of Modern Art, Glenn Lowry (Haus auf Henrys Wiese, Vale Perkins, Kanada, 2008–09, Seite 372). Der am Westufer des Lake Memphremagog gelegene Bau, unweit der Grenze zwischen Quebec und Vermont, greift ein vertrautes Motiv der Region auf: an den Wänden der Farmen gestapeltes Kaminholz. Der Holzstapeleffekt ebenso wie die Verarbeitung regionaltypischer Materialien (etwa weißes Pinienholz für den Innenausbau) ordnen den Bau typologisch der ländlichen Architektur zu. Dennoch bietet auch dieses Haus an Ausblick und Komfort, was der zeitgenössische Lebensstil fordert.

Shim-Sutcliffe zeichnen darüber hinaus für einen Wohnbau verantwortlich, den Glenn Lowry „eines der bedeutendsten Privathäuser Nordamerikas" nannte. Das Integral House (Toronto, Kanada, 2005–09, Seite 366) mit 1394 m² Nutzfläche gibt dem Begriff „Herrenhaus" eine völlig neue Bedeutung. Das in einer bewaldeten Schlucht in Toronto gelegene Anwesen umfasst u. a. Musikräume und einen Konzertsaal mit 150 Plätzen. Die komplexen Kurven des Grundrisses spielen auf das berufliche Fachgebiet des Bauherren an, der zahlreiche klassische Unterrichtswerke zum Thema Mathematik verfasste. Die geschosshohe, zwischen „synkopisch angeordnete Eichenholzlamellen" gesetzte Verglasung prägt Innenräume und Außenbau in weiten Teilen und bietet einen großzügigen Ausblick in die bewaldete Umgebung. So entsteht ein Wohnkonzept, das sich zur Natur und dem Außenraum öffnet, selbst im Winter, der hier sehr kalt sein kann. Einzige Vorgaben des Bauherren an die Planer waren: „Kurven und ein Konzertsaal". Dem *Toronto Star* zufolge war der Eigentümer bereit, 5,4 Millionen Dollar in das Grundstück mit einem Vorgängerbau zu investieren, den er abreißen ließ, um Platz für das neue Meisterwerk zu schaffen. „Von der Straße aus", so der Artikel, „sind nur zwei Geschosse sichtbar. Die Hauptwohnbereiche liegen unterhalb des Straßenniveaus, sodass man den Eindruck hat, in die Schlucht hinabzusteigen. Die Rückseite des Hauses wird von Verglasung und Eichenholzlamellen dominiert. Die Innenarchitektur ist minimalistisch – eigentlicher Blickpunkt sind die Bäume der Umgebung. Sie sind von allen fünf Wohnebenen aus sichtbar. ‚Unser Wunsch war es, ein zeitloses Projekt zu realisieren', so die Architektin Brigitte Shim."[5] Über Kosten zu sprechen, ist oft ein Tabu, wenn es um große Privatanwesen geht, und doch gehört dieser Aspekt zu ihrer Geschichte. Tatsächlich ist es ein Privileg im privaten Wohnbau, wenn Bauherren über finanzielle Mittel verfügen und bereit sind, diese in den Bau eines außergewöhnlichen Hauses zu investieren. Bei James Stewart, dem Auftraggeber des Integral House, war dies ganz offensichtlich der Fall.

ALLES IST MÖGLICH

Besonders ein Büro in diesem Band vermittelt mit seinen Entwürfen das Potenzial und die Bandbreite der privaten Wohnbauarchitektur. Christian Pottgiesser, geboren 1965 in Deutschland, gründete sein Büro architecturespossibles 2005 in Paris. Wie der Name des Büros vermuten lässt, ist für den Architekten zu Beginn eines neuen Projekts grundsätzlich jede bauliche Form möglich. Sein Haus L (Yvelines, Frankreich, 2007–11, Seite 328) ist ein gutes Beispiel für diesen Ansatz, denn die Konfiguration des Hauses ist alles andere als gewöhnlich. Statt eines Einzelbaus schlug Pottgiesser seinen Auftraggebern, einer Familie mit vier Kindern, fünf Türme vor – einen für jedes Kind und einen für die Eltern – das Ganze auf einem Gartengrundstück unweit einer Orangerie aus dem 18. Jahrhundert. Die Türme setzen auf einem 47 m langen, „amöbenförmigen" Sockel auf. Klassische Wohnbautypologien hätten eine solche Lösung wohl kaum nahegelegt, und doch war sie nicht nur möglich, sondern scheint den Bedürfnissen der Bauherrenfamilie auch bestens zu entsprechen. Auch wenn die Prioritäten hier in Yvelines offenkundig gänzlich andere sind als die eines Architekten in Tokio, belegt dieses Projekt doch, dass zu Beginn einer Hausplanung jede Form denkbar ist. Pottgiesser suchte bei seinem Haus L nach Bezugspunkten zu einer Schlossruine aus dem 18. Jahrhundert und verstand es dennoch, den Wohnbau dezidiert in zeitgenössischer Formensprache zu verankern. Architekten wie Sou Fujimoto suchen nach Wegen, den Typus Haus neu zu erfinden – und lösen sich dabei von jahrzehnte-, mitunter jahrhundertealten Vorstellungen des Hausbaus, seinen Funktionen und seiner Raumgestaltung. Das von Fujimoto angesprochene Netz(werk) ist zweifellos ein Spiegel unserer Zeit, und es gibt keinen Grund, warum ein Haus kein Netzwerk aus Räumen sein sollte, das man auf verschiedenste Weise nutzen kann – ein Netzwerk, das seinen Bewohnern nicht länger seine eigene Logik diktiert. Stellen wir uns eine Architektur vor, die längst nicht mehr so unbeweglich ist, wie die Materialien von Wänden und Decken, kurzum, stellen wir uns einfach dies vor: *Architektur heute!*

[1] Ezra Klein, „The Rich Get Richer in One Chart", in: *The Washington Post,* 9. September 2010, http://voices.washingtonpost.com/ezra-klein/2010/09/the_rich_getting_richer_in_one.html, Zugriff am 23. April 2012.

[2] Vgl. http://www.businessinsider.com/new-charts-about-inequality-2011-11#the-top-001-the-super-elite-claim-a-greater-share-of-the-income-than-any-time-on-record-3, Zugriff am 23. April 2012.

[3] Yoree Koh, „Building Anew Out of Tsunami's Rubble", in: *The Wall Street Journal,* Asien-Ausgabe, 6. Juni 2011, http://online.wsj.com/article/SB100014240527023049060045763666439797668 36.html, Zugriff am 23. April 2012.

[4] Jean-Pierre Raynaud in einer E-mail an den Autor, 28. April 2012.

[5] Katie Daubs, „The House that Math Built", in: *Toronto Star,* 4. Februar 2011, http://www.thestar.com/news/article/933017--the-house-that-math-built, Zugriff am 23. April 2012.

INTRODUCTION

VIVRE EN RÉSEAU

Les temps sont difficiles, du moins pour certains. On aurait pu penser que l'architecture contemporaine allait souffrir, ou même que sa créativité s'émousserait sous les coups brutaux et conjugués du fonctionnalisme et de l'économie. Néanmoins, dans la sphère architecturale, les résidences privées constituent encore une sorte de microcosme qui reflète les hauts et les bas de la profession de façon un peu décalée ou amplifiée. Il est certain que les membres des « classes moyennes » font rarement appel à un architecte de qualité pour concevoir leur maison. C'est un privilège habituellement réservé aux classes sociales aisées. La crise récente n'a pas modifié la tendance constatée depuis une trentaine d'années qui, pour le dire brutalement, permet aux riches de devenir plus riches. Aux États-Unis, par exemple, 64 % de la croissance des revenus de la période précédant la crise actuelle (1979–2007) sont allés aux 10 % des mieux rémunérés[1]. Un fossé encore plus prononcé existe avec les très riches, ce 0,01 % des ménages américains qui possèdent aujourd'hui une plus grande part du revenu national qu'à n'importe quelle période connue de l'histoire[2]. La vérité est donc qu'il n'y a pas de temps difficiles pour les très riches, ce qui explique que l'on continue à construire des maisons de luxe un peu partout dans le monde. La sélection des projets publiés dans cet ouvrage a volontairement opté pour une autre approche, pour d'autres types de projets que ces « palais » surgis de terre du Sri Lanka à Toronto, pour s'intéresser aux efforts dépensés dans la conception de petites, voire de très petites, mais très fonctionnelles résidences. C'est souvent le cas au Japon, par exemple. L'acceptation par les Japonais de maisons mesurant nettement moins de 100 mètres carrés est due à des facteurs historiques, culturels et démographiques. La densité de la population et le coût des terrains dans des villes comme Tokyo rend presque impossible la construction de grandes résidences. Cette tendance à une modestie naturelle est parfois compensée par la volonté des clients japonais de faire appel à de jeunes architectes novateurs. Bien qu'il n'y ait aucune raison objective pour qu'une gigantesque maison ne soit pas un chef-d'œuvre architectural, il est clair que l'on peut trouver beaucoup plus d'innovation dans les petites résidences conçues sous la double contrainte de budgets limités et de terrains de dimensions réduites.

LA VAGUE ET LES ARBRES

Certains architectes se sont récemment concentrés sur des domaines où leur talent était requis. C'est le cas de Shigeru Ban qui propose de nouvelles solutions d'architecture d'urgence pratiquement chaque fois que se produit un tremblement de terre ou un tsunami majeurs. Il l'a encore récemment fait pour le séisme de Tohoku suivi d'un tsunami qui a frappé le Japon du Nord-Est le 11 mars 2011. Tadao Ando, auteur de deux des plus spectaculaires maisons publiées dans ces pages, à Monterrey (Mexique) et Mirissa (Sri Lanka), a été nommé membre du comité créé par le gouvernement japonais pour guider les efforts de la reconstruction après le séisme de 2011. Dépassant les considérations sur le besoin de reconstruire immédiatement, Ando a envisagé les vrais enjeux à long terme : « Je pense que le Japon a besoin de repenser ses connexions avec la famille, l'amour de son pays, son rôle en Asie et les responsabilités des individus vivant sur une même planète. Le Japon a oublié tout cela au cours de ces trente dernières années », a-t-il déclaré au *Wall Street Journal*. Il s'était déjà engagé auparavant en faveur de la plantation massive d'arbres dans l'île de Seto en mer du Japon, par exemple. Dans le cas du séisme de Tohoku, il a déclaré : « Dans le but de revivifier l'esprit japonais, j'ai proposé l'idée d'une "Forêt de repos". Je pense que ce serait une bonne

12

12
*Sou Fujimoto, House NA,
Tokyo, Japan, 2010*

idée de planter une forêt ouverte à tout le monde dans chaque préfecture dévastée – Miyagi, Iwate et Fukushima –, ce qui a été autorisé par le Parlement.» Ando a aussi suggéré que l'entretien de ces arbres «serait une barrière naturelle entre la mer et les villes qui seront construites à l'intérieur des terres, et les regarder pousser rappellerait aux habitants ce qui s'est déroulé en 2011». Selon le *Wall Street Journal*, il ajoutait : «Ce type de mémorial vivant de "forme naturelle" serait plus approprié que la construction d'un bâtiment de plus[3].»

Aux États-Unis, où les cicatrices laissées par l'ouragan Katrina ne se referment qu'à grand-peine, le projet en cours d'exécution lancé par l'acteur Brad Pitt, appelé Make it Right, a néanmoins obtenu des résultats intéressants. Le projet de Maison flottante (Float House, Nouvelle-Orléans, Louisiane, 2008–09, page 284) conçu par le Prix Pritzker Thom Mayne et l'agence Morphosis, s'intéresse aux moyens de construire des maisons non seulement de coût accessible, mais en mesure de résister aux futurs désastres naturels. Accrochée à des mâts en acier ancrés dans des piliers de béton enfouis sur 13,70 mètres de profondeur, cette maison est capable de flotter à la surface de l'inondation car elle peut s'élever à 3,65 mètres au-dessus de son emplacement et s'y reposer sans aucun dommage lorsque l'eau se retire. Comme l'écrit l'agence Morphosis : «Les changements climatiques globaux provoquent des inondations et des catastrophes naturelles toujours plus violentes. Dans le monde, près de 200 millions de personnes vivent dans des zones côtières inondables et, aux États-Unis mêmes, plus de 36 millions d'habitants vivent sous la menace d'inondations. Le prototype de la Float House propose une façon de vivre durable en mesure de s'adapter à cette réalité incertaine.»

LE BON, LE MAUVAIS ET LE LAID

L'idée qui a présidé à la création de la collection *Architecture Now!* est de ne privilégier aucune zone géographique, aucun style architectural. La seule limite de cet ouvrage présent tient donc à celles des connaissances de son auteur, mais comme ces livres sont des best-sellers depuis plus de dix ans, les propositions et les offres d'information affluent. Ainsi *Architecture Now! Houses 3* peut-il être considéré comme un large survol des différents types de maisons individuelles construites au cours de ces trois ou quatre dernières années dans le monde. Son contenu espère présenter le meilleur de ce qui a été édifié. Le terme de «meilleur» étant évidemment subjectif, certains lecteurs peuvent ne pas être d'accord avec nos choix. Nous sollicitons leur indulgence. Ceci dit, ce livre offre des avantages directement liés à cette subjectivité. Des sites Internet affirmant offrir le panorama de tout ce qui se passe dans l'architecture contemporaine existent certainement, mais proposent curieusement tous en même temps plus ou moins les mêmes photos et les mêmes textes et font aussi peu de distinctions entre ce que nous pourrions appeler «le bon, le mauvais et le laid». L'intérêt de la forme même du livre n'est pas encore mort.

DE LA CHINE AU CHILI

Un des messages que souhaiterait transmettre cet ouvrage est qu'aujourd'hui, la «bonne» architecture se trouve presque partout sur la planète dès lors que l'on dispose des moyens et de la volonté de construire plus qu'un simple abri. Dans les pages qui suivent se trouvent des maisons chiliennes, paraguayennes, mexicaines, péruviennes et brésiliennes, des résidences construites aux États-Unis, au Canada, en

France, aux Pays-Bas, en Allemagne, en Suisse, au Portugal et en Espagne. D'autres ont été sélectionnées en Nouvelle-Zélande, au Japon, en Corée et en Chine, et même au Sri Lanka et au Ghana. Bien sûr, cette liste n'est pas exhaustive et de vastes régions ne sont pas représentées, mais, dans l'ensemble, de belles maisons sont construites chaque année un peu partout et il y a quelque chose de vraiment nouveau dans cette extension géographique. Il y a de cela quelques années, il eut été quasi impossible d'entendre parler d'une splendide résidence privée de 1200 mètres carrés en Chine. Aujourd'hui, un architecte chinois âge de quarante-huit ans, Wang Shu, vient de remporter le Prix Pritzker, la distinction la plus prestigieuse de la profession d'architecte. Une maison en Corée a été conçue par un architecte américain (Daeyang Gallery and House, Séoul, Corée-du-Sud, 2010–12, page 214) et une autre, à Pasadena, est l'œuvre d'un célèbre praticien chinois (Glen Oaks Residence, Pasadena, Californie, 2009–11, page 262). Les frontières, les barrières et les distances disparaissent face à l'incroyable développement de la communication à l'échelle de la planète. L'architecture ne peut plus se développer dans l'isolement et le nationalisme sans entraves. Les voyages et l'Internet rendent tout possible, partout et à chaque instant.

Par ailleurs, ce livre n'est certainement pas conçu pour promouvoir un style ou un certain modèle de maison. Dans ces pages, comme dans le monde plus large et fédérateur de l'architecture contemporaine, les types les plus divers coexistent. Les références au passé, à l'histoire de l'architecture ont laissé leur empreinte sur les nouvelles résidences présentées ici. Il ne s'agit plus du pastiche superficiel du désormais « ancien » postmodernisme, mais le fruit d'une réflexion approfondie et d'une intégration qui illustre finalement le rejet complet de l'idée de *tabula rasa* défendue avec tant de panache par Walter Gropius et d'autres au début du XXᵉ siècle. Nous sommes « modernes », même si le modernisme a considérablement évolué jusqu'au point de ne plus être reconnaissable, même lorsque des architectes comme John Pawson ou David Chipperfield sont impliqués. « Moderne » signifie « du temps présent ou lié à lui ». Comme d'autres disciplines créatives, l'architecture s'est toujours fortement appuyée sur le passé. L'art de construire n'a jamais été ignoré, même à l'apogée du Style international. Des changements notables dans les attitudes envers le passé sont peut-être survenus avec l'émergence du postmodernisme de la fin des années 1960 et le manifeste de Robert Venturi *De l'ambiguïté en architecture* (1966, 1971 pour la traduction française). En 1972, il revint à la charge avec un second ouvrage intitulé *A Significance for A&P Parking Lots, or Learning from Las Vegas*, plus connu dans sa version révisée publiée en 1977 sous le titre *L'Enseignement de Las Vegas* (1978 pour la traduction française). D'une certaine façon les titres de ces ouvrages annonçaient la couleur, mais les projets parfois extravagants sortis des agences de Michael Graves, Robert A. M. Stern ou de Venturi lui-même relevaient plus de l'embaumement propret du cadavre du modernisme que de la naissance d'une architecture nouvelle.

C'EST DANS L'ADN
Si cette nouvelle vie existe aujourd'hui, c'est parce que les architectes ont redécouvert leur propre ADN, les siècles de l'histoire de l'art de construire qui ont précédé et nourri leur capacité de création. Regardez la Maison sur l'eau de Li Xiaodong (Water House, village de Yuhu, Lijiang, Chine, 2006–09, page 7) et demandez-vous si le passé et le présent n'ont pas engendré ici la vraie modernité. Même non initié à l'histoire de la Chine, chacun peut ressentir le poids de ces pierres et la présence de l'eau. Ce qui sépare ce type de projet de l'ancien post-

modernisme ou « contextualisme » est que des architectes acceptent l'idée que le passé n'est pas qu'une question de façade mais une continuité qui concerne les matériaux, les formes, mais aussi les fonctions.

Les maisons japonaises publiées dans cet ouvrage, y compris la maison NA de Sou Fujimoto (House NA, Tokyo, 2010, page 186) s'aventurent à leur manière dans un nouveau territoire, et redéfinissent l'espace de vie tout en expérimentant une ouverture physique radicale à la limite des contraintes qui pèsent d'habitude sur une résidence privée. Là encore, ceci vient de la tradition japonaise dans laquelle les écrans *shoji* ou les panneaux coulissants ont généré depuis des siècles un « espace souple », mais témoigne également de la densité extrême de la population, en particulier le long du corridor oriental Tokyo-Osaka. Ici, la tradition omniprésente est une force, toujours sous-jacente à l'innovation. Il s'agit peut-être de la manière la plus simple de définir les changements survenus depuis que Venturi faisait l'éloge du parking A&P. Le titre de son premier livre, *De l'ambiguïté en architecture*, est peut-être plus proche de ce qui se passe aujourd'hui. De préférence au plan clair, net et rigoureux, des architectes du monde entier acceptent, ou même amplifient l'inhérence de l'ambiguïté dans différents types de constructions. Ceci ne signifie pas la fin de la fonctionnalité, mais, en particulier dans les résidences privées, la flexibilité est devenue le cri de ralliement : les familles se composent différemment, les espaces s'utilisent d'autres manières. À la place du modèle de la banlieue résidentielle américaine d'après-guerre qui avait créé des espaces différenciés pour le séjour, la salle à manger et cuisine, les architectes et leurs clients distinguent aujourd'hui zones « publiques » et zones « privées ». La plupart du temps, l'espace de séjour est devenu un lieu ouvert où se détendre, s'alimenter, préparer la cuisine. Les chambres et les salles de bain restent « privées » pour des raisons évidentes, mais lorsque le climat le permet, les limites naguère strictes entre l'intérieur et l'extérieur sont estompées par l'utilisation de vitrages toute hauteur ou de panneaux coulissants.

À LA RECHERCHE DU JARDIN

Les résidences les plus ambitieuses et les plus dispendieuses publiées ici créent presque systématiquement un dialogue fructueux avec leur cadre naturel, que ce soit le bord de la mer, la forêt ou la rive d'un lac. On peut noter ici un lien avec l'architecture moderniste dans laquelle le verre, par exemple dans la Farnsworth House de Mies van der Rohe (Plano, Illinois, 1951), a marqué une grande partie de la conception résidentielle actuelle et de l'intégration au cadre naturel comme dans la fameuse Maison sur la cascade de Frank Lloyd Wright (Fallingwater, Mill Run, Pennsylvanie, 1935), comme si la plus pure expression des privilèges du riche propriétaire d'une maison était la redécouverte de la nature dans un environnement entièrement contemporain et protégé, dans une recherche du jardin d'Éden qui a animé une grande partie de l'histoire de l'architecture. Lorsque la nature est trop lointaine, comme dans les villes japonaises, les architectes et leurs clients la cherchent néanmoins, sous forme de plantes en pot et de vues sur le ciel.

Les lecteurs familiers de la collection *Architecture Now !* ont sans doute noté la présence d'œuvres d'artistes où la relation entre leur art et l'architecture apparaît évidente. Dans cet ouvrage est présentée une maison de l'artiste Jean-Pierre Raynaud, mais également

*13
Susanne Nobis, Toward
Landscape, Lake Starnberg,
Berg, Germany, 2006–10*

13

plusieurs maisons conçues par des architectes pour eux-mêmes. La tradition (ou l'humour) voudrait que l'architecte soit souvent le plus mal logé, mais les maisons d'architectes présentées ici semblent faire exception à la règle. L'Espagnol Antón García-Abril, par exemple, n'a pas hésité à tenter une expérience dans son petit abri (25 mètres carrés) appelé La Truffe (La Trufa, Costa da Morte, Espagne, 2010, page 8). « La Trufa est un petit morceau de nature construit en terre et rempli d'air », dit-il. Un espace dans un rocher qui se trouvait là et qui se fond dans le terrain. Il se camoufle, en imitant le processus de la formation minérale par sa structure et s'intègre dans l'environnement naturel pour se plier à ses lois. En dehors de la manière dont il a conçu cette construction en béton en utilisant 50 mètres cubes de foin pour son coffrage, Antón García se réfère explicitement au Cabanon de Le Corbusier (Roquebrune, Cap Martin, France, 1951), ce petit bungalow où l'architecte suisse passa sa dernière nuit avant de se noyer dans la mer en 1965.

POURPRE, ORGANIQUE, EXTRATERRESTRE

La résidence de Glen Oaks de Ma Qingyun est une maison d'architecte de taille beaucoup plus importante. Cette extension de 340 mètres carrés qui prolonge une maison datant du milieu du XXe siècle est décrite par le doyen de l'École d'architecture de l'université de Californie du Sud (USC) comme « pourpre, organique et extraterrestre ». Ma Qingyun est le fondateur de MADA s.p.a.m., l'une des premières grandes agences d'architecture apparues après la libéralisation de la règlementation chinoise qui permit enfin à chaque praticien de signer ses réalisations au lieu de se fondre dans de grands « instituts ». Comprenant une galerie double hauteur semi-publique, une cuisine, un bureau et un studio de danse au deuxième étage pour l'épouse de Ma, Shouning Li, la maison dotée de fenêtres circulaires est habillée de béton projeté qui donne à sa « peau » un aspect relativement brut. La circulation en rampe vers l'ancienne construction correspond à une greffe de la maison de banlieue américaine et permet de proposer de nouvelles fonctionnalités à une résidence conçue pour une autre époque. De par sa formation, Ma Qingyun est pleinement conscient des traditions et de la typologie architecturales américaines. Qu'il ose remettre en question et réinventer une « icône » aussi fondamentale que la maison familiale de l'après-guerre peut être pris pour un signe des temps. Si la Californie est le lieu où Rudolf Schindler, Richard Neutra, John Lautner et Frank Gehry ont conçu des maisons révolutionnaires pour leur époque, il reste que l'extension imaginée par l'architecte chinois aborde de façon encore plus fondamentale les défis que de nouveaux styles de vie font peser sur l'architecture de la maison, en Amérique comme ailleurs.

Suzanne Nobis, née à Munich en 1963, a travaillé pour Renzo Piano et Herzog & de Meuron avant de créer son agence à Berg en 2000. Non loin de ses bureaux, elle a conçu sa propre maison sur les agréables rives du lac de Starnberg (Toward Landscape, lac Starnberg, Berg, Allemagne, 2006–10, page 296). S'inspirant de la forme des hangars à bateaux de ce lac, elle a créé deux volumes, l'un en galerie ouverte et l'autre appelé « la maison des chambres ». Elle a opté pour une peau en titane « repliée » sur une ossature en bois pour créer des espaces à la fois chaleureux et modernes. Les deux volumes donnent sur le lac par des façades entièrement vitrées. En voyant cette maison, qui bouscule nombre de barrières entre divers types de construction (le hangar à bateau et la résidence), on pourrait presque penser qu'être architecte est vraiment un merveilleux métier, surtout si l'on a la chance de pouvoir vivre dans une telle maison.

14

UNE TORTUE ET UN POT DE FLEUR

La ville de Cape Coast au Ghana, à 165 kilomètres à l'ouest d'Accra sur le golfe de Guinée, est sans doute un des lieux les plus éloignés de la scène de l'art contemporain européen que l'on puisse imaginer. Pourtant, c'est plus précisément à Biriwa qu'un artiste allemand connu, Carsten Höller, et un célèbre artiste vidéo, Marcel Odenbach, ont décidé de construire une maison de vacances, la Maison tortue (House Turtle, 1999–2009, page 220). Comme l'écrit Höller, elle a été conçue à partir des considérations suivantes : a) disposer d'une circulation d'air maximum à travers et sous la maison pour éviter toute climatisation mécanique ; b) rendre la construction aussi peu attirante que possible pour les moustiques et garder à distance les autres animaux, serpents compris ; c) favoriser les angles à 87 ou 93° par rapport à l'angle droit pour augmenter/diminuer la perception des distances et de l'aspect rectiligne ; d) collecter l'eau de pluie du toit et des terrasses en sous-sol ; e) donner à la maison un aspect «non achevé». Posée sur de minces colonnes et suspendue au-dessus de l'océan, elle a une apparence très singulière. Quasi isolée au-dessus de la plage, c'est un lieu pour s'échapper vers un autre univers, au bout du monde.

Jean-Pierre Raynaud, né en 1939, est un célèbre artiste français qui a cherché à sa façon à s'isoler du bruit et de l'agitation de Paris en vivant naguère dans une maison souterraine qu'il avait pour l'essentiel dessinée lui-même (Le Mastaba, en collaboration avec l'architecte Jean Dedieu, 1986) à La Garenne-Colombes, à dix kilomètres du centre de la capitale. Là, il pouvait créer et exposer ses œuvres, allant de pots de fleurs géants dorés à la feuille à des drapeaux étrangers transformés en œuvre d'art par son intervention. Plus récemment, avec l'assistance de son ami l'architecte Jean-Michel Wilmotte, Raynaud a créé un nouveau lieu à Barbizon (France, 2009, page 406) à 58 kilomètres de Paris. Barbizon est un village connu pour avoir abrité une école de peinture éponyme à laquelle participèrent d'illustres peintres tels Théodore Rousseau et Jean-François Millet au XIXᵉ siècle. Après avoir débarrassé une maison ancienne appelée le Clos d'Hortense d'extensions ultérieures à sa construction, l'architecte l'a agrandie d'un vaste volume de verre où Raynaud expose une bonne partie de ses œuvres. Cette verrière permet aussi d'ouvrir la maison vers son cadre boisé et un jardin de 1000 mètres carrés dessiné par l'artiste qui a travaillé avec l'architecte paysagiste Neveux Rouyer pour obtenir une sorte d'unité entre l'art, l'architecture et la nature qu'il aime. «Plus qu'un problème d'architecture, c'est l'espace qui est en jeu. Comme les œuvres d'art, c'est à l'intérieur d'une surface que tout se joue, d'où l'importance dans les autres siècles du cadre qui marquait le territoire de l'œuvre. Depuis une cinquantaine d'années, le tableau s'est affranchi de cette frontière pour créer une osmose entre le projet et la vie, c'est totalement évident dans les grands *Nymphéas* de Monet, dans les drippings de Pollock ou un monochrome de Klein. L'espace pour moi a toujours été l'espace de la pensée, l'espace de tous les possibles.» Jean-Pierre Raynaud a beaucoup travaillé à la frontière de l'art et de l'architecture à travers sa maison de La Celle-Saint-Cloud, par exemple, commencée en 1969 et démolie vingt-quatre ans plus tard. Avec les déblais de sa démolition, il organisa en 1993 une exposition fameuse au CAPC de Bordeaux. Dans ce cas exceptionnel, l'architecture de l'atelier de l'artiste peut être considérée comme partie intégrante de son travail artistique, ici en collaboration étroite avec Jean-Michel Wilmotte. Jean-Pierre Raynaud conclut : «Je ne sais pas consommer au sens où on l'entend. Mes espaces n'ont jamais été construits pour rencontrer la vie, mais seulement pour qu'ils existent [4]. »

15
Shigeru Ban, Villa Vista, Weligama,
Sri Lanka, 2007–10

UNE FALAISE SUR LA MER

La pointe extrême sud du Sri Lanka, face à l'océan Indien, est un site presque tout aussi surprenant pour une œuvre majeure d'architecture résidentielle contemporaine que le golfe de Guinée. Les deux localités voisines de Mirissa et Weligama ont récemment vu se construire deux maisons signées de grands architectes japonais. Leurs commanditaires sont belges, un père et son fils, directeurs d'une prospère entreprise locale de pneumatiques. La première achevée a été la maison au Sri Lanka (House in Sri Lanka, Mirissa, Sri Lanka, 2006–09, page 54) de Tadao Ando. Ne mesurant pas moins de 2577 mètres carrés, cette importante résidence a vu sa construction retardée par le tsunami de décembre 2004 qui avait ravagé la région. Consulté par Pierre Pringiers au début de cette même année, Ando n'a pu achever le chantier que cinq ans plus tard. Des spécialistes vinrent du Japon pour que le béton utilisé par Ando soit au niveau de ses critères habituels de qualité. Le projet est pleinement fidèle au vocabulaire géométrique du Prix Pritzker et alterne avec maestria des effets de transparence et d'opacité. Une spectaculaire piscine à débordement, geste architectural demandé par le client, se projette de l'étage de la maison vers l'immensité de l'océan.

Le même tsunami a exercé une influence directe sur la seconde maison, la villa Vista (Weligama, Sri Lanka, 2007–10, page 68), résidence de 825 mètres carrés construite pour Koenraad Pringiers par Shigeru Ban. Celui-ci s'était beaucoup impliqué dans la conception de maisons pour l'après-tsunami dans la localité côtière d'Hambantota, non loin de Weligama. Le tremblement de terre survenu le 26 décembre 2004 en Indonésie avait provoqué un tsunami catastrophique qui avait entraîné la mort d'environ 38 000 personnes au Sri Lanka. Un programme caritatif d'un million de dollars fut lancé par le groupe immobilier Colliers International pour aider à la reconstruction dans la région et l'agence Shigeru Ban Architects offrit son temps et ses efforts pour ce projet. Construites en blocs de terre compressée et bois, 50 maisons – dont 36 furent achevées en avril 2006 – avaient été programmées. Chaque maison mesure 71 mètres carrés pour un coût approximatif de 13 000 dollars. Écologiques et de dimensions suffisantes pour offrir un certain confort, ces maisons en matériaux naturels restent fraîches malgré les températures extérieures élevées. Le mobilier en bois de caoutchoutier local faisait également partie du projet. La villa Vista semble bien loin de ce type d'action humanitaire mais comme l'architecte est le même, des liens dans le temps et l'espace peuvent être retracés. Implantée comme la précédente au sommet d'une colline, la résidence cadre des vues spectaculaires sur l'océan. Shigeru Ban a utilisé du bois massif, des planches de fibrociment et des feuilles de cocotier tissées qui permettent de « se fondre dans l'ambiance locale ». Pour les plafonds, l'architecte a dessiné un « cannage » en bandeaux de teck de 80 millimètres de large et 3 millimètres d'épaisseur. À l'évidence, Shigeru Ban a davantage cherché à intégrer les traditions constructives locales que Tadao Ando. C'est un trait inscrit dans l'essence de son architecture, dont l'aspect peut considérablement varier en fonction de la situation géographique. Ban utilise également souvent des matériaux écologiques comme les tubes de carton structurels (mais pas sur ce projet). Il ne s'agirait pas de croire qu'Ando n'est pas sensible à la situation de sa Sri Lanka House, bien au contraire. Sa grande force est toujours de savoir implanter un bâtiment dans un cadre naturel et de tirer le maximum du potentiel du site. Les approches des deux architectes japonais sont par nature différentes.

16
Rick Joy, Woodstock Farm Estate,
Woodstock, Vermont, USA, 2007–09

16

PRESQU'AU PARADIS

Les architectes brésiliens Thiago Bernardes et Paulo Jacobsen sont habitués aux clients désirant des maisons à la fois très grandes et très luxueuses. La maison Joá (Rio de Janeiro, Brésil, 2010–11, page 116) d'une surface de près de 3500 mètres carrés n'est donc pas pour eux une exception. Elle est située sur un vaste plateau de 16 000 mètres carrés qui offre des vues spectaculaires sur les quartiers de São Conrado et de Barra da Tijuca où la plupart des compétitions des Jeux olympiques de 2016 se dérouleront, et sur le fameux monolithe de Pedra da Gávea de 840 mètres de haut qui domine la résidence. Dans ce cadre, les architectes ont pris la liberté de créer une continuité réelle entre l'intérieur et l'extérieur. Les matériaux les plus visibles sont la brique, le bois et le verre qui se prêtent à l'interpénétration du dedans et du dehors en renforçant une impression d'espace ininterrompu. Dans cette atmosphère de jardin tropical, les photos de cette maison réussissent mal à rendre ses dimensions impressionnantes alors que le sentiment d'espace est, en soi, l'expression ultime du luxe. Ses résidents vivent dans la grande ville tout en bénéficiant des vues et de l'environnement d'un lieu de villégiature. Même si l'on n'y trouve pas de courbes, elle peut rappeler la maison beaucoup plus modeste qu'Oscar Niemeyer s'était construite sur la Estrada das Canoas au-dessus du quartier de São Conrado à Rio (1952–53). À l'époque, les riches et les puissants ne jugeaient pas convenable de vivre au-dessus de la ville, zone plutôt réservée aux favelas. La tradition peut changer, surtout quand des architectes comme Niemeyer ouvrent la voie.

VIVRE DANS UN ARBRE

Bien qu'il soit à de nombreux égards un pays de traditions profondément enracinées, le Japon semble en même temps accepter facilement les expérimentations architecturales radicales, y compris dans le domaine de la maison. Cette acceptation vient certainement de ce que les architectes expliquent leurs défis par des arguments et un constat des réalités qui ne sont pas sans liens avec le passé. L'une des plus étonnantes résidences publiées ici est la maison NA de Sou Fujimoto. Né en 1971, Fujimoto est déjà très connu dans les cercles architecturaux pour son approche novatrice, à la limite du concevable. Ici, il a imaginé une résidence presque entièrement ouverte sur la rue. L'architecte compare sa maison en acier laqué blanc et à niveaux décalés, à une cabane dans les arbres. Dans un jeu fascinant sur la connexion entre le passé, le présent et le futur de l'architecture, il se réfère directement à « la vie dans les arbres », celle peut-être de lointains ancêtres et à « une plate-forme pour un type de communication en réseau dans l'espace ». Bien qu'il soit assez difficile de percevoir les aspects pratiques de cette proposition, on note une volonté de répondre à une attitude jeune, dont la référence est davantage l'Internet qu'un univers tiré du passé et soumis à la machine.

Une autre réalisation tokyoïte, mais cette fois de la célèbre agence SANAA, Prix Pritzker 2010, s'appuie également sur des plateaux décalés ou des « dalles à différents niveaux ». ici, comme dans la House NA, l'idée n'est pas de créer un espace souple et bidimensionnel mais bien de chercher à obtenir une souplesse en trois dimensions. Le contact avec la nature, le ciel, le vent ou même les plantes en pot de l'immeuble d'appartements Shakuji (Tokyo, 2009–10, page 360) est dans la tradition de la culture japonaise. De conception radicale, ces appartements n'en sont pas moins attentivement intégrés à l'échelle de la rue. Si certains pionniers modernistes cherchaient une rupture avec l'environnement immédiat afin de créer des objets « uniques », ce n'est certainement pas le cas de SANAA. Il s'agit d'une architecture différente, nouvelle, qui correspond cependant à de nombreux égards à de très anciens besoins et attentes culturels. Si la souplesse sur un seul plan a souvent été considérée comme une nouvelle façon de construire une maison, ces architectes ont littéralement porté l'argument à un niveau supérieur, entièrement différent.

UN NID EN FORÊT

Keisuke Maeda, né en 1974, est encore plus jeune que Sou Fujimoto. Il ne vient ni de Tokyo ni d'Osaka mais d'Hiroshima où il a ouvert son agence, UID architects, en 2003. Sa Maison-nid (Nest House, Onomichi, Hiroshima, 2010, page 378) explore les liens avec la nature de façon plus ouverte que les maisons tokyoïtes présentées dans ces pages. « C'est un peu comme un principe qui se développerait du nid en forêt vers la forêt, puis vers la terre et enfin vers l'univers », explique-t-il. Cette petite maison de 121 mètres carrés fait en effet penser à un nid de bois stylisé, mais non sans de grandes ouvertures et une relation évidente à son environnement boisé. Également influencée par son cadre naturel, la Maison sur pilotis en forêt (Pilotis in a Forest House, Kita-Karuizawa, Gunma, Japon, 2010, page 198) de Go Hasegawa (né en 1977) semble au premier regard plus proche d'une cabane perchée dans les arbres que d'une construction traditionnelle ancrée dans le sol. « La forêt forme les murs de la construction », explique Hasegawa. Il compare le séjour suspendu à un « petit espace genre grenier » dans lequel le plafond de 1,80 mètre de haut et une table de repas surbaissée sur un sol de verre cherchent « à donner le sentiment que l'environnement naturel extérieur est plus vaste et plus proche ». Si l'architecte ne précise pas les caractéristiques écologiques de ce projet, il a clairement cherché à protéger les grands arbres et à rapprocher ses clients de la nature. « Par beau temps, vous pouvez vous détendre sous les pilotis au milieu de la forêt, dit-il, et après le coucher du soleil, dormir dehors au pied des grands arbres. » C'est une résidence de week-end et ses propriétaires, comme la plupart des Japonais, passent probablement plus de temps dans un cadre urbain hyperdensifié qu'en forêt, et surtout dans une forêt où l'on peut vivre et dormir. De 77 mètres carrés, cette maison, comme la House NA de Fujimoto, cherche à retrouver un instinct remontant à la nuit des temps, le sentiment de vivre parmi les arbres.

L'AMÉRIQUE TOUJOURS PRÉSENTE

Bien que les expérimentations radicales sur la typologie résidentielle soient moins fréquentes en Amérique du Nord aujourd'hui que lorsque Frank Gehry jouait en artiste avec les matériaux de la maison Norton (Norton House, Venice, Californie, 1983), quelques très belles maisons y voient néanmoins encore le jour, souvent dans un cadre rural ou naturel. Un bon exemple est celui du domaine de la ferme de Woodstock (Woodstock Farm Estate, Woodstock, Vermont, page 236) de Rick Joy perdu dans les Green Mountains. Cette maison « à pignon de pierre allongé » doit davantage son aspect aux constructions agricoles qu'à l'architecture moderne, de même que la grange sur deux niveaux qui fait partie du complexe. L'aménagement intérieur rappelle l'austérité extérieure, mais offre certainement le confort et la modernité auquel les clients de « maisons d'architectes » sont maintenant habitués. Les architectes canadiens Shim-Sutcliffe ont conçu une maison de vacances pour le directeur du Musée d'art moderne de New York, Glenn Lowry (House on Henry's Meadow, Vale Perkins, Canada,

2008–09, page 372). Située sur la rive ouest du lac Memphremagog, près de la frontière entre le Québec et le Vermont, cette Maison sur la prairie d'Henry tient compte de traditions locales qui consistent à empiler le bois de chauffage autour des fermes. L'effet d'empilement de ce bois et l'utilisation de matériaux comme des bardeaux de pin peints en blanc pour l'habillage intérieur rappellent les constructions d'inspiration agricole tout en offrant le confort et les vues qui vont de pair avec un style de vie contemporain.

L'agence Shim-Sutcliffe est également à l'origine d'une résidence que Glenn Lowry a qualifiée de « l'une des plus importantes résidences privées d'Amérique du Nord ». De 1394 mètres carrés, la Maison intégrale (Integral House, Toronto, 2005–09, page 366) relève de la catégorie des « demeures ». Implantée dans une étroite vallée boisée à Toronto, elle possède un espace dédié à la musique et aux spectacles qui peut accueillir jusqu'à 150 personnes. Son plan complexe, en courbes, n'est pas sans rapport avec le propriétaire, auteur à succès de manuels de mathématiques. Des baies vitrées toute hauteur insérées entre « des ailettes de chêne syncopées », qui sont une des caractéristiques les plus visibles de la maison vue de l'extérieur, offrent des perspectives généreuses sur le site boisé et donnent l'impression qu'elle est immergée dans la nature, voire même ouverte sur elle, malgré la rigueur du climat hivernal. Le client voulait « des courbes et un espace pour spectacles » et était d'accord, selon le journal de Toronto, le *Star*, pour acheter une maison déjà présente sur le site pour 5,4 millions de dollars et la raser afin de laisser au futur chef-d'œuvre toute sa place. « De la rue, explique le journal, seuls deux niveaux sont visibles. Le séjour principal est creusé dans le sol, ce qui donne l'impression de descendre dans les profondeurs de la petite vallée. La moitié arrière de la maison est en pans de verre entrecoupés d'ailettes de bois. La décoration intérieure est minimaliste, les arbres de l'extérieur étant le principal élément d'attraction. Ils sont visibles des cinq niveaux. "Le souhait était que ce projet donne une impression d'intemporalité", a déclaré l'architecte Brigitte Shim [5]. » La référence au prix d'un projet est souvent un tabou, du moins pour les grandes résidences, mais ici, elle fait partie de l'histoire. Qu'un client ait les moyens et la volonté de faire construire une résidence exceptionnelle est pour l'architecte un privilège, et c'était le cas pour James Stewart, client de l'Integral House.

TOUT EST POSSIBLE

D'une certaine façon, le travail de l'une des agences présentées dans ce livre donne une certaine idée de l'importance et de l'étendue du champ de l'architecture résidentielle. Christian Pottgiesser, né en Allemagne en 1965, a créé son agence architecturespossibles en 2005 à Paris. Le nom de cette agence implique qu'au départ d'un projet toute forme d'architecture est possible. Sa maison L (Yvelines, France, 2007–11, page 328) semble en être la preuve tant sa configuration est loin de l'ordinaire. Plutôt qu'un seul « bâtiment, » Pottgiesser a suggéré de construire cinq tours pour un client et ses quatre enfants, une pour chaque enfant et une pour les parents, sur un terrain voisin d'une orangerie du XVIIIe siècle. Les tours sont réparties sur un socle « amiboïde » de 47 mètres de long. Les typologies classiques de l'habitat n'auraient jamais permis une telle solution qui pourtant, non seulement était possible, mais semble en fait assez bien répondre aux attentes du client. Bien que les priorités soient différentes dans les Yvelines de celle d'un architecte œuvrant à Tokyo, le projet confirme à de nombreux égards l'idée qu'une maison peut prendre n'importe quelle forme. Si Pottgiesser a recherché une relation avec les vestiges d'un ancien

17
Christian Pottgiesser, L House,
Yvelines, France, 2007–11

17

château du XVIIIᵉ siècle tout en imaginant une forme résolument contemporaine, les architectes comme Sou Fujimoto veulent réinventer la maison, en mettant de côté des décennies et parfois des siècles d'a priori sur ses fonctions et son espace. Le réseau auquel se réfère Fujimoto est bien dans l'esprit de notre époque et il n'y a aucune raison apparente pour qu'une maison ne ressemble pas à un réseau d'espaces dans lequel on pourrait naviguer de multiples façons, sans qu'il n'impose sa « logique » sur ses occupants. Imaginer une architecture n'est plus une démarche aussi rigide que les matériaux qui constituent les murs et les toits, il faut imaginer « l'Architecture, maintenant ! ».

[1] Esra Klein, « The Rich Get Richer in One Chart », *The Washington Post*, 9 septembre 2010, http://voices.washingtonpost.com/ezra-klein/2010/09/the_rich_getting_richer_in_one.html, consulté le 23 avril 2012.

[2] http://www.businessinsider.com/new-charts-about-inequality-2011-11#the-top-001-the-super-elite-claim-a-greater-share-of-the-income-than-any-time-on-record-3, consulté le 23 avril 2012.

[3] Yoree Koh, « Building Anew Out of Tsunami's Rubble », *The Wall Street Journal*, Asie, 6 juin 2011. http://online.wsj.com/article/SB10001424052702304906004576366643979766836.html, consulté le 23 avril 2012.

[4] Jean-Pierre Raynaud, courriel à l'auteur, le 28 avril 2012.

[5] Katie Daubs, « The House that Math Built », *Toronto Star*, 4 février 2011, http://www.thestar.com/news/article/933017--the house-that-math-built, consulté le 23 avril 2012.

AIRES MATEUS

Aires Mateus e Associados
Rua Silva Carvalho 193
1250–250 Lisbon
Portugal

Tel: +351 21 381 56 50 / Fax: +351 21 381 56 59
E-mail: m@airesmateus.com / Web: www.airesmateus.com

MANUEL ROCHA DE AIRES MATEUS was born in Lisbon, Portugal, in 1963. He graduated as an architect from the Faculty of Architecture at the Technical University of Lisbon (FA-UTL; 1986). He worked with Gonçalo Byrne beginning in 1983 and with his brother Francisco Xavier Rocha de Aires Mateus beginning in 1988. He has taught at the Harvard GSD (2002, 2005), and the Accademia di Architettura (Mendrisio, Switzerland, since 2001). **FRANCISCO XAVIER ROCHA DE AIRES MATEUS** was born in Lisbon in 1964. He also graduated from the FA-UTL (1987) and began working with Gonçalo Byrne beginning in 1983, before his collaboration with his brother. He, too, has taught at Harvard and in Mendrisio. Their work includes the Sines Cultural Center (Sines, 2000); the Casa No Litoral (Litoral Alentejano, 2000); the Alenquer House (Alenquer, 2002); a plan for the Park Hyatt Hotel (Dublin, Ireland, 2003); the Fontana Park Hotel (Lisbon, 2002–07); the Santa Marta Light House Museum (Cascais, 2003–07); the Highway Toll and Control Building (Benavente, 2006–07); a school complex (Vila Nova da Barquinha, 2006–08); 14 private houses, Vila Utopia-Wise (Lisbon, 2005–09); social housing (Madrid, Spain, 2007–09); EDP headquarters, Portuguese Electric Company (Lisbon, 2008–09); Portugal Telecom Call Center (Santo Tirso, 2008–09); Parque de los Cuentos Museum (Málaga, Spain, 2008–09); an urban plan for the Parque Mayer and Botanical Gardens (Lisbon, 2008–09); a House in Leiria (Leiria, 2008–10); and a House in Aroeira (Aroeira, 2009–10, published here), all in Portugal unless stated otherwise. They participated in the 2010 Venice Architecture Biennale curated by Kazuyo Sejima.

MANUEL ROCHA DE AIRES MATEUS wurde 1963 in Lissabon geboren. Sein Studium schloss er an der Fakultät für Architektur der Universidade Técnica de Lisboa ab (FA-UTL, 1986). Ab 1983 arbeitete er mit Gonçalo Byrne, seit 1988 auch mit seinem Bruder Francisco Xavier Rocha de Aires Mateus zusammen. Nach Lehraufträgen an der Harvard GSD (2002, 2005) unterrichtet er nun an der Accademia di Architettura (Mendrisio, Schweiz, seit 2001). **FRANCISCO XAVIER DE AIRES MATEUS** wurde 1964 in Lissabon geboren. Auch er absolvierte sein Architekturstudium an der FA-UTL (1987). Ab 1983 arbeitete er mit Gonçalo Byrne, die Kooperation mit seinem Bruder folgte. Auch er lehrte in Harvard und Mendrisio. Zu ihren Projekten zählen das Kulturzentrum in Sines (2000), die Casa No Litoral (Litoral Alentejano, 2000), die Casa Alenquer (Alenquer, 2002), ein Entwurf für das Park Hyatt Hotel (Dublin, 2003), das Fontana Park Hotel (Lissabon, 2002–07), das Santa-Marta-Leuchtturmmuseum (Cascais, 2003–07), eine Mautstelle und Autobahnwacht (Benavente, 2006–07), ein Schulkomplex (Vila Nova da Barquinha, 2006–08), Vila Utopia-Wise, 14 Einfamilienhäuser (Lissabon, 2005–09), ein soziales Wohnbauprojekt (Madrid, 2007–09), die Firmenzentrale der portugiesischen Elektrizitätswerke EDP (Lissabon, 2008–09), ein Callcenter für Portugal Telecom (Santo Tirso, 2008–09), das Museum im Parque de los Cuentos (Málaga, 2008–09) sowie die Stadtplanung für den Parque Mayer und den Botanischen Garten (Lissabon, 2008–09), ein Haus in Leiria (Leiria, 2008–10) sowie ein Haus in Aroeira (Aroeira, 2009–10, hier vorgestellt). 2010 war das Büro auf der Architekturbiennale von Venedig vertreten, die von Kazuyo Sejima kuratiert wurde.

MANUEL ROCHA DE AIRES MATEUS est né à Lisbonne en 1963. Diplômé de la faculté d'architecture de l'Université technique de Lisbonne (FA-UTL, 1986), il a travaillé avec Gonçalo Byrne à partir de 1983 et avec son frère Francisco Xavier Rocha de Aires Mateus à partir de 1988. Il a enseigné à la Harvard GSD (2002, 2005) et à l'Accademia di Architettura (Mendrisio, Suisse, depuis 2001). **FRANCISCO XAVIER DE AIRES MATEUS,** né à Lisbonne en 1964, est également diplômé de la FA-UTL (1987) et a commencé à travailler avec Gonçalo Byrne en 1983, avant de rejoindre son frère. Il a lui aussi enseigné à Harvard et à Mendrisio. Parmi leurs réalisations, essentiellement au Portugal sauf mention contraire : le Centre culturel Sines (Sines, 2000) ; la Casa No Litoral (Litoral Alentejano, 2000) ; la maison d'Alenquer (Alenquer, 2002) ; un plan pour le Park Hyatt Hotel (Dublin, Irlande, 2003) ; le Fontana Park Hotel (Lisbonne 2002–07) ; le Musée du phare de Santa Marta (Cascais, 2003–007) ; un bâtiment de péage et de surveillance d'autoroute (Benavente, 2006–07) ; un complexe scolaire (Vila Nova da Barquinha, 2006–08) ; 14 résidences privées, Vila Utopia-Wise (Lisbonne, 2005–09) ; des logements sociaux (Madrid, 2007–09) ; le siège de la compagnie portugaise d'électricité EDP (Lisbonne, 2008–09) ; un centre d'appel pour Portugal Telecom (Santo Tirso, 2008–09) ; le musée du Parque de los Cuentos (Málaga, Espagne, 2008–09) ; un plan d'urbanisme pour le Parque Mayer et ses jardins botaniques (Lisbonne, 2008–09) ; une maison à Leiria (Leiria, 2008–10) et la maison à Aroeira (Aroeira, 2009–10, publiée ici). En 2010, ils ont participé à la Biennale d'architecture de Venise, dirigée par Kazuyo Sejima.

HOUSE IN AROEIRA

Aroeira, Portugal, 2009–10

Area: 268 m². Client: not disclosed
Cost: €350 000. Collaboration: Francisco Caseiro

The architects contrast opaque white blocks with the much more open, and recessed, center of the house.

Die Architekten schaffen Kontraste zwischen den geschlossenen weißen Blöcken und dem ungleich offeneren, zurückgesetzten Kern des Hauses.

Les ailes latérales aux façades aveugles et blanches contrastent avec la partie centrale en retrait, beaucoup plus ouverte.

The irregular shape of this white house encloses a generous central green space. The site, located outside Lisbon, is surrounded by pine trees and is known for its golf course. The interior of the house, where white surfaces also dominate, is divided into a living room, library, dining room, studio, a master bedroom, and two rooms for children, as well as a garage. The architects explain: "The site's hexagonal shape goes unnoticed due to the lack of fencing, which dilutes the land into the surrounding pine trees. This house covers the maximum possible area, echoing the shape of the site. It is arranged around a courtyard, articulating its spaces as an extension of this central space. Beginning from a capricious shape, this house encounters its first sharp boundary in the outline of the awning. The auxiliary zones resolve the geometry, tranquilizing the main spaces."

Das asymmetrische Haus rahmt einen großzügigen grünen Innenhof. Das kiefernumstandene Grundstück in der Nähe Lissabons liegt in einer für seine Golfplätze bekannten Gegend. Das Innere des Hauses, das von weißen Oberflächen dominiert ist, gliedert sich in Wohnbereich, Bibliothek, Essbereich, Studio, ein Elternschlafzimmer und zwei Kinderzimmer sowie eine Garage. Die Architekten führen aus: „Durch den Verzicht auf eine Umzäunung geht das Grundstück nahtlos in den nahen Kiefernwald über, die hexagonale Grundform bleibt fast unbemerkt. Der Bau nutzt das Grundstück maximal, indem es seinen Konturen folgt. Er ist um einen Innenhof angeordnet und artikuliert seine Räume als Fortführung dieser zentralen Zone. Das Haus, auf den ersten Blick formal eigenwillig, zeigt erst mit dem Vordach scharfe Konturen. Die funktionalen Nebenräume mildern die strenge Geometrie und beruhigen die Hauptwohnbereiche."

Le plan irrégulier de cette maison intégralement blanche s'organise autour d'un vaste espace vert central. Non loin de Lisbonne, son site planté de pins est connu pour sa proximité d'un terrain de golf. L'intérieur de la maison, où le blanc prédomine également, est divisé en un séjour, une bibliothèque, une salle à manger, un studio, une chambre principale, deux chambres d'enfants et un garage. « En l'absence de clôture, explique l'architecte, la forme hexagonale du terrain n'est pas perceptible, ce qui donne l'impression d'une dilution de l'espace dans la forêt de pins. Le bâti couvre le maximum de la surface de la parcelle dont il suit la forme. Il s'organise autour d'une cour qui articule ses volumes en une extension de l'espace central. Se développant à partir d'une forme capricieuse, la maison butte sur une première limite marquée par le profil de l'auvent. Les zones auxiliaires résolvent l'équation géométrique du plan et apaisent les espaces principaux. »

This view, taken from the roof, shows the curving, pointed central space of the house with the green background in sharp contrast with the white forms.

Die vom Dach aufgenommene Ansicht zeigt die geschwungene, spitz zulaufende Kontur des zentralen Baukörpers. Die grüne Kulisse ist ein auffälliger Kontrast zu den weißen Formen.

Prise de la toiture, cette vue montre l'espace central incurvé et en pointe ainsi que l'environnement verdoyant en fort contraste avec les masses blanches de la construction.

A plan makes the inner courtyard legible, with its almost organic forms in contrast with the essentially rectilinear external lines of the house.

Ein Grundriss macht den Innenhof nachvollziehbar. Seine organische Form kontrastiert mit den geradlinigen Außenkanten des Hauses.

Plan montrant la cour intérieure de forme presque organique contrastant avec les contours extérieurs essentiellement rectilignes.

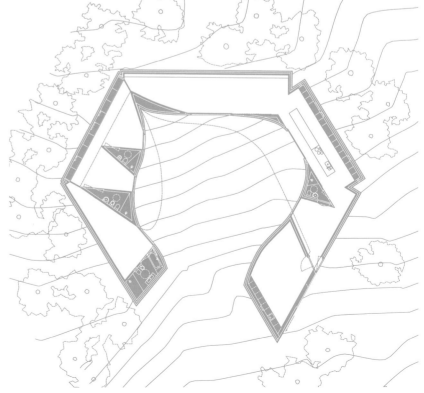

Interior views show the same contrast between opacity and large openings seen on the exterior of the house. White is the rule here, as it is for the outside surfaces of the house.

Innenansichten bestätigen den schon am Außenbau erkennbaren Kontrast von geschlossenen Flächen und groß-zügigen Öffnungen. Weiß dominiert hier ebenso wie am Außenbau.

Ces vues de l'intérieur montrent la même confrontation entre plans aveugles et grandes ouvertures déjà observée en façade. Comme à l'extérieur, le blanc est de règle.

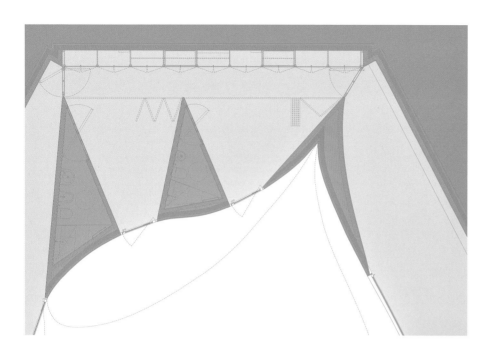

A plan and a photo emphasize the opening in the house, with the slight overhang and curving inner surface of the residence.

Grundriss und Aufnahme zeigen die Öffnung des Hauses mit den leicht auskragenden Vordächern und der geschwungener Innenfassade.

Le plan et la photo ci-dessous font ressortir l'importance des dimensions des ouvertures ainsi que l'auvent qui protège la façade concave de la maison.

Inside the house, modern furniture and books add a certain amount of warmth to the otherwise very strict and white environment. A large glazed surface brings in ample lateral light.

Im Haus sorgen modernes Mobiliar und Bücher für eine gewisse Wärme im sonst recht strengen weißen Interieur. Die großzügige Verglasung lässt reichlich Seitenlicht einfallen.

À l'intérieur, le mobilier moderne et la présence des livres confèrent une certaine chaleur à cet environnement immaculé, dessiné avec rigueur. Une grande baie fournit un généreux éclairage naturel.

TADAO ANDO

Tadao Ando Architect & Associates
Osaka
Japan

Born in Osaka in 1941, **TADAO ANDO** was self-educated as an architect, largely through his travels in the United States, Europe, and Africa (1962–69). He founded Tadao Ando Architect & Associates in Osaka in 1969. He has received the Alvar Aalto Medal, Finnish Association of Architects (1985); the Medaille d'or, French Academy of Architecture (1989); the 1992 Carlsberg Prize; and the 1995 Pritzker Prize. Notable buildings include Church on the Water (Hokkaido, Japan, 1988); Japan Pavilion Expo '92 (Seville, Spain, 1992); Forest of Tombs Museum (Kumamoto, Japan, 1992); Rokko Housing (Kobe, Japan, 1983–93); the Suntory Museum (Osaka, Japan, 1994); Awaji Yumebutai (Awajishima, Hyogo, Japan, 1997–2000); the Pulitzer Foundation for the Arts (Saint Louis, Missouri, USA, 1997–2000); the Modern Art Museum of Fort Worth (Fort Worth, Texas, USA, 1999–2002); and the Chichu Art Museum on the Island of Naoshima in the Inland Sea (Japan, 2004). More recently he has completed the Omote Sando Hills complex (Tokyo, Japan, 2006); 21_21 Design Sight (Tokyo, Japan, 2004–07); Tokyu Toyoko Line Shibuya Station (Shibuya-ku, Tokyo, Japan, 2006–08); an expansion of the Clark Art Institute (Williamstown, Massachusetts, USA, 2006–08); a House in Sri Lanka (Mirissa, Sri Lanka, 2006–09, published here); and the renovation of the Punta della Dogana (Venice, Italy, 2007–09). In 2010, Tadao Ando completed the Stone Sculpture Museum (Bad Kreuznach, Germany, 1996–2010); the Shiba Ryotaro Memorial Museum (Higashiosaka, Osaka, Japan, 1998–2001/2010); the WSJ-352 Building on the Novartis Campus (Basel, Switzerland, 2004–10); and the Lee Ufan Museum (Naoshima, Kagawa, Japan, 2007–10). He has recently completed a House in Monterrey (Monterrey, Mexico, 2008–11, also published here); and is working on the Abu Dhabi Maritime Museum (Abu Dhabi, UAE, 2006–); and a house for the designer Tom Ford near Santa Fe (New Mexico, USA).

TADAO ANDO wurde 1941 in Osaka geboren. Als Architekt ist er Autodidakt und bildete sich in erster Linie durch Reisen in die USA, nach Europa und Afrika (1962–69). 1969 gründete er sein Büro Tadao Ando Architect & Associates in Osaka. 1985 erhielt er die Alvar-Aalto-Medaille des finnischen Architektenverbands, 1989 die Medaille d'Or der französischen Académie d'Architecture, 1992 den Carlsberg-Preis sowie 1995 den Pritzker-Preis. Zu seinen beachtenswerten Bauten zählen die Kirche auf dem Wasser (Hokkaido, 1988), der japanische Pavillon auf der Expo '92 (Sevilla, 1992), das Wald-der-Gräber-Museum (Kumamoto, 1992), die Wohnanlage Rokko (Kobe, 1983–93), das Suntory Museum (Osaka, 1994), Awaji Yumebutai (Awajishima, Hyogo, 1997–2000), die Pulitzer Foundation for the Arts (St. Louis, Missouri, 1997–2000), das Modern Art Museum in Fort Worth (Fort Worth, Texas, 1999–2002) und das Chichu Art Museum auf der Insel Naoshima in der Seto-Inlandsee (Japan, 2004). Jüngere Projekte sind u. a. der Omote-Sando-Hills-Komplex (Tokio, 2006), das 21_21 Design Sight (Tokio, 2004–07), der U-Bahnhof Shibuya der Tokyu-Toyoko-Linie (Shibuya-ku, Tokio, 2006–08), eine Erweiterung des Clark Art Institute (Williamstown, Massachusetts, 2006–08), ein Haus in Sri Lanka (Mirissa, Sri Lanka, 2006 bis 2009, hier vorgestellt) sowie der Umbau der Punta della Dogana (Venedig, 2007–09). 2010 konnte Tadao Ando das Steinskulpturenmuseum (Bad Kreuznach, 1996 bis 2010) fertigstellen, das Shiba Ryotaro Memorial Museum (Higashiosaka, Osaka, 1998–2001/2010), das Gebäude WSJ-352 auf dem Novartis Campus (Basel, 2004–10) und das Lee Ufan Museum (Naoshima, Kagawa, 2007–10). Unlängst realisiert wurde ein Haus in Monterrey (Mexiko, 2008–11, ebenfalls hier vorgestellt). Aktuell arbeitet Ando an dem Meeresmuseum in Abu Dhabi (VAE, seit 2006) und einem Haus für den Designer Tom Ford bei Santa Fe (New Mexico, USA).

Né à Osaka en 1941, **TADAO ANDO** est un architecte autodidacte formé en grande partie par ses voyages aux États-Unis, en Europe et en Afrique (1962–69). Il fonde Tadao Ando Architect & Associates à Osaka en 1969. Il est titulaire de la médaille Alvar Aalto de l'Association finlandaise des architectes (1985), de la médaille d'or de l'Académie d'architecture (Paris, 1989), du prix Carlsberg (1992) et du prix Pritzker (1995). Il a notamment réalisé l'Église sur l'eau (Hokkaido, Japon, 1988); le pavillon du Japon pour Expo '92 (Séville, Espagne, 1992); le musée de la Forêt des tombes (Kumamoto, Japon, 1992); les immeubles de logement Rokko (Kobe, Japon, 1983–93); le musée Suntory (Osaka, Japon, 1994); le Centre de conférences Awaji Yumebutai (Awajishima, Hyogo, Japon, 1997–2000); la Fondation Pulitzer pour les arts (Saint Louis, Missouri, 1997–2000); le Musée d'art moderne de Fort Worth (Texas, 1999–2002) et le Musée d'art Chichu sur l'île de Naoshima en mer Intérieure du Japon (2004). Plus récemment, il a achevé le complexe Omote Sando Hills (Tokyo, 2006); le Centre de design 21_21 Design Sight (Tokyo, 2004–07); la gare de Shibuya de la ligne Tokyu Toyoko (Shibuya-ku, Tokyo, 2006–08); une extension du Clark Art Institute (Williamstown, Massachusetts, 2006–08); la maison au Sri Lanka (Mirissa, Sri Lanka, 2006–09, publiée ici) et la rénovation des entrepôts de la Punta della Dogana (Venise, 2007–09). En 2010, Tadao Ando a achevé le Musée de la sculpture sur pierre (Bad Kreuznach, Allemagne, 1996–2010); le Musée du mémorial Shiba Ryotaro (Higashiosaka, Osaka, Japon, 1998–2001/2010); l'immeuble WSJ-352 sur le Campus Novartis (Bâle, Suisse, 2004–10); le musée Lee Ufan (Naoshima, Kagawa, Japon, 2007–10) et une maison à Monterrey (Monterrey, Mexique, 2008–11, publiée ici). Il travaille actuellement au projet du Musée maritime d'Abou Dhabi (Abou Dhabi, EAU, 2006–) et à une maison pour le styliste Tom Ford près de Santa Fe (Nouveau-Mexique, États-Unis).

HOUSE IN MONTERREY

Monterrey, Mexico, 2008–11

Area: 1519 m². Client: not disclosed
Cost: not disclosed

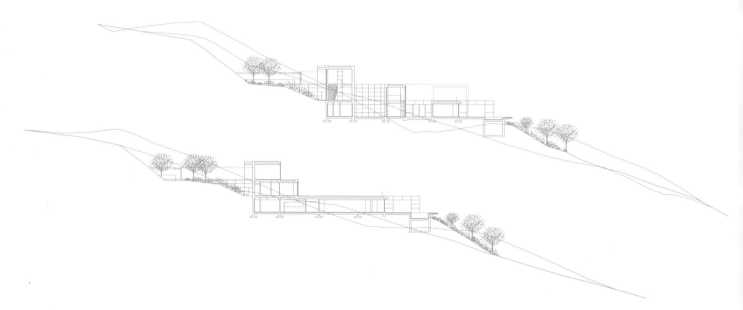

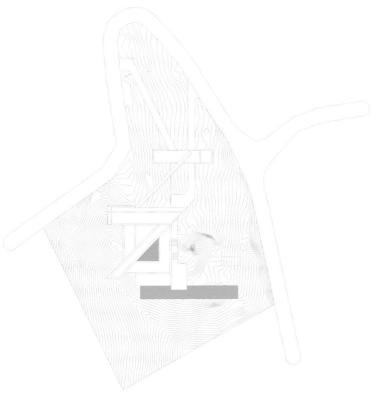

Section drawings and an aerial view (opposite), together with a plan (left), show the entirely rectilinear design in its hilly setting. Above, a pool seems to disappear into the horizon.

Querschnitte und ein Luftbild (gegen-über) sowie ein Grundriss zeigen deutlich die strenge Geradlinigkeit des Entwurfs auf hügeligem Terrain. Oben ein Pool, der mit dem Horizont zu verschmelzen scheint.

Les coupes, la vue aérienne (page ci-contre) et le plan de gauche montrent la rigueur géométrique du projet dans son cadre de collines. Ci-dessus, la piscine semble dispa-raître à l'horizon.

Monterrey is the capital of the state of Nuevo León and one of the richest cities of Mexico. The 10 824-square-meter site is located at the foot of a mountainous national park. Tadao Ando explains that "the client requested a house which merges into the surrounding environment, bringing the beautiful views inside with perfect privacy. I conceived the house to realize this theme—open but closed to the outside, but using geometry corresponding to the theme." The composition consists of a main square volume with a Z-shaped element above, forming a large three-story residence. The public areas, located in the "Z," include a private gallery. A library connects the private and public spaces. The main materials employed are exposed concrete, steel sash windows, granite, and limestone both exterior and interior. Tadao Ando says quite clearly that he "pays his best respects" to the Mexican architect Luis Barragán with this house, developing, as he puts it, "his essences of modern architecture in my own way."

Monterrey, Hauptstadt des Bundesstaats Nuevo León, zählt zu den reichsten Städten Mexikos. Das 10 824 m² große Grundstück liegt in einem Nationalpark am Fuß der Berge. Tadao Ando erzählt: „Der Bauherr wollte ein Haus, das mit seiner Umgebung verschmilzt, die wunderbare Aussicht erschließt, jedoch völlige Privatsphäre bietet. Ich entwarf das Haus also entsprechend dieser Vorgaben – offen, dabei nach außen geschlossen, dem Thema mit geometrischen Mitteln gerecht werdend." Die Komposition besteht aus einem quadratischen Baukörper, überschnitten von einem Z-förmigen Element: insgesamt eine großzügige dreistöckige Villa. Zu den öffentlichen Bereichen im „Z"-Riegel gehört auch eine private Galerie. Eine Bibliothek verbindet private und öffentliche Wohnbereiche. Zentrale Materialien – innen wie außen – sind Sichtbeton, Schiebefenster mit Stahlrahmen, Granit und Kalkstein. Tadao Ando betont, mit diesem Haus einerseits dem mexikanischen Architekten Luis Barragán seine Reverenz zu erweisen, andererseits jedoch die „Kernelemente der modernen Architektur Barragáns auf eigene Weise" zu interpretieren.

Monterrey, capitale de l'État de Nuevo Leon, est l'une des villes les plus riches du Mexique. Le terrain de 10 824 m² se trouve au pied d'un parc national de montagnes. « Le client souhaitait une maison qui se fonde dans son cadre, explique Tadao Ando, et laisse entrer les magnifiques vues sur le paysage tout en respectant l'intimité de ses habitants. J'ai conçu la maison sur ce thème : elle est ouverte mais fermée sur l'extérieur en utilisant une géométrie particulière adaptée. » La composition consiste en un volume principal de plan carré surmonté d'un élément en Z contenant la résidence étagée sur trois niveaux. Les zones publiques, comprises dans ce Z, comprennent, entre autres, un musée privé. Une bibliothèque fait le lien entre les espaces privés et publics. Les principaux matériaux sont le béton brut, l'acier pour les huisseries, le granit et le calcaire aussi bien à l'extérieur qu'à l'intérieur. Tadao reconnaît « rendre hommage » ici à l'architecte mexicain Luis Barragán et développer à sa façon « l'essence de son architecture moderniste ».

With an elegance hitherto seen mainly in Japan, Ando juxtaposes his smooth concrete in this setting where interior and exterior come together.

Mit einer Eleganz, die man hauptsächlich aus Japan kennt, komponiert Ando dort, wo innen und außen aufeinandertreffen, seine glatten Betonflächen.

Avec son élégance habituelle, d'esprit très japonais, Ando utilise son fameux béton lissé dans une composition où l'intérieur et l'extérieur se fondent.

A dining and living area faces the swimming pool with a fully glazed wall. Below, plans of the main part of the house.

Ein Wohn- und Essbereich ist mit einer geschosshohen Glaswand zum Pool orientiert. Unten Grundrisse des zentralen Baukörpers.

L'espace de séjour-salle à manger fait face à la piscine aperçue derrière une immense baie vitrée. Ci-dessous, plans de la partie principale de la maison.

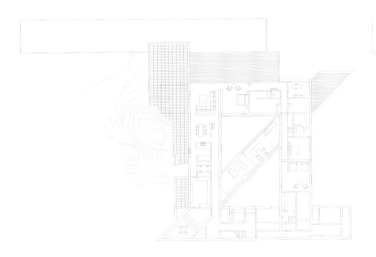

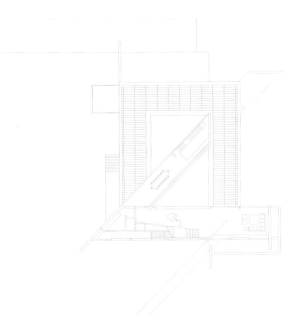

HOUSE IN SRI LANKA

Mirissa, Sri Lanka, 2006–09

Area: 2577 m². Client: Saskia and Pierre Pringiers
Cost: not disclosed. Collaboration: PWA Architects

Located on a cliff-top site facing the Indian Ocean, this substantial house was built in southernmost Sri Lanka for a Belgian couple. Tadao Ando received the commission for this project in 2004 before the December 26 tsunami of that year severely damaged the area. The client created the Solideal Loadstar Rehabilitation Trust (SLRT) to rebuild part of the southern coast of Sri Lanka subsequent to the tsunami. The architect selected a local construction company with ties to Japan and brought two former construction site managers from Japan to manage the poured-in-place concrete work. The building is made up of the actual residence, guest areas, and an atelier for the client's wife, who is an artist. As Tadao Ando states: "These programs were distributed within zigzagging volumes, and the interstitial voids created between them were provided as places for entering into a dialogue with the natural Sri Lankan environment." Numerous "semi-outdoor" spaces are included in the house. A "horizon pool" that extends toward the ocean was included in the plan on the second-level terrace at the request of the client. Local temple stone, cut concrete, and timber were used for finishing, together with natural stone for the perimeter areas. The steel door and windows were made in Belgium.

Das an einem Steilhang an der Südspitze Sri Lankas gelegene großzügige Anwesen mit Blick auf den Indischen Ozean wurde für ein belgisches Ehepaar geplant. Tadao Ando erhielt den Auftrag 2004 noch vor dem großen Tsunami, der die Region am 26. Dezember desselben Jahres heimsuchte. Als Beitrag zum Wiederaufbau der südlichen Küstenregion Sri Lankas stiftete der Bauherr den Solideal Loadstar Rehabilitation Trust (SLRT). Ando entschied sich, mit einer ortsansässigen Baufirma zu arbeiten, die Verbindungen nach Japan hat, und betraute zwei ehemalige Bauleiter aus Japan mit den gesamten Ortbetonarbeiten. Das Haus umfasst einen privaten Wohnbereich, Gästeräume sowie ein Atelier für die Bauherrin, eine Künstlerin. Ando erklärt: „Das Raumprogramm wurde in Z-förmigen Volumina untergebracht, die entstehenden Zwischenräume genutzt, um in den Dialog mit der Landschaft Sri Lankas zu treten." Zum Haus zählen auch zahlreiche „halboffene" Bereiche. Auf Wunsch des Bauherrn befindet sich auf einer Terrasse im Obergeschoss ein Infinity Pool, der sich zum Meer orientiert. Für den Ausbau wurde mit Stein aus Tempelanlagen der Region, geschnittenem Betonstein und Holz gearbeitet, bei den Einfassungsmauern auch mit Naturstein. Stahltür und -fenster sind belgische Fabrikate.

Appartenant à un couple belge, cette vaste demeure a été édifiée au sommet d'une falaise qui domine l'océan Indien à l'extrême Sud du Sri Lanka. Tada Ando en avait reçu la commande peu avant le tsunami du 26 décembre 2004 qui a ravagé cette région. Le client a d'ailleurs fondé le Solideal Loadstar Rehabilitation Trust (SLRT), pour aider à la reconstruction de la région de la côte sud du pays. Ando a choisi une entreprise de construction déjà en lien avec le Japon et a fait venir deux anciens chefs de chantier japonais pour superviser la mise en œuvre du béton coulé sur place. La résidence se compose de la maison des propriétaires, d'une aile pour invités et d'un atelier d'artiste pour la femme du commanditaire. « Le programme se distribue dans des volumes en zigzag, explique l'architecte, tandis que les vides interstitiels sont traités comme des lieux ouvrant un dialogue avec l'environnement naturel du Sri Lanka. » La maison possède de nombreux espaces « semi-extérieurs ». À la demande du client, une piscine à débordement qui se projette vers l'océan a été aménagée au niveau de la terrasse du premier étage. Une pierre locale, du béton scié et du bois figurent parmi les principaux matériaux de second œuvre ainsi que de la pierre naturelle autour de la maison. Les portes et les fenêtres en acier ont été réalisées en Belgique.

Very much alone on the water's edge, the house opposes a rigorous geometric plan to the curving hillside on which it is set, visible in the site plan below.

Isoliert an der Küste gelegen, bildet das Haus mit seinem streng geometrischen Grundriss ein Pendant zum geschwungenen Hügelgrundstück, wie der Lageplan unten zeigt.

Très isolée au bord de l'océan, la maison oppose la rigueur de son plan géométrique à un paysage vallonné, comme le confirme le plan ci-contre.

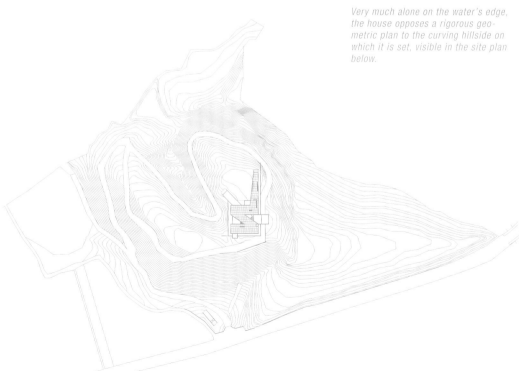

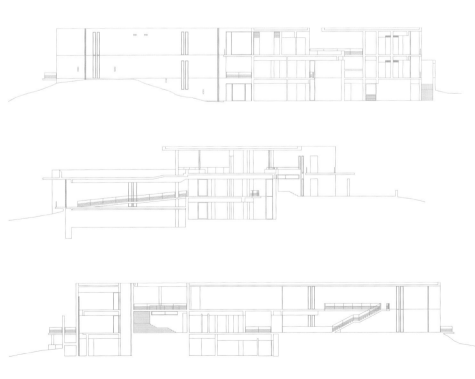

Section drawings, and two images
show a number of Tadao Ando's sig-
nature gestures, such as the suspended staircase (left page) or the
gently inclined ramp seen in the
image above.

Die Querschnitte und Aufnahmen zeigen etliche typische Gesten Andos,
etwa die schwebende Treppe (linke
Seite) oder die sanft geneigte Rampe
oben im Bild.

Les plans de coupe et ces deux
photographies montrent un certain
nombre de gestes typiques de Tadao
Ando comme l'escalier suspendu (à
gauche) ou la rampe en pente douce
(ci-dessus).

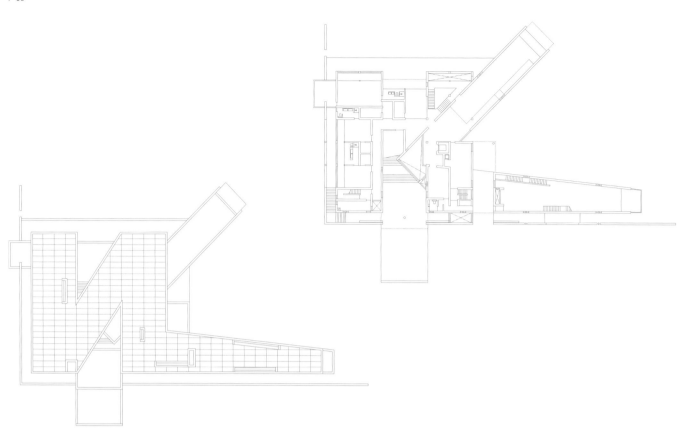

Some windows open fully, allowing the sensation of being both outside and inside. Furnishing is relatively sparse, as might have been the case were this house to have been in Japan.

Einige Fenster lassen sich vollständig öffnen; es entsteht der Eindruck, sich zugleich innen und außen aufzuhalten. Die Möblierung ist sparsam, wie sie dies auch in Japan wäre.

Certaines fenêtres s'ouvrent entièrement pour donner aux occupants l'impression d'être à la fois dedans et dehors. Les meubles sont en nombre limité, comme dans une maison japonaise.

On the left page, plans of the house and a view of a double-height space with a fully glazed face opposite the ocean.

Auf der linken Seite Grundrisse des Hauses und der Blick in einen doppelgeschossigen Raum mit voll verglaster, zum Ozean orientierter Fassade.

Page de gauche : plans de la maison et vue d'un espace double hauteur se terminant par une grande baie vitrée qui donne sur l'océan.

RICARDO BAK GORDON

Bak Gordon Arquitectos
Rua do Alecrim 19A
1200–014 Lisbon
Portugal

Tel: +351 21 347 11 07
Fax: +351 21 347 11 09
E-mail: bakgordon@bakgordon.com
Web: www.bakgordon.com

RICARDO BAK GORDON was born in Lisbon, Portugal, in 1967 and studied at the Faculty of Architecture of Porto University, the Faculty of Architecture of Lisbon's Technical University (FA-UTL), and at the Milan Polytechnic Institute, from which he graduated in 1990. During that year he created Vilela & Gordon, with Carlos Vilela Lúcio. In 2000 he created the firm Bak Gordon Arquitectos, where he currently works. He also teaches at the Architecture Faculty of the Instituto Superior Técnico in Lisbon. Projects and competitions include first prize in the international competition for the residence of the Portuguese Ambassador in Brasilia; first prize in the international competition for the preservation of the historic center of Sintra; first prize for the Human Sciences and Arts Complex for Polo in Aviz, Évora; and first prize in the invited competition for the Municipal Archives Building in Palmela. He was the author of the first exhibition project for the International Architecture Triennale of Lisbon in 2007; the Pavilion of Portugal for the São Paulo Biennial in 2007; the Portuguese Pavilion at Expo Zaragoza 2008; and the Sobral da Lagoa House (Óbidos, Portugal, 2008, published here). Together with Álvaro Siza, Carrilho da Graça, and Aires Mateus, he represented Portugal at the Venice Architecture Biennale in 2010.

RICARDO BAK GORDON wurde 1967 in Lissabon geboren und studierte an der Architekturfakultät der Universität von Porto, der Technischen Universität Lissabon (FA-UTL) sowie am Polytechnikum Mailand, wo er 1990 sein Studium abschloss. Im gleichen Jahr gründete er mit Carlos Vilela Lúcio das Büro Vilela & Gordon. 2000 folgte die Gründung von Bak Gordon Arquitectos, wo Gordon gegenwärtig arbeitet. Darüber hinaus lehrt er an der Architekturfakultät des Instituto Superior Técnico in Lissabon. Zu seinen Projekten und Wettbewerben zählen der erste Preis im internationalen Wettbewerb für die Residenz des portugiesischen Botschafters in Brasília, der erste Preis im internationalen Wettbewerb für das Denkmalschutzprogramm der historischen Altstadt von Sintra, der erste Preis für den Gebäudekomplex Geisteswissenschaften und Kunst, Polo de Aviz in Évora, sowie der erste Preis des geladenen Wettbewerbs für das Stadtarchiv in Palmela. Bak Gordon gestaltete das erste Ausstellungsprojekt der Internationalen Architekturtriennale Lissabon 2007, den portugiesischen Pavillon für die Biennale São Paulo 2007, den portugiesischen Pavillon auf der Expo in Saragossa 2008 sowie das Haus Sobral da Lagoa (Óbidos, Portugal, 2008, hier vorgestellt). Gemeinsam mit Álvaro Siza, Carrilho da Graça und Aires Mateus vertrat er Portugal auf der Architekturbiennale von Venedig 2010.

RICARDO BAK GORDON, né à Lisbonne en 1967, a étudié à la faculté d'architecture de l'université de Porto, à celle de l'Université technique de Lisbonne (FA-UTL) ainsi qu'à l'École polytechnique de Milan dont il est sorti diplômé en 1990. La même année, il a ouvert l'agence Vilela & Gordon, avec Carlos Vilela Lúcio et a créé son agence actuelle, Bak Gordon Arquitectos, en 2000. Il a remporté le premier prix du concours international pour la résidence de l'ambassadeur du Portugal à Brasilia ; le premier prix du concours international pour la préservation du centre historique de Sintra ; le premier prix pour le concours du Complexe des sciences humaines et des arts de Polo à Aviz (Évora) et le premier prix au concours sur invitation pour les Archives municipales de Palmela. Il est l'auteur du premier projet d'exposition pour la Triennale d'architecture de Lisbonne en 2007 ; du Pavillon portugais pour la Biennale of São Paulo en 2007 et de celui de l'Expo Zaragoza 2008, en Espagne et de la maison Sobral da Lagoa (Obidos, Portugal, 2008, publiée ici). Avec Álvaro Siza, Carrilho da Graça et Aires Mateus, il a représenté le Portugal à la Biennale d'architecture de Venise en 2010.

SOBRAL DA LAGOA HOUSE

Óbidos, Portugal, 2008

Area: 124 m². Client: not disclosed
Cost: not disclosed. Collaboration: Ana Durão, Luis P. Pinto, Walter Perdigão

Built in a rural village near the coast of Portugal, with numerous white single-family houses with red clay tile roofs, this house occupies a void between two existing residences, with one side facing a street and the other opening into the landscape. The space not occupied by the building is given over to a pool and garage. The pool sits above the garage and a storage space. The two-story white-plaster house stands out from the older, neighboring structures, with its colored window openings. The architect states: "All the spaces are 'contaminated' by both the framed landscape view and the pastel-colored filtered light brought inside by the reflections of the painted window shutters. Although the interior finishes point to a more conventional comfort with the wood floor and the white painted walls and ceiling, the outside spaces are quite the opposite, searching for fresh and durable materials that give way to the smooth breeze passing by the pool water."

Das in einem Dorf unweit der portugiesischen Küste gelegene Haus steht zwischen weißen Einfamilienhäusern mit roten Ziegeldächern und wurde in einer Baulücke zwischen zwei älteren Nachbarbauten realisiert. Während eine Seite des Baus zur Straße orientiert ist, öffnet sich die andere zur Landschaft. Die nicht bebaute Fläche wurde für Garage und Pool genutzt: Der Pool liegt über der Garage und einem Abstellraum. Das zweigeschossige, weiß verputzte Haus kontrastiert mit seinen farbig akzentuierten Fensteröffnungen mit der nachbarschaftlichen Bebauung. Der Architekt erklärt: „Atmosphärisch sind die Räume geprägt von gerahmten Landschaftsblicken und dem pastellfarbigen Widerschein der lackierten Fensterläden. Während der Innenausbau mit Holzböden und weiß gestrichenen Wänden und Decken von konventionellem Komfort ist, sind die Außenbereiche das Gegenteil, sie stehen für die Suche nach ungewöhnlichen und witterungsbeständigen Materialien, die es der sanften Brise ermöglichen, über das Wasser des Pools zu streichen."

Proche de la côte portugaise, dans un petit village aux multiples maisons individuelles blanches à toits de tuiles rouges, cette maison a rempli un vide entre deux bâtiments anciens, une de ses façades donnant sur la rue, l'autre sur le paysage. Un bâtiment adjacent regroupe un garage et un espace de stockage au-dessus duquel a été aménagée une piscine. La maison de deux niveaux aux façades d'enduit blanc se distingue de ses voisines par des volets de couleurs contrastées. « Tous les espaces sont comme "contaminés" par la présence de ces vues sur le paysage et la lumière pastel filtrée par sa réflexion sur les volets peints, explique l'architecte. Si l'intérieur offre un confort plus conventionnel avec ses planchers de bois et ses murs et plafonds blancs, les espace extérieurs, en revanche, ont été traités en matériaux frais et durables, qui renforcent l'effet de la brise légère régnant autour de la piscine. »

The sober lines of the house and its unified finish make it contrast even more clearly with the village environ- ment. Above, a drawing shows the relation of the house to neighboring structures.

Die strengen Linien des Hauses und sein einheitlicher Verputz heben es umso stärker vom dörflichen Umfeld ab. Oben eine Zeichnung, die das Haus in seinem nachbarschaftlichen Kontext zeigt.

Les lignes sobres de la maison et son aspect unifié contrastent fortement avec l'environnement du village. Ci- dessus, dessin montrant la relation entre la maison et les constructions adjacentes.

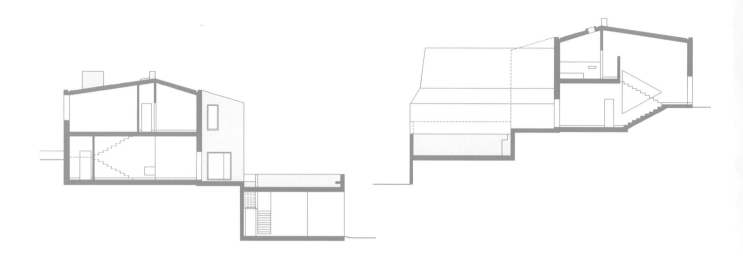

Two section drawings reveal the design's approach to the sloped site. Below, wood and light form a contrast with the clean, white walls.

Zwei Querschnitte illustrieren die Integration des Entwurfs in das Hang-grundstück. Holz und Licht (unten) sorgen für Kontraste mit den klaren weißen Wänden.

Deux dessins de coupe montrent l'implantation de la maison dans la pente. Ci-dessous, les planchers et des jeux de lumière contrastent avec les murs intégralement blancs.

A small swimming pool looks out onto the countryside. Right, an interior with an open door and window, both painted in light green.

Ein kleiner Pool mit Blick auf die ländliche Umgebung. Rechts ein Raum mit geöffneter hellgrüner Tür und Fenster.

La petite piscine est comme suspendue au-dessus du paysage. À droite, vue de l'intérieur : la porte et les volets sont peints en vert anisé.

SHIGERU BAN

Shigeru Ban Architects
5–2–4 Matsubara, Setagaya-ku
Tokyo 156–0043, Japan
Tel: +81 3 3324 6760 / Fax: +81 3 3324 6789
E-mail: tokyo@shigerubanarchitects.com / Web: www.shigerubanarchitects.com

Born in 1957 in Tokyo, **SHIGERU BAN** studied at SCI-Arc from 1977 to 1980. He attended the Cooper Union School of Architecture, where he studied under John Hejduk (1980–82). He worked in the office of Arata Isozaki (1982–83), before founding his own firm in Tokyo in 1985. His work includes numerous exhibition designs (Alvar Aalto show at the Axis Gallery, Tokyo, 1986). His buildings include the Odawara Pavilion (Kanagawa, 1990); the Paper Gallery (Tokyo, 1994); the Paper House (Lake Yamanaka, 1995); and the Paper Church (Takatori, Hyogo, 1995), all in Japan. He has also designed ephemeral structures such as his Paper Refugee Shelter made with plastic sheets and paper tubes for the United Nations High Commissioner for Refugees (UNHCR). He designed the Japanese Pavilion at Expo 2000 in Hanover. Recent work includes the Schwartz Residence (Sharon, Connecticut, USA, 2002); Hanegi Forest Annex (Setagaya, Tokyo, Japan, 2004); Mul(ti)houses (Mulhouse, France, 2001–05); the Takatori Church (Kobe, Hyogo, Japan, 2005); a small museum of canal history in Pouilly-en-Auxois (France, 2005); disaster relief post-tsunami rehabilitation houses (Kirinda, Hambantota, Sri Lanka, 2005); the Papertainer Museum (Seoul Olympic Park, Songpa-Gu, South Korea, 2006); Sagaponac House, Furniture House-05 (Long Island, New York, USA, 2006); the Nicolas G. Hayek Center (Tokyo, Japan, 2007); the Paper Teahouse (London, UK, 2008); Haesley Nine Bridges Golf Clubhouse (Yeoju, South Korea, 2009); the Paper Tube Tower (London, UK, 2009); Villa Vista (Weligama, Sri Lanka, 2007–10, published here); and the Metal Shutter Houses on West 19th Street in New York (New York, USA, 2010). He installed his Paper Temporary Studio on top of the Centre Pompidou in Paris to work on the new Centre Pompidou-Metz (Metz, France, 2010).

SHIGERU BAN, 1957 in Tokio geboren, studierte von 1977 bis 1980 am Southern California Institute of Architecture (SCI-Arc). Anschließend besuchte er die Cooper Union School of Architecture, wo er bei John Hejduk studierte (1980–82). Bevor er 1985 sein eigenes Büro in Tokio gründete, arbeitete er bei Arata Isozaki (1982–83). Zu seinen Entwürfen zählen zahlreiche Ausstellungsarchitekturen (Alvar-Aalto-Ausstellung, Axis Gallery, Tokio, 1986). Realisierte Bauten sind u. a. der Odawara-Pavillon (Kanagawa, 1990), die Paper Gallery (Tokio, 1994), das Paper House (Yamanaka-See, 1995) und die Paper Church (Takatori, Hyogo, 1995). Ban entwarf auch temporäre Bauten, etwa Flüchtlingsquartiere aus Papier, die er aus Plastikplanen und Pappröhren für den UNHCR realisierte, und den japanischen Pavillon für die Expo 2000 in Hannover. Jüngere Projekte sind die Schwartz Residence (Sharon, Connecticut, USA, 2002), eine Erweiterung der Wohnanlage Hanegi Forest (Setagaya, Tokio, 2004), Mul(ti)houses (Mulhouse, Frankreich, 2001–05), die Takatori-Kirche (Kobe, Hyogo, 2005), ein kleines Museum zur Kanalgeschichte in Pouilly-en-Auxois (Frankreich, 2005), Häuser für Katastrophenhilfe nach dem großen Tsunami (Kirinda, Hambantota, Sri Lanka, 2005), das Papertainer Museum (Olympiapark Seoul, Songpa-Gu, Südkorea, 2006), das Sagaponac House, Furniture House-05 (Long Island, New York, 2006), das Nicolas G. Hayek Center (Tokio, 2007), das Paper Teahouse (London, 2008), das Clubhaus für den Haesley Nine Bridges Golfclub (Yeoju, Südkorea, 2009), den Paper Tube Tower (London, 2009), die Villa Vista (Weligama, Sri Lanka, 2007–10, hier vorgestellt) und die Metal Shutter Houses an der West 19th Street in New York (2010). Auf dem Dach des Centre Georges Pompidou in Paris hatte Ban sich ein temporäres Atelier aus Pappröhren eingerichtet, um dort am neuen Centre Pompidou Metz (2010) zu arbeiten.

Né en 1957 à Tokyo, **SHIGERU BAN** a étudié au SCI-Arc de 1977 à 1980 et à la Cooper Union School of Architecture, auprès de John Hejduk (1980–82). Il a travaillé dans l'agence d'Arata Isozaki (1982–83) avant de fonder la sienne à Tokyo en 1985. Son œuvre comprend de nombreuses installations d'expositions (« Alvar Aalto », galerie Axis, Tokyo, 1986) et des bâtiments comme le pavillon Odawara (Kanagawa, 1990) ; la Galerie de papier (Tokyo, 1994) ; la Maison en carton (lac Yamanaka, 1995) et l'Église en carton (Takatori, Hyogo, 1995), tous au Japon. Il a également conçu des structures éphémères comme un Abri d'urgence en carton pour réfugiés fait de film plastique et de tubes de carton pour le Haut Commissariat des Nations Unies pour les réfugiés (HCR). Il a aussi dessiné le Pavillon japonais pour Expo 2000 à Hanovre. Parmi d'autres réalisations récentes : la résidence Schwartz (Sharon, Connecticut, 2002) ; l'annexe de la Forêt d'Hanegi (Setagaya, Tokyo, 2004) ; les logements Mul(ti)houses (Mulhouse, France, 2001–05) ; l'église de Takatori (Kobé, Hyogo, 2005–07) ; un petit musée sur l'histoire du canal de Bourgogne à Pouilly-en-Auxois (France, 2005) ; les maisons d'un programme de reconstruction post-tsunami (Kirinda, Hambantota, Sri Lanka, 2005) ; le musée Papertainer (Séoul, parc Olympique, Songpa-Gu, Corée-du-Sud, 2006) ; les maison Sagaponac et Maison-meubles-05 (Long Island, New York, 2006) ; le Centre Nicolas G. Hayek (Tokyo, 2007) ; la Maison de thé en papier (Londres, 2008) ; le club-house du golf de Haesley Nine Bridges (Yeoju, Corée-du-Sud, 2009) ; la Tour en tubes de carton (Londres, 2009) ; la villa Vista (Weligama, Sri Lanka, 2007-10, publiée ici) et les Maisons à volets de métal (19e Rue Ouest, New York, 2010). Il avait installé un Studio temporaire en carton au sommet du Centre Pompidou à Paris pour servir d'annexe à son agence pendant la construction du Centre Pompidou-Metz (Metz, 2010).

VILLA VISTA

Weligama, Sri Lanka, 2007–10

*Area: 825 m². Client: Koenraad Pringiers. Cost: not disclosed
Collaboration: PWA Architects*

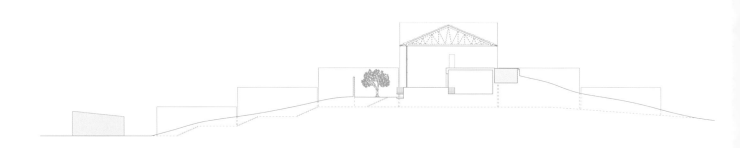

A section drawing shows the main
house with its pool to the right.
Below, concrete and wood are the
main materials employed.

*Der Querschnitt zeigt das Haupthaus
mit dem Pool rechts im Bild. Beton
und Holz sind die zentralen Baumaterialien (unten).*

*Dessin de coupe montrant la maison
et sa piscine (à droite). Ci-dessous, le
béton et le bois sont les principaux
matériaux utilisés.*

The architect employs a layered
effect with a stone wall, a concrete
screen, and then a wooden screen in
an effect that appears to be relatively
complex.

Der Architekt entschied sich für ein
Staffelprinzip und erzielte mit einer
Steinmauer, einem Wandschirm aus
Betonformstein und einem dahinter-
geschalteten hölzernen Wandschirm
eine komplexe Wirkung.

L'architecte a obtenu un effet de
stratification complexe et sophistiqué
par le biais d'un mur de pierre, d'un
écran de béton et d'un écran de bois.

The client for this house is the son of Pierre Pringiers, who built his own house with Tadao Ando (page 54). He contacted Shigeru Ban subsequent to the architect's work on post-tsunami reconstruction in Sri Lanka. It is set on a hilltop site facing the ocean. The architect explains that there are three different framed views at the origin of the design: "The first is the view of the ocean seen from the jungle in the valley, framed perpendicularly by the external corridor from the existing house to this house and the roof. The next is the horizontal scenery of the ocean from the hilltop framed by the large roof supported by a truss frame of 22-meter span and the floor. The last is the view of the cliff which glows red during sunset; this is viewed through a square frame composed of four meters of solid wood in the main bedroom." The roof is covered in light corrugated sheets and woven coconut leaves that permit it to "blend into the local ambiance." Shigeru Ban created a woven "wickerwork" pattern for the ceiling of the residence with bands of teak 80 millimeters wide and 3 millimeters thick. Here, as always, the architect shows an ability to renew his style and structural approaches according to the task at hand.

Bauherr der Villa ist Koenraad Pringiers, der Sohn von Pierre Pringiers, der Tadao Ando mit dem Bau seines Hauses betraut hatte (Seite 54). Koenraad Pringiers kontaktierte Shigeru Ban erstmals, als sich dieser nach dem Tsunami für Wiederaufbauprojekte in Sri Lanka engagiert hatte. Die Villa liegt auf einem Hügel mit Blick aufs Meer. Ausgangspunkt für den Entwurf waren, so der Architekt, drei gerahmte Ausblicke: „Der erste ist der Seeblick vom Dschungel im Tal, welcher vertikal von einem Korridor zwischen Alt- und Neubau gerahmt wird. Der nächste ist der horizontale Panoramablick auf den Ozean vom Hügel, gerahmt vom großen Dach, das auf einem Hängewerk mit 22 m Spannweite und der Geschossplatte ruht. Letzter Ausblick ist der Blick auf das Kliff, das bei Sonnenuntergang rot leuchtet: Dieser Blick bietet sich vom Hauptschlafzimmer aus durch einen vier Meter großen Massivholzrahmen." Das Dach wurde mit leichten Wellblechplatten und Palmblättern gedeckt und knüpft so „an lokales Ambiente an". Für die Decken im Haus entwarf Shigeru Ban ein Flechtwerk aus 80 mm schmalen und 3 mm dünnen Teakholzbändern. Wie immer beweist der Architekt auch hier die Fähigkeit, seinen Stil und die konstruktiven Methoden der jeweiligen Aufgabe anzupassen.

Le commanditaire de cette résidence est le fils de Pierre Pringiers pour lequel Tadao Ando a construit une résidence non loin de là (page 54). Koenraad Pringiers avait contacté Shigeru Ban suite à son travail de reconstruction de la région après le tsunami de 2004. La villa se dresse au sommet d'une colline, face à l'océan Indien. Ban a expliqué que trois vues cadrées avec précision étaient à l'origine du projet : la première, une vue de l'océan à partir de la jungle de la vallée, cadrée perpendiculairement par le passage extérieur qui relie une maison existante à la nouvelle construction et à son toit ; la seconde, une vision panoramique de l'océan du haut de la colline cadrée entre la toiture de 22 m de portée soutenue par une ferme et le sol ; la dernière, une vue de la falaise qui se teinte de rouge au coucher du soleil, prise dans un cadre carré de bois massif dans la chambre principale. » Le toit est recouvert de tôle ondulée et d'un tissage de feuilles de cocotier qui lui permettent de « se fondre dans l'atmosphère locale ». Pour l'habillage des plafonds, l'architecte a dessiné un « cannage » en bandeaux de teck de 80 millimètres de large et 3 millimètres d'épaisseur. Ici, comme toujours, Shigeru Ban montre sa capacité à renouveler son style et son approche structurelle en fonction du problème posé et du site.

The house stands in splendid isolation on its cliff-top setting, just above the sea. The pool, seen above, offers an open view of the water. Below, floor plans.

Das Haus in privilegierter Einsamkeit ruht auf einem Steilabhang unmittelbar über dem Ozean. Der Pool (oben) bietet einen unverstellten Blick auf das Meer. Unten Etagengrundrisse.

La maison se dresse dans son splendide isolement au sommet d'une falaise qui domine la mer. La piscine (ci-dessus) offre une vue directe sur la côte. Ci-dessous, plans au sol.

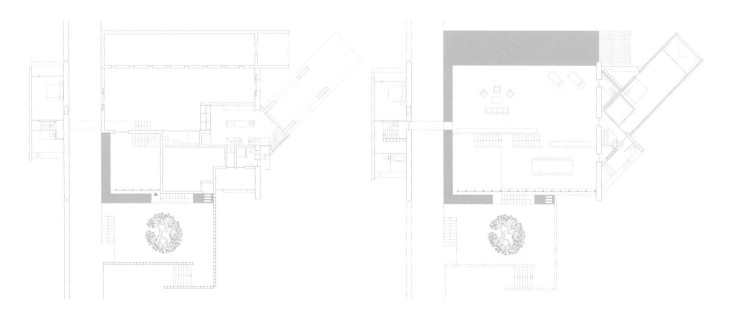

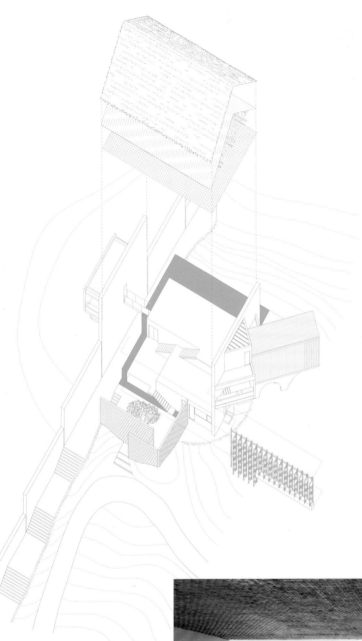

An exploded axonometric drawing shows the house and its relation to local building traditions, also expressed in the woven "wickerwork" pattern for the ceiling.

Eine Explosionszeichnung veranschaulicht die Konstruktion und ihre Verwandtschaft mit traditionellen regionalen Bauweisen, was sich etwa im „Flechtwerk" der Decke zeigt.

Vue axonométrique éclatée montrant la maison et certains liens avec les traditions constructives locales, également notables dans le « cannage » du plafond.

BARCLAY & CROUSSE

Barclay & Crousse Architecture
Choquehuanca 199
Chorillos
Lima 09
Peru
Tel: +51 1 252 0503
E-mail: atelier@barclaycrousse.com
Web: www.barclaycrousse.com

7 Passage Saint Bernard
75011 Paris
France
Tel: +33 1 49 23 51 36
E-mail: atelier@barclaycrousse.com
Web: www.barclaycrousse.com

JEAN-PIERRE CROUSSE was born in Lima, Peru, in 1963. He was educated at the Universidad Ricardo Palma in Lima and at Milan Polytechnic in Italy, where he received a European architecture degree (1989). **SANDRA BARCLAY** was born in Lima in 1967 and also studied at the Universidad Ricardo Palma, before getting a French architecture degree (D.P.L.G.) at the École d'Architecture de Paris-Belleville (1993). Their built work includes the reconstruction of the Musée Malraux (Le Havre, France, 1999); B House (Cañete, Peru, 1999); the M House (Cañete, Peru, 2001); an office building in Malakoff (Paris, France, 2003); and a renovation of the city hall of Epinay sur Seine (France, 2004). More recently, they have worked on the F House (Lima, Peru, 2009–10, published here); the Vedoble Houses (Cañete, Peru, 2008–11, also published here); a 170-unit housing project (Nantes, France, 2009); Montreuil Student Apartments (Paris, France, 2011); the Museo Paracas (Ica, Peru, 2012); and the Lugar de la Memoria (Lima, Peru, 2010–13).

JEAN-PIERRE CROUSSE wurde 1963 in Lima geboren. Er studierte an der Universidad Ricardo Palma in Lima und am Mailänder Polytechnikum, wo er seine Studien mit einem europäischen Architekturdiplom abschloss (1989). **SANDRA BARCLAY** wurde 1967 in Lima geboren, studierte ebenfalls zunächst an der Universidad Ricardo Palma und schloss ihr Studium mit einem französischen Architekturdiplom (D.P.L.G.) an der École d'Architecture de Paris-Belleville (1993) ab. Zu ihren realisierten Bauten zählen das Musée Malraux (Le Havre, Frankreich, 1999), die Casa B (Cañete, Peru, 1999), die Casa M (Cañete, Peru, 2001), ein Bürogebäude in Malakoff (Paris, 2003) und die Sanierung des Rathauses in Epinay sur Seine (Frankreich, 2004). Jüngere Projekte des Büros sind die Casa F (Lima, 2009–10, hier vorgestellt), die Casas Vedoble (Cañete, Peru, 2008–11, ebenfalls hier vorgestellt), ein Wohnbauprojekt mit 170 Wohneinheiten (Nantes, 2009), Studentenwohnungen in Montreuil (Paris, 2011), das Museo Paracas (Ica, Peru, 2012) sowie der Lugar de la Memoria (Lima, 2010–13).

JEAN-PIERRE CROUSSE, né à Lima (Pérou) en 1963, a étudié à l'université Ricardo Palma de Lima et à l'École polytechnique de Milan où il a obtenu un diplôme européen d'architecte (1989). **SANDRA BARCLAY**, née à Lima en 1967, a également étudié à l'université Ricardo Palma de Lima et obtenu son diplôme d'architecte D.P.L.G. à l'École d'architecture de Paris-Belleville (1993). Leurs réalisations comprennent la reconstruction du musée André Malraux (Le Havre, France, 1999) ; la maison B (Cañete Pérou, 1999) ; la maison M (Canete, Pérou, 2001) ; l'immmeubles de bureaux à Malakoff (Paris, 2003) et la rénovation de l'hôtel de ville d'Épinay-sur-Seine (France, 2004). Plus récemment ils ont réalisé la maison F (Lima, Pérou, 2009–10, publiée ici) ; les maisons Vedoble (Canete, Pérou, 2008–11, également publiées ici) ; un immeuble de 170 appartements (Nantes, France, 2009) ; des logements pour étudiants à Montreuil (France, 2011) ; le musée Paracas (Ica, Pérou, 2012) et le Lugar de la Memoria (Lima, 2010–13).

VEDOBLE HOUSES

Cañete, Peru, 2008–11

Area: 917 m². Client: not disclosed
Cost: $720 000

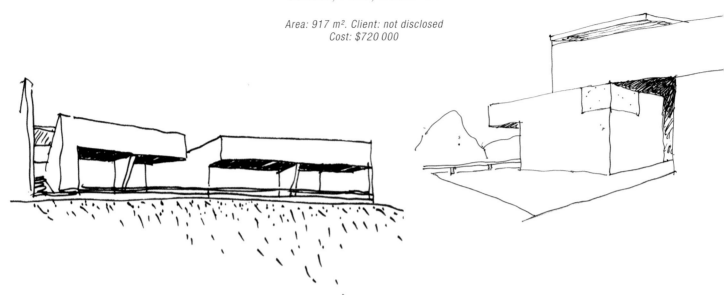

The rough concrete and long, wide openings give these houses something of the appearance of defensive bunkers from a distance, and yet they are fully open to the ocean.

Durch den rauen Sichtbeton und die niedrigen breiten Fassadenöffnungen wirken die Häuser von Weitem wie Festungsanlagen, öffnen sich jedoch vollständig zum Meer.

Vues de loin, les vastes ouvertures des façades de ces maisons en béton leur donnent un aspect de bunkers, mais de bunkers généreusement ouverts sur l'océan.

Located on a cliff above La Escondida Beach in the province of Cañete, this project is made up of four summer houses. The architects explain: "These houses were not designed at the same time, nor were they conceived as a whole, but they share the same approach to the site, to the extraordinary climate of this region, and their relationship to the landscape." They describe the houses as "inhabited platforms" where "cracks" have been created to provide for open stairs and common patios. An ochre or "sand" color with rough exposed concrete was used to avoid the effects of layers of dust from the nearby desert. In fact, the situation of the houses, on a line between the ocean and the desert, defines their character, with such elements as long narrow pools that create a link between the two environments.

Der Komplex aus vier Sommerhäusern in der Provinz Cañete liegt an einem Steilabhang über dem Strand von La Escondida. Die Architekten führen aus: „Der Entwurf für die Häuser entstand nicht zeitgleich, sie wurden auch nicht als Gesamtensemble konzipiert, teilen aber dieselbe Ausrichtung auf dem Grundstück, das außergewöhnliche Klima der Region und ihr Verhältnis zur Landschaft." Sie beschreiben die Häuser als „bewohnte Plattformen" mit „Zwischenräumen" für offene Treppen und gemeinschaftliche Terrassen. Die mit Sichtbeton kombinierten, ocker- bzw. sandfarben gestrichenen Oberflächen kaschieren die auffälligen Sandablagerungen aus der nahegelegenen Wüste. Tatsächlich prägt die landschaftliche Lage die Bauten, die wie ein Band zwischen Ozean und Wüste liegen; lange schmale Schwimmbecken fungieren als Bindeglied zwischen den beiden klimatischen Zonen.

Ces quatre résidences d'été ont été édifiées au sommet d'une falaise dominant la plage de La Escondida dans la province de Cañete. « Ces maisons n'ont été ni conçues en même temps, ni comme un ensemble, expliquent les architectes, mais partagent une approche identique du site, du climat extraordinaire de cette région et une même relation au paysage. » Ils les décrivent comme des « plateformes habitées » entre lesquelles auraient été aménagées des « fissures » pour implanter des escaliers ou des patios communs. La couleur ocre ou sableuse et le béton brut ont été choisis pour limiter les effets de la poussière de sable venue du désert voisin. En fait, la situation de ces maisons sur une mince ligne de relief entre l'océan et le désert définit leur caractère, certains éléments comme les piscines allongées faisant le lien entre ces deux environnements naturels.

Above, the houses seen from the beach on top of their rather arid hillside.

Oben die Häuser auf dem Kamm des wüstenähnlichen Steilabhangs, vom Strand aus gesehen.

Ci-dessus, les maisons perchées au sommet de la falaise aride, vues de la plage.

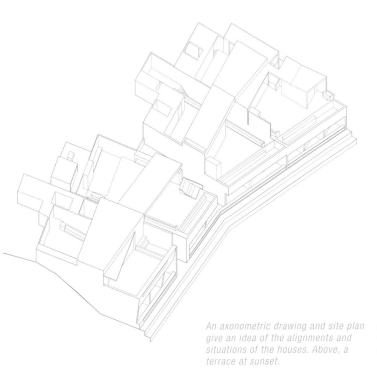

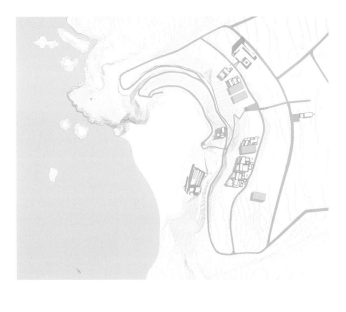

An axonometric drawing and site plan give an idea of the alignments and situations of the houses. Above, a terrace at sunset.

Axonometrie und Lageplan geben eine Vorstellung von der Anordnung und Lage der Häuser. Oben eine der Terrassen bei Sonnenuntergang.

Cette axonométrie et le plan du site font comprendre les alignements et les articulations des maisons. Ci-dessus, une terrasse au coucher du soleil.

Left, a swimming pool passes above a terrace. Below, a view from a pool down to the rocky beach.

Links ein Pool, der als Brücke eine der Terrassen quert. Unten der Blick von einem Schwimmbecken hinunter auf die Felslandschaft am Strand.

À gauche, une piscine passe au-dessus d'une terrasse. Ci-dessous, vue d'une des piscines dominant une plage de galets.

Even if they appear to be rather rough from the outside, the houses provide for considerable comfort in this unexpected setting. Here, inside and outside seem to come together as one in the house.

Trotz ihrer von außen so strengen Anmutung bieten die Häuser gehobenen Komfort in ungewöhnlicher Lage. Hier gehen Innen- und Außenraum fließend ineinander über.

Même si elles peuvent sembler un peu « brutes » vues de l'extérieur, ces maisons offrent un confort remarquable dans leur cadre étonnant. Ici, l'intérieur et l'extérieur semblent ne faire qu'un.

Right page, a living area is directly connected to the outside terrace thanks to sliding windows. Below, section drawings of the houses show their insertion into the hillside.

Ein Wohnbereich (rechte Seite) ist durch Schiebefenster direkt mit der Terrasse verbunden. Querschnitte (unten) illustrieren die Einbindung der Häuser in das Hanggrundstück.

Page de droite : le séjour se trouve ici directement dans la continuité de la terrasse grâce à des baies vitrées coulissantes. Ci-dessous : coupes montrant l'insertion des maisons dans le flanc de la colline.

Full-height glazing offers a stunning view of the shoreline from one of the bedrooms. Right, a concrete stair rises toward the daylight, like a slit through the concrete of the house.

Dank raumhoher Verglasung bietet dieses Schlafzimmer einen beeindruckenden Panoramablick auf den Strand. Rechts eine Sichtbetontreppe, die wie ein Schnitt durch den Baukörper zum Licht führt.

Dans une des chambres, une baie vitrée toute hauteur offre une vue stupéfiante sur la côte. À droite, un escalier en béton monte vers la lumière telle une fente entaillant le béton de la maison.

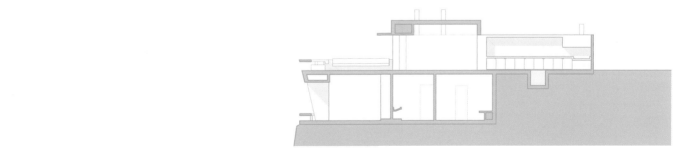

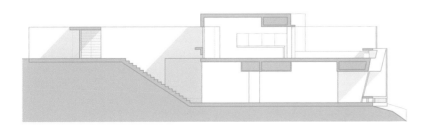

F HOUSE

Lima, Peru, 2009–10

*Area: 1235 m². Client: not disclosed
Cost: not disclosed*

Section drawings show that a considerable part of the large house is below grade, thus obviating any feeling of its bulk from the outside.

Querschnitte machen deutlich, dass ein erheblicher Teil des großzügigen Hauses unter Straßenniveau liegt, wodurch der Eindruck von Masse vermieden wird.

Ces coupes montrent qu'une partie considérable de la maison est enterrée, ce qui, vu de l'extérieur, réduit la perception de sa masse.

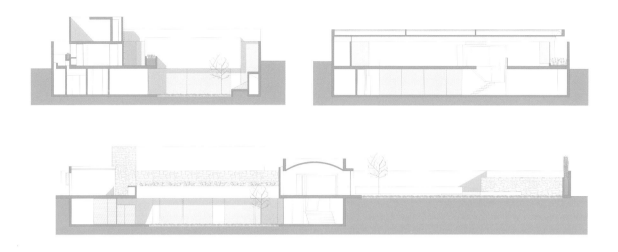

In describing this project, the architects recall that there is an inherent contradiction in the houses of Lima that are meant to adhere to the "paradigm of the garden city" but in fact are closed in by fences and protective walls. They do not hesitate to call the 1200-square-meter residence a "palace," but sought to reconcile the client's desire for privacy with a form of "anti-monumentality." This task was surely rendered more complex by the fact that the site (1367 m²) is not much larger than the house. Basing their concept on a combination of the Mediterranean courtyard house and the "pre-Columbian strategy of enclosure," Barclay & Crousse basically obviated the considerable size of the structure. "The enclosure, the intimacy, and the architectural promenade combine to create the impression of a small house of which the real dimensions are only revealed by movement and time through the polycentric space," they state. A large domed roof unifies the "public" spaces of the living and dining rooms.

Mit Blick auf ihr Projekt erinnern die Architekten an die grundlegende Widersprüchlichkeit der Wohnbebauung Limas, die sich einerseits am „Paradigma der Gartenstadt" orientieren will, sich andererseits jedoch mit Zäunen und schützenden Mauern umgibt. Obwohl sie das 1200 m² große Anwesen durchaus als „Wohnpalast" bezeichnen, legten sie Wert darauf, dem Wunsch des Bauherrn nach Privatsphäre eine gewisse „Antimonumentalität" entgegenzustellen. Die Aufgabe wurde zweifellos durch den Umstand erschwert, dass das 1367 m² große Grundstück kaum größer als das Haus ist. Dank eines konzeptuellen Brückenschlags zwischen mediterranem Hofhaus und dem „präkolumbischen Prinzip der Umbauung" gelang es Barclay & Crousse, die Größe des Baus zurückzunehmen. „Durch das Zusammenspiel von Umbauung, Privatsphäre und *promenade architecturale* entsteht der Eindruck eines kleineren Hauses, dessen wahre Dimensionen sich erst nach und nach durch Bewegung im polyzentrischen Raum erschließen", so die Planer. Ein großes Tonnendach überspannt die „öffentlichen" Bereiche von Wohn- und Esszimmer.

Décrivant ce projet, ses architectes rappellent la contradiction inhérente à Lima entre des maisons relevant du « paradigme de la cité-jardin », mais en fait entourées de clôtures protectrices. Ils n'hésitent pas à parler de « palais » pour décrire cette résidence de 1200 m², mais ont cherché à concilier le désir d'intimité du client avec une certaine anti-monumentalité. Leur tâche a sans doute été compliquée par le fait que le terrain de 1367 m² est à pleine plus grand que la résidence même. Partant d'un concept de maison à cour méditerranéenne et de « stratégie de clôture précolombienne », Barclay et Crousse ont su amadouer les dimensions considérables de cette résidence. « L'effet de clôture, l'intimité et l'organisation d'un parcours architectural se combinent pour donner l'impression d'une petite maison dont les dimensions réelles ne se révèlent qu'à travers les mouvements et le passage du temps à travers cet espace polycentrique. »

Plaster and stone façades give a sheltered, or perhaps rather closed, appearance to the house.

Gipsputz- und Steinfassaden lassen den Bau geschützt und geschlossen wirken.

Les façades de pierre et de béton enduit créent un sentiment de protection, voire même de clôture.

Plans show courtyard and garden space: above, an image of a living area that opens into a court with a sliding full-height glass wall.

Grundrisse zeigen Hof- und Gartenanlagen. Oben der Blick in einen Wohnbereich, der dank raumhoher Glasschiebetüren fließend in einen Hof übergeht.

Plans montrant la cour et le jardin. Ci-dessus, un séjour ouvre sur une cour à travers un mur de verre coulissant toute hauteur.

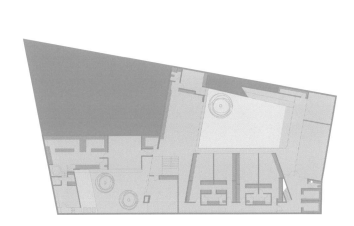

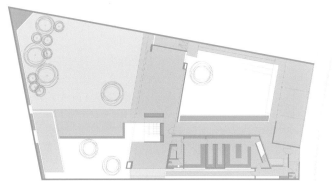

Above, a dining area with a curved ceiling, wooden floors, and a full-height opening that allows ample natural light to enter from the side.

Oben ein Essbereich mit Tonnengewölbe, Holzboden und geschosshoher Verglasung, durch die seitlich reichlich Tageslicht einfällt.

Ci-dessus, l'espace salle à manger sous un plafond en berceau. Le plancher est en bois. La lumière pénètre par une immense baie vitrée toute hauteur.

Dark surfaces are contrasted with light ones. Natural light penetrates the interior without sacrificing the intimacy or protective nature of the architecture.

Dunkle Oberflächen kontrastieren mit hellen Flächen. Tageslicht durchflutet die Räume; Privatsphäre oder Schutzfunktion der Architektur werden dennoch nicht in Mitleidenschaft gezogen.

Des surfaces de couleur sombre contrastent avec les murs blancs et les sols de bois. La lumière naturelle inonde l'intérieur sans porter atteinte à l'intimité de la maison ou la nature protectrice de cette architecture.

The curved ceiling gives a sense of movement to the space, where wooden floors or furnishings warm the palette and the feeling of the interiors, which might otherwise seem cold.

Durch die gewölbte Decke gewinnen die Räume dynamische Spannung; dank Böden und Mobiliar aus Holz wirkt das Interieur, das leicht kühl hätte erscheinen können, farblich und atmosphärisch warm.

Les plafonds voûtés créent une certaine impression de mouvement tandis que les sols et les meubles en bois réchauffent la palette chromatique de ces pièces qui auraient pu paraître froides.

HAGY BELZBERG

Belzberg Architects
2919 1/2 Main Street
Santa Monica, CA 90405
USA

Tel: +1 310 453 9611
Fax: +1 310 453 9166
E-mail: hb@belzbergarchitects.com
Web: www.belzbergarchitects.com

HAGY BELZBERG received his M.Arch degree from the Harvard GSD and began his professional career with explorations of non-standardized construction methodology involving digital manufacturing. In 2000, he was awarded the contract to design the interior space of Frank Gehry's Walt Disney Concert Hall (Los Angeles, 2003), where he utilized digital machining and prefabrication to work within the complex existing structure. In 2008, he was selected as an "Emerging Voice" by the Architectural League of New York. His work includes 20th Street Offices (Santa Monica, California, 2009); Skyline Residence (Los Angeles, California, 2008–10, published here); Kona Residence (Kona, Hawaii, 2010, also published here); Los Angeles Museum of the Holocaust (Los Angeles, California, 2010); 9800 Wilshire Boulevard Offices (Beverly Hills, California, 2012); City of Hope Cancer Research Museum (Duarte, California, 2013); and the Occidental College Center for Global Affairs (Los Angeles, 2013), all in the USA.

HAGY BELZBERG schloss sein Studium mit einem M. Arch. an der Harvard GSD ab und forschte zu Beginn seiner Laufbahn zu Konstruktionsmethoden mit nicht-standardisierten Bauteilen und digitaler Fertigung. 2000 gewann er die Ausschreibung für den Innenausbau der Walt Disney Concert Hall von Frank Gehry (Los Angeles, 2003). Dort arbeitete er mit digitalen Fertigungsmethoden und digitaler Vorfertigung, um dem komplexen Bau gerecht zu werden. 2008 zeichnete ihn der Architektenverband New York als „Neues Talent" aus. Zu seinen Projekten zählen Büros an der 20th Street (Santa Monica, Kalifornien, 2009), die Skyline Residence (Los Angeles, Kalifornien, 2008–10, hier vorgestellt), das Holocaust-Museum in Los Angeles (2010), die Kona Residence (Kona, Hawaii, 2010, ebenfalls hier vorgestellt), Büros am 9800 Wilshire Boulevard (Beverly Hills, Kalifornien, 2012), das City of Hope Museum für Krebsforschung (Duarte, Kalifornien, 2013) sowie das Occidental College am Center for Global Affairs (Los Angeles, 2013), alle in den USA.

HAGY BELZBERG a obtenu son diplôme de M.Arch. à la Harvard GSD et entamé sa carrière professionnelle par l'exploration de méthodologies de constructions non-standard dont les techniques de fabrication pilotées par ordinateur. En 2000, il a été chargé de l'aménagement intérieur du Walt Disney Concert Hall de Frank Gehry (Los Angeles, 2003) où il a utilisé des techniques d'usinage numérique et de préfabrication pour s'adapter à une structure complexe. En 2008, il a été désigné «Voix émergente» par l'Architectural League de New York. Parmi ses réalisations, toutes aux États-Unis : les bureaux de la 20ᵉ Rue (Santa Monica, Californie, 2009) ; la Skyline Residence (Los Angeles, Californie, 2008–10, publiée ici) ; la Kona Residence (Kona, Hawaï, 2010, publiée ici) ; le musée de l'Holocauste de Los Angeles (Los Angeles, 2010) ; les bureaux du 9800 Wilshire Boulevard (Beverly Hills, Californie, 2012), le musée de la Recherche sur le cancer City of Hope (Duarte, Californie, 2013) et l'Occidental College Center for Global Affairs (Los Angeles, 2013).

KONA RESIDENCE

Kona, Hawaii, USA, 2010

Area: 725 m². Client: not disclosed. Cost: not disclosed
Collaboration: Barry Gartin (Project Manager), David Cheung, Cory Taylor

Below, the asymmetric entrance archway of the house, apparently inspired by local crafts. A drawing of the entrance canopy is seen on the right page.

Unten der asymmetrische Bogengang am Eingang, inspiriert von lokalen Handwerkstraditionen (rechts unten in einer Zeichnung).

Ci-dessous, la pergola asymétrique de l'entrée, apparemment inspirée de traditions artisanales locales. À droite, dessin de cette même arche.

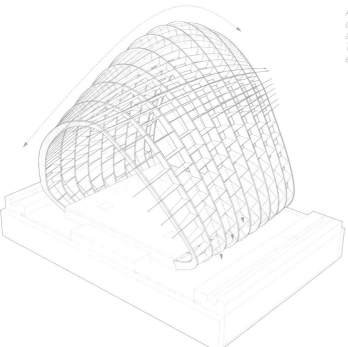

Above, dining and sunning areas come together in space that takes advantage of the warm local climate. The distinction between interior and exterior is absent.

Essbereich und Sonnenterrasse profitieren vom warmen Klima der Region und gehen fließend ineinander über. Auf eine Trennung von Innen- und Außenraum wurde verzichtet.

Ci-dessus, la terrasse-salle à manger couverte et le solarium bénéficient pleinement du climat local. La distinction entre l'intérieur et l'extérieur a été gommée.

The architect based the alignments of this house, built between hardened lava flows, on the views of volcanic mountains to the east and the ocean to the west available from the site. According to the designers: "The program is arranged as a series of pods distributed throughout the property, each having its own unique features and view opportunities. The pods are programmatically assigned as two sleeping pods with common areas, media room, master suite, and main living space. An exterior gallery corridor becomes the organizational and focal feature for the entire house, connecting the two pods along a central axis." Rooftop photovoltaic panels, rainwater collection, and drywells are part of the environmental aspects of the design. Recycled teak wood and local cut lava make reference to local building tradition, as does the entry pavilion inspired by Hawaiian basket weaving. Wood ceilings and screen sculpted with digital technology "continue the abstract approach to traditional Hawaiian wood carving, further infusing traditional elements into the contemporary arrangement."

Der Architekt plante das Haus, das zwischen erstarrten Lavafeldern liegt, entlang von Sichtachsen zu den Vulkanbergen im Osten und zum Meer im Westen. Die Planer erklären: „Das Programm wurde in einer Reihe von Raumeinheiten untergebracht, die über das gesamte Gelände verteilt sind und jeweils besondere Highlights und Ausblicke bieten. Die Einheiten gliedern sich programmatisch in zwei Schlafeinheiten mit Gemeinschaftsbereichen, Medienzimmer, Hauptschlafzimmer mit Nebenräumen und Hauptwohnraum. Ein als Galerie gestalteter Außenkorridor bildet den organisatorischen Kern des gesamten Hauses und verbindet die zwei Raumeinheiten entlang einer Mittelachse." Ökologische Aspekte des Entwurfs sind Solarmodule auf dem Dach, Regenwassernutzung sowie Vorfluter. Mit recyceltem Teakholz, vor Ort gebrochenem Lavagestein und dem Eingangspavillon, einer Reminiszenz an hawaiianische Korbflechttechniken, erweist der Entwurf lokalen Bautraditionen seine Reverenz. Holzdecken und ein digital gefertigter Wandschirm „setzen die abstrakte Interpretation traditioneller hawaiianischer Holzschnitztechniken fort und lassen weitere traditionelle Elemente in das zeitgenössische Ensemble einfließen".

Les axes de cette maison, construite entre d'anciennes coulées de lave, matérialisent des vues sur une chaîne de volcans à l'est et l'océan à l'ouest. « Le programme est décliné dans une série d'unités réparties sur la parcelle, chacun possédant ses caractéristiques et ses perspectives propres. Chacune remplit en effet une fonction : deux chambres avec des espaces communs, un salon média, une grande chambre et un séjour principal. Une galerie extérieure constitue l'axe visuel et organisationnel de la maison toute entière en reliant les unités le long de son axe central. » Des panneaux photovoltaïques en toiture, la collecte des eaux de pluie et des puits secs illustrent le caractère écologique du projet. Le bois de teck recyclé et la pierre de lave renvoient aux traditions constructives locales, de même que le pavillon d'entrée inspiré de l'art du cannage hawaïen. Des plafonds et des écrans sculptés par technologies numériques « reprennent l'approche abstraite de la sculpture du bois hawaïenne, ce qui renforce la présence des éléments traditionnels dans cet aménagement contemporain ».

Stone, wood, and plaster surfaces are brought together in a coherent whole where the architecture seems more like a shelter than a closed house.

Stein, Holz und Putz verbinden sich zu einem stimmigen Ganzen: Hier wirkt die Architektur eher wie ein schützendes Dach als ein geschlossenes Haus.

La pierre, le bois et le stuc forment un tout cohérent par lequel l'architecture devient davantage un abri qu'une structure close.

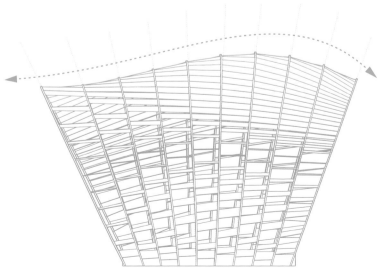

Fully opening walls allow private space to be almost entirely outside, while still within the protection of the house.

Private Wohnbereiche lassen sich durch vollständig zu öffnende Wände geradezu als Außenbereich definieren und liegen dennoch unter einem schützenden Dach.

Les murs de verre qui s'ouvrent entièrement dilatent les pièces vers l'extérieur, tout en les maintenant dans l'enveloppe protectrice de la maison.

On this page, the wooden detailing of the house is extensive and sometimes takes on organic forms, as in the bedroom screen and ceiling to the left.

Im Haus finden sich auffällig viele Holzarbeiten, oft in organischen Formen, wie der Raumteiler und die Decke im Schlafzimmer links.

La présence du bois dans certains détails d'aménagement est très forte. Elle prend parfois une forme organique comme dans la claustra et le plafond de la chambre à gauche.

Wood and stone finishes are juxtaposed in the exterior design. The warm interiors, where wood dominates, can be seen through the generously glazed façades.

Am Außenbau, rechts im Bild, kontrastieren Fassadenelemente aus Holz und Stein. Durch die großzügige Verglasung fällt der Blick auf das warme Interieur, in dem Holz dominiert.

À l'extérieur, on retrouve la juxtaposition de la pierre et du bois. L'intérieur chaleureux, où prédomine le bois, se perçoit à travers les immenses baies vitrées.

SKYLINE RESIDENCE

Los Angeles, California, USA, 2008–10

Area: 446 m². Client: not disclosed
Cost: not disclosed. Collaboration: Bill Bowen (Project Manager),
Dan Rentsch, Barry Gartin

Located on a ridge in the Hollywood Hills, the Skyline Residence seeks an "economical approach to creating an environmentally sensitive building within a limited budget." It was the budget allocated by the client that imposed the use of materials that could be obtained locally. The architect makes a virtue of this limitation by referring to " carbon neutral economics," or the purchasing of goods that are manufactured locally to save on carbon emissions due to transport. Photovoltaic panels, wind turbines, or recycled products were ruled out for cost reasons, thus, as Hagy Belzberg states: "The **SKYLINE RESIDENCE** reverted back to purchasing locally, minimized grading, and capitalizing on natural characteristics of the site." The project won an AIA California Council Design Award and a Los Angeles Architecture Award for Single Family Housing given by the Los Angeles Business Council.

Die auf einem Kamm in den Hollywood Hills gelegene Skyline Residence steht für die „wirtschaftliche Realisierung eines umweltbewussten Baus mit begrenztem Budget". Aufgrund finanzieller Vorgaben des Bauherrn fiel die Entscheidung zwingend auf vor Ort erhältliche Materialien. Der Architekt machte die Einschränkung zur Tugend und setzte ganz auf „CO₂-neutrales Wirtschaften" und den Einkauf von lokal gefertigten Baustoffen, was unnötige transportbedingte CO_2-Emissionen erspart. Aus Kostengründen wurde auf Solarmodule, Windturbinen oder recycelte Baustoffe verzichtet. Laut Hagy Belzberg setzt, „die **SKYLINE RESIDENCE** bewusst auf lokale Baustoffe, die Planierung des Baugrunds wurde auf ein Minimum beschränkt und der landschaftliche Vorzug des Grundstücks optimal genutzt". Das Projekt wurde mit dem Design Award des AIA Kalifornien und dem Architekturpreis für Einfamilienhäuser ausgezeichnet, der von der Handelskammer Los Angeles vergeben wird.

Implantée sur une crête des collines d'Hollywood, cette résidence traduit la recherche « d'une approche économique de la création d'une construction respectueuse de l'environnement pour un budget limité ». Le budget alloué par le client imposait l'utilisation de matériaux disponibles localement. L'architecte a fait de ces contraintes une vertu et signale son « empreinte carbone neutre » ou l'achat de produits fabriqués localement pour réduire les émissions de gaz dues aux transports. Les panneaux photovoltaïques, les éoliennes ou certains produits recyclés ont été écartés pour des raisons de coût. Hagy Belzberg précise également que « la **SKYLINE RESIDENCE** est revenue à des achats locaux, des produits de qualité standard et a cherché à tirer profit des caractéristiques naturelles du site ». Le projet a remporté un prix de conception de l'AIA-California Council et un prix d'architecture du logement familial de Los Angeles décerné par le Los Angeles Business Council.

Full-height glazing and views on the pool and city beyond give this house all the glamour of some earlier Los Angeles houses designed by the likes of Lautner or Neutra. Right, a site plan shows the house in its context.

Raumhohe Verglasung und der Ausblick auf den Pool und die Stadt dahinter verleihen diesem Haus all den Glamour, den schon Lautners und Neutras Bauten in Los Angeles auszeichneten. Der Lageplan rechts zeigt das Haus in seiner Umgebung.

Des baies vitrées toute hauteur et des vues sur la piscine et la ville à l'horizon confèrent à cette maison tout le glamour d'anciennes demeures de Los Angeles conçues par des architectes comme Lautner ou Neutra. À droite, un plan du site montre l'édifice dans son contexte.

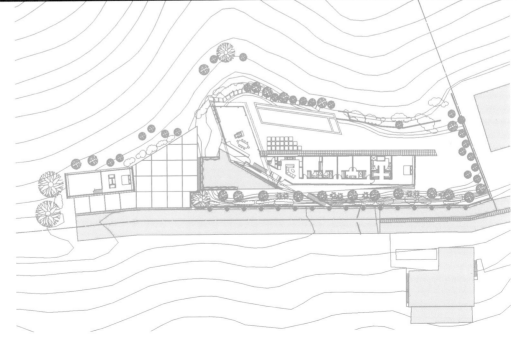

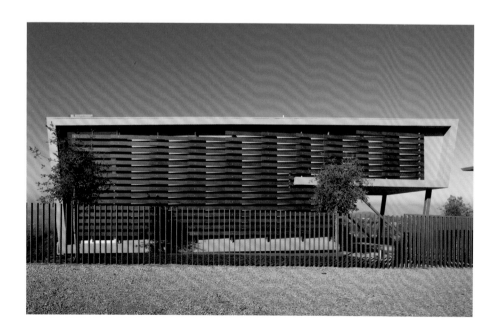

A cantilevered volume and a wood slat facing mark one side of the house, which also has sharply angled, nearly blank areas, such as the one seen above.

Die Seitenansicht zeigt ein auskragendes Volumen und einen Holzwandschirm; das Haus hat außerdem schiefwinklige, nahezu geschlossene Fassadenflächen (oben).

Une des deux façades principales se caractérise par un grand volume en porte-à-faux et un immense écran de bois. Fortement inclinées, les deux extrémités de la maison sont pratiquement aveugles (ci-dessus).

The real, substantial size of the residence is evident in the photo to the right. Wood slats protect the long opening seen in the image below.

Die wahre Größe des ausgedehnten Komplexes wird rechts im Bild deutlich. Holzlamellen liegen schützend vor einer großflächigen Fassadenöffnung (unten).

Les dimensions réelles de cette résidence sont mises en évidence dans la photographie de droite. Ci-dessous, un lattis de bois protège la façade vitrée.

Terraces and large openings bring ample contact with the exterior and natural light into the house. As is the case in some exterior elevations, angled openings vary the interior architectural effects.

Terrassen und große Fenster sorgen für eine klare Anbindung an den Außenraum und lassen Tageslicht in das Haus. Wie bei einigen Fassadenansichten ergeben sich auch im Interieur Effekte durch schiefe Winkel.

Des terrasses et de grandes baies assurent un généreux contact avec l'extérieur et l'éclairage naturel. À certains moments, des ouvertures trapézoïdales multiplient les effets visuels.

Full-height glazing, or glazing covered with slats, assures the light is
admitted in a controlled way into the
very modern interiors.

Geschosshohe Verglasung und Fenster mit Sonnenschutzblenden sorgen
für kontrollierten Lichteinfall in die
dezidiert modernen Räume.

Des murs de verre ou des baies protégées par un lattis de bois apportent
un éclairage naturel contrôlé.

SOLANO BENÍTEZ

Solano Benítez
Gabinete de Arquitectura
Padre Cardozo 489
Asunción 1409
Paraguay

Tel/Fax: +595 21 20 1524
E-mail: gabinetedearquitectura@hotmail.com

SOLANO BENÍTEZ was born in Asunción, Paraguay, in 1963. He graduated in architecture from the Facultad de Arquitectura, Universidad Nacional de Asunción in 1986. He created the Gabinete de Arquitectura in 1987, currently in partnership with Alberto Marinoni and Gloria Cabral. In 1999, he won the National Architecture Prize of Paraguay for the building Edificio de Publicitaria Paraná. In 2008, he won the first edition of BSI Swiss Architectural Award in Lugano. Mario Botta, the Chairman of the BSI jury, cited: "The architectural research of Solano Benítez, carried out in a difficult political and economic context, with objectively complex operational issues, stands apart from the production processes dictated by globalization and reveals astonishing quality." Benítez has represented his country at the Biennales of Venice, São Paulo, and Lisbon. His projects include a vacation complex (Ytú, 1998); an architect's studio (Asunción, 2000); a tomb (Piribebuy, 2001); Unilever Headquarters (Asunción, 2001); Esmeraldina House (Asunción, 2002); Fanego House (Asunción, 2003); Abu y Font House (Asunción, 2004); L. A. Farm House (Santani, 2005, published here); and Teletón (Lambare, 2009), all in Paraguay.

SOLANO BENÍTEZ wurde 1963 in Asunción, Paraguay, geboren. Sein Architekturstudium schloss er 1986 an der Architekturfakultät der Universidad Nacional de Asunción ab. 1987 gründete er sein Büro Gabinete de Arquitectura, das er derzeit zusammen mit Alberto Marinoni und Gloria Cabral führt. 1999 erhielt er den Nationalen Architekturpreis von Paraguay für das Edificio de Publicitaria Paraná, 2008 wurde er in Lugano mit dem ersten BSI Swiss Architectural Award ausgezeichnet. Mario Botta, Vorsitzender der BSI-Jury, erklärte: „Die architektonische Forschungsarbeit von Solano Benítez, entstanden unter schwierigen politischen und ökonomischen Bedingungen, thematisiert objektiv komplexe funktionale Fragen, sticht hervor inmitten von Produktionsprozessen, die die Globalisierung diktiert, und ist von erstaunlicher Qualität." Benítez vertrat sein Heimatland bereits auf den Biennalen von Venedig, São Paulo und Lissabon. Zu seinen Projekten zählen eine Ferienanlage (Ytu, 1998), das Studio für einen Architekten (Asunción, 2000), ein Grabmal (Piribebuy, 2001), die Zentrale von Unilever in Asunción (2001), die Casa Esmeraldina (Asunción, 2002), die Casa Fanego (Asunción, 2003), die Casa Abu y Font (Asunción, 2004), das Landhaus L. A. (Santani, 2005, hier vorgestellt) sowie Teletón (Lambare, 2009), alle in Paraguay.

SOLANO BENÍTEZ, né à Asunción (Paraguay) en 1963, est diplômé de la faculté d'architecture de l'Université nationale d'Asunción (1986). Il a créé son Gabinete de Arquitectura en 1987, aujourd'hui associé avec Alberto Marinoni et Gloria Cabral. En 1999, il a remporté le prix national d'architecture du Paraguay pour l'immeuble Edificio de Publicitaria Paraná et, en 2008, le prix d'architecture suisse BSI, décerné pour la première fois à Lugano. Mario Botta, président du jury BSI a déclaré à cette occasion : « La recherche architecturale de Solano Benítez, menée dans un contexte politique et économique difficile, et face à des enjeux opérationnels objectivement complexes, se détache des processus de production dictés par la globalisation et révèle une étonnante qualité. » Benítez a représenté son pays aux biennales de Venise, de São Paulo et de Lisbonne. Parmi ses réalisations, toutes au Paraguay, figurent un complexe de vacances (Ytu, 1998) ; un studio d'architecte (Asunción, 2000) ; un tombeau (Pirebebuy, 2001) ; le siège d'Unilever (Asunción, 2001) ; la maison Esmeraldina (Asunción, 2002) ; la maison Fanego (Asunción, 2003) ; la maison Abu y Font (Asunción, 2004) ; la maison de campagne L. A. (Santani, publiée ici) et le siège de Teletón (Lambare, 2009).

L. A. FARM HOUSE

Santani, Paraguay, 2005

Area: 570 m². Client: not disclosed
Cost: not disclosed

This large, unusual home is called Las Anitas and is located in rural Paraguay, where the fog seen in these images is frequent. Its forms appear to be relatively closed, but, on the front side, sliding glass doors and a large curved steel awning allow it to open into the countryside. An unusual trapezoidal interior brick wall made with pieces of broken bricks mixed with concrete divides the living area from private spaces over a 35-meter length. The bedroom area is located to the north of the structure. V-shaped concrete beams are used because, as the architect explains, "they resolve a complex structure with a small number of elements." The bedroom area is formed as a rectangle north of the building. Two bedrooms have access to two mezzanines: one with a view to the living area, the other, as a terrace, to the northern landscape." Made essentially with bricks, the L. A. House justifies the commentary of Mario Botta: "Solano Benítez uses simple materials that he obtains locally, which enables him to achieve expressive forms with major impact and poetic power. The poverty of the materials used is inversely proportional to the emotions that the architect conveys. The environmental values of Latin America are reinforced through his architecture, with a fresh language, new concepts and unexpected qualities for living spaces."

Das große, außergewöhnliche Haus Las Anitas liegt in einer ländlichen Gegend Paraguays, für die der Nebel auf diesen Aufnahmen typisch ist. Der Bau wirkt zunächst recht geschlossen, öffnet sich zur Stirnseite jedoch mit Glasschiebetüren und einem geschwungenen Stahlvordach zur Landschaft. Im Innern des Baus trennt eine ungewöhnliche Bruchsteinmauer mit reliefartigem Trapezmotiv über eine Länge von 35 m die offenen Wohnbereiche von den privaten Zonen. Die Schlafzimmer liegen im nördlichen Trakt. Der Architekt arbeitete mit V-förmigen Betonträgern, die „eine komplexe Konstruktion mit wenigen Elementen ermöglichen. Der Schlafbereich bildet ein Rechteck am Nordende des Baus. Zwei der Schlafzimmer haben Zugang zu einem Mezzaningeschoss: das eine bietet einen Blick auf den Wohnbereich, das andere in Form einer Terrasse ermöglicht die Aussicht auf die Landschaft im Norden." Das primär als Backsteinbau realisierte Haus L. A. scheint Mario Bottas Urteil zu bestätigen: „Solano Benítez arbeitet mit einfachen, lokal verfügbaren Baustoffen, was ihm erlaubt, expressive Formen von eindrucksvoller Wirkung und poetischer Kraft zu gestalten. Die Einfachheit der verarbeiteten Materialien verhält sich antiproportional zur emotionalen Wirkung, die der Architekt erzeugt. Seine Architektur verleiht den umweltpolitischen Anliegen Lateinamerikas Nachdruck – mit einer frischen Formensprache, neuen Konzepten und überraschendem Gewinn für den Wohnraum."

Cette vaste et étonnante maison appelée Las Anitas a été construite en pleine campagne dans une région où le brouillard est fréquent, comme le montrent ces images. Si elle semble de loin relativement fermée, une façade percée de portes de verre coulissantes sous un grand auvent métallique incurvé l'ouvre sur le paysage. Un mur intérieur trapézoïdal, monté en briques brisées mélangées à du béton, sépare la zone de séjour de celle des chambres sur 35 m de long. Des poutres de béton en V ont été utilisées parce qu'« elles résolvent le problème d'une structure complexe à l'aide d'un petit nombre d'éléments seulement », précise l'architecte. La zone des chambres, rectangulaire, se trouve au nord. Deux chambres ont accès à deux mezzanines, l'une donnant sur le séjour, l'autre sur une terrasse extérieure. Essentiellement construite en briques, la maison justifie ce commentaire de Mario Botta : « Solano Benítez utilise des matériaux simples, trouvés localement, qui lui permettent d'obtenir des formes expressives exerçant un puissant impact visuel et poétique. La pauvreté de ces matériaux est inversement proportionnelle aux émotions exprimées par l'architecte. Les valeurs environnementales de l'Amérique latine sont renforcées par cette architecture, qui apporte un langage neuf, des concepts nouveaux et une qualité des espaces de vie inattendue. »

These strict lines immediately make it evident that a talented architect has designed this house. Though it appears quite closed, it exudes a mastery of proportions and design.

Die strenge Linienführung macht sofort deutlich, dass dieser Entwurf von einem talentierten Architekten stammt. Zwar wirkt das Haus eher geschlossen, doch sind Proportionierung und Gestaltung meisterhaft.

Au premier regard, la rigueur des lignes témoigne de l'intervention d'un architecte de talent. Bien qu'elle semble assez fermée, la maison manifeste une grande maîtrise des proportions.

A large curving canopy, black columns, and drainpipes create an alternation with the brick and stone surfaces of the building.

Ein großes geschwungenes Vordach, schwarze Stützen und Traufrohre sorgen für Variation an den Backstein- und Steinfassaden des Gebäudes.

Un important auvent incurvé, des colonnes peintes en noir et les tuyaux d'évacuation des eaux contrastent avec la brique et la pierre des murs de la maison.

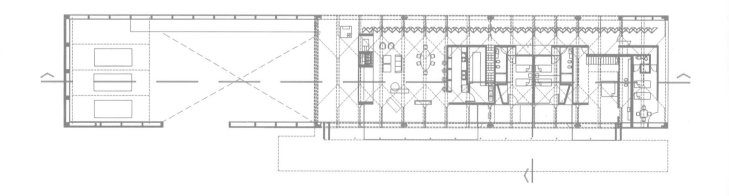

The rough materials of the exterior also find their place inside, but the massive wood dining table and generous openings give unexpected warmth to the interior volumes.

Die rauen Materialien des Außenbaus finden sich im Innenraum wieder. Der massive Holztisch und die großzügigen Fensteröffnungen geben den Interieurs eine unerwartete Wärme.

Les matériaux bruts vus en façade sont également utilisés à l'intérieur, mais la massive table en bois et les généreuses ouvertures confèrent à l'espace intérieur une chaleur inattendue.

BERNARDES + JACOBSEN

Bernardes + Jacobsen Arquitetura
Rua Corcovado 250
Jardim Botânico
22460–050 Rio de Janeiro, RJ
Brazil

Tel/Fax: +55 21 2512 7743
E-mail: contato@bernardesarq.com.br
Web: www.bernardesarquitetura.com.br

THIAGO BERNARDES was born in Rio de Janeiro in 1974. The office of Bernardes + Jacobsen was created in 1980 by his father, **CLAUDIO BERNARDES**, and Paulo Jacobsen, pioneers of a new type of residential architecture based on an effort to combine contemporary design and Brazilian culture. Thiago Bernardes worked in his father's office from 1991 to 1996, when he left to create his own firm, working on more than 30 residential projects between that date and 2001. With the death of his father, Thiago Bernardes reintegrated the firm and began to work with **PAULO JACOBSEN**, who was born in 1954 in Rio. Jacobsen studied photography in London before graduating from the Bennett Methodist Institute in 1979. The office of Bernardes + Jacobsen currently employs approximately 50 people in Rio de Janeiro and São Paulo and works on roughly 40 projects per year. Some of their significant projects include the Gerdau Headquarters (Santa Catarina, 2005); Villa Isabela (Henriksberg, Finland, 2005); Hotel Leblon (Rio de Janeiro, 2005); FW House (Guaruja, 2005); and the MPM Agency Main Office (São Paulo, 2006). Recent work includes the JH House (São Paulo, 2008); the JZ House (Bahia, 2008); RW House (Búzios, Rio de Janeiro, 2009); the FN and DB Houses (both in São Paulo, 2009); and the Joá House (Rio de Janeiro, 2010–11, published here), all in Brazil unless stated otherwise. The office has also created temporary projects such as Container Art (São Paulo, Brazil, 2008) for an international video art exhibition.

THIAGO BERNARDES wurde 1974 in Rio de Janeiro geboren. 1980 gründete sein Vater **CLAUDIO BERNARDES** mit Paulo Jacobsen das Büro Bernardes + Jacobsen. Die Partner waren Pioniere einer neuen Wohnbauarchitektur, die zeitgenössische Gestaltung und brasilianische Kultur miteinander vereinte. Von 1991 bis 1996 war Thiago Bernardes im Büro seines Vaters tätig und gründete schließlich sein eigenes Büro, mit dem er zwischen 1996 und 2001 über 30 Wohnbauprojekte realisierte. Nach dem Tod seines Vaters führte Thiago Bernardes die Büros zusammen und arbeitet seither mit **PAULO JACOBSEN**, geboren 1954 in Rio. Jacobsen studierte Fotografie in London, bevor er 1979 sein Studium am Bennett Methodist Institute abschloss. Das Büro Bernardes + Jacobsen beschäftigt derzeit rund 50 Mitarbeiter in Rio de Janeiro und São Paulo und arbeitet an etwa 40 Projekten pro Jahr. Ausgewählte Schlüsselprojekte sind u. a. die Gerdau-Zentrale (Santa Catarina, 2005), die Villa Isabela (Henriksberg, Finnland, 2005), das Hotel Leblon (Rio de Janeiro, 2005), das Haus FW (Guaruja, 2005) sowie die Hauptniederlassung der Agentur MPM (São Paulo, 2006). Neuere Projekte sind u. a. das Haus JH (São Paulo, 2008), das Haus JZ (Bahia, 2008), das Haus RW (Búzios, Rio de Janeiro, 2009), das Haus FN und das Haus DB (beide in São Paulo, 2009) sowie das Haus Joá (Rio de Janeiro, 2010–11, hier vorgestellt), alle in Brasilien, soweit nicht anders angegeben. Das Büro realisierte außerdem temporäre Bauten wie das Projekt Container Art (São Paulo, 2008) für eine internationale Videokunstausstellung.

THIAGO BERNARDES est né à Rio de Janeiro en 1974. L'agence Bernardes + Jacobsen a été fondée en 1980 par son père, **CLAUDIO BERNARDES**, et par Paulo Jacobsen, pionniers d'un nouveau type d'architecture résidentielle qui souhaitait associer principes de la conception architecturale contemporaine et culture brésilienne. Thiago Bernardes a travaillé dans l'agence paternelle de 1991 à 1996, puis a créé sa propre structure, réalisant plus de 30 projets résidentiels jusqu'en 2001. Après le décès de son père, il a réintégré l'agence de celui-ci et commencé à collaborer avec **PAULO JACOBSEN**, né en 1954 à Rio de Janeiro. Jacobsen avait étudié la photographie à Londres, avant d'être diplômé de l'Institut méthodiste Bennett de Rio en 1979. L'agence Bernardes + Jacobsen emploie actuellement environ 50 personnes à Rio de Janeiro et São Paulo, et travaille sur une quarantaine de projets chaque année. Parmi leurs réalisations les plus significatives, la plupart au Brésil : le siège de Gerdau (Santa Catarina, 2005) ; la villa Isabella (Henriksberg, Finlande, 2005) ; l'hôtel Leblon (Rio de Janeiro, 2005) ; la maison FW (Guaruja, 2005) et le siège de l'agence MPM (São Paulo, 2006). Parmi leurs travaux actuels : la maison JH (São Paulo, 2008) ; la maison JZ (Bahia, 2008) ; la maison RW (Búzios, Rio de Janeiro, 2009) ; les maisons FN et DB (São Paulo, 2009) et la maison Joá (Rio de Janeiro, 2010–11, publiée ici). L'agence a également conçu des projets d'installations temporaires comme Container Art (São Paulo, 2008) pour une exposition internationale sur l'art vidéo.

JOÁ HOUSE
Rio de Janeiro, Brazil, 2010–11

Area: 3500 m². Client: not disclosed
Cost: not disclosed

This very large residence is located at the highest point of the Joá neighborhood, in Rio de Janeiro, on a 16 000-square-meter plateau offering views of São Conrado, Barra da Tijuca, and Pedra da Gávea. As is often the case in local architecture, the continuity between indoor and outdoor space is emphasized, as are natural lighting and ventilation. Made up essentially of two volumes, each two stories high with a third, functional level below each, the house is linked together by a pergola and a glass catwalk. The wood and glass pergola marks the entrance to the house and provides access to the living room, dining room, gallery, a downstairs home theater, and the exterior spaces. A wooden staircase leads up to the bedrooms. As for the appearance of the volumes, the architects explain: "With the use of a few predominant materials such as apparent wood, natural brick, Navona Travertine marble, rough finishes, and aluminum frames in weathering steel, the residence consists of a mixed structure concept including concrete, steel, and laminated wood, streamlining the identification with a straightforward and easy 'visual' identity."

Das ungewöhnlich große Anwesen liegt auf dem höchsten Punkt des Joá-Viertels in Rio de Janeiro auf einem 16 000 m² großen Plateau mit Blick auf die Bezirke São Conrado, Barra da Tijuca und Pedra da Gávea. Wie so oft in der Architektur der Region wird die Kontinuität von Innen- und Außenraum betont, besonderer Wert wird auf natürliche Belichtung und Durchlüftung gelegt. Das Haus besteht im Kern aus zwei zweigeschossigen Volumina (mit darunterliegendem Funktionsgeschoss), die durch eine Pergola und einen verglasten Korridor miteinander verbunden sind. Die Pergola bildet den Eingang und gewährt Zugang zu Wohn- und Esszimmer, einer Galerie, einem Kinoraum im Untergeschoss sowie den Außenbereichen. Eine Holztreppe führt hinauf zu den Schlafzimmern. Mit Blick auf die Gestaltung der Baukörper erklärt der Architekt: „Mit dominierenden Materialien wie Holz, Naturziegeln, Navona-Travertin, naturbelassenen Oberflächen und Aluminiumrahmen in Cor-Ten-Stahl setzt der Bau konzeptuell auf gemischte Strukturen aus Beton, Stahl und Schichtholz. So entsteht der Eindruck einer ungezwungenen ‚visuellen Identität' von großer Leichtigkeit."

Cette très vaste résidence a été édifiée au point le plus élevé du quartier de Joá à Rio de Janeiro, sur un plateau de 16 000 m² offrant des vues superbes sur les quartiers du São Conrado, de Barra da Tijuca et de Pedra da Gávea. Comme souvent dans l'architecture locale, une continuité entre l'intérieur et l'extérieur est recherchée, de même que l'éclairage et la ventilation naturels. La maison se compose essentiellement de deux volumes, chacun de deux niveaux et d'un troisième en sous-sol. Ses divers éléments sont reliés par une pergola et une coursive vitrée. La pergola de bois et de verre de l'entrée donne accès au séjour, à la salle à manger, à une galerie, à un salon de télévision en sous-sol et aux jardins. Un escalier en bois conduit aux chambres. Sur l'aspect des volumes, les architectes précisent : « Grâce à quelques matériaux prédominants comme le bois apparent, la brique naturelle, le travertin de Navona, des finitions simples et des huisseries en aluminium dans des cadres en acier patiné, cette résidence propose un mix de béton, d'acier et de bois lamellé, qui favorise la perception de son identité "visuelle" directe et simple. »

This very large residence is largely clad in wood on the upper level and glazed at ground level. The roof overhangs and protects terraces with a view on the Bay of Rio.

Das großzügige Anwesen ist im oberen Bereich weitgehend mit Holz verblendet, zu ebener Erde verglast. Das auskragende Dach spannt sich schützend über die Terrassen mit Blick auf die Bucht von Rio.

Cette très vaste résidence est en grande partie habillée de bois en partie supérieure et vitrée au niveau du sol. Les surplombs des toitures protègent les terrasses qui ont une vue sur la baie de Rio.

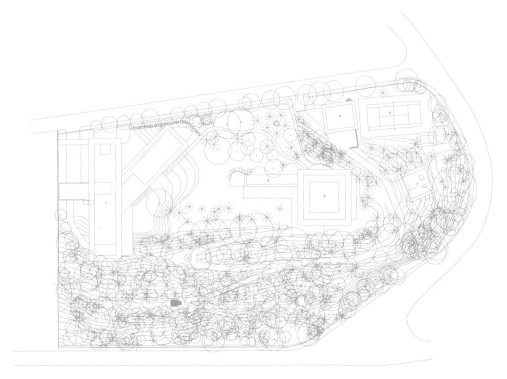

The Pedra da Gávea looms over the house, but the lush natural setting above all gives an impression of close proximity to nature.

Der Pedra da Gávea ragt majestätisch hinter dem Haus auf. Durch die üppige Vegetation entsteht der Eindruck besonderer Nähe zur Natur.

Au pied de la montagne de la Pedra da Gávea, la maison et le cadre naturel luxuriant donnent une impression de relation très proche.

Section drawings show the slope of the site and the broad, largely straight floor alignments. Glazing at ground level brings views and ample light into the house.

Querschnitte illustrieren die Hanglage des Grundstücks und die großzügige, geradlinige Anordnung der Ebenen. Das Erdgeschoss profitiert dank der Verglasung von den Ausblicken und reichlich Tageslicht.

Les dessins de coupe montrent la pente du terrain et l'alignement des niveaux. Le vitrage au niveau du sol assure un excellent éclairage de l'intérieur de la maison tout en offrant des perspectives sur le paysage.

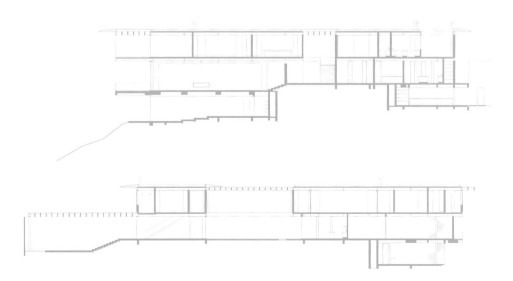

Brick surfaces on the first floor overhang the largely open ground level,
while sliding doors, in the image
above, directly connect interior and
exterior.

Backsteinflächen im ersten Stockwerk
schweben über dem weitgehend offen
gehaltenen Erdgeschoss. Glasschiebetüren verbinden die Innen- und
Außenräume.

Les plans de brique des étages
semblent parfois en suspension au-
dessus des baies vitrées, plus encore
lorsque les baies vitrées coulissantes
sont ouvertes sur l'extérieur.

An artful juxtaposition of a glazed
walkway, an overhanging brick
volume, and an open terrace permit
proximity to nature in a setting where
every detail appears to be under
control.

Die gekonnte Kombination des verglasten Korridors mit einem back-
steinverklinkerten Volumen und einer
offenen Terrasse sorgt für eine enge
Anbindung an die Landschaft. Hier ist
jedes Detail bewusst gewählt.

La juxtaposition habile d'une passerelle vitrée, d'un volume clos en
brique et d'une terrasse ouverte
assure une grande proximité avec la
nature, dans un cadre où chaque
détail semble parfaitement contrôlé.

TATIANA BILBAO

Tatiana Bilbao S.C.
Paseo de la Reforma 382–301
Colonia Juárez
Delegación Cuauhtémoc
México D.F. 06600
Mexico

Tel/Fax: +52 55 8589 8822
E-mail: info@tatianabilbao.com
Web: www.tatianabilbao.com

TATIANA BILBAO was born in Mexico City in 1972. She graduated in Architecture and Urbanism from the Universidad Iberoamericana in 1996. She was an Advisor for Urban Projects at the Urban Housing and Development Department of Mexico City (1998–99). In 2004, she created Tatiana Bilbao S.C., with projects in China, Spain, France, and Mexico. In 2005, she cofounded the urban research center MXDF with Derek Dellekamp, Arturo Ortiz, and Michel Rojkind, and also became a Professor of Design at the Universidad Iberoamericana. Her office was selected as one of the top 10 emerging firms in the 2007 Architectural Record Design Vanguard. In 2010, two new partners, David Vaner and Catia Bilbao, joined her firm. She curated the Ruta del Peregrino (with Derek Dellekamp), a 117-kilometer pilgrimage route where numerous architects created stopping points and small buildings from Ameca to Talpa de Allende (Jalisco, Mexico, 2009–11). Her built work includes Ajijic House, Chapala Lake (Jalisco, 2011, published here); the Culiacán Botanical Garden (Culiacán, Sinaloa, 2004–under construction); Veracruz Towers (Veracruz, 2011–); and Casa Demialma (Zihuatanejo, Joluta, 2011–), all in Mexico.

TATIANA BILBAO wurde 1972 in Mexiko-Stadt geboren. 1996 schloss sie ihr Studium der Architektur und Stadtplanung an der Universidad Iberoamericana ab. Sie war als beratende Stadtplanerin für die Wohnungsbau- und Stadtentwicklungsbehörde in Mexiko-Stadt (1998–99) tätig. 2004 gründete sie ihr Büro Tatiana Bilbao S. C., das Projekte in China, Spanien, Frankreich und Mexiko realisierte. 2005 gründete sie mit Derek Dellekamp, Arturo Ortiz und Michel Rojkind darüber hinaus das experimentelle Studio MXDF. Ebenfalls seit 2005 ist sie Professorin für Entwerfen an der Universidad Iberoamericana. 2007 präsentierte sie der *Architectural Record* als eines von zehn herausragenden Nachwuchsbüros. 2010 kamen David Vaner und Catia Bilbao als neue Partner hinzu. Gemeinsam mit Derek Dellekamp kuratierte Tatiana Bilbao die Ruta del Peregrino, einen 117 km langen Pilgerweg zwischen Ameca und Talpa de Allende (Jalisco, Mexiko, 2009–11), entlang dessen Route zahlreiche Architekten kleinere Bauten und Rastplätze bauten. Zu ihren realisierten Projekten zählen die Casa Ajijic am Chapalasee (Jalisco, 2011, hier vorgestellt), der Botanische Garten in Culiacán (Culiacán, Sinaloa, 2004–im Bau), die Veracruz Towers (Veracruz, seit 2011) sowie die Casa Demialma (Zihuatanejo, Joluta, seit 2011), alle in Mexiko.

TATIANA BILBAO, née à Mexico en 1972, est diplômée en architecture et urbanisme de l'Université ibéro-américaine (1996). Elle a été conseillère en urbanisme au département du Logement urbain et du Développement de Mexico (1998–99). En 2004, elle a créé l'agence Tatiana Bilbao S.C. et a réalisé des projets en Chine, en Espagne, en France et au Mexique. En 2005, elle a par ailleurs fondé le Centre de recherches urbaines MXDF avec Derek Dellekamp, Arturo Ortiz et Michel Rojkind et, la même année, a été nommée professeur de conception à l'Université ibéro-américaine. Son agence a été désignée comme l'une des dix agences émergentes dans le Design Vanguard 2007 de l'*Architectural Record*. En 2010, deux nouveaux partenaires, David Vaner et Catia Bilbao, l'ont rejointe. Elle a été commissaire pour la Ruta del Peregrino (avec Derek Dellekamp), un chemin de pèlerinage de 117 km entre Ameca et Talpa de Allende (Jalisco, Mexique, 2009–11) le long duquel divers architectes ont créé des arrêts et des petites constructions. Parmi ses réalisations, toutes au Mexique : la maison Ajijic (lac de Chapala, Jalisco, 2011, publiée ici) ; le jardin botanique de Culiacán (Culiacán, Sinaloa, 2004, en cours) ; les tours de Veracruz (Veracruz, 2011–) et la Casa Demialma (Zihuatanejo, Joluta, 2011–).

AJIJIC HOUSE

Chapala Lake, Jalisco, Mexico, 2011

Area: 280 m². Client: Vivian Charpenel
Cost: $150 000

This is a weekend house located on Lake Chapala near Guadalajara. Four cubes, two of which are oriented to the lake and two toward the town of Ajijic, form the concept. These cubes symbolically represent the members of the client's family. The cubes offer private space but also overlap, creating semipublic areas. Three circular traces are also inscribed in the design, defining the landscape and its relationship to the architecture. "We needed to find a low-cost, low-maintenance construction system that could fit to the budget (the client) had," says Bilbao. "We needed a very gentle material that could be a strong statement allowing us to play with different deep concepts but also to play with high contrasts such as opacity, transparency, and reflectivity of the inner space and the surroundings but at the same time be shining as this family is. We decided to use one of the most long-lasting and long-used materials in construction: rammed earth, a strong direct material that could be the structure, the isolation, and the aesthetic definition of the space at the same time. This completed the definition of the systems and is also the point of intersection between them: the ground." The artists Rodolfo Díaz and Marco Rountree, and Cynthia Gutiérrez were invited to participate in the project in specific areas. Six lamps were specially designed for the client by the noted Cuban artist Jorge Pardo.

Das Wochenendhaus liegt am Chapalasee, nicht weit von Guadalajara. Das Entwurfskonzept basiert auf vier sich überlagernden Kuben, von denen zwei zum See, zwei zur Kleinstadt Ajijic orientiert sind. Die Kuben stehen symbolisch für die vier Mitglieder der Bauherrenfamilie – sie bilden private Räume sowie an ihren Schnittstellen Gemeinschaftsbereiche. Eingeschrieben in den Entwurf sind darüber hinaus drei Kreismotive, die die Landschaft und ihren Bezug zur Architektur andeuten. „Wir waren auf der Suche nach einem kostengünstigen, wartungsarmen Baukonzept, das den Budgetvorgaben (der Bauherren) entsprach", so Bilbao. „Wir brauchten ein formbares Material, ein deutliches Statement, das uns erlauben würde, mit verschiedenen Konzepten zu spielen, dazu mit auffälligen Kontrasten wie Opazität, Transparenz und Spiegelungen von Innenraum und Umgebung – eine Aussage, die ebensolche Ausstrahlung besitzt wie die Familie selbst. Wir entschieden uns, mit einem der beständigsten und ältesten Baustoffe überhaupt zu arbeiten: mit Stampflehm, einem ausdrucksstarken, unverfälschten Material, das zugleich als Tragwerk, Dämmung und ästhetisches Markenzeichen fungiert. So waren die verschiedenen Systeme definiert und zugleich ein Bindeglied gefunden: der Lehm, der Boden." Die Künstler Rodolfo Díaz, Marco Rountree und Cynthia Gutiérrez wurden an der Gestaltung bestimmter Bereiche beteiligt. Der kubanische Künstler Jorge Pardo entwarf eigens für den Bauherrn sechs Leuchten.

Cette maison de week-end est située au bord du lac Chapala près de Guadalajara. Son concept repose sur quatre cubes, dont deux sont orientés vers le lac et deux vers la ville d'Ajijic. Ils représentent symboliquement les membres de la famille du client. Chacun constitue un espace privé, mais ils délimitent ensemble des zones communes à travers leur imbrication. Trois tracés circulaires figurant également dans le plan précisent la relation du paysage et de l'architecture. « Nous devions trouver un système constructif économique et de faible entretien, adapté au budget du client, précise l'architecte. Nous avions besoin d'un matériau simple mais de présence forte nous permettant de jouer avec différents concepts profonds mais aussi avec des contrastes puissants comme l'opacité, la transparence et la réflectivité de l'espace intérieur et de l'environnement, mais qui soit aussi intéressant que l'est cette famille. Nous avons opté pour l'un des matériaux de construction les plus durables et les plus anciens, le pisé, un matériau simple et direct qui pouvait à la fois constituer la structure, l'isolation et donner une définition esthétique à l'espace. Ce choix complétait la définition des systèmes tout en étant à leur point d'intersection entre eux, à savoir le sol. » Les artistes Rodolfo Díaz, Marco Rountree et Cynthia Gutiérrez ont été invités à participer au projet à travers des interventions ponctuelles. Six lampes ont été spécialement conçues pour le client par le célèbre artiste cubain Jorge Pardo.

The Ajijic House is small, but its disposition, site, and the way in which
the angled roof creates more ample
interior space are carefully calculated
to make it architecturally interesting.

Die Casa Ajijic ist klein, doch Auftei-
lung und Lage sowie das schräge
Dach, das großzügige Räume schafft,
sind auf eine reizvolle architektonische Wirkung hin angelegt.

Si la maison Ajijic est petite, son
plan, son cadre et la façon dont ses
toitures amplifient les volumes inté
rieurs la rendent néanmoins architec-
turalement intéressante.

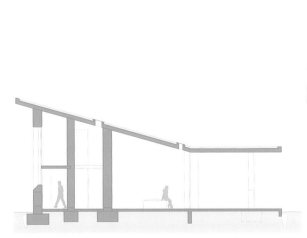

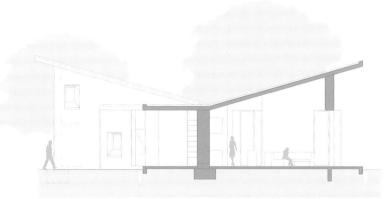

Right, a model shows the precise configuration of the house with its angled roofs and two main sections. Above, an interior view showing the use of rammed-earth walls.

Das Modell (rechts) veranschaulicht die exakte Konfiguration des Hauses mit Dachschrägen und den beiden zentralen Volumina. Oben eine Innenansicht mit Stampflehmmauern.

À droite, une maquette montre la configuration de la maison répartie en deux sections sous des toitures très inclinées. Ci-dessus, vue de l'intérieur illustrant la forte présence des murs en pisé.

Materials and surfaces remain relatively rough and simple, but the house is both bright and spacious.

Materialien und Oberflächen sind weitgehend unbearbeitet und schlicht gehalten, dennoch wirkt das Haus hell und großzügig.

Si la maison est à la fois lumineuse et spacieuse, matériaux et surfaces restent relativement bruts et simples.

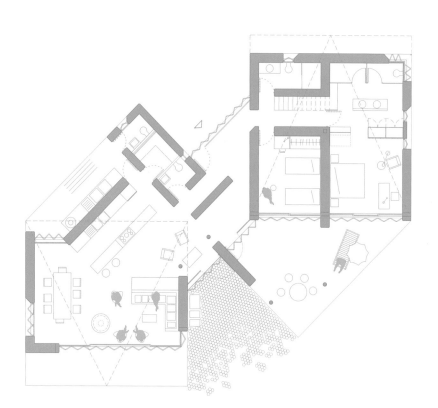

A plan shows the division of the house into two areas—one of which is "public"—the living space (above)—and one of which is private—the bedrooms (right).

Der Grundriss veranschaulicht die Gliederung des Hauses in zwei Bereiche: einen öffentlichen – den Wohnbereich (oben) – sowie einen privaten – die Schlafzimmer (rechts).

Le plan montre la division de la maison en deux parties, l'une « publique » – le séjour (ci-dessus) – et l'autre « privée », les chambres (à droite).

PETE BOSSLEY

Bossley Architects
2/55 Mackelvie Street
Ponsonby
Auckland 1021
New Zealand

Tel: +64 9 361 2201
Fax: +64 9 361 2202
E-mail: mail@bossleyarchitects.co.nz
Web: www.bossleyarchitects.co.nz

PETE BOSSLEY was born in 1950 in New Zealand. After his studies, he was an architect in the Ministry of Works (Auckland, 1978–81). From 1987 to 1989, he was Director of Bossley Cheshire Architects; from 1989 to 1996, Director of Jasmax Architects; and since 1996, he has been the Director of Bossley Architects in Auckland. He was the joint principal responsible for design and documentation of the architecture and interior design of the Museum of New Zealand Te Papa Tongarewa (Wellington, 1998), including the subsequently expanded art galleries (2001) and the "Treaty of Waitangi" exhibition. **ANDREA BELL** was born in 1972 in New Zealand. She obtained her B.Arch degree from the Unitec Institute of Technology (Auckland 1994–98), and has been a Senior Associate, Design and Project Architect at Bossley Architects since 1999. Their recent work includes the Forman House, Thorne Bay House, Voyager NZ Maritime Museum, and the Brown Vujcich House (published here), all completed in Auckland, New Zealand, in 2009.

PETE BOSSLEY wurde 1950 in Neuseeland geboren. Nach seinem Studium war er zunächst als Architekt beim Ministerium für Bauen und Infrastruktur tätig (Auckland, 1978–81). Von 1987 bis 1989 war er Direktor bei Bossley Cheshire Architects, von 1989 bis 1996 Direktor bei Jasmax Architects, seit 1996 ist er Direktor bei Bossley Architects in Auckland. Als Koplaner verantwortete er Architektur und Innenarchitektur des Neuseeland-Museums Te Papa Tongarewa (Entwurf und Dokumentation; Wellington, 1998), eine spätere Galerieerweiterung (2001) sowie die Ausstellungsarchitektur für *Treaty of Waitangi*. **ANDREA BELL** wurde 1972 in Neuseeland geboren. Sie schloss ihren B. Arch. am Unitec Institute of Technology (Auckland 1994–98) ab und ist seit 1999 Seniorpartnerin und entwerfende Projektarchitektin bei Bossley Architects. Zu ihren jüngeren Projekten zählen das Forman House, das Thorne Bay House, das Voyager NZ Maritime Museum und das Brown Vujcich House (hier vorgestellt), alle 2009 in Auckland, Neuseeland.

Né en 1950 en Nouvelle-Zélande, **PETE BOSSLEY** a débuté comme architecte au ministère néozélandais des Travaux publics (Auckland, 1978–81). De 1987 à 1989, il dirige l'agence Bossley Cheshire Architects ; de 1989 à 1996 Jasmax Architects puis, à partir de 1996, sa propre agence, Bossley Architects à Auckland. Il a été responsable du design et de la documentation sur l'architecture et de l'architecture intérieure du musée de Nouvelle-Zélande Te Papa Tongarewa (Wellington, 1998) dont l'agrandissement des galeries d'art en 2001 et l'exposition sur le « Traité de Waitangi ». **ANDREA BELL**, née en 1972 en Nouvelle-Zélande, a obtenu son diplôme de B.Arch. de l'Institut de technologie Unitec (Auckland, 1994–98) et est associée senior, architecte de conception et de projet chez Bossley Architects depuis 1999. Parmi leurs réalisations récentes, toutes à Auckland en 2009 : la Forman House ; la Thorne Bay House ; le Musée maritime Voyager NZ et la Brown Vujcich House (publiée ici).

BROWN VUJCICH HOUSE

Auckland, New Zealand, 2008–09

Area: 265 m². Client: not disclosed
Cost: not disclosed

The house is located in the Herne Bay area of Auckland on a narrow, sloping urban site. The glazed entry includes an access bridge and has a vertical cedar screen. A stairway leads up to the main public areas and down to the bedrooms and a private living space. Each room has its own terrace, and, at the lowest level, the house opens out to a terrace and pool near the family space. Full-height cedar and aluminum vertical fins regulate light and privacy for the upper levels. Cedar and brick are used for the exteriors, while colors inspired by the clients' interest in 1950s and 1960s furniture, art, and ceramics are seen inside the house.

Das Haus in Herne Bay, Auckland, liegt auf einem schmalen Hanggrundstück in der Stadt. Der verglaste Eingang mit vorgesetztem vertikalem Zedernwandschirm wird über einen Brückensteg erschlossen. Das Treppenhaus führt hinauf zu den öffentlichen Wohnbereichen und hinunter zu den Schlafzimmern und einem privaten Wohnbereich. Jeder Raum verfügt über eine eigene Terrasse. Im Untergeschoss öffnet sich das Wohnzimmer zu einer Terrasse mit Pool. Oben filtern vertikale Lamellen aus Zedernholz und Aluminium das Licht und sorgen für Privatsphäre. Am Außenbau kamen Zedernholz und Backstein zum Einsatz; die Palette orientiert sich farblich an Möbeln, Kunst und Keramik der 1950er- und 1960er-Jahre – eine Sammelleidenschaft des Bauherrn, die sich im gesamten Haus spiegelt.

Cette maison est située dans le quartier de Herne Bay à Auckland sur une étroite parcelle en pente. L'entrée vitrée, protégée par un écran de cèdre, intègre la passerelle d'accès. Un escalier monte au séjour principal et descend vers les chambres et un séjour plus privé. Chaque pièce possède une terrasse et, au niveau le plus bas, la maison s'ouvre sur une terrasse et une piscine. Des ailettes verticales de cèdre et d'aluminium régulent l'éclairage et protègent l'intimité des niveaux supérieurs. L'extérieur est traité en brique et bardeaux de cèdre tandis qu'à l'intérieur, les coloris révèlent l'intérêt du client pour le mobilier, la céramique et l'art des années 1950 et 1960.

The cedar and metal finishings give the house an almost industrial appearance from certain angles, such as the one above.

Durch die Zedernholzfassade mit Metalldetails gewinnt das Haus aus bestimmten Blickwinkeln (wie oben) fast eine industrielle Anmutung.

Sous certains angles, les éléments de second œuvre en cèdre et en métal donnent à cette maison, un aspect presque industriel.

With its generous openings and terraces, the house is well conceived to assure the privacy of the owners. The plan (below) shows the terraces, and the relatively small lot.

Mit seinen großzügigen Öffnungen und Terrassen wahrt das Haus dank geschickter Planung dennoch die Privatsphäre der Eigentümer. Der Grundriss (unten) zeigt die Terrassen und das recht kleine Grundstück.

Généreusement ouverte et dotée de terrasses, la maison a été néanmoins conçue pour assurer l'intimité de ses occupants. Le plan ci-dessous montre les terrasses et le terrain de dimensions assez réduites.

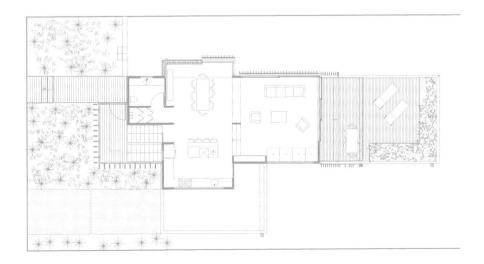

Inside spaces are bright and open, especially in the directions where there is some protection from neighboring residences, as is the case with the trees (above).

Die Räume sind hell und offen, besonders in Richtungen, in denen Sichtschutz zu Nachbargrundstücken besteht, hier etwa durch den Baumbestand (oben).

À l'intérieur, les espaces restent lumineux et ouverts, en particulier dans les axes de vue protégés des résidences voisines, entre autres par des arbres (ci-dessus).

The interiors are fairly simple and modern with large openings on either side, as seen in the living-room space (above).

Die Interieurs sind vergleichsweise schlicht und modern, mit großflächigen Öffnungen zu beiden Seiten, wie hier im Wohnbereich (oben).

Les aménagements intérieurs assez simples sont modernes, parfois à double exposition, comme dans le séjour (ci-dessus).

Translucent glass and different wood or metal surfaces are used to enliven the space. Above, a bathroom and the kitchen. Below, a floor plan of the house.

Transluzente Verglasung sowie unterschiedliche Holz- und Metallflächen beleben den Raum. Oben ein Bad und die Küche. Unten ein Etagengrundriss des Hauses.

Le verre translucide et les plans habillés de métal ou de bois animent l'espace. Ci-dessus, une salle de bains et la cuisine. Ci-dessous, le plan au sol de la maison.

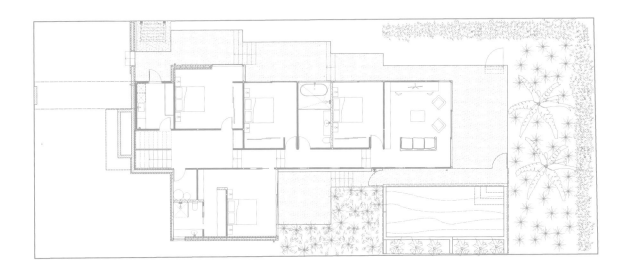

FLORIAN BUSCH

Florian Busch Architects
14–10–312 Sakuragaokacho
Shibuya-ku
Tokyo 150–0031
Japan

Tel: +81 3 6277 5190
Fax: +81 3 6277 5199
E-mail: info@florianbusch.com
Web: www.florianbusch.com

FLORIAN BUSCH was born in Munich, Germany, in 1973. After graduating from the Bauhaus University in Weimar and the Architectural Association in London, he worked for Toyo Ito & Associates in Tokyo (2004–08). In 2009 he founded Florian Busch Architects, an office practicing architecture, urbanism, and sociocultural analysis. Based in Tokyo, the office currently consists of seven architects and designers. Recent work includes the House in Takadanobaba (Shinjuku, Tokyo, 2011, published here); show design for the Tokyo Designers Week 2011; the "Tohoku to the Future" exhibition for Japan's Ministry of Economics, Trade, and Industry (Tokyo, 2011); House at the Ocean (Kisami, 2010–12); Loh House in Niseko (Hokkaido, under construction); the Outside-Inside Prototype (Chiba, under construction), all in Japan; and several research projects focusing on the development of materials.

FLORIAN BUSCH wurde 1973 in München geboren. Nach Abschlüssen an der Bauhaus-Universität in Weimar sowie der Architectural Association in London arbeitete er zunächst für Toyo Ito & Associates in Tokio (2004–08). 2009 gründete er Florian Busch Architects mit den Schwerpunkten Architektur, Stadtplanung und soziokultureller Forschung. Das Büro mit Sitz in Tokio beschäftigt derzeit sieben Architekten und Planer. Jüngere Projekte sind u. a. das Haus in Takadanobaba (Shinjuku, Tokio, 2011, hier vorgestellt), eine Ausstellungsarchitektur für die Tokyo Designers Week 2011, eine Ausstellungsarchitektur für *Tohoku to the Future,* eine Ausstellung des japanischen Ministeriums für Wirtschaft, Handel und Industrie (Tokio, 2011), das Haus am Meer (Kisami, 2010–12), Haus Loh in Niseko (Hokkaido, im Bau), Outside-Inside (Prototyp; Chiba, im Bau), alle in Japan, sowie mehrere Forschungsprojekte zur Materialentwicklung.

FLORIAN BUSCH, né à Munich en 1973, est diplômé de l'université du Bauhaus à Weimar et de l'Architectural Association de Londres. Il a travaillé chez Toyo Ito & Associates à Tokyo (2004–08) et, en 2009, a fondé Florian Busch Architects, agence spécialisée en architecture, urbanisme et analyse socioculturelle. Basée à Tokyo, elle compte actuellement sept architectes et designers. Parmi ses récentes réalisations : la maison à Takadanobaba (Shinjuku, Tokyo, 2011, publiée ici) ; une exposition de design pour la Designers Week de Tokyo en 2011 ; l'exposition « Tohoku to the Future » pour le ministère japonais de l'Économie, du Commerce et de l'Industrie (Tokyo, 2011) ; une maison au bord de l'océan (Kisami, 2010–12) ; la maison Loh à Niseko (Hokkaido, Japon, en construction) ; le Prototype Extérieur-Intérieur (Chiba, Japon, en construction) et plusieurs projets de recherche sur le développement de matériaux.

HOUSE IN TAKADANOBABA

Shinjuku, Tokyo, Japan, 2011

Area: 153 m². Client: not disclosed
Cost: ¥46 million

Typical of many urban Japanese lots, the site of this house measures 22 meters in depth and just 4.7 meters in width. The architect states: "When the brief asked for a wide-open living space where breathing within the confines of the city was possible, we proposed an architecture of the exterior that claims the space around it by extending beyond its limits." The concept consists in creating a single, folded plane with the house opening on alternate sides as it rises to a height of three stories. In this sense, Busch is correct in saying that the house has "no inside." With no fixed partitions, fabrics are used to contrast with the concrete used for construction. Florian Busch explains: "The structural concept was developed with Masato Araya. It is an ingenious composition of conventional structural principles that play together strikingly: they break up each other's rigidity and make the building impossibly light."

Das Grundstück des Hauses ist, typisch für viele Bauflächen in japanischen Städten, 22 m lang und nur 4,7 m breit. Der Architekt berichtet: „Die Vorgaben sahen offene Wohnräume vor, die befreites Atmen in der Enge der Stadt ermöglichen sollten. Wir entwarfen also eine Freiraumarchitektur, die ihr Umfeld besetzt, indem sie über ihre Grenzen hinauswächst." Vom Konzept her besteht der Bau aus einem einzigen, gefalteten Band, das sich über drei Geschosse wechselseitig öffnet. Mit der Aussage, das Haus habe „keinen Innenraum", trifft Busch den Punkt. Statt fester Trennwände kontrastieren Textilvorhänge mit dem Tragwerk aus Beton. Florian Busch führt aus: „Das bautechnische Konzept wurde mit Masato Araya entwickelt. Es ist eine raffinierte Komposition aus konventionellen Konstruktionsprinzipien, die ein faszinierendes Zusammenspiel erzeugen: Sie brechen ihre typische Strenge auf und verleihen dem Bau eine geradezu unglaubliche Leichtigkeit."

Typique de la faible taille des parcelles constructibles au Japon, le terrain de cette maison ne mesure que 22 m de long par 4,70 m de large. « Alors que le brief demandait un espace de séjour très ouvert, permettant de respirer dans la ville étriquée, explique l'architecte, nous avons proposé une architecture de l'extérieur revendiquant l'espace qui l'entoure et l'amplifiant au-delà de ses limites. » Le concept est celui d'un plan unique qui se plie et s'ouvre alternativement sur trois niveaux. En ce sens, Busch a raison de dire que la maison ne possède « pas d'intérieur. » En l'absence de cloisonnements fixes, des rideaux de séparation contrastent avec le béton de la construction. « Le concept structurel a été mis au point avec Masato Araya. C'est une composition ingénieuse de principes structurels conventionnels qui jouent ensemble de façon saisissante ; ils annulent mutuellement leur rigidité et confèrent au bâtiment une incroyable légèreté. »

The structure of the house as seen in the street-side view (left) creates a zigzag form in space. Right, an axonometric drawing of the house (center of the drawing) and, below, the very simple concrete and glass living space.

Die Konstruktion des Hauses, links auf einer Straßenansicht, bildet eine Zickzackform im Raum. Rechts eine Axonometrie (in der Mitte der Bau) und unten der ausgesprochen schlichte Wohnbereich in Glas und Beton.

La structure de la maison, telle que perçue de la rue (à gauche) a pris une forme de « grecque ». À droite, dessin axonométrique de la maison (au centre) et ci-dessous, le très simple séjour en verre et béton.

*Concrete walls, ceilings, and floors
are pierced by a spiral staircase and
a number of full-height windows.*

*Sichtbetonwände und -böden, durch-
brochen von einer Wendeltreppe und
zahlreichen geschosshohen Fenstern.*

*Les murs, les plafonds et les sols
sont en béton, percés de baies toute
hauteur et d'un escalier en spirale.*

*The kitchen space is inserted into
the concrete forms of the house. The
dining area in the background of the
photo above is seen from another
angle on the left.*

*Die Küche wurde in das Betonband
des Hauses eingeschrieben. Der Essbereich im Hintergrund der Aufnahme
oben erscheint links aus einem anderen Blickwinkel.*

*La cuisine suit les formes en béton
de la maison. Ci-dessus au fond,
l'espace des repas, vu sous un autre
angle à gauche.*

ARTHUR CASAS

Studio Arthur Casas SP
818 Itápolis Street
01245–000 São Paulo, SP
Brazil

Tel: +55 11 2182 7500
Fax: +55 11 3663 6540
E-mail: sp@arthurcasas.com
Web: www.arthurcasas.com

ARTHUR CASAS was born in 1961 and graduated as an architect from the Mackenzie University of São Paulo, Brazil, in 1983. He has concentrated on both interiors and constructions, developing residential and commercial projects with a distinctive vocabulary of forms. He has participated in the Architecture Biennial in São Paulo, in 1997 and 2003, and in the Buenos Aires Biennial, in 2003 and 2005. In 2008, Arthur Casas won the prestigious Red Dot Design Award, in Germany, for developing creative cutlery and dinner-set lines for Riva. His completed commercial projects include the Natura Store (Paris, France, 2005); Alexandre Herchcovitch Store (Tokyo, Japan, 2007); Huis Clos Store (São Paulo, 2008); Cidade Jardim Mall (São Paulo, 2008); Zeferino Store, Oscar Freire Street (São Paulo, 2008); Kosushi Restaurant (São Paulo, 2008); C-View Bar and C-House Restaurant, Affinia Hotel (Chicago, Illinois, USA, 2008); KAA Restaurant (São Paulo, 2008); the Jack Vartanian Store (New York, New York, USA, 2008); and the Quinta da Baroneza (Bragança Paulista, São Paulo, 2009, published here), all in Brazil unless stated otherwise.

ARTHUR CASAS, Jahrgang 1961, schloss sein Architekturstudium 1983 an der Mackenzie-Universität in São Paulo, Brasilien, ab. Seine Schwerpunkte sind sowohl Innengestaltung wie Architektur; seine Wohn- und Geschäftsbauten zeichnen sich durch eine charakteristische Formensprache aus. 1997 und 2003 war Casas auf den Architekturbiennalen in São Paulo vertreten, 2003 und 2005 zudem auf der Biennale in Buenos Aires. 2008 wurde seine kreative Besteck- und Geschirrserie für Riva mit dem renommierten deutschen Red Dot Design Award ausgezeichnet. Zu seinen realisierten Projekten zählen Ladengeschäfte für Natura (Paris, 2005), Alexandre Herchcovitch (Tokio, 2007) und Huis Clos (São Paulo, 2008), das Einkaufszentrum Cidade Jardim (São Paulo, 2008), die Zeferino-Boutique an der Rua Oscar Freire (São Paulo, 2008), das Restaurant Kosushi (São Paulo, 2008), die C-View Bar und das C-House Restaurant im Affinia Hotel (Chicago, Illinois, 2008), das Restaurant KAA (São Paulo, 2008), ein Ladengeschäft für Jack Vartanian (New York, 2008) sowie die Quinta da Baroneza (Bragança Paulista, São Paulo, 2009, hier vorgestellt).

Né en 1961, **ARTHUR CASAS** est diplômé en architecture de l'université Mackenzie à São Paulo (1983). Il se consacre à la fois à l'aménagement intérieur et à l'architecture et met en œuvre dans ses projets résidentiels ou commerciaux un vocabulaire formel personnel. Il a participé à deux biennales d'architecture de São Paulo (1997 et 2003) et à la Biennale de Buenos Aires en 2003 et 2005. En 2008, ses lignes de couverts et ses services de table pour Riva ont remporté le prestigieux prix allemand Red Dot Design Award. Parmi ses projets d'architecture commerciale réalisés : le magasin Natura (Paris, 2005) ; le magasin Alexandre Herchcovitch (Tokyo, 2007) ; le magasin Huis Clos (São Paulo, 2008) ; le Cidade Jardim Mall (São Paulo, 2008) ; le magasin Zeferino, rue Oscar Freire (São Paulo, 2008) ; le restaurant Kosushi (São Paulo, 2008) ; le bar C-View et le restaurant C-House de l'Affinia Hotel (Chicago, 2008) ; le restaurant KAA (São Paulo, 2008) ; le magasin Jack Vartanian (New York, 2008) et la Quinta da Baroneza (Bragança Paulista, São Paulo, 2009, publiée ici).

QUINTA DA BARONEZA

Bragança Paulista, São Paulo, Brazil, 2009

Area: 1576 m². Client: not disclosed
Cost: not disclosed

The architect blends a surprising variety of forms—seemingly suspended, or in wood or stone according to their placement.

Der Architekt verbindet eine erstaunliche Bandbreite von Formen: scheinbar schwebend oder – je nach Funktion – gemauert oder aus Holz.

L'architecte a associé un nombre étonnant d'éléments, suspendus ou non, habillés de bois ou de pierre en fonction de leur implantation.

A canopy juts out over the swimming pool and a volume with a high window is interposed between the formal rectilinear elements of the design. Right, a site plan.

Ein Dach greift über den Pool aus, ein Baukörper mit hohem Fenster ist in die formalen, geradwinkligen Elemente des Entwurfs eingespannt. Rechts ein Lageplan.

Un auvent se projette au-dessus de la piscine tandis qu'un volume vertical vitré s'interpose entre des éléments horizontaux. À droite, plan du site.

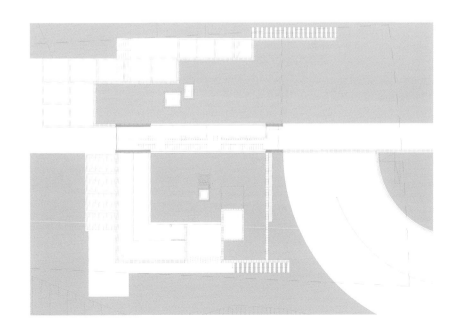

This substantial residence is in fact a weekend house for a 35-year-old couple with two children. The architect was asked only that the house should be "bright" and have a view of the nearby golf course. Arthur Casas explains: "My intention was to have the house unnoticed from the street perspective, therefore the rugged topography of the land was important." Casas used organic materials, such as sustainably produced Cumaru and old bricks recovered from construction demolition. The house is characterized by its numerous openings and view of the golf course, its "interconnected spaces, generous convenience areas, and high level of comfort," according to the architect. The integration of the house into its sloped site minimizes the impression of mass that such a large house might otherwise generate. The architect willfully contrasts opaque wood or brick surfaces with large horizontal and vertical openings.

Das großzügige Anwesen wird von einem 35-jährigen Paar mit zwei Kindern als Wochenendhaus genutzt. Einzige Vorgabe für den Architekten war der Wunsch nach einem „hellen" Haus mit Blick über den nahe gelegenen Golfplatz. Arthur Casas erklärt: „Mein Ziel war es, das Haus von der Straße aus nicht einsehbar zu halten; deshalb spielte die hügelige Topografie des Geländes eine entscheidende Rolle." Casas arbeitete mit ökologischen Baustoffen, etwa mit Cumaroholz aus nachhaltiger Forstwirtschaft und alten Ziegeln aus Abrissbauten. Markante Kennzeichen des Hauses sind seine zahlreichen Öffnungen und der Blick auf den Golfplatz, die „ineinander übergehenden Räume, die großzügigen Wohnbereiche und hoher Komfort", so der Architekt. Die Integration des Hauses in das Hanggrundstück lässt die bauliche Masse geringer scheinen, als dies bei einem solchen Bau zu erwarten wäre. Bewusst kontrastiert der Architekt opake Oberflächen aus Holz oder Ziegel mit großflächigen horizontalen und vertikalen Fensterbändern.

Cette importante résidence est la maison de week-end d'un couple et de ses deux enfants. La seule demande du client était que la maison soit « lumineuse » et ait une vue sur un terrain de golf voisin. « Mon intention était que la maison reste discrète du côté de la rue et la topographie accidentée du terrain a donc joué un rôle important », a expliqué l'architecte. Casas s'est servi de matériaux écologiques comme du bois cumaru de production durable et de vieilles briques récupérées sur des chantiers de démolition. La maison se caractérise par ses multiples ouvertures, ses vues sur le golf et ses « espaces interconnectés, ses zones de commodités généreuses et son niveau élevé de confort ». L'intégration dans le site escarpé minimise l'impression de masse qu'une construction aussi volumineuse aurait pu donner. L'architecte a multiplié les contrastes entre les plans fermés en brique ou en bois et les grandes ouvertures verticales ou horizontales.

A full-height window swings up to open the house entirely on one side of the living room (above).

Ein raumhohes Fenster lässt sich nach oben schwenken und öffnet den Wohnraum an der Stirnseite vollständig nach außen (oben).

Une baie toute hauteur se replie contre le plafond pour totalement ouvrir une extrémité du séjour sur la nature (ci-dessus).

A floor plan of the house on the right.
The long narrow volume of the house
has a stairway that leads directly to a
tree, planted in the axis of the
passage.

Rechts ein Etagengrundriss des Hauses. Im langen schmalen Baukörper
liegt eine Treppe, die direkt auf einen
Baum zuläuft, der in der Flucht der
Hauptachse liegt.

À droite, le plan au sol de la maison.
Le volume vertical et étroit vu page
précédente contient un escalier qui
semble directement mener à un arbre
planté dans son axe.

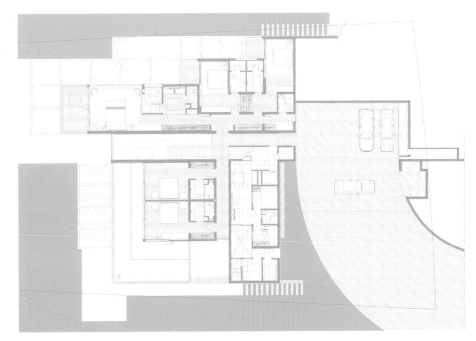

Inside the relatively closed walls of the house, the natural surroundings are nonetheless very present because of the full-height glazing or the swinging glazed façade seen below.

Selbst innerhalb der eher geschlossenen Wände des Hauses ist die landschaftliche Umgebung durch raumhohe Fenster und hochklappbare Glasfronten (unten) deutlich präsent.

Cadrée entre les murs assez présents de la maison, la nature reste néanmoins toujours proche grâce aux baies toute hauteur ou aux murs de verre basculants (ci-dessous).

Despite the apparently rural setting of
the house, its level of sophistication
is apparent in the images on this
double page. The plan of the house is
entirely rectilinear.

Trotz der ländlichen Lage des Hauses
ist der Wohnkomfort (auf den Aufnahmen dieser Doppelseite) offensichtlich hoch. Der Grundriss ist konsequent rechtwinklig angelegt.

Malgré un cadre naturel apparemment rural, le niveau de sophistication de la maison est impressionnant.
Le plan de la maison est entièrement
orthogonal.

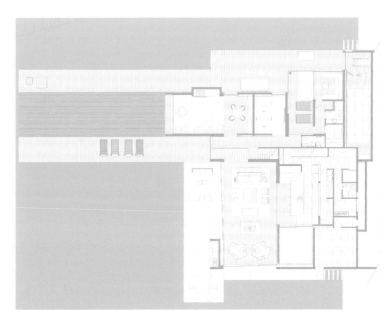

CC-STUDIO

cc-studio
Krelis Louwenstraat 1-b29
1055 KA Amsterdam
The Netherlands

Tel: +31 652 01 70 97
E-mail: info@cc-studio.nl
Web: www.cc-studio.nl / www.b29studios.nl

PETER HEIDEMAN was born in Utrecht, the Netherlands, in 1967, and graduated from the Building Technology College (1993) and from the Academy of Architecture in Amsterdam (2000). From 1996 to 1998 he worked on Neuteling Riedijk's Amsterdam Borneo Sporenburg projects, and from 1998 to 2008 as an architect for VenhoevenCS, where he codesigned projects such as the fire station of Den Helder and the VWA Laboratory in Zwijndrecht. Since 1993 he has also worked on a number of independent projects and alterations for private clients. **GERALD LINDNER** was born in Mombasa, Kenya, in 1966. He graduated in Civil Engineering from the Technical University of Delft (1990), and then worked for various engineering firms in general engineering and as a specialist in glass structures. In 1997, he made the switch to architecture and designed the Kraanspoor project for OTH with Trude Hooykaas (Amsterdam). He founded cc-studio in 2010 with Peter Heideman. Recent cc-studio projects include the Fabric Façade Studio Apartment (Almere, 2010–11, published here); the design study of a UHPC structural joint using 3D printing (2011); testing of a lightweight reflective insulating inner façade for GenieLoods (Vijfhuizen, 2011); a landscaped garden studio (Amsterdam, 2012); and research on sustainable and adaptable housing for the Dutch government body SEV (Stuurgroep Experimenten Volkshuisvesting, 2012), all in the Netherlands.

PETER HEIDEMAN wurde 1967 in Utrecht geboren und schloss sein Studium der Bautechnologie an der Hogeschool van Amsterdam (1993) sowie ein Architekturstudium an der Academie van Bouwkunst Amsterdam (2000) ab. Von 1996 bis 1998 arbeitete er für Neutelings Riedijk an der Borneo Sporenburg in Amsterdam sowie von 1998 bis 2008 als Architekt für VenhoevenCS, wo er Projekte wie die Feuerwache in Den Helder oder das VWA-Labor in Zwijndrecht entwarf. Seit 1993 arbeitet er außerdem an verschiedenen freien Projekten und Umbauten für private Auftraggeber. **GERALD LINDNER** wurde 1966 in Mombasa, Kenia, geboren. Er schloss sein Studium als Bauingenieur an der TU Delft ab (1990) und arbeitete für verschiedene Ingenieurbüros als Bauingenieur und Spezialist für konstruktiven Glasbau. 1997 wandte er sich der Architektur zu und entwarf mit Trude Hooykaas das Kraanspoor-Projekt für OTH (Amsterdam). 2010 gründete er mit Peter Heidemann das cc-studio. Jüngere Projekte des Büros sind u. a. das Studio- und Wohngebäude Fabric Façade (Almere, 2010–11, hier vorgestellt), eine 3D-Entwurfsstudie für Arbeitsfugen in ultrahochfestem Beton (2011), der Test einer dämmenden und reflektierenden Leichtbau-Innenfassade für GenieLoods (Vijfhuizen, 2011), ein Gartenatelier mit Landschaftsgestaltung (Amsterdam, 2012) sowie Studien zu nachhaltigen und variablen Wohnkonzepten für die niederländische Regierungskommission SEV (Stuurgroep Experimenten Volkshuisvesting, 2012), alle in den Niederlanden.

PETER HEIDEMAN, né à Utrecht (Pays-Bas) en 1967, est diplômé de l'Université des sciences appliquées (1993) et de l'Académie d'architecture d'Amsterdam (2000). De 1996 à 1998, il a travaillé pour l'agence Neuteling Riedijk sur ses projets pour le quartier de Borneo Sporenburg à Amsterdam et de 1998 à 2008, comme architecte chez VenhoevenCS où il est intervenu sur divers projets comme un centre de secours incendie à Den Helder ou le laboratoire VWA à Zwijndrecht. Depuis 1993, il travaillait également à son compte sur divers projets et aménagements pour des clients privés. **GERALD LINDNER**, né à Mombasa (Kenya) en 1966, est diplômé en ingénierie civile de l'Université polytechnique de Delft (1990) et a ensuite travaillé pour plusieurs agences d'ingénierie puis comme spécialiste des constructions en verre. En 1997, il s'est tourné vers l'architecture et conçu le bâtiment de bureaux Kraanspoor pour OTH en collaboration avec Trude Hooykaas à Amsterdam. Il a fondé cc-studio en 2010 avec Peter Heideman. Parmi leurs récentes réalisations : l'atelier appartement Fabric Façade (Almere, 2010–11, publié ici) ; l'étude de projet d'un joint structurel UHPC en impression 3D (2011) ; le test d'une façade intérieure isolante légère réfléchissante pour GenieLoods (Vijfhuizen, 2011) ; un atelier de jardin paysagé (Amsterdam, 2011) et des recherches sur des logements durables et adaptables pour l'agence gouvernementale néerlandaise SEV (Stuurgroep Experimenten Volkshuisvesting, 2012).

FABRIC FAÇADE STUDIO APARTMENT

Almere, The Netherlands, 2010–11

Address: Zeussingel 41, Almere, The Netherlands
Area: 193 m² floor; 30 m² atrium; 31 m² roof terrace. Client: Rob Veening
Cost: €150 000 (shell), €70 000 (finishing)
Collaboration: design cc-studio and studiotx, in collaboration with Rob Veening

This structure was built on a small site (168 m²), one of 350 plots designated in the OMA master plan for construction by private owners in the Homerus area of Almere. The client, a painter, requested a studio and exhibition space downstairs with living areas above. Furthermore, he requested a "spacious and open" feeling. The strict limitations on building size imposed by the master plan and the limited budget provided made the task of the architects complex. A central atrium and 4.5-meter ceiling height in part of the living room provided the spaciousness requested by Veening. With the agreement of the client, cc-studio found a way to save on the building's cladding, using rolls of PTFE (Teflon)–coated fiberglass fabric, used in the industrial manufacture of conveyors belts for the food industry. This durable and non-combustible material was provided free of charge by the German firm Verseidag-Indutex. The architects state: "We are very happy with the result as the flexible material moves with wind and with a storm it really becomes alive and kicking."

Der Bau wurde auf einer Fläche von nur 168 m² realisiert, einem von 350 Grundstücken, die der Masterplan von OMA in Almere-Homerus für private Wohnbauten vorsieht. Der Bauherr, ein Maler, wünschte sich ein Studio und Ausstellungsflächen im unteren Geschoss mit Wohnbereich darüber sowie „Großzügigkeit und Offenheit". Die strengen Größenvorgaben des Masterplans sowie das knappe Budget stellten die Architekten vor komplexe Herausforderungen. Durch einen zentralen Lichthof und einer Deckenhöhe von bis zu 4,5 m im Wohnbereich konnte der gewünschten Großzügigkeit Rechnung getragen werden. In Abstimmung mit dem Bauherrn entwickelte cc-studio eine Technik, die Einsparungen bei der Verschalung des Gebäudes erlaubte: Sie arbeiteten mit PTFE-(Teflon)-beschichtetem Glasfasertextil, das üblicherweise für Förderbänder in der Lebensmittelindustrie genutzt wird. Das strapazierfähige nichtbrennbare Material wurde kostenfrei vom deutschen Hersteller Verseidag-Indutex zur Verfügung gestellt. Die Architekten erklären: „Wir sind hoch zufrieden mit dem Ergebnis: Das flexible Material bewegt sich im Wind – und erwacht bei stürmischem Wetter erst recht zum Leben."

Cette maison a été construite sur une petite parcelle de 168 m², l'une des 350 prévues par le plan directeur d'OMA pour la construction de résidences privées dans le quartier Homerus d'Almere. Le client, un peintre, voulait disposer au rez-de-chaussée d'un atelier et d'un espace d'exposition et d'un appartement à l'étage. Par ailleurs, il recherchait un sentiment « d'espace et d'ouverture. » Les contraintes dimensionnelles du plan directeur et le budget limité rendaient la tache complexe. Un atrium central et une hauteur de plafond de 4,50 m dans une partie du séjour ont fourni l'espace souhaité. Avec l'accord du client, cc-studio a trouvé le moyen d'économiser sur le bardage extérieur en utilisant des rouleaux de tissu de fibre de verre enduit de PTFE (Téflon) utilisée pour les convoyeurs de l'industrie alimentaire. Ce matériau durable et non combustible a été offert par la firme allemande Verseidag-Indutex. « Nous sommes très heureux du résultat, ont déclaré les architectes, le matériau bouge avec le vent et en cas de tempête devient littéralement vivant. »

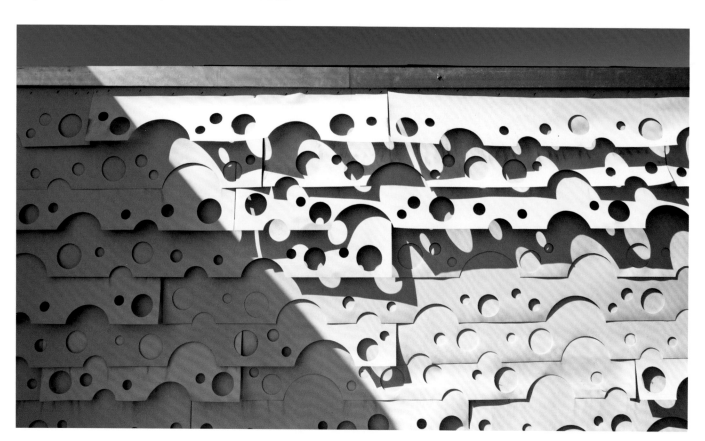

Seen from a distance, the façade of the building appears to be rusticated or made of rough stone. On the contrary, as seen from a closer vantage point, it is covered with fabric patterns.

Aus der Distanz wirkt die Fassade wie bossiert oder aus rauem Mauerwerk. Aus der Nähe zeigt sich jedoch, dass sie stattdessen mit Textilelementen verblendet wurde.

Vue d'une certaine distance, les murs de la façade semblent faits d'un appareillage de pierres rustiquées ou de moellons grossiers. De près, on réalise qu'elle est recouverte d'une sorte de textile découpé.

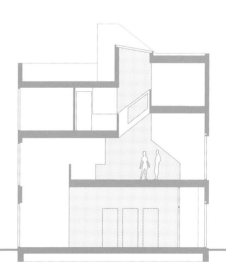

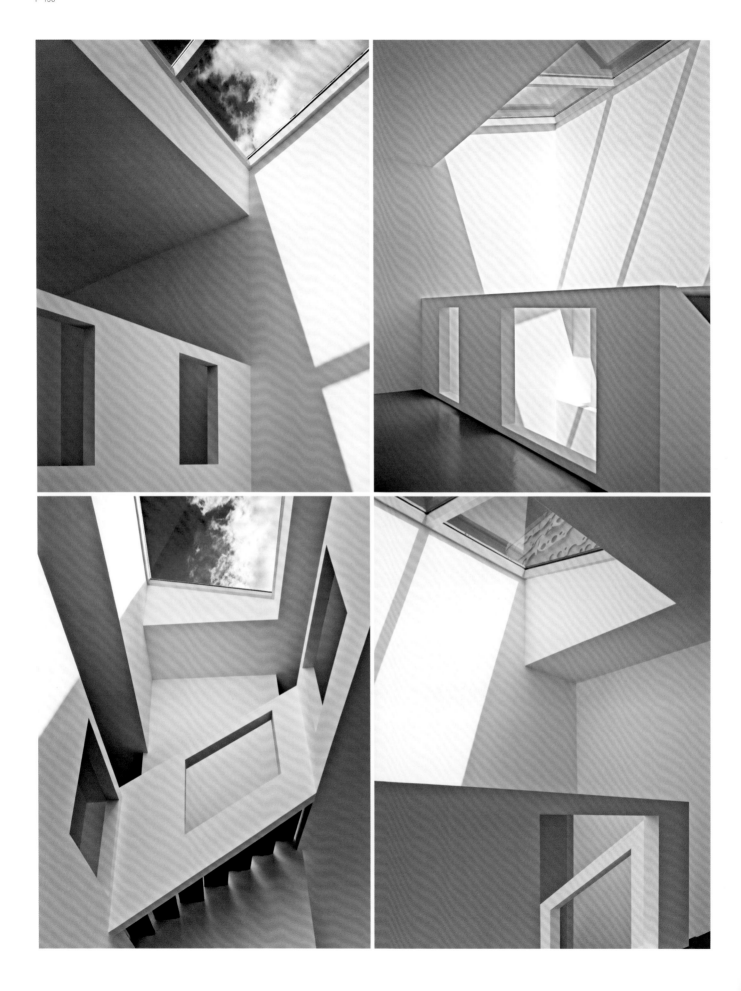

Interiors are rendered complex by forms and openings that are located in unexpected places. Natural light is admitted in a generous manner.

Der Innenraum gewinnt durch überraschend positionierte Formen und Öffnungen an Komplexität. Tageslicht fällt großzügig ein.

La composition volumétrique de l'intérieur a été volontairement rendue plus complexe par des éléments et des ouvertures présents là où on ne les attend pas. Une généreuse lumière naturelle baigne l'intérieur de la maison.

The roughness of the exterior makes the building look like some renovated industrial structures, and yet the interior affirms the fully contemporary nature of the project.

Die raue Außenfassade lässt den Bau wie ein saniertes Industriegebäude wirken. Der Innenraum bekräftigt jedoch, wie zeitgenössisch dieses Projekt ist.

Le traitement brut des façades fait penser à une structure industrielle rénovée, alors que l'intérieur affirme clairement la nature contemporaine du projet.

PRESTON SCOTT COHEN

Preston Scott Cohen, Inc.
179 Sidney Street, 1st floor
Cambridge, MA 02139
USA

Tel: +1 617 441 2110
Fax: +1 617 441 2113
E-mail: info@pscohen.com
Web: www.pscohen.com

Born in 1961, **PRESTON SCOTT COHEN** received his B.Arch degree from the Rhode Island School of Design (1983) and his M.Arch degree from the Harvard GSD (1985). Cohen is the Chair and Gerald M. McCue Professor of Architecture at Harvard GSD. Recent projects completed or under construction include the Goodman House (Pine Plains, New York, USA, 2003–04); the Goldman Sachs Arcade Canopy (New York, New York, USA, 2005–08); the Inman House (Cambridge, Massachusetts, USA, 2008, published here); the Nanjing Performing Arts Center (China, 2007–09); the Tel Aviv Museum of Art Amir Building (Israel, 2009–11); the Taiyuan Museum of Art (China, 2007–12); Datong City Library (China, 2008–13); and the Fahmy Residence (Los Gatos, California, USA, 2007, 2011–13).

PRESTON SCOTT COHEN, geboren 1961, absolvierte einen B. Arch. an der Rhode Island School of Design (1983) sowie einen M. Arch. an der Harvard GSD (1985). Cohen ist Dekan und Gerald-M.-McCue-Professor für Architektur an der Harvard GSD. Jüngere realisierte bzw. im Bau befindliche Projekte sind das Goodman House (Pine Plains, New York, 2003–04), ein Vordach für die Goldman Sachs Arcade (New York, 2005–08), das Inman House (Cambridge, Massachusetts, 2008, hier vorgestellt), das Performing Arts Center der Universität von Nanjing (China, 2007–09), das Amir Building am Tel Aviv Museum of Art (Israel, 2009–11), das Taiyuan Museum of Art (China, 2007–12), die Stadtbibliothek in Datong (China, 2008–13) und die Fahmy Residence (Los Gatos, Kalifornien, 2007, 2011–13).

PRESTON SCOTT COHEN a obtenu ses diplômes de B.Arch. (1983) à la Rhode Island School of Design et de M.Arch. à la Harvard GSD (1985). Il est président du département d'Architecture et Gerald M. McCue Professor of Architecture à la Harvard GSD. Parmi ses réalisations récentes ou en cours : la maison Goodman (Pine Plains, New York, 2003–04) ; l'auvent de la Goldman Sachs Arcade (New York, 2005–08) ; la maison Inman (Cambridge, Massachusetts, 2008, publiée ici) ; le Centre des arts du spectacle de l'université de Nankin (Nankin, Chine, 2007–09) ; l'immeuble Amir du Musée des beaux-arts de Tel Aviv (Israël, 2009–11) ; le Musée des beaux-arts de Taiyuan (Chine, 2007–12) ; la bibliothèque de Datong (Chine, 2008–13) et la maison Fahmy (Los Gatos, Californie, 2007, 2011–13).

INMAN HOUSE

Cambridge, Massachusetts, USA, 2008

Area: 158 m². Client: Scott Cohen
Cost: not disclosed. Collaboration: Charles Welsh (General Contractor)

The interior of the house has been made fully contemporary, which is somewhat unexpected within the frame of a traditional residence.

Das Interieur des Hauses ist konsequent zeitgenössisch – eher eine Überraschung hinter der Fassade eines traditionellen Altbaus.

L'aménagement intérieur d'esprit très contemporain surprend un peu dans cette maison familiale d'aspect extérieur si traditionnel.

Seen from the outside, and even in plan, the house looks as though it might fit in well with its Cambridge neighborhood, but modernity lurks within.

Von außen, und selbst auf dem Grundriss, scheint sich das Haus nahtlos in seine Nachbarschaft in Cambridge zu fügen, doch im Innern zeigt es sein modernes Gesicht.

Vue de l'extérieur et en plan, la maison semble parfaitement adaptée à l'environnement de Cambridge, mais sa modernité se cache à l'intérieur.

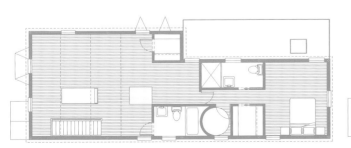

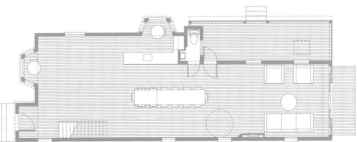

This project involved the complete renovation of an 1870s farmhouse, providing for an open living, dining and kitchen area, a study, one bedroom, and two and a half bathrooms. A steel beam and tension rods stabilized the existing structure once it was gutted. The architect explains: "The historically restored clapboard exterior contrasts with the radically reconceived interior. Essentially, the house is a collage of three architectural typologies: a modernist, one-story villa with a clear view to a walled garden beyond; a one-room schoolhouse-type of space; and a Cape Cod cottage." The second floor of the house has a floor window and a light well "which allow the house to be seen altogether as a unified vessel of space." Wooden floors and an overall reflective white plaster finish inside, together with the unexpected floor openings, do, indeed, make this apparently very traditional wooden house, modern.

Ein Farmhaus aus den 1870er-Jahren sollte grundlegend renoviert werden: Entstanden sind ein offener Wohnraum mit Essbereich und Küche, ein Arbeitszimmer, ein Schlafzimmer sowie zwei Bäder und ein Gästebad. Nach der Entkernung des Altbaus sorgten ein Stahlträger und Zuganker für die Stabilisierung des Hauses. Der Architekt erklärt: „Das Äußere des historisch sanierten Schindelbaus ist ein Kontrastprogramm zum radikal umgestalteten Innenraum. Das Haus ist im Grunde eine Collage aus drei baulichen Typologien: eines modernen Bungalows mit freiem Blick in den umfriedeten Garten und darüber hinaus; eines Dorfschulhauses mit großem Hauptraum und eines Cape-Cod-Cottage." Das Obergeschoss des Hauses hat ein Bodenfenster und einen Lichtschacht, wodurch „das Haus als räumliches Gesamtkontinuum" erscheint. Holzböden und glänzender Weißputz runden das Interieur ab und geben dem scheinbar traditionellen Holzhaus ein modernes Gesicht.

Ce projet de rénovation entière d'une maison des années 1870 avait pour programme un séjour ouvert avec cuisine et coin salle à manger, un bureau, une chambre, deux salles de bains et une salle d'eau. La structure ancienne, une fois équipée de gouttières, a été stabilisée par une poutre d'acier et des câbles en tension. « La façade extérieure en bardeaux de bois restaurée dans son style ancien contraste avec l'intérieur radicalement repensé, explique l'architecte. Essentiellement, la maison est un collage de trois typologies architecturales : la première moderniste, inspirée de la villa sur un niveau avec vue sur jardin clos à l'arrière, la seconde celle d'un espace ouvert type école et la troisième, le style cottage de Cape Cod. » L'étage est doté d'une baie descendant jusqu'au sol et d'un puits de lumière « qui permet de considérer la maison toute entière comme un espace unifié ». À l'intérieur, les planchers en bois, un enduit de plâtre blanc brillant sur les murs et de surprenants percements à travers les sols font de cette maison en bois apparemment très traditionnelle une résidence contemporaine.

Slicing through the house as he did with the circular opening, as seen on this page, the architect brings both light and contemporary feeling into the interiors, where wood clads the floors and other surfaces remain white.

Durch Einschnitte, wie die runde Öffnung auf dieser Seite, lässt der Architekt Licht in das Interieur und setzt zeitgenössische Akzente. Die Böden sind aus Holz, die übrigen Oberflächen bleiben weiß.

Par des percements, comme l'ouverture circulaire ci-dessus, l'architecte apporte à la fois davantage de lumière et un sentiment de modernité dans cet intérieur dominé par le bois des planchers et la blancheur des murs.

JAMES CUTLER

Cutler Anderson Architects
135 Parfitt Way SW
Bainbridge Island, WA 98110
USA

Tel: +1 206 842 4710
Fax: +1 206 842 4420
E-mail: contact@cutler-anderson.com
Web: www.cutler-anderson.com

JAMES L. CUTLER was born in 1949 in Wilkes-Barre, Pennsylvania. He received an M.Arch degree from the Louis I. Kahn Studio program, and B.A. (1971) and M.Arch (1973) degrees from the University of Pennsylvania. He has lived on Bainbridge Island, Washington, since 1974 and is a founding member of the Bainbridge Island Land Trust, a non-profit organization which acquires interests in land having significant conservation values such as scenic vistas, wetlands, wildlife corridors, and protection of animal habitat. Since 1977, he has been principal of his own design firm, Cutler Anderson Architects (formerly James Cutler Architects). Their recent work includes a private residence on Mallorca (Spain, 2003); the Famous Tree Residence (Sisters, Oregon, USA, 2007–08, published here); Catskills Artist Studio (Catskills, New York, USA, 2011); Awtrey Bed and Breakfast (Manzanita, Oregon, USA, 2011); and Howe Residence (Block Island, Rhode Island, USA, 2011). Ongoing work includes the Edith Green Wendall Wyatt Federal Building (Portland, Oregon, 2013); the Narty Wellness Spa and Resort (Olsztyn, Poland, −2015); a Private Residence (Lake Pelnik, Poland, −2016); and the North East Development Medical Research Facility (Bratislava, Slovakia, −2017).

JAMES L. CUTLER wurde 1949 in Wilkes-Barre, Pennsylvania, geboren. Er absolvierte einen M. Arch. im Rahmen des Louis-I.-Kahn-Studioprogramms sowie einen B. A. (1971) und einen M. Arch. (1973) an der University of Pennsylvania. Seit 1974 lebt Cutler auf Bainbridge Island, Washington, und ist Gründungsmitglied des gemeinnützigen Bainbridge Island Land Trust, der Nutzungsrechte für schützenswerte Landstriche erwirbt, wie landschaftlich besonders reizvolle Aussichtspunkte, Feuchtgebiete oder Biotopverbünde zum Schutz der Lebensräume von Tieren. Seit 1977 leitet er sein Büro Cutler Anderson Architects (vormals James Cutler Architects). Jüngere Projekte sind u. a. ein privates Wohnhaus auf Mallorca (2003), die Famous Tree Residence (Sisters, Oregon, 2007–08, hier vorgestellt), das Catskills Artist Studio (Catskills, New York, 2011), das Awtrey Bed & Breakfast (Manzanita, Oregon, 2011) sowie die Howe Residence (Block Island, Rhode Island, 2011). Gegenwärtig fertiggestellt wird u. a. das Edith Green Wendall Wyatt Federal Building (Portland, Oregon, 2013), das Wellness-Spa und Hotel Narty (Olsztyn, Polen, bis 2015), ein privates Wohnhaus an einem See (Pelnik, Polen, bis 2016) sowie das Medizinische Forschungszentrum Nordost (Bratislava, Slowakei, bis 2017).

JAMES L. CUTLER, né en 1949 à Wilkes-Barre en Pennsylvanie est diplômé (M.Arch.) du programme Louis I. Kahn Studio et a obtenu son B.A. (1971) et son M.Arch. (1973) à l'université de Pennsylvanie (1993). Il vit sur Bainbridge Island (Washington) depuis 1974 et est membre fondateur du Bainbridge Island Land Trust, association sans but lucratif qui achète des terrains de valeur environnementale significative – marais, corridors pour le passage d'espèces sauvages, vues spectaculaires – et s'occupe de la protection de l'habitat animal. Il anime son agence, Cutler Anderson Architects (anciennement James Cutler Architects), depuis 1977. Parmi ses réalisations récentes : une résidence privée (Majorque, Espagne, 2003) ; la Famous Tree Residence (Sisters, Oregon, 2007–08, publiée ici) ; un atelier d'artiste dans les Catskills (Catskills, New York, 2011) ; le Bed and Breakfast Awtrey (Manzanita, Oregon, 2011) ; la résidence Howe (Block Island, Rhode Island, 2011) et, en cours de chantier, l'immeuble fédéral Edith Green Wendall Wyatt (Portland, Oregon, 2013) ; le spa et hôtel Narty (Olsztyn, Pologne, −2015) ; une résidence privée (lac de Pelnik, Pologne, −2016) et le Centre de recherche médicale Nord-Est à Bratislava (Slovaquie, −2017).

FAMOUS TREE RESIDENCE

Sisters, Oregon, USA, 2007–08

Area: 203 m². Client: Mark and Melanie Monteiro
Cost: $1.2 million

The architects colored the concrete walls of this residence "to match the shade of the exposed soils, and they were scaled to the 3.7-meter high native flora." A semicircular opening in a vertical cliff face was used to provide views both of a canyon below and the more distant mountains. The architects explain: "The wooden part of the structure was designed to visually reveal the tectonic response to the lateral loads that exist in this volcanic zone. The whole of this wooden structure was encased in glass to protect it from the elements and display its fabrication." Full-height glazing provides spectacular, uninterrupted views of the landscape of the site, contrasting with the visible wood frame of the building.

Mit den Sichtbetonwänden des Hauses griffen die Architekten „die Farbigkeit der offen liegenden Gesteinsschichten auf und orientierten die Wände von der Größe her an der bis zu 3,7 m hohen einheimischen Flora". Ein halbrunder Einschnitt in einem Felskliff wurde genutzt, um Sichtachsen auf einen tiefergelegenen Canyon und eine Bergkette am Horizont zu erschließen. Die Architekten erklären: „Die Holzelemente der Konstruktion machen die tektonische Ableitung der Seitenlasten in dieser vulkanischen Zone sichtbar. Die Holzkonstruktion wurde mit Glas ummantelt, um Schutz vor den Elementen zu bieten und die Struktur zu zeigen." Dank geschosshoher Verglasung – ein Kontrast zum offenen Holztragwerk des Hauses – bietet sich ein spektakulärer, unverstellter Panoramablick auf die Landschaft.

L'architecte a teinté les murs en béton de cette résidence « pour l'harmoniser avec la couleur de la terre… la hauteur des murs est de 3,70 m ce qui correspond à l'échelle de la flore locale ». Le site est une sorte d'encoche semi-circulaire dans une falaise verticale qui offre des vues sur la vallée en contrebas et les montagnes dans le lointain. « La partie en bois de la structure a été conçue pour mettre visuellement en valeur la réponse tectonique aux charges latérales qui existent dans cette zone volcanique. L'ensemble est enchâssé dans une enveloppe de verre pour le protéger des éléments tout en laissant les détails de sa fabrication apparents », a expliqué l'architecte. Ce vitrage toute hauteur permet également de bénéficier de vues spectaculaires sur le paysage.

Low, generously glazed, and inserted into its natural setting, the house is seen in the sketch below, with pine trees around it.

Das Haus, niedrig, großzügig verglast und in die Landschaft eingebunden, ist unten auf der Skizze inmitten von Kiefern zu sehen.

Croquis ci-dessous : de profil relativement bas, généreusement vitrée et bien insérée dans son cadre naturel, la maison est entourée de pins.

The light frame structure seems to be
gently present in its site, looking out,
open, and yet allowing for a comfort-
able, modern existence.

Der leichte Holzrahmenbau fügt sich
behutsam in sein Umfeld – offen,
nach außen orientiert – und bietet
doch zugleich komfortablen und
modernen Wohnraum.

Légère, cette construction à ossature
en bois, n'impose aucunement sa
présence. Elle semble ouverte, tour-
née vers le paysage tout en permettant un style de vie confortable et
actuel.

The lightness of the frame and the extent of the glazing are evident in the pictures above.

Auf den Ansichten oben wird deutlich, wie leicht die Holzrahmenkonstruktion wirkt und wie großzügig verglast wurde.

Ci-dessus, la légèreté de l'ossature et l'importance des vitrages sont parfaitement visibles.

MASAKI ENDOH

Masaki Endoh
EDH Endoh Design House
101, 2–13–8 Honnmachi
Shibuya-ku
Tokyo 151–0071
Japan

Tel/Fax: +81 3 3377 6293
E-mail: endoh@edh-web.com
Web: www.edh-web.com

MASAKI ENDOH was born in Tokyo, Japan, in 1963. He graduated from the Science University of Tokyo in 1987 and completed an M.Arch in 1989, at the same university. He worked for the KAI-Workshop (1989–94), and established his firm EDH Endoh Design House in 1994. He has been a Professor at Chiba Institute of Technology since 2008. He was awarded the Tokyo House Prize for Natural Shelter in 2000; the Yoshioka Award for Natural Shelter in 2000; and the JIA "Rookie of the Year 2003" for Natural Ellipse in 2003. His works include Natural Shelter (Tokyo, 1999); Natural Illuminance (Tokyo, 2001); Natural Slats (Tokyo, 2002); Natural Ellipse (Tokyo, 2002); Natural Wedge (Tokyo, 2003); Natural Strata (Kawasaki, 2003); and, more recently, Natural Illuminance II (Tokyo, 2010–11, published here); and Natural Strip IV (Tokyo, 2010–11, also published here), all in Japan.

MASAKI ENDOH wurde 1963 in Tokio geboren. Er schloss sein Studium 1987 an der Naturwissenschaftlichen Universität Tokio ab und absolvierte dort 1989 seinen M. Arch. Nach seiner Tätigkeit für den KAI-Workshop (1989–94) gründete er 1994 sein Büro EDH Endoh Design House. Endoh ist seit 2008 Professor am Chiba Institute of Technology. 2000 wurde er für sein Projekt Natural Shelter mit dem Tokyo House Prize und dem Yoshioka Award ausgezeichnet sowie 2003 mit dem JIA „Rookie of the Year 2003" für das Projekt Natural Ellipse. Zu seinen Projekten zählen Natural Shelter (Tokio, 1999), Natural Illuminance (Tokio, 2001), Natural Slats (Tokio, 2002), Natural Ellipse (Tokio, 2002), Natural Wedge (Tokio, 2003), Natural Strata (Kawasaki, 2003) sowie in jüngerer Zeit Natural Illuminance II (Tokio, 2010–11, hier vorgestellt) und Natural Strip IV (Tokio, 2010–11, ebenfalls hier vorgestellt).

MASAKI ENDOH, né à Tokyo en 1963, est diplômé de l'Université des sciences de Tokyo (1987) et a obtenu son M.Arch. de la même institution en 1989. Il a travaillé pour l'agence KAI-Workshop (1989-94) et fondé sa propre structure EDH (Endoh Design House) en 1994. Il est professeur à l'Institut de technologie de Chiba depuis 2008. En 2000, il a reçu le prix de la maison de Tokyo et le prix Yoshioka pour son Natural Shelter et le « Rookie of the Year » 2003 de la JIA pour Natural Ellipse en 2003. Ses réalisations récentes, toutes au Japon, comprennent les maisons Natural Shelter (Tokyo, 1999) ; Natural Illuminance (Tokyo, 2001) ; Natural Slats (Tokyo, 2002) ; Natural Ellipse (Tokyo, 2002) ; Natural Wedge (Tokyo, 2003) ; Natural Strata (Kawasaki, 2003) et, plus récemment, Natural Illuminance II (Tokyo, 2010–11, publiée ici) et Natural Strip IV (Tokyo, 2010-11, publiée ici).

NATURAL ILLUMINANCE II

Tokyo, Japan, 2010–11

Area: 37.50 m². Client: not disclosed
Cost: not disclosed

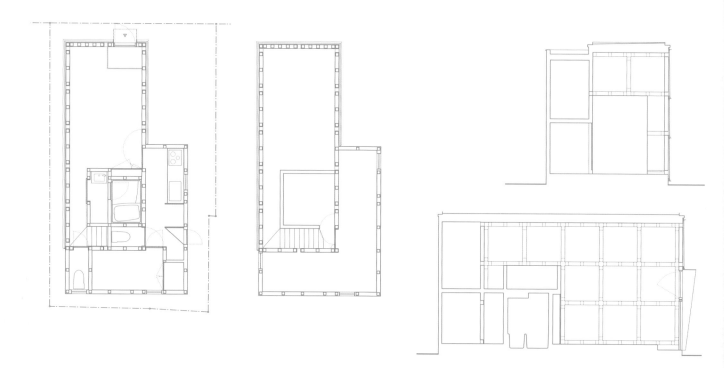

This small house was designed with a wood-beam frame clad on the exterior with translucent glass. A grid of wooden squares forms the interior walls, with the gaps between the squares covered with translucent plastic that allow daylight in from all angles. Masaki Endoh explains that these strips form a surface equivalent to a single large window and yet they provide light from every side. The architect explains that the design actually consists of two structures—one being the high-ceilinged living room and the other a wood-framed loft with steel walls containing the kitchen, master bedroom, and children's bedroom. The architects explain: "This is the smallest house ever designed by EDH, built for Mr. Endoh's brother. The land plot and volume (cubic meters) are of an average size for central Tokyo. Building area is limited by law, so space must be used efficiently. The house is just as small as any other in the neighborhood but the high-ceilinged living room, loft, and smaller bedrooms allocate more room to areas used by the entire family and give a sense of spaciousness."

Das kleine Haus ist im Prinzip eine transluzent verschalte Holzrahmenkonstruktion. Markantes Merkmal des Innenraums ist ein Raster aus Holzquadraten, durch dessen Zwischenräume aus transluzentem Kunststoff allseitig Tageslicht einfällt. Masaki Endoh zufolge entspricht die Gesamtfläche der Lichtstreifen einem großen Einzelfenster, erlaubt jedoch Lichteinfall von allen Seiten. Der Architekt verweist auf die Gliederung des Entwurfs in zwei Volumina – einen hohen Wohnraum sowie einen Holzrahmenanbau mit Stahlwänden für Küche, Elternschlafzimmer und Kinderzimmer. Den Architekten zufolge ist „das Haus der kleinste bis dato von EDH entworfene Wohnbau, geplant für den Bruder von Masaki Endoh. Grundstücksgröße und -volumen (in m³) sind für Tokioter Verhältnisse durchschnittlich. Die Bebauungsfläche ist gesetzlich vorgeschrieben, weshalb eine effiziente Raumnutzung unverzichtbar ist. Das Haus ist ebenso klein wie seine Nachbarbauten, doch der hohe Wohnbereich, der Anbau und die kleinen Schlafzimmer bieten eine bessere Raumnutzung für die gemeinschaftlich von der Familie genutzen Bereiche und vermitteln Großzügigkeit."

Cette petite maison à ossature en bois construite pour le frère de Masaki Endoh est en grande partie habillée de verre translucide. À l'intérieur, l'ossature en bois montée sur une trame carrée reste visible, les vides étant remplis par des panneaux de plastique translucide. Masaki Endoh explique que ces bandeaux de lumière forment une surface équivalente à une grande baie, mais éclairent en même temps de tous les côtés. Le projet se compose en fait de deux éléments : le premier est un séjour sous grande hauteur de plafond et le second un loft à ossature de bois également mais à murs d'acier, contenant la cuisine, la chambre principale et la chambre des enfants. « C'est la plus petite maison jamais conçue par EDH, explique l'architecte. La taille de la parcelle et le volume disponible sont de dimensions normales pour le centre de Tokyo. La constructibilité des terrains est limitée par la réglementation et l'espace doit donc être utilisé de manière efficace. Si la maison est aussi petite que ses voisines, le séjour à hauts plafonds, le loft, et les petites chambres accordent à la famille davantage de place que d'habitude et donne le sentiment de volumes spacieux. »

The plan of the house and its elevations (seen above) do not fully prepare the viewer for its unusual pattern of openings and its essentially closed nature.

Grund- und Aufrisse (oben) bereiten den Besucher nicht wirklich auf die Wirkung der ungewöhnlichen Öffnungen und die prinzipielle Geschlossenheit des Hauses vor.

Le plan et les élévations de la maison (ci-dessus) ne préparent pas vraiment le visiteur à l'aspect très fermé de la maison et au rythme surprenant des ouvertures.

NATURAL STRIP IV

Tokyo, Japan, 2010–11

Area: 26 m². Client: not disclosed
Cost: not disclosed

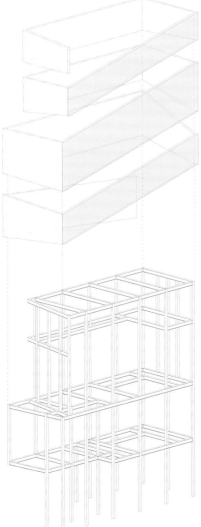

Like many narrow row houses in Japanese cities, this residence seems to announce a traditional plan, but the upper levels are surprisingly skewed.

Wie bei vielen schmalen Reihenhäusern in japanischen Städten wirkt der Grundriss auch hier zunächst konventionell, doch die oberen Geschosse zeigen überraschende Winkel.

Comme beaucoup des maisons étroites fréquentes dans les villes japonaises, cette petite résidence paraît suivre un plan traditionnel, alors que les niveaux supérieurs semblent partir complètement en biais.

Despite its very small size, **NATURAL STRIP IV** is comprised of two apartments on three floors, the main apartment upstairs and a second apartment downstairs. Both bedrooms and the main bathroom are on the second floor. The two apartments are not connected so each has its own entrance and staircase. Steel columns take on the role of "a skeleton with wraparound walls and windows functioning as skin and muscle, giving a larger sense of space inside." The wraparound windows are translucent and the wraparound walls are made of cement boards on the exterior and wood on the inside, sandwiched with insulation.

Trotz der ungewöhnlich kleinen Baufläche umfasst **NATURAL STRIP IV** zwei Wohnungen, verteilt auf insgesamt drei Ebenen: eine Hauptwohnung in den oberen Etagen sowie eine zweite Wohnung zu ebener Erde. Schlafzimmer und Bäder liegen im ersten Stock. Dank separater Eingänge und Treppen sind beide Wohnungen räumlich voneinander unabhängig. Stahlstützen dienen als „Skelett, während Wände und Fenster dem Bau wie Haut und Muskeln spiralförmig vorgehängt sind, was den Innenraum großzügiger macht". Die vorgehängte Verglasung ist transluzent, die vorgehängten Wandelemente bestehen aus Faserzementplatten (außen) und Holz (innen) mit einer Dämmschicht.

Malgré sa très petite taille, **NATURAL STRIP IV** comprend deux appartements répartis sur trois niveaux. Les deux chambres principales et leurs salles de bains se trouvent au premier étage. Les deux appartements ne sont pas connectés, chacun possédant son entrée et son escalier. Des colonnes d'acier jouent le rôle de « squelette enveloppé de murs et de fenêtres fonctionnant comme la peau et les muscles, donnant un sentiment d'espace intérieur plus vaste ». Le bandeau de fenêtres enveloppant est translucide et les murs se composent d'un sandwich de plaques de fibrociment à l'extérieur, d'isolant et de bois à l'intérieur.

The interior is bright, but austere, with light entering from unexpected angles, such as the low triangle seen near the floor in the image above.

Das Interieur wirkt hell, wenn auch streng. Licht fällt aus unerwarteten Winkeln ein, etwa durch das flache Dreieck am Boden, oben im Bild.

L'intérieur est lumineux mais austère. La lumière entre parfois par des angles inattendus, comme à travers l'ouverture triangulaire pratiquée près du sol (photo ci-dessus).

ERIC FISHER

FISHER ARCHitecture
928 South Aiken Avenue
Pittsburgh, PA 15232
USA

Tel: +1 412 657 4153
E-mail: eric@fisherarch.com
Web: www.fisherarch.com

ERIC FISHER was born in 1959 in Philadelphia. He studied visual arts and engineering at Dartmouth College (B.A., 1982), before obtaining his M.Arch degree from Harvard GSD (1988). He worked in the office of Richard Meier (1993–96), spending time there on detail design for the Getty Center. He was Senior Project Manager at Frederick Fisher and Partners (1997–2000), Senior Associate at Perfido Weiskopf Architects (2001–03), and founded FISHER ARCHitecture in 2004. His recent work includes the Fisher House (Pittsburgh, 2008); the Emerald Art Glass House (Pittsburgh, 2007–11, published here); the zero-energy Irwin Studio (Pittsburgh, 2012); the Edgar House and Ewing House, two woodland homes that share a site (Sarver, 2010–); and the Vandergrift Community Center (Vandergrift, 2011–), all in Pennsylvania, USA.

ERIC FISHER wurde 1959 in Philadelphia geboren. Er studierte zunächst Kunst und Bauingenieurwesen am Dartmouth College (B. A., 1982) und absolvierte später einen M. Arch. an der Harvard GSD (1988). Er arbeitete für Richard Meier (1993–96), u. a. an Details für das Getty Center. Er war Projektleiter bei Frederick Fisher and Partners (1997–2000), Seniorteilhaber bei Perfido Weiskopf Architects (2001–03) und gründete 2004 sein Büro FISHER ARCHitecture. Zu seinen jüngeren Projekten zählen das Fisher House (Pittsburgh, 2008), das Emerald Art Glass House (Pittsburgh, 2007–11, hier vorgestellt), das energieautarke Irwin Studio (Pittsburgh, 2012), das Edgar House und das Ewing House, zwei Einfamilienhäuser auf einem gemeinsamen Waldgrundstück (Sarver, seit 2010) sowie das Vandergrift Community Center (Vandergrift, seit 2011), alle in Pennsylvania.

ERIC FISHER est né en 1959 à Philadelphie. Il a étudié les arts plastiques et l'ingénierie au Dartmouth College (diplôme de B.A. en 1982), avant d'obtenir son diplôme de M.Arch. de la Harvard GSD (1988). Il a travaillé dans l'agence de Richard Meier (1993–96), en particulier sur l'aménagement du Getty Center. Il a été directeur de projet senior chez Frederick Fisher and Partners (1997–2000), associé senior chez Perfido Weikskopf Architects (2001–03) et à fondé FISHER ARCHitecture en 2004. Parmi ses réalisations récentes, toutes en Pennsylvanie : la Fisher House (Pittsburgh, 2008) ; l'Emerald Art Glass House (Pittsburgh, 2007–11, publiée ici) ; le Studio Irwin énergie zéro (Pittsburgh, 2012) ; l'Edgar House et la Ewing House, deux maisons en forêt partageant un même site (Sarver, 2010–) et le Vandergrift Community Center (Vandergrift, 2011–).

EMERALD ART GLASS HOUSE

Pittsburgh, Pennsylvania, USA, 2007–11

Area: 641 m². Client: Kim and Bob Zielinski
Cost: not disclosed

This residence is dramatically cantilevered above the glass-manufacturing facility of the client, Bob Zielinski, and named for his firm. Inspired by industrial forms, the house is clad in Cor-ten steel. The north-facing façade is made with "Greenheat" radiant-heated glass, while a glass rain screen is used to cover a concrete core containing a glass stairway that links the ground floor to the kitchen. Recycled materials and a geothermal well complement the overall "green" credentials of the house, which was the winner of a Pennsylvania AIA award. Eric Fisher ventures that "the **EMERALD ART GLASS HOUSE** may be the world's longest residential cantilever." In any case the engineering involved has more to do with bridge design than that of the average house. According to *The New York Times* ("An Industrial Strength House in Pittsburgh," February 8, 2012): "Acting as the contractor, Mr. Zielinski brought costs down to about $225 a square foot (0.09 m²). Construction challenges included digging two seven-foot-wide (2.13-meter) holes 35 feet (10.6 meters) into bedrock and filling them with concrete and steel to support the cantilevered sections of the five-level, 6900-square-foot (641 m²) house."

Das Haus schwebt dramatisch über der Glasfabrik des Bauherrn Bob Zielinski, nach der das Domizil benannt ist. Das von Industriebauten inspirierte Haus wurde mit Cor-Ten-Stahl verblendet. Die Nordfassade wurde mit „Greenheat"-Sicherheitsglas realisiert, eine zusätzliche Glashaut ummantelt als Witterungsschutz den Betongebäudekern. Dort verläuft eine Treppe mit Glasgeländer, die das Erdgeschoss mit der Küche verbindet. Weitere Aspekte des „grünen" Hauses (Preis des AIA-Verbands Pennsylvania) sind recycelte Baustoffe und eine Wärmepumpe. Fisher zufolge ist „das **EMERALD ART GLASS HOUSE** der wohl längste bewohnte Ausleger der Welt". Ingenieurtechnisch hat der Bau mehr mit Brückenbau als einem typischen Wohnhaus gemein. Die *New York Times* („An Industrial Strength House in Pittsburgh", 8. Februar 2012) schrieb: „Mr. Zielinski fungierte zugleich als Bauunternehmer und konnte die Kosten auf 225 Dollar per Quadratfuß (0,09 m²) senken. Bauliche Herausforderungen waren u. a. zwei 7 Fuß (2,13 m) breite und 35 Fuß (10,6 m) tiefe Bohrungen im Gesteinsgrund, die mit Beton und Stahl ausgegossen wurden, um den Ausleger des fünfstöckigen, 6900 Fuß (641 m²) großen Hauses zu tragen."

Cette résidence se projette en un porte-à-faux spectaculaire au-dessus des ateliers de verrerie de son propriétaire, Bob Zielinski, dont elle porte le nom de l'entreprise. Inspirée de formes industrielles, elle est habillée d'acier Corten. La façade nord est en verre radiant « Greenheat » tandis qu'un écran de verre recouvre un noyau en béton contenant un escalier de verre reliant le rez-de-chaussée à la cuisine. Des matériaux recyclés et un puits géothermique figurent parmi les équipements écologiques de cette maison qui a remporté le prix de l'AIA de Pennsylvanie. Selon Eric Fisher : « L'**EMERALD ART GLASS HOUSE** est peut-être le plus long porte-à-faux résidentiel du monde. » Son ingénierie relève en tous cas davantage des ouvrages d'art que de celui de l'architecture résidentielle classique. Selon le *New York Times* (« An Industrial Strength House in Pittsburgh », 8 février 2012) : « Agissant en tant que maître d'ouvrage, M. Zielinski a réduit les coûts à environ 2400 $ le m². Parmi les défis de ce chantier figuraient le creusement dans la roche de deux puits de 10,60 m de profondeur sur 2,13 m de large, qui ont été remplis de béton et d'acier pour soutenir les parties en porte-à-faux de cette maison de 641 m² sur cinq niveaux. »

The house sits above the factory of
its owner, producing an unusual juxtaposition of a modern architectural
form in an industrial environment.

Das Haus wurde auf die Fabrik des
Bauherrn aufgestockt – in seinem
industriell geprägten Umfeld sorgt der
moderne Baukörper für ungewöhnliche Kontraste.

La maison est en suspension au-
dessus de l'usine de son propriétaire,
ce qui produit une curieuse juxtaposition entre une forme architecturale
moderne et un environnement
industriel.

The interior of the house is both luminous and generous in its spaces. Wood is combined with steel, glass, and wooden floors.

Das Interieur ist lichtdurchflutet, die Räume großzügig. Holz wird mit Stahl, Glas und Holzböden kombiniert.

Lumineux, l'intérieur de la maison est de dimensions généreuses. Le bois s'y combine avec le verre et l'acier.

The steel structure visible in the living and dining area (above) recalls the industrial area that the house is built in and its unusual setting.

Die im Wohn- und Essbereich offen-liegende Stahlrahmenkonstruktion (oben) ist eine Reminiszenz an die ungewöhnliche Lage des Hauses inmitten eines Industriegebiets.

L'ossature en acier laissée apparente dans le séjour-salle à manger (ci-dessus) rappelle la nature industrielle du quartier et l'implantation inatten-due de la maison.

SOU FUJIMOTO

Sou Fujimoto Architects
10–3 Ichikawa-Seihon Building 6F
Higashi-Enoki-Cho Shinjuku
Tokyo 162–0807
Japan

Tel: +81 3 3513 5401
Fax: +81 3 3513 5402
E-mail: media@sou-fujimoto.net
Web: www.sou-fujimoto.net

SOU FUJIMOTO was born in 1971. He received a B.Arch degree from the University of Tokyo, Faculty of Engineering, Department of Architecture (1990–94). He established his own firm, Sou Fujimoto Architects, in 2000. He is considered one of the most interesting rising Japanese architects, and his forms usually evade easy classification. He has been a Lecturer at the Tokyo University of Science (2001–), Tokyo University (2004), and Kyoto University (2007–). His work includes the Industrial Training Facilities for the Mentally Handicapped (Hokkaido, 2003); Environment Art Forum, Annaka (Gunma, 2003–06); Treatment Center for Mentally Disturbed Children (Hokkaido, 2006); House O (Chiba, 2007); N House (Oita Prefecture, 2007–08); and the Final Wooden House (Kumamura, Kumamoto, 2007–08). Other recent work includes his participation in Toyo Ito's Sumika Project (House Before House, Utsunomiya, Tochigi, 2008); Musashino Art University Museum and Library (Tokyo, 2007–09); House H (Tokyo, 2008–09); Tokyo Apartment (Itabashiku, Tokyo, 2009–10); the Uniqlo Store in Shinsaibashi (Osaka, 2010); and House NA (Tokyo, 2010, published here), all in Japan.

SOU FUJIMOTO wurde 1971 geboren. Sein Architekturstudium an der Fakultät für Bauingenieurwesen der Universität Tokio schloss er mit einem B. Arch. ab (1990–94). Sein eigenes Büro, Sou Fujimoto Architects, gründete er 2000. Er gilt als einer der interessantesten jungen Architekten Japans, seine Formensprache entzieht sich einfachen Zuordnungen. Als Dozent lehrt er an der Tokioter Universität der Wissenschaften (seit 2001) sowie den Universitäten von Tokio (2004) und Kioto (seit 2007). Zu seinen Projekten zählen Ausbildungsstätten für geistig Behinderte (Hokkaido, 2003), das Environment Art Forum, Annaka (Gunma, 2003–06), ein Behandlungszentrum für psychisch erkrankte Kinder (Hokkaido, 2006), Haus O (Chiba, 2007), Haus N (Präfektur Oita, 2007–08) und das Final Wooden House in Kumamoto (2007–08). Weitere jüngere Arbeiten sind u. a. seine Beteiligung an Toyo Itos Sumika-Projekt (House Before House, Utsunomiya, Tochigi, 2008), Museum und Bibliothek der Kunsthochschule Musashino (Tokio, 2007–09), das Haus H (Tokio, 2008–09), ein Apartment in Tokio (Itabashiku, 2009–10), der Uniqlo Store in Shinsaibashi (Osaka, 2010) und das Haus NA (Tokio, 2010, hier vorgestellt), alle in Japan.

Né en 1971, **SUO FUJIMOTO** a obtenu son diplôme de B.Arch. à l'université de Tokyo (faculté d'ingénierie, département d'Architecture, 1990–94). Il crée sa propre agence, Sou Fujimoto Architects, en 2000. Considéré comme l'un des plus intéressants jeunes architectes japonais du moment, son vocabulaire formel échappe à toute classification aisée. Il a été assistant à l'Université des sciences de Tokyo (2001–), à l'université de Tokyo (2004) et à l'université de Kyoto (2007–). Parmi ses réalisations, toutes au Japon : des installations de formation pour handicapés mentaux (Hokkaido, 2003) ; l'Environment Art Forum d'Annaka (Gunma, 2003–06) ; un Centre de traitement pour enfants souffrant de troubles mentaux (Hokkaido, 2006) ; la maison O (Chiba, 2007) ; la maison N (préfecture d'Oita, 2007–08) ; la Maison de bois "définitive" (Kumamura, Kumamoto, 2007–08). Plus récemment, il a participé au projet Sumika de Toyo Ito (Maison d'avant la maison, Utsunomiya, Tochigi, 2008) ; le musée et la bibliothèque de l'Université d'art Musashino (Tokyo, 2007–09) ; la maison H (Tokyo, 2008–09) ; un appartement à Tokyo (Itabashiku, Tokyo, 2009–10) ; le magasin Uniqlo à Shinsaibashi (Osaka, 2010) et la maison NA (Tokyo, 2010, publiée ici).

HOUSE NA

Tokyo, Japan, 2010

*Area: 83 m². Client: not disclosed
Cost: not disclosed*

As has been the case for many of his structures, this house by Sou Fujimoto, located in a residential area of central Tokyo, breaks with architectural traditions. He compares it to "living within a tree," though he admits that the "white steel-frame structure itself shares no resemblance to a tree." He has "stratified the floor plates" in an almost "furniture-like" scale that effectively makes the entire small residence into a continuous space. He seeks "the richness once experienced" by our ancestors "from the time when they inhabited trees." As usual though, Fujimoto is not preoccupied with looking back to ancient times so much as he looks to the future. In this house, as he says, "when accommodating a group of guests, the distribution of people across the entire house will form a platform for a network type of communication in space." The house is a three-dimensional network.

Wie so viele Bauten Fujimotos, bricht auch dieses Haus in einem zentralen Wohngebiet Tokios mit architektonischen Traditionen. Fujimoto spricht vom „Wohnen in einem Baum", auch wenn er einräumt, dass „die weiße Stahlrahmenkonstruktion einem Baum nicht wirklich ähnelt". Durch die „Schichtung der Geschossplatten" in fast „mobiliarhaftem" Maßstab lässt Fujimoto das kleine Haus effektiv zum Raumkontinuum verschmelzen. Es ist die Suche nach einem „Erfahrungsschatz", den unsere Ahnen „besaßen, als sie noch in Bäumen lebten". Doch wie bei ihm üblich, geht es Fujimoto weniger um die Vergangenheit als vielmehr um den Blick in die Zukunft. In diesem Bau, so der Architekt, „entsteht, wenn Gäste im Haus sind, durch die Verteilung der Personen im Bau eine räumliche Plattform für netzwerkähnliche Kommunikation". Das Haus wird zum dreidimensionalen Netzwerk.

Comme beaucoup des réalisations de Sou Fujimoto, cette maison située dans un quartier résidentiel central de Tokyo rompt avec la tradition architecturale. Il la compare avec « la vie dans un arbre » tout en admettant que « la structure à ossature en acier laqué blanc n'a aucune ressemblance avec un arbre ». Il a « échelonné les dalles des sols » à une échelle « presque de mobilier » pour faire de cette petite maison un continuum spatial. Il a recherché « la richesse jadis vécue [par nos ancêtres] à l'époque où ils vivaient dans les arbres ». Cependant, comme à son habitude, Fujimoto n'est pas tant préoccupé par l'histoire que par le futur. Dans cette maison « lorsque sera reçu un groupe d'invités, dit-il, la distribution des hôtes dans la totalité de la maison formera une plate-forme de communication dans l'espace, de type réseau ». Cette maison est un réseau en trois dimensions.

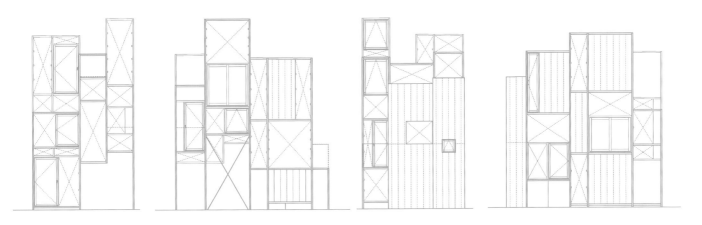

As is often the case in Fujimoto's work, House NA challenges the usual concepts of interior space and floor levels. Interior and exterior are also mixed together in ways that make it difficult to distinguish between them.

Wie oft bei Fujimoto, so stellt auch das Haus NA traditionelle Innenraumkonzepte und Etagenanordnungen infrage. Innen- und Außenraum sind so miteinander verschränkt, dass eine klare Unterscheidung schwerfällt.

Comme souvent chez Fujimoto, la maison NA défie les concepts classiques d'espace intérieur et de niveaux. L'intérieur et l'extérieur se mélangent d'une façon qui les rend indistinguables.

The astonishing, bright, curtainless space seen in these images seems to be nearly as far as possible from the prototypical private residence—all the more so in the Japanese context of privacy.

Die erstaunliche, helle und vorhang-lose Raumsituation auf diesen Ansichten scheint Welten entfernt vom klassischen privaten Wohnbau – besonders ungewöhnlich vor dem Hintergrund japanischer Vorstellungen von Privatsphäre.

Étonnant, lumineux et sans cloisonne-ment, cet espace semble aussi éloi-gné que possible des archétypes de la maison individuelle et encore plus de la recherche habituelle d'intimité des foyers japonais.

GO HASEGAWA

Go Hasegawa & Associates
2–18–7 Gaien Building 5F, Jingumae
Shibuya-ku
Tokyo 150–0001
Japan

Tel: +81 3 3403 0336
Fax: +81 3 3403 0337
E-mail: office@hsgwg.com
Web: www.hsgwg.com

GO HASEGAWA was born in 1977 in Saitama, Japan. He completed a Master's degree at the Tokyo Institute of Technology, Graduate School of Science and Engineering (2002), before working in the office of Tiara Nishizawa (2002–04). He founded Go Hasegawa & Associates in 2005, and has been a Lecturer at the Tokyo Institute of Technology, Tokyo University of Science, and Hosei University since 2009. He won the Grand Prize in the Tokyo Gas House Design Competition in 2007 for his House in a Forest. His work includes the House in a Forest (Nagano, 2006); House in Sakuradai (Mie, 2006); House in Gotanda (Tokyo, 2006); House in Komae (Tokyo, 2009); Nerima Apartment (Tokyo, 2010); Pilotis in a Forest (Gunma, 2010, published here); Townhouse in Asakusa (Tokyo, 2010); House in Komazawa (Tokyo, 2011); House in Kyodo (Tokyo, 2011, also published here); Nippon Design Center (Tokyo, 2012); and a belfry (Ishinomaki, Miyagi, 2012), all in Japan.

GO HASEGAWA wurde 1977 in Saitama, Japan, geboren. Er schloss sein Masterstudium an der Fakultät für Natur- und Ingenieurwissenschaften am Tokyo Institute of Technology ab (2002) und arbeitete anschließend im Büro von Tiara Nishizawa (2002–04). 2005 gründete er Go Hasegawa & Associates; seit 2009 ist er Dozent am Tokyo Institute of Technology, der Naturwissenschaftlichen Universität Tokio und der Universität Hosei. 2007 gewann er mit seinem Entwurf House in a Forest den Großen Preis des Hauswettbewerbs von Tokyo Gas. Zu seinen Projekten zählen das Haus in einem Wald (Nagano, 2006), das Haus in Sakuradai (Mie, 2006), das Haus in Gotanda (Tokio, 2006), das Haus in Komae (Tokio, 2009), das Nerima-Apartment (Tokio, 2010), das Projekt Pilotis in a Forest (Gunma, 2010, hier vorgestellt), das Stadthaus in Asakusa (Tokio, 2010), das Haus in Komazawa (Tokio, 2011), das Haus in Kyodo (Tokio, 2011, ebenfalls hier vorgestellt), das Nippon Design Center (Tokio, 2012) sowie ein Glockenturm (Ishinomaki, Miyagi, 2012), alle in Japan.

GO HASEGAWA est né en 1977 à Saitama (Japon). Il a obtenu son diplôme de mastère de l'École supérieure des sciences et de l'ingénierie de l'Institut de technologie de Tokyo (2002), puis a travaillé dans l'agence de Tiara Nishizawa (2002–04). Il a fondé Go Hasegawa & Associates en 2005 et est assistant à l'Institut de technologie de Tokyo, à l'Université des sciences de Tokyo et à l'université Hosei depuis 2009. Il a remporté le Grand Prix du concours de conception de la Tokyo Gas House en 2007 pour sa Maison en forêt. Parmi ses réalisations, toutes au Japon : la Maison en forêt (Nagano, 2006) ; une maison à Sakuradai (Mie, 2006) ; une maison à Gotanda (Tokyo, 2006) ; une maison à Komae (Tokyo, 2009) ; l'appartement Nerima (Tokyo, 2010) ; la maison Pilotis in a forest (Gunma, 2010, publiée ici) ; une maison de ville à Asakusa (Tokyo, 2010) ; une maison à Komazawa (Tokyo, 2011) ; une maison à Kyodo (Tokyo, 2011, publiée ici) ; le Centre du design japonais (Tokyo, 2012) et un beffroi (Ishinomaki, Miyagi, 2012).

HOUSE IN KYODO

Tokyo, Japan, 2011

Area: 68 m². Client: not disclosed
Cost: not disclosed

This two-story house was designed for a married couple with a large collection of books. "As a result," says Go Hasegawa, "I decided to make the entire first floor a book vault and insert the bathroom, sink area, entrance, study, bedroom, and closets in the gaps between the shelves." The bookshelves are 1.8-meters in height, which creates a relation between the body and the books, according to the architect. Interior and exterior walls were made with fiber-reinforced cement panels. A very thin (60-mm) steel sandwich panel roof covers the second-floor living room and terrace. Hasegawa explains: "The silver roof softly reflects light and greenery from the neighboring garden on undersurfaces and the ground, and fills the interior of the house. The light and landscape are reflected on the ceiling like the surface of a pond, causing the roof to disappear, and imbuing the second floor with the open quality of a rooftop."

Das zweistöckige Haus ist ein Entwurf für ein Ehepaar mit einer umfangreichen Bibliothek. „Deshalb entschied ich mich", so Go Hasegawa, „das gesamte Erdgeschoss als Bücher-‚Wunderkammer' zu planen und Bad, Waschecke, Eingang, Arbeitszimmer, Schlafzimmer und Wandschränke zwischen die Regale zu setzen". Dem Architekten zufolge entsteht durch die 1,8 m hohen Bücherregale eine maßstäbliche Bezugsgröße zwischen Büchern und Körper. Innen- und Außenwände wurden mit Glasfaserbetonplatten realisiert. Besonders dünne (60 mm starke) Stahlsandwichpaneele überdachen Wohnraum und Terrasse im ersten Stock. Hasegawa führt aus: „Das silbrige Dach reflektiert verhalten Licht und Grün aus dem angrenzenden Garten auf die Böden und prägt das Interieur. Licht und Landschaft spiegeln sich in der Decke wie in einem Teich: Das Dach tritt optisch zurück und der erste Stock gewinnt die Atmosphäre einer Dachterrasse."

Cette maison d'un seul étage a été conçue pour un couple propriétaire d'une abondante collection de livres. « C'est pourquoi, explique Go Hasegawa, j'ai décidé de faire du rez-de-chaussée dans son entier une réserve de livres et d'insérer la salle de bains, l'évier, l'entrée, le bureau, la chambre et des placards dans des vides entre les rayonnages. » Ceux-ci mesurent 1,8 m de haut ce qui, selon l'architecte, crée une relation physique entre les livres et le corps. Les murs extérieurs et intérieurs sont des panneaux de fibrociment armé. Des panneaux en sandwich d'acier très fins (60 mm) habillent l'étage et la terrasse. « La toiture argentée, explique Hasegawa, reflète délicatement la lumière naturelle et la verdure du jardin voisin sur ses sous-faces et sur le sol, effet lumineux qui baigne l'intérieur de la maison. La lumière et le paysage se reflètent au plafond comme à la surface d'un étang, faisant disparaître le toit… »

The forms of the house are expected, but its rhythm of openings and closed surfaces is not, nor are its materials really.

Formal wirkt das Haus zunächst konventionell, doch die rhythmische Anordnung von Öffnungen und geschlossenen Flächen ist alles andere als das – was auch für die Materialwahl gilt.

Si la forme de la maison semble classique, le rythme de ses ouvertures et ses façades aveugles ne l'est pas, de même que ses matériaux de construction.

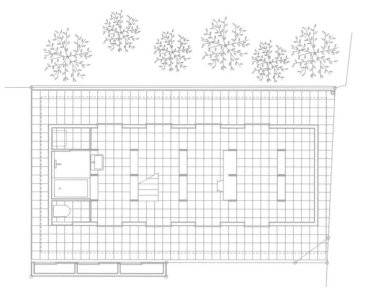

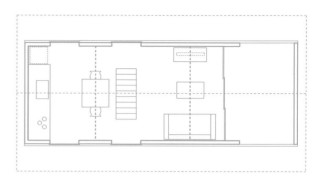

The house is narrow and generously glazed, with wooden floors somewhat alleviating the otherwise "modern" appearance in the image below.

Das schmale Haus ist großzügig verglast. Holzböden bringen Wärme in die sonst eher „moderne" Strenge des Interieurs (unten im Bild).

La maison est étroite et généreusement vitrée. Les planchers en bois atténuent un peu l'aspect « moderne » de l'aménagement intérieur (ci-dessous).

The library space is covered in wood, as is the ceiling, as well as elements such as the staircase. Japanese houses are generally very modest in scale, and this 68-square-meter residence is no exception.

Der Bibliotheksbereich wird von Holz dominiert, etwa bei der Deckenvertäfelung und der Treppe. Japanische Häuser sind generell eher bescheiden und dieses 68 m² große Domizil ist keine Ausnahme.

La bibliothèque est entièrement habillée de bois, y compris son plafond et l'escalier. Les maisons japonaises sont généralement d'échelle très modeste et cette résidence de 68 m² ne fait pas exception.

A sliding glass screen recalls Japanese tradition, allowing the living space to be easily subdivided as required.

Die Schiebetür ist ein Rückgriff auf traditionelle japanische Elemente und erlaubt die Teilung der Räume nach Bedarf.

Un écran de verre coulissant rappelle la tradition japonaise. Il permet de diviser facilement l'espace en fonction des besoins.

On the right, a wooden ceiling and an exceptionally large opening (far right) show a constant and innovative interpretation of traditional designs.

Eine holzvertäfelte Decke (rechts) und eine ungewöhnlich große Öffnung (ganz rechts) zeugen von innovativer Interpretation traditioneller Elemente.

À droite, le plafond de bois et la grande baie que l'on aperçoit au fond à droite illustrent une réinterprétation de pratiques traditionnelles.

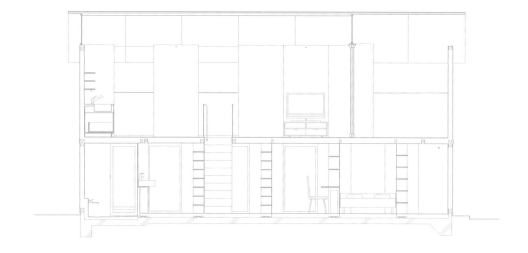

Right, a section shows that the upper level has a greater ceiling height than the ground level. Volumes are in general lightly defined, allowing for open, flexible space.

Der Querschnitt (rechts) zeigt in der oberen Ebene eine größere Raumhöhe als im Erdgeschoss. Die Volumina sind zurückhaltend gegliedert, was eine offene, flexible Raumnutzung ermöglicht.

À droite, coupe montrant que la hauteur du plafond est plus élevée à l'étage qu'au rez-de-chaussée. Les volumes sont en règle générale peu définis, ce qui donne un sentiment d'espace souple et ouvert.

PILOTIS IN A FOREST

Kita-Karuizawa, Gunma, Japan, 2010

Area: 77 m². Client: not disclosed
Cost: not disclosed

This weekend house was designed with the intention to allow its owners and visitors to see the trunks of neighboring trees even when they are in the bottom section of the structure. Since this large lower space is entirely open, the architect explains, "I used the forest as the building's walls." He compares the suspended living area to a "small attic-like space" where a 1.8-meter ceiling and a low dining table sitting on a glass floor seek to "convey the sense that the natural environment outside is larger and closer." Though the architect does not specifically emphasize the ecological credentials of this structure, he clearly sought to preserve mature trees, and to bring the clients closer to nature. "In good weather, you can relax under the pilotis in the middle of the forest," he says, "and after the sun goes down, sleep outside among the towering trees."

Das Wochenendhaus wurde so konzipiert, dass Bauherren und Gäste einen Ausblick auf die Bäume des angrenzenden Waldstücks haben, auch in der Zone unterhalb des aufgeständerten Hauses. Dieser großzügige untere Bereich ist gänzlich offen gehalten, wobei der Architekt „den Wald als Wand interpretierte". Den darüber schwebenden Wohnbereich beschreibt er als „kleinen Raum, einem Dachboden ähnlich". Die 1,8 m hohen Decken und ein niedriger Esstisch über einem Bodenfenster „lassen den landschaftlichen Außenraum größer wirken und näher rücken". Obwohl der Architekt die ökologischen Aspekte seines Entwurfs nicht ausdrücklich betont, bemühte er sich offensichtlich darum, den älteren Baumbestand zu erhalten und den Bewohnern eine große Nähe zur Natur zu ermöglichen. „Bei gutem Wetter kann man unter den Piloten mitten im Wald entspannen", so Hasegawa, „und nach Sonnenuntergang unter den großen Bäumen schlafen."

Cette maison a été conçue pour que ses occupants puissent voir les troncs des arbres qui l'entourent en particulier lorsqu'ils se trouvent dans sa partie inférieure. Le grand volume au ras du sol est entièrement ouvert : « J'ai fait des arbres les murs de la maison », explique l'architecte. Il compare la partie suspendue à un « petit espace, comme une sorte de grenier » dont le plafond à 1,80 m de haut et la table des repas posée sur un sol de verre cherchent à « exprimer l'idée que l'environnement naturel extérieur est plus vaste et plus proche ». Bien que l'architecte ne parle pas spécialement des avantages écologiques de ce projet, il a cherché à respecter le cadre boisé et à rapprocher les résidents de la nature. « Par beau temps, vous pouvez vous reposer entre les pilotis au milieu de la forêt, dit-il, et après que le soleil se soit couché, dormir ainsi en plein air au milieu des arbres. »

In its forest setting the house might bring to mind certain industrial structures, but its height off the ground is exceptional, allowing for a supplementary level, which is at once outdoors and yet covered from above (left page).

Das Haus im Wald erinnert in gewisser Weise an Industriebauten, doch seine Aufständerung ist ungewöhnlich und schafft eine zusätzliche Nutzungsebene, die einerseits draußen liegt, andererseits jedoch von oben geschützt ist (linke Seite).

Malgré son cadre forestier, la maison peut rappeler certaines constructions industrielles, mais sa hauteur par rapport au sol est exceptionnelle, ce qui dégage au sol un niveau supplémentaire, à la fois extérieur et couvert (page de gauche).

The wood clad interior has an unusual feature—a glass-top dining table that corresponds to a glazed section in the floor allowing diners to look down to ground level.

Ein ungewöhnliches Element des von Holz dominierten Interieurs ist ein Esstisch mit Glasfläche über einem Bodenfenster, durch das die Tischgäste einen Blick hinunter auf die ebenerdige Ebene haben.

Entièrement habillé de bois, le niveau supérieur a été doté d'une curiosité : le plateau en verre de la table surplombe une ouverture vitrée percée dans le sol pour permettre aux hôtes de voir le niveau inférieur de la maison.

The very highly perched structure allows for a surprisingly free and open space below—whether inside or out, residents feel like they are very much in the forest.

Durch die hohe Aufständerung des Baus wirkt der untere Nutzbereich erstaunlich frei und offen – die Bewohner fühlen sich innen wie außen unmittelbar dem Wald verbunden.

Très haut perchée, la maison dégage au niveau du sol un étonnant espace ouvert où les résidents peuvent se sentir déjà en forêt.

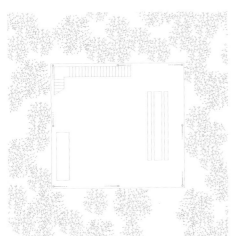

HANS VAN HEESWIJK

Hans van Heeswijk Architects bv BNA
Ertskade 111
1019 BB Amsterdam
The Netherlands

Tel: +31 20 622 57 17
Fax: +31 20 623 82 84
E-mail: info@heeswijk.nl
Web: www.heeswijk.nl

HANS VAN HEESWIJK was born in Breda, the Netherlands, in 1952. He graduated from the Faculty of Architecture, Technical University of Delft, in 1980, and worked in the office of Aldo van Eyck from 1981 to 1985. He created Hans van Heeswijk Architects in Amsterdam in 1985 and currently employs 23 people. His work includes the Zouthaven Pedestrian Bridge (Amsterdam, 2004); an extension of the town hall and a new library in Heerhugowaard (2008); the MOTI (Museum of the Image, Breda, 2008); the Hermitage Museum (Amsterdam, 2009); the Rieteiland House (Amsterdam, 2010–11, published here); the town hall in Lansingerland (2012); and the extension and renovation of the Mauritshuis (The Hague, 2014), all in the Netherlands.

HANS VAN HEESWIJK wurde 1952 in Breda, Niederlande, geboren. Sein Studium schloss er 1980 an der Architekturfakultät der TU Delft ab, anschließend arbeitete er von 1981 bis 1985 im Büro von Aldo van Eyck. 1985 gründete er sein Büro Hans van Heeswijk Architects in Amsterdam, das derzeit 23 Mitarbeiter beschäftigt. Zu seinen Projekten zählen eine Fußgängerbrücke in Zouthaven (Amsterdam, 2004), die Erweiterung des Rathauses und eine neue Bibliothek in Heerhugowaard (2008), das MOTI (Museum of the Image, Breda, 2008), die Eremitage in Amsterdam (2009), das Haus Rieteiland (Amsterdam, 2010–11, hier vorgestellt), das Rathaus von Lansingerland (2012) sowie die Erweiterung und Sanierung des Mauritshuis (Den Haag, 2014), alle in den Niederlanden.

HANS VAN HEESWIJK, né à Breda (Pays-Bas) en 1952, est diplômé de la faculté d'architecture de l'Université polytechnique de Delft (1980) et a travaillé chez Aldo van Eyck de 1981 à 1985. Il a créé l'agence Hans van Heeswijk Architects à Amsterdam en 1985, qui compte aujourd'hui 23 collaborateurs. Parmi ses réalisations, toutes aux Pays-Bas : la passerelle piétonnière de Zouthaven (Amsterdam, 2004) ; une extension d'un hôtel de ville et une nouvelle bibliothèque (Heerhugowaard, 2008) ; le musée MOTI (musée de l'image, Breda, 2008) ; le musée de l'Hermitage (Amsterdam, 2009) : la maison Rieteiland (Amsterdam, 2010–11, publiée ici) ; un hôtel de ville (Lansingerland, 2012) et l'extension et rénovation du Mauritshuis (La Haye, 2014).

RIETEILAND HOUSE

Amsterdam, The Netherlands, 2010–11

Address: Larikslaan 1, Amsterdam, The Netherlands. Area: 235 m²
Clients: Hans van Heeswijk and Natascha Drabbe
Cost: not disclosed. Collaboration: Richard Gouverneur, Rob Hulst, Richard Teeling

This house, the architect's residence, includes the kitchen, three bedrooms, and utility areas on the ground floor, with a lounge area and two studies on the first floor and a sleeping area, bathroom, Turkish bath, and roof terrace on the second floor. Located on the water on Ijburg Island, the house is clad in aluminum panels on one side and fully glazed on the other. A service core clad in wenge wood containing closets, toilets, and a dumbwaiter, as well as cabling, rises up through the interior. Double-height spaces were created for the kitchen area and first-floor living room. A triple height of nine meters was created between the dining room and the second-floor master bedroom. The architect designed the kitchen, bathroom cabinets, fireplace, dining tables, bookshelves, and the door and window hardware.

Der private Wohnsitz des Architekten umfasst eine Küche, drei Schlafzimmer und Hauswirtschaftsräume im Erdgeschoss, einen Wohnbereich sowie zwei Büros im ersten Stock und einen Schlafbereich, Bad, ein Türkisches Bad und eine Dachterrasse im zweiten Obergeschoss. Das auf der Insel Ijburg am Wasser gelegene Haus ist zu einer Seite mit Aluminiumpaneelen verblendet, an der anderen vollständig verglast. Im mit Wengeholz vertäfelten Gebäudekern, der sich durch den Bau zieht, sind Wandschränke, Toiletten sowie ein Speiseaufzug und Versorgungsleitungen untergebracht. Die Küche und der Wohnbereich im ersten Stock wurden doppelgeschossig angelegt. Zwischen Essbereich und Hauptschlafzimmer im zweiten Stock ist die Raumhöhe sogar mit 9 m dreigeschossig. Der Architekt entwarf darüber hinaus Küche, Badeinbauten, Kamin, Esstische, Regale sowie Tür- und Fensterbeschläge.

La maison que Hans van Heeswijk a construite pour son propre usage comprend : au rez-de-chaussée, une cuisine, trois chambres et des pièces de service ; au premier étage, le séjour, deux bureaux, une zone pour dormir ; au deuxième étage, la chambre principale, une salle de bains, un bains de vapeur et une terrasse. Construite au bord de l'eau sur l'île de Ijburg, la maison est habillée de panneaux d'aluminium côté rue et entièrement vitrée de l'autre côté. Le noyau central paré de wengé, qui s'élève sur toute la hauteur de la construction, contient des placards, des toilettes, un dressing et les circulations techniques. La cuisine et le séjour bénéficient d'une double hauteur tandis qu'elle atteint 9 m entre la salle à manger et la chambre principale du deuxième étage. L'architecte a également conçu les rayonnages, les salles de bains, des bancs, des rangements, la cheminée et les tables pour les repas.

Relatively closed from the entrance side (left), the house is, on the contrary, fully glazed and open at the rear—with the double-height living area visible on the left.

Der zur Straßenseite hin eher geschlossene Bau (links) ist auf der Rückseite vollständig verglast und offen – der Wohnbereich mit doppelter Raumhöhe ist oben links im Bild zu sehen.

Relativement fermée du côté de l'entrée (à gauche), la maison est au contraire entièrement vitrée et ouverte sur l'arrière. Le séjour double hauteur figure sur la gauche de l'image.

Only certain areas are closed for the sake of privacy, otherwise the house is amazingly open, and even vertiginous, as seen from some angles.

Nur ausgewählte Bereiche sind zur Wahrung der Privatsphäre geschlossen, ansonsten ist das Haus erstaunlich offen: aus manchen Blickwinkeln sogar schwindelerregend offen.

Seules certaines parties sont fermées, pour des raisons d'intimité. Étonnement ouvert, le reste de la maison paraît presque vertigineux sous certains angles.

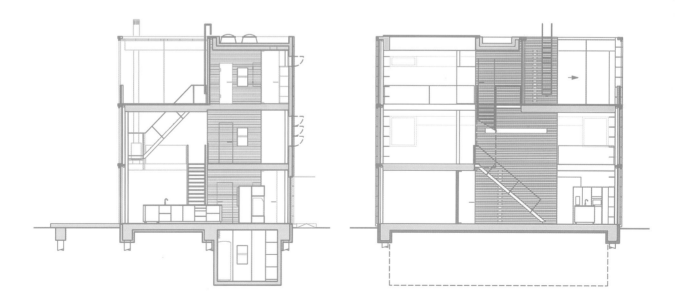

A plunging view of the double-height dining area with suspended metallic staircases that to some extent bring to mind industrial spaces.

Ein Blick hinunter in den doppelgeschossigen Essbereich mit abgehängten Stahltreppen, die in gewisser Weise an Industriearchitektur denken lassen.

Une vue plongeante de la partie salle à manger à double hauteur et de son escalier métallique suspendu rappelle certaines atmosphères industrielles.

The dining table seen in the image on the left page is again photographed here from ground level. Below, plans show the interpenetration of the different levels.

Der links im Bild zu sehende Esstisch hier aus einem Blickwinkel im Erdgeschoss. Etagengrundrisse (unten) illustrieren die Verschränkung der verschiedenen Ebenen.

La table des repas, vue page de gauche, photographiée ici du sol. Ci-dessous, plans montrant l'interpénétration des différents niveaux.

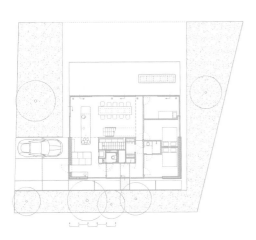

STEVEN HOLL

Steven Holl Architects, P.C.
450 West 31st Street, 11th floor
New York, NY 10001, USA

Tel: +1 212 629 7262 7 Fax: +1 212 629 7312
E-mail: nyc@stevenholl.com / Web: www.stevenholl.com

Born in 1947 in Bremerton, Washington, **STEVEN HOLL** obtained his B.Arch degree from the University of Washington (1970). He studied in Rome and at the Architectural Association in London (1976). He began his career in California and opened his own office in New York in 1976. His notable buildings include Void Space / Hinged Space, Housing (Nexus World, Fukuoka, Japan, 1991); Stretto House (Dallas, Texas, USA, 1992); Makuhari Housing (Chiba, Tokyo, Japan, 1997); Chapel of Saint Ignatius, Seattle University (Seattle, Washington, USA, 1997); Kiasma Museum of Contemporary Art (Helsinki, Finland, 1998); and an extension to the Cranbrook Institute of Science (Bloomfield Hills, Michigan, USA, 1999). Winner of the 1998 Alvar Aalto Medal, Steven Holl, won the competition (2009) for the Glasgow School of Art (Glasgow, UK), and has completed an expansion and renovation of the Nelson-Atkins Museum of Art (Kansas City, Missouri, USA, 1999–2007); Linked Hybrid (Beijing, China, 2005–08); the Knut Hamsun Center (Hamarøy, Norway, 2006–09); HEART: Herning Museum of Contemporary Art (Herning, Denmark, 2007–09); and the Vanke Center / Horizontal Skyscraper (Shenzhen, China, 2008–09), which won the 2011 AIA Honor Award for Architecture. Current projects include Cité de l'Océan et du Surf (Biarritz, France, 2005–10, with Solange Fabião); the Nanjing Museum of Art and Architecture (China, 2008–10); Daeyang Gallery and House (Seoul, South Korea, 2010–12, published here); Shan-Shui Hangzhou (master plan, Hangzhou, China, 2010–); and the Hangzhou Music Museum (Hangzhou, China, 2010–).

STEVEN HOLL, geboren 1947 in Bremerton, Washington, absolvierte seinen B. Arch. an der University of Washington (1970) und studierte darüber hinaus in Rom sowie an der Architectural Association in London (1976). Nach beruflichen Anfängen in Kalifornien gründete er 1976 ein Büro in New York. Zu seinen meist beachteten Projekten zählen die Wohnanlage Void Space/Hinged Space (Nexus World, Fukuoka, Japan, 1991), das Stretto House (Dallas, Texas, 1992), die Wohnanlage Makuhari (Chiba, Tokio, 1997), die Sankt-Ignatius-Kapelle, Seattle University (Seattle, Washington, 1997), das Kiasma Museum für zeitgenössische Kunst (Helsinki, 1998) sowie eine Erweiterung des Cranbrook Institute of Science (Bloomfield Hills, Michigan, 1999). 1998 wurde Steven Holl mit der Alvar-Aalto-Medaille ausgezeichnet, er konnte den Wettbewerb für die Glasgow School of Art (2009, Glasgow) für sich entscheiden und realisierte die Renovierung und Erweiterung des Nelson-Atkins Museum of Art (Kansas City, Missouri, 1999–2007), das Linked Hybrid (Peking, 2005–08), das Knut-Hamsun-Zentrum (Hamarøy, Norwegen, 2006–09), das Herning Museum für zeitgenössische Kunst (HEART, Herning, Dänemark, 2007–09) sowie das Vanke Center/Horizontal Skyscraper (Shenzhen, China, 2008–09), das 2011 mit dem Ehrenpreis des AIA ausgezeichnet wurde. Aktuelle Projekte sind u. a. die Cité de l'Océan et du Surf (Biarritz, 2005–10, mit Solange Fabião), das Nanjing Museum für Kunst und Architektur (China, 2008–10), ein Haus mit Galerie Daeyang (Seoul, Südkorea, 2010–12, hier vorgestellt), ein Masterplan für Shan-Shui Hangzhou (Hangzhou, China, seit 2010) sowie das Museum für Musik in Hangzhou (China, seit 2010).

Né en 1947 à Bremerton (État de Washington), **STEVEN HOLL** a obtenu son diplôme de B.Arch. à l'université de Washington (1970). Il a étudié à Rome et à l'Architectureal Association de Londres (1976), il a débuté sa carrière en Californie et ouvert son agence à New York la même année. Il a reçu la médaille Alvar Aalto en 1998. Parmi ses réalisations les plus notables : l'immeuble d'appartements Void Space/Hinged Space (Nexus World, Fukuoka, Japon, 1991) ; la maison Stretto (Dallas, Texas, 1992) ; les logements Makuhari (Chiba, Tokyo, 1997) ; la chapelle Saint-Ignace, université de Seattle (Seattle, Washington, 1997) ; le Musée d'art contemporain Kiasma (Helsinki, Finlande, 1998) et une extension de l'Institut des sciences de Cranbrook (Bloomfield Hills, Michigan, 1999). En 2009, il a remporté le concours pour l'École d'art de Glasgow et a réalisé l'extension et rénovation du musée d'art Nelson Atkins (Kansas City, Missouri, 1999–2007) ; le Linked Hybrid (Pékin, 2005–08) ; le Centre Knut Hamsun (Hamarøy, Norvège, 2006–09) ; le musée d'art contemporain Herning (HEART, Herning, Danemark, 2007–09) ; le Vanke Center/Gratte-ciel horizontal (Shenzhen, Chine, 2008–09) qui a remporté le prix d'honneur d'architecture de l'AIA en 2011. Parmi ses réalisations actuelles : la Cité de l'océan et du surf (Biarritz, France, 2005-10, avec Solange Fabiao) ; le Musée d'art et d'architecture de Nankin (Chine, 2008–10) ; la galerie et résidence Daeyang (Séoul, Corée-du-Sud, 2010–12, publiée ici) ; Shan-Shui Hangzhou (plan directeur, Hangzhou, Chine, 2010–) et le Musée de la musique d'Hangzhou (Hangzhou, 2010–).

DAEYANG GALLERY AND HOUSE

Seoul, South Korea, 2010–12

*Area: 994 m². Client: Daeyang Shipping Co. Ltd.
Cost: not disclosed*

The presence of water and the forms of the house that jut into the central pool gives this structure an unusual presence and obvious architectural appeal.

Das Wasser und die in das zentrale Bassin ragenden Volumina verleihen dem Haus eine ungewöhnliche Erscheinung und offensichtliche architektonische Reize.

La présence de l'eau et la forme des différentes parties de la maison qui se projettent au-dessus du bassin central confèrent à cette résidence une présence inhabituelle et une réelle séduction architecturale.

Located in the hilly Kangbuk area of Seoul, this structure bears a relation to music according to the architect. The basic geometry of the building is inspired by "a 1967 sketch for a music score by the composer Istvan Anhalt, 'Symphony of Modules,' which was discovered in a book by John Cage called *Notations*." The complex is divided into three pavilions, one for the entrance, another for the residence, and an event space. These volumes are set juxtaposed around the central, angular basin. The whole composition echoes the irregular, angled shape of the site. Five glass strips in the pavilions allow daylight into the spaces. Holl explains that the architectural proportions are based on the series 3, 5, 8, 13, 21, 34, 55. The reflecting pool and gardens form an integral part of the design, with full-height glazing opening from the pavilions onto the basin. Red- and charcoal-stained wood strips clad the interiors, while a custom patinated copper rain screen covers the exterior surfaces.

Der in Kangbuk, einem hügeligen Stadtviertel von Seoul, gelegene Bau geht konzeptuell auf eine musikalische Komposition zurück: Die Geometrie des Gebäudes ist, so der Architekt, von „*Symphony of Modules,* einem 1967 entstandenen Partiturentwurf des Komponisten Istvan Anhalt" inspiriert, „den ich in *Notations,* einem Buch von John Cage, entdeckt habe". Die Anlage gliedert sich in drei Pavillons: Eingang, Wohnhaus sowie Veranstaltungsbereich. Die Baukörper sind um das zentrale eckige Wasserbassin gruppiert. Die Gesamtkomposition spiegelt die asymmetrischen Konturen des Grundstücks. Fünf Lichtbänder in den Pavillons lassen Tageslicht in die Räume fallen. Holl zufolge basieren die architektonischen Proportionen auf der [Fibonacci-]Folge 3, 5, 8, 13, 21, 34, 55. Der Wasserspiegel und die Gartenanlagen sind integraler Bestandteil des Entwurfs, die geschosshohe Verglasung öffnet den Blick auf das Wasserbecken. Das Interieur ist mit gebeizten Holzpaneelen in Rotbraun und Anthrazit vertäfelt; eine speziell patinierte, hinterlüftete Fassade aus Kupfer ummantelt den Außenbau.

Situé dans le quartier vallonné de Kangbuk à Séoul, cette maison n'est pas sans relation avec la musique explique son architecte. La simplicité de sa géométrie lui a été inspirée par « une esquisse de partition musicale de 1967 du compositeur Istvan Anhalt, *Symphony of Moduli*, découverte dans un livre de John Cage intitulé *Notations* ». Holl explique également que les proportions architecturales reprennent la série de nombres 3, 5, 8, 13, 21, 34, 55. Le petit complexe se divise en trois pavillons, un pour l'entrée, l'autre pour la résidence et un troisième pour des évènements. Ces volumes se juxtaposent autour d'un bassin central de forme anguleuse. L'ensemble de la composition rappelle la forme irrégulière et anguleuse du terrain. Dans les pavillons, cinq bandeaux vitrés verticaux laissent pénétrer la lumière naturelle. Le bassin et les jardins, sur lesquels ouvrent les pavillons par d'immenses baies vitrées toute hauteur, font partie intégrale du projet. Des plans de bois teint en rouge et graphite habillent l'intérieur. À l'extérieur des panneaux de cuivre qui se patineront avec le temps protègent les façades de la pluie.

A combination of opaque columns clad in wood, full-height glazing, and the ground-level pool enliven the space and create ambiguities, such as the feeling that the water might cascade into the house.

Eine Kombination aus geschlossenen, holzvertäfelten Wandabschnitten, raumhoher Verglasung und dem Bassin auf Bodenniveau sorgt für räumliche Dynamik und Mehrdeutigkeit, etwa den Eindruck, das Wasser könne jederzeit in das Haus fluten.

La combinaison de colonnes habillées de bois, de baies vitrées toute hauteur et d'un bassin anime l'espace et crée des ambiguïtés, comme le sentiment que l'eau pourrait déborder dans la maison.

CARSTEN HÖLLER
AND MARCEL ODENBACH

CARSTEN HÖLLER is a German artist, born in 1961 in Brussels. He has a doctorate in agricultural science from the University of Kiel and he lives and works in Stockholm. Noted projects are his winding, tubular slides such as "Test Site" (Tate Modern, London, UK, 2006) and his Congolese/Western nightclub, bar, and restaurant "The Double Club," created in London with the Prada Foundation (2008). His solo exhibitions include "Divided Divided" (Museum Boijmans Van Beuningen, Rotterdam, the Netherlands, 2010); "SOMA" (Hamburger Bahnhof, Museum für Gegenwart, Berlin, Germany, 2010); and "Carsten Höller: Experience" (New Museum, New York, USA, 2011). **MARCEL ODENBACH** was born in 1953 in Cologne, Germany. He studied architecture and art at the RWTH (Aachen). He is a freelance video artist, surely one of the best known in Germany, who lives and works in Cologne and Ghana, and is a Professor in Film and Video at the Düsseldorf Kunstakademie. His solo exhibitions include "Marcel Odenbach" (New Museum of Contemporary Art, New York, USA, 1999); "Marcel Odenbach: In stillen Teichen lauern Krokodile" (Hamburger Bahnhof, Museum für Gegenwart, Berlin, Germany, 2006); "Marcel Odenbach: Das im Entwischen Erwischte" (Kunsthalle Bremen, Bremen, Germany, 2008); and "Marcel Odenbach: Works on Paper" (Kunstmuseum Bonn, Bonn, Germany, 2013). Together they completed House Turtle (Biriwa, Ghana, 1999–2009, published here).

Der deutsche Künstler **CARSTEN HÖLLER** wurde 1961 in Brüssel geboren. Er promovierte in Agrarwissenschaften an der Universität Kiel und lebt und arbeitet in Stockholm. Bekannt gewordene Arbeiten sind etwa seine geschwungenen Röhrenrutschen wie *Test Site* (Tate Modern, London, 2006) oder sein Double Club, ein kongolesisch/westlicher Nachtklub mit Bar und Restaurant, den er in London mit der Prada Foundation realisierte (2008). Zu seinen Einzelausstellungen zählen *Divided Divided* (Museum Boijmans Van Beuningen, Rotterdam, 2010), *SOMA* (Hamburger Bahnhof, Museum für Gegenwart, Berlin, 2010) und *Carsten Höller: Experience* (New Museum, New York, 2011). **MARCEL ODENBACH** wurde 1953 in Köln geboren. Er studierte Architektur und Kunst an der RWTH Aachen. Er ist freischaffender Videokünstler, einer der bekanntesten Deutschlands, lebt und arbeitet in Köln und Ghana und ist Professor für Film und Video an der Düsseldorfer Kunstakademie. Zu seinen Einzelausstellungen zählen *Marcel Odenbach* (New Museum of Contemporary Art, New York, 1999), *Marcel Odenbach: In stillen Teichen lauern Krokodile* (Hamburger Bahnhof, Museum für Gegenwart, Berlin, 2006), *Marcel Odenbach: Das im Entwischen Erwischte* (Kunsthalle Bremen, 2008) und *Marcel Odenbach: Works on Paper* (Kunstmuseum Bonn, 2013). Gemeinsames Projekt der Künstler ist das House Turtle (Biriwa, Ghana, 1999–2009, hier vorgestellt).

CARSTEN HÖLLER est un artiste allemand, né à Bruxelles en 1961. Docteur en sciences de l'agriculture de l'université de Kiel, il vit et travaille à Stockholm. Parmi ses projets remarqués, on notera ses toboggans tubulaires hélicoïdaux tels le *Test Site* (Tate Modern, Londres, 2006) ainsi que son club, bar et restaurant congolais/occidental *Double Club* crée à Londres avec la Fondation Prada (2008). Ses expositions personnelles incluent « Divide Divided » (Museum Boijmans Van Beuningen, Rotterdam, 2010), « SOMA » (Museum für Gegenwart, Hamburger Bahnhof, Berlin, 2010) et « Carsten Höller : Experience » (New Museum, New York, 2011). **MARCEL ODENBACH**, né en 1953 à Cologne en Allemagne a étudié l'art et l'architecture à l'École supérieure RWTH à Aix-la-Chapelle. Un des plus célèbres artistes vidéo allemands, il vit et travaille à Cologne et au Ghana et enseigne le film et la vidéo à la Kunstakademie de Düsseldorf. Ses expositions personnelles incluent « Marcel Odenbach » (New Museum of Contemporary Art, New York, 1999) ; « Marcel Odenbach: In stillen Teichen lauern Krokodile » (Hamburger Bahnhof, Museum für Gegenwart, Berlin, 2006) ; « Marcel Odenbach: Das im Entwischen Erwischte » (Kunsthalle Bremen, Brême, 2008) et « Marcel Odenbach: Works on Paper » (Kunstmuseum Bonn, Bonn, 2013). Ils ont conçu ensemble la House Turtle (Biriwa, Ghana, 1999–2009, publiée ici).

HOUSE TURTLE

Biriwa, Ghana, 1999–2009

Area: 434 m² (not including roof). Client: Carsten Höller and Marcel Odenbach
Cost: not disclosed. Collaboration: Dornbracht

Standing on its irregular pilotis or stilts, the house looks from the exterior as though it might be a temporary structure. Like the coastline it looks out on, it is intentionally rough in its appearance and materials.

Das Haus ruht auf unregelmäßigen Piloten oder Stützen und wirkt von außen fast wie ein temporärer Bau. Wie die Küste, zu der es sich öffnet, ist es in Erscheinung und Materialwahl bewusst rau.

Posée sur des pilotis plantés de façon irrégulière, la maison fait penser à une structure temporaire. Comme la côte rocheuse sur laquelle elle donne, elle a adopté un aspect brut qu'expriment bien ses matériaux.

According to Carsten Höller, the **HOUSE TURTLE**, located near Cape Coast (Ghana) on the Gulf of Guinea in the town of Biriwa "was designed with the following considerations: a) to have a maximum of air flow through and under the house to avoid the necessity of air conditioning; b) to make the construction unattractive for mosquitos and keep animals, including snakes, at bay; c) to favor 87 or 93° angles over 90° angles, in order to increase/decrease the perception of distance and straightness; d) to collect rainwater from the roof and the terraces underground; e) to make the house look 'unfinished.'" As a basic, hand-drawn floor plan shows, the house is made up of parallelograms as opposed to rectangles. The artist's rooms are located at opposite ends of the house, with a shared living area and kitchen between. "We are like dilettante architects, and we made so many mistakes […] But since this is Africa, it takes ages to build anything, so we had time to think about the mistakes and find the right solutions," says Höller in the online magazine *WWD* ("Cliff Hanger," 2012). They encountered numerous difficulties due to the administrative complications and the site, which is not located on any road.

Laut Carsten Höller wurde das **HOUSE TURTLE** in Biriwa, unweit von Cape Coast (Ghana) am Golf von Guinea „unter Berücksichtigung folgender Kriterien geplant: a) maximale Luftzirkulation durch und unter dem Haus, um auf Klimatisierung verzichten zu können, b) Schutzmaßnahmen gegen Moskitos und andere Tiere wie Schlangen, c) Planung von 87°- oder 93°-Winkeln statt der üblichen 90°-Winkel, um das Empfinden von Raumtiefe und Geradwinkligkeit zu verstärken/mindern, d) Sammeln von Regenwasser über das Dach und unterhalb der Terrassen, e) das Haus ‚unfertig' erscheinen zu lassen." Wie ein einfacher handgezeichneter Grundriss zeigt, basiert das Haus auf Parallelogrammen statt auf Rechtecken. Die Quartiere der beiden Künstler liegen an den entgegengesetzten Enden des Hauses, dazwischen befinden sich ein gemeinsamer Wohnbereich und eine Küche. „Wir sind dilettantische Architekten, haben alles Mögliche falsch gemacht", so Carsten Höller in dem Onlinemagazin *WWD* („Cliff Hanger". 2012). „Aber hier in Afrika dauert es ewig, etwas zu bauen, weshalb genug Zeit blieb, unsere Fehler zu analysieren und bessere Lösungen zu finden." Es waren zahlreiche Schwierigkeiten zu bewältigen: bürokratischer Natur ebenso wie im Hinblick auf den Bauplatz, der alles andere als gewöhnlich ist.

Selon Carsten Höller, la **HOUSE TURTLE**, située près de Cape Coast (Ghana) sur le golfe de Guinée dans la ville de Biriwa « a été conçue à partir des considérations suivantes : a) disposer d'une circulation d'air maximum à travers et sous la maison pour éviter toute climatisation mécanique ; b) rendre la construction aussi peu attirante que possible pour les moustiques et garder à distance les autres animaux, serpents compris ; c) favoriser les angles à 87 ou 93° par rapport à l'angle droit pour augmenter/diminuer la perception des distances et de l'aspect rectiligne ; d) collecter l'eau de pluie du toit et des terrasses en sous-sol ; e) donner à la maison un aspect « non achevé ». Comme le montre un plan au sol dessiné à la main, la maison se compose de parallélogrammes et non de rectangles. Les chambres des artistes sont disposées aux deux extrémités, séparées par un séjour et une cuisine communes. « Nous sommes un peu des architectes dilettantes et avons fait beaucoup d'erreurs, dit Höller, mais comme nous sommes en Afrique et qu'il faut des années pour construire quoi que ce soit, nous avons eu le temps de réfléchir à nos fautes et de trouver des solutions. » Les deux artistes ont également rencontré de multiples difficultés d'ordre administratif ou d'autres dues à la nature du site, non relié à une route.

Spaces in the house are largely open to the exterior, providing sheltered areas that are neither entirely inside, nor really outside.

Die Räume sind überwiegend offen gehalten. So entstehen geschützte Bereiche, die weder gänzlich Innen- noch ganz Außenraum sind.

Les pièces de la maison largement ouvertes sur l'extérieur sont des espaces à vivre ni entièrement intérieurs ni vraiment extérieurs.

The weathering of the concrete gives an enigmatic appearance to the house—though its forms are modern, it looks as though it might have been there forever. Right, a wooden terrace with a pool in front of the house.

Die Witterungserscheinungen des Sichtbetons geben dem Haus etwas Rätselhaftes – trotz moderner Formensprache wirkt es, als sei es schon immer da gewesen. Rechts eine Holzterrasse mit Pool vor dem Haus.

La patine du béton confère à la maison son aspect un peu énigmatique. Bien que ses formes soient modernes, elle semble avoir toujours été là. À droite, une terrasse en bois et une piscine prolongent le séjour.

SEBASTIÁN IRARRÁZAVAL

Sebastián Irarrázaval Arquitectos
General John O'Brien 2458
Vitacura
Santiago
Chile

Tel: +56 2 245 6252
E-mail: sebastian@sebastianirarrazaval.com
Web: www.sebastianirarrazaval.com

SEBASTIÁN IRARRÁZAVAL was born in 1967. He studied architecture at the Universidad Católica in Santiago de Chile and at the Architectural Association in London. In 1993 he set up his own practice in Santiago. He has taught a design studio at the Universidad Católica since 1994. He has participated in the XV Chilean Architectural Biennial, Venice Biennale, and Shenzhen and Hong Kong Bi-City Biennial. His work includes the Reserva House (Santiago, 2006); Lira House (Santiago, 2007); Hotel Indigo Patagonia (Puerto Natales, 2007); Container House 1 (Santiago, 2009); modular spaces for earthquake victims (Retiro, 2010); the Cultural Center of the Embassy of Chile (Buenos Aires, Argentina, 2010); Design School and Institute of Urban Studies, Universidad Católica de Chile (Santiago, 2010); Caterpillar House (Santiago, 2011–12, published here); and Hotel Drake (Toronto, Canada, 2012), all in Chile unless stated otherwise.

SEBASTIÁN IRARRÁZAVAL, geboren 1967, studierte an der Universidad Católica in Santiago de Chile und der Architectural Association in London. 1993 gründete er sein Büro in Santiago. Seit 1994 leitet er Studioworkshops für Entwerfen an der Universidad Católica. Er war vertreten auf der XV. Chilenischen Architekturbiennale, der Biennale in Venedig und der Shenzhen and Hong Kong Bi-City Biennial. Zu seinen Projekten zählen das Haus Reserva (Santiago, 2006), das Haus Lira (Santiago, 2007), das Hotel Indigo Patagonia (Puerto Natales, 2007), das Container-Haus 1 (Santiago, 2009), Modulbauten für Erdbebenflüchtlinge (Retiro, 2010), das Kulturzentrum der Chilenischen Botschaft (Buenos Aires, Argentinien, 2010), das Institut für Entwerfen und das Institut für Urbanistik der Universidad Católica de Chile (Santiago, 2010), das Caterpillar-Haus (Santiago, 2011–12, hier vorgestellt) sowie das Hotel Drake (Toronto, Kanada, 2012), alle in Chile, sofern nicht anders vermerkt.

SEBASTIÁN IRARRÁZAVAL est né en 1967. Après avoir étudié l'architecture à l'Université catholique de Santiago de Chile et à l'Architectural Association de Londres, il a ouvert son agence à Santiago. Il enseigne un atelier de conception de l'Université catholique depuis 1994. Il a participé à la XVe Biennale d'architecture chilienne, à la Biennale de Venise et à la Biennale de Shenzhen et de Hong Kong Bi-City. Parmi ses réalisations, la plupart au Chili : la maison Reserva (Santiago, 2006) ; la maison Lira (Santiago, 2007) ; l'hôtel Indigo Patagonia (Puerto Natales, 2007) ; la Container House 1 (Santiago, 2009) ; des espaces modulaires pour les victimes d'un tremblement de terre (Retiro, 2010) ; le centre culturel de l'ambassade du Chili (Buenos Aires, Argentine, 2010) ; l'École de dessin et l'Institut d'études urbaines, Université catholique du Chili (Santiago, 2010) ; la maison Caterpillar (Santiago, 2011–12, publiée ici) et l'hôtel Drake (Toronto, 2012).

CATERPILLAR HOUSE

Santiago, Chile, 2011–12

Area: 320 m². Client: Ricardo Bezanilla Montes
Cost: $680 000. Collaboration: Eric Caro

This house was built for an art collector and his family with 12 standard used shipping containers of different sizes on a 900-square-meter site on the outskirts of Santiago. One of the 12-meter containers was used with an open top as a swimming pool. The site has a view of the Andes that the architect wished to take into account and he also sought to encourage natural airflows in order to avoid mechanical cooling. The house is integrated into a slope, which produces inclined interior spaces in the children's bedrooms, for example. A horizontal plane was created in the site with retaining walls, and the containers were put in place before being "wrapped," in order to unify their appearance but also to create "ventilated façades" that help to control interior temperatures. The architect states: "The material palette was chosen having in mind not only low-cost materials but low maintenance as well. In the choice of materials it was also important to analyze their capacity to age well and to incorporate passing time as something that adds value to materials."

Das Haus für einen Kunstsammler und seine Familie wurde aus zwölf alten Frachtcontainern unterschiedlicher Standardgrößen auf einem 900 m² großen Grundstück am Stadtrand von Santiago realisiert. Ein oben offener 12-m-Container dient als Swimmingpool. Der Architekt berücksichtigte den Blick auf die Anden und die Möglichkeiten natürlicher Durchlüftung, um auf Klimatechnik verzichten zu können. Das Haus wurde in den Hang integriert, wodurch sich etwa in den Kinderzimmern Schrägen ergaben. Durch Stützmauern entstanden horizontale Flächen, die Container selbst wurden vor Ort positioniert, bevor sie „ummantelt" wurden, um ein einheitliches Erscheinungsbild zu schaffen und „belüftete Fassaden" zu realisieren, die eine Temperierung des Innenraums ermöglichen. Die Architekten erklären: „Die Materialpalette ergab sich aus der Wahl kostengünstiger und pflegeleichter Baustoffe. Ein weiterer entscheidender Faktor bei der Wahl des Materials war es, eines zu finden, das gut altert und im Lauf der Zeit an Wert gewinnt."

Cette maison a été construite pour un collectionneur d'art et sa famille à l'aide de 12 conteneurs de récupération de différentes dimensions sur un terrain de 900 m² situé en banlieue de Santiago. Le site présente une vue sur les Andes que l'architecte a pris en compte, de même qu'il a cherché à favoriser la ventilation naturelle afin d'éviter toute climatisation mécanique. La maison est à flanc de coteau, ce qui explique l'inclinaison de certains volumes, telle que dans les chambres d'enfants. La terrasse horizontale bordée de murs de soutènement a d'abord été mise en place, puis les conteneurs montés avant d'être « enveloppés » pour unifier leur aspect mais aussi créer des « façades ventilées » contribuant à un meilleur contrôle de la température. « La palette des matériaux a été choisie en fonction à la fois de leur coût et de leur facilité de maintenance, explique l'architecte. Dans ce choix, il était également important d'analyser leur capacité au vieillissement en intégrant le passage du temps comme un élément qui leur donnera une valeur supplémentaire. » L'un des conteneurs de 12 m de long a été équipé d'un toit ouvrant et transformé en piscine.

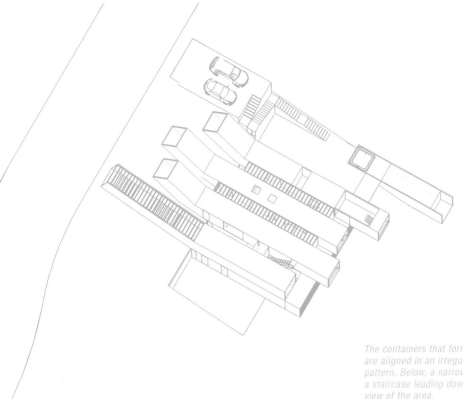

Die Container, aus denen das Haus besteht, sind parallel versetzt angeordnet. Unten ein schmaler Raum mit einer nach unten führenden Treppe; auf der linken Seite ein Blick ins Umland.

Les conteneurs de dimensions inégales qui constituent la maison sont parallèles. Ci-dessous, un volume étroit se termine par un escalier qui conduit au sous-sol. Page de gauche, une vue de l'environnement.

The containers that form the house are aligned in an irregular, parallel pattern. Below, a narrow interior with a staircase leading down; left page, a view of the area.

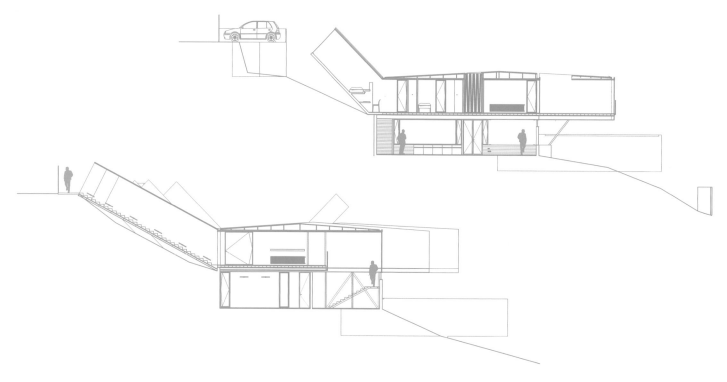

The kitchen is entirely glazed and opens onto a terrace. Section drawings show the angled elements, one of which has a stairway.

Die Küche ist vollständig verglast und öffnet sich zu einer Terrasse. Querschnitte zeigen die schräg positionierten Elemente; durch eines verläuft eine Treppe.

La cuisine entièrement vitrée ouvre sur une terrasse. Les coupes montrent les inclinaisons de certains éléments, dont l'un est une cage d'escalier.

There is an interesting alternation between the expected, industrial side of the house and the more refined, or "smooth" surfaces that are also part of its character.

Interessant ist der Wechsel zwischen der zu erwartenden industriellen Anmutung des Hauses und aufwendigeren, „glatteren" Oberflächen, die seinen Charakter ebenso prägen.

On note une opposition intéressante entre l'aspect industriel de la maison et le traitement plus raffiné et plus « lisse » de certaines surfaces qui lui donnent son caractère.

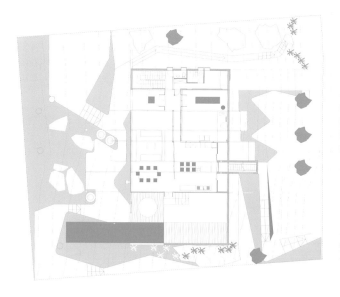
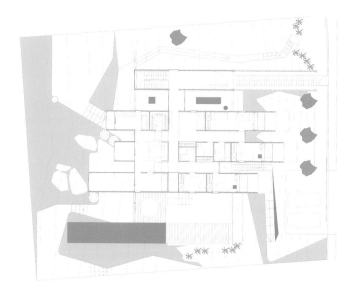

Above, plans of the house. Below, the bathroom has an old-style bathtub and fully exposed copper pipes.

Oben Grundrisse des Hauses. Unten ein Bad mit einer Wanne alten Stils und offen liegenden Kupferleitungen.

Ci-dessus, les plans de la maison. Ci-dessous, la salle de bains à baignoire à l'ancienne et aux arrivées d'eau en cuivre apparentes.

Large openings and white surfaces with black finishings give the interior a sophistication and lightness that might not be expected, given the use of containers as the basic construction element.

Großzügige Öffnungen und weiße Flächen mit schwarzen Details verleihen dem Interieur eine Hochwertigkeit und Helligkeit, die angesichts der Nutzung von Containern als zentralem Bauelement überraschen mag.

Les grandes ouvertures, les murs, blancs, les huisseries laquées noir apportent une sophistication et un sentiment de légèreté inattendus quand on sait que les éléments de base sont des conteneurs de transport.

RICK JOY

Rick Joy
400 South Rubio Avenue
Tucson, AZ 85701
USA

Tel: +1 520 624 1442
Fax: +1 520 791 0699
E-mail: studio@rickjoy.com
Web: www.rickjoy.com

RICK JOY was born in Dover-Foxcroft, Maine, in 1958. His first working experience was not as an architect, but as a musician and a carpenter in Maine. He obtained his degree in architecture in 1990, and spent three years in the office of Will Bruder, working on the design team for the Phoenix Central Library. He then set up his own practice in Tucson in 1993. The same year Joy received the Young Architects Award from Progressive Architecture magazine, and in 1994 an AIA Honor Award for Arizona Home of the Year. He received the 2002 American Academy of Arts and Letters Award in Architecture and in 2004 won the National Design Award from the Smithsonian Institute / Cooper-Hewitt Museum. Recent and current work of the firm includes Woodstock Farm Estate (Woodstock, Vermont, 2007–09, published here); Casa Ciprés (Key Biscayne, Florida, 2011); the Princeton University restaurant and café (Princeton, New Jersey, 2012–14); the Princeton train station and store (Princeton, New Jersey, 2012–14); a New York City loft (2010–); and El Sargento, a master plan and architecture for a family estate (El Sargento, Baja California, Mexico, 2011–), all in the USA unless stated otherwise.

RICK JOY wurde 1958 in Dover-Foxcroft, Maine, geboren. Er arbeitete zunächst nicht als Architekt, sondern als Musiker und Tischler in Maine. Sein Studienabschluss in Architektur folgte 1990; drei Jahre arbeitete er für Will Bruder im Planungsteam der Phoenix Central Library. 1993 gründete er sein eigenes Büro in Tucson. Im selben Jahr wurde er mit dem Young Architects Award der Zeitschrift *Progressive Architecture* ausgezeichnet; 1994 erhielt er den Ehrenpreis der AIA für das „Haus des Jahres in Arizona". 2002 folgte der Architekturpreis der Amerikanischen Akademie der Künste sowie 2004 der National Design Award des Smithsonian Institute/Cooper-Hewitt Museum. Jüngere und aktuelle Projekte des Büros sind die Woodstock Farm (Woodstock, Vermont, 2007–09, hier vorgestellt), ein Restaurant und Café für die Princeton University (Princeton, New Jersey, 2012–14), Bahnhof und Bahnhofsshop Princeton (Princeton, New Jersey, 2012–14), Casa Ciprés (Key Biscayne, Florida, 2011), ein Loft in New York City (seit 2010) sowie El Sargento, ein Masterplan und Bauten für ein Familiengut (El Sargento, Baja California, Mexiko, seit 2011), alle in den USA, sofern nicht anders angegeben.

RICK JOY est né à Dober-Foxcroft (Maine) en 1958. Il a débuté non pas comme architecte mais comme menuisier et musicien. Diplômé en architecte en 1990, il a travaillé pendant trois ans chez Will Bruder, en particulier dans l'équipe chargée du projet de la bibliothèque centrale de Phoenix. Il a ensuite ouvert son agence à Tucson en 1993. La même année, il a reçu le prix jeunes architectes du magazine *Progressive Architecture* ; un prix d'honneur de l'AIA pour la maison de l'année 1994 en Arizona ; le prix d'architecture de l'American Academy of Arts and Letters en 2002 et, en 2004, le prix national de conception du Smithsonian Institute/Cooper-Hewitt Museum. Parmi ses réalisations récentes ou en cours : le Woodstock Farm Estate (Woodstock Vermont, 2007–09, publiée ici) : le Princeton University Restaurant and Café (Princeton, New Jersey, 2012–14) ; la gare ferroviaire et magasin de Princeton (Princeton, New Jersey, 2012–14) ; la Casa Ciprés (Key Biscayne, Floride, 2011) ; un loft à New York (2010–) et El Sargento, plan directeur et projet d'architecture pour un domaine familial (El Sargento, Basse-Californie, Mexique, 2011–).

WOODSTOCK FARM ESTATE

Woodstock, Vermont, USA, 2007–09

Area: 358 m² (main house); 209 m² (barn); 249 m² (porch/deck)
Client: Paul Palandjian and family. Cost: not disclosed
Collaboration: Dale Rush (Project Architect), Nicolas Norero, Klara Valent

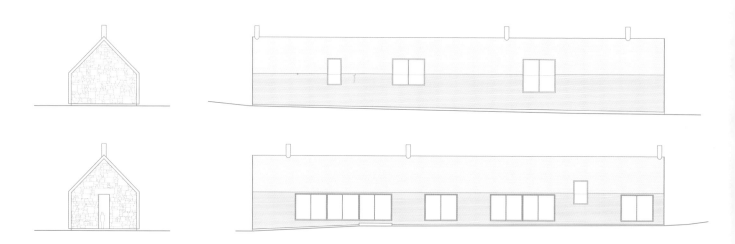

Above, elevations of the house, and an image of the structure seen in its rural setting in Vermont.

Oben Aufrisse des Hauses und eine Aufnahme der Anlage inmitten seiner ländlichen Umgebung in Vermont.

Ci-dessus, quatre élévations de la maison et une image de la « ferme » dans le cadre rural du Vermont.

Left, a site plan with the pond at the center. Above, a photo showing the house in the background and a typical rural barn in the foreground.

Links ein Lageplan mit dem See in der Mitte. Die Aufnahme oben zeigt das Haus im Hintergrund und eine typische Scheune im Vordergrund.

À gauche, un plan du terrain montrant un étang en son centre. Ci-dessus, une vue de la maison avec, au premier plan, une vieille grange traditionnelle.

Located on the site of a previous farmhouse, this residence and barn were built in a valley of the Green Mountains in Vermont. The house, states the architect, "is a simple elongated stone-ended gable with major view orientation to the fields and pond to the north and large notched openings to the south that allow filtered light and shadows through the trees." The interior walls of the house are clad in vertical narrow spruce boards. The two-story barn is aligned on a pond and contains a guest "bunkhouse" upstairs and a garage and enclosed basketball court on the ground level. Referring to both structures, the architect explains: "Each are constructed of primary steel post-and-beam bents supporting a structural insulated panel system skin which is clad on the exterior with flush detailed cedar shingles." The overall project succeeds in providing considerable comfort within forms that are inspired by the rural setting.

Auf dem Grundstück eines früheren Farmhauses entstand in einem Tal der Green Mountains in Vermont ein neues Wohnhaus mit Scheune. Das Haus, so der Architekt, „ist ein schlichter gestreckter Giebelbau, nach Norden mit gemauerter Stirnseite und betonter Orientierung zu den Feldern und einem kleinen See sowie nach Süden mit eingeschnittenen Fensteröffnungen und Bäumen, durch die gefiltertes Licht und Schattenspiele einfallen". Die Innenwände des Wohnhauses wurden mit vertikalen Fichtenbrettern vertäfelt. Die zweistöckige Scheune orientiert sich zum See. Hier gibt es im Obergeschoss ein „Bettenlager" für Gäste, im Erdgeschoss ist Platz für eine Garage und einen Basketballcourt. Der Architekt erklärt: „Beide Bauten wurden als Stahlfachwerk errichtet, das ein Gebäudehautsystem aus gedämmten Paneelen stützt, das außen mit bündig liegenden Zedernschindeln verblendet wurde." Als Gesamtensemble überzeugt das Projekt durch seinen beträchtlichen Komfort und eine Formensprache, die von der ländlichen Umgebung inspiriert ist.

Construite sur le site d'une ancienne ferme, cette résidence et sa grange annexe se trouvent dans une vallée des Green Mountains dans l'État du Vermont. La maison, expliquent l'architecte « est un simple pignon de pierre en projection, essentiellement orienté vers les prés et un étang au nord et ouvert au sud par de grandes découpes vitrées qui laissent passer une lumière filtrée par des arbres et leur ombre ». À l'intérieur, les murs sont habillés d'étroites lattes verticales d'épicéa. De deux niveaux, la grange se dresse dans l'axe d'un étang et contient au rez-de-chaussée un garage et un terrain de basketball et à l'étage un « baraquement » qui sert de chambre d'amis. « Chaque [structure] est constituée de portiques à piliers et poutres d'acier soutenant une peau structurelle isolante en panneaux habillés à l'extérieur de shingles de cèdre posés à vif », explique l'architecte. Le projet réussit à offrir un remarquable confort dans des formes inspirées de son cadre rural.

The "elongated barn" design of the house, which is clad in cedar shingles, is clearly visible in the image above.

Oben ist das Gestaltungsprinzip des Baus als „lange Scheune" deutlich zu erkennen. Das Haus ist mit Zedernholzschindeln verblendet.

La maison a été conçue comme une « grange allongée ». Elle est parée de shingles de cèdre.

The stone end of the gabled house
directly recalls local architecture,
though the elongated form of the
residence is an extrapolation of this
vernacular genre.

*Die gemauerte Stirnseite des Giebel-
baus knüpft an lokale Bauweisen an,
auch wenn die überlange Hausform
eine Abwandlung der üblichen Form
ist.*

*Le pignon de pierre rappelle nette-
ment l'architecture locale, de même
que la forme allongée de la maison
est l'extrapolation d'un type
constructif vernaculaire.*

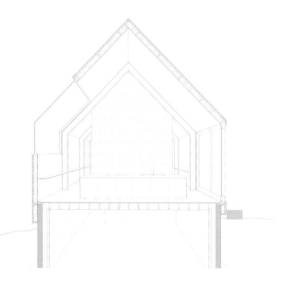

The interior of the house is bright and has a full-height ceiling in the living area, seen above. Below, a site plan, with the house at the bottom of the page, and the barn to its right.

Das Interieur des Hauses ist hell; der Wohnbereich hat einen offenen Giebel (oben). Unten ein Lageplan mit dem Wohnhaus unten und der Scheune rechts davon.

L'intérieur de la maison est lumineux. Le séjour bénéficie d'un plafond cathédrale (ci-dessus). Ci-dessous, plan au sol de la maison, en bas, et de la grange, à droite.

The stone end of the house provides
a variation in surface treatment, with
a fireplace inserted into its mass. The
bedroom has a bathtub to the right of
the bed.

Die gemauerte Stirnwand des Hauses – mit integriertem Kamin – sorgt
für Abwechslung in der Oberflächen-
behandlung. In dem Schlafzimmer
steht die Badewanne rechts neben
dem Bett.

Côté intérieur, le pignon en pierre
apporte une texture différente. Une
cheminée a été insérée dans son
épaisseur. La chambre dispose d'une
baignoire à droite du lit.

MATHIAS KLOTZ

Mathias Klotz
Los Colonos 0411
Providencia
Santiago 753 0115
Chile

Tel: +56 2 233 6613 / Fax: +56 2 232 2479
E-mail: estudio@mathiasklotz.com
Web: www.mathiasklotz.com

MATHIAS KLOTZ was born in 1965 in Viña del Mar, Chile. He received his architecture degree from the Pontificia Universidad Católica de Chile in 1991. He created his own office in Santiago the same year. He has taught at several Chilean universities and was Director of the School of Architecture of the Universidad Diego Portales in Santiago (2001–03) and Dean since 2004. Recent work includes the Casa Viejo (Santiago, 2001); the Smol Building (Concepción, 2001); 20 one-family houses in La Dehesa (Santiago, 2003); the Faculty of Health, Universidad Diego Portales (Santiago, 2004); the remodeling of the Cerra San Luis House (Santiago, 2004); the Ocho al Cubo House (Marbella, Zapallar, 2005); La Roca House (Punta del Este, Uruguay, 2006); the Techos House (Nahuel Huapi Lake, Patagonia, Argentina, 2006–07); the 11 Mujeres House (Cachagua, 2007); Raul House (Aculeo, 2007, published here); Bitran House (Cachagua, 2010, also published here); Casa L (Buenos Aires, Argentina, 2011); and the Buildings Department San Isidro (Buenos Aires, Argentina, 2011–12). Ongoing projects include the H Building and the O Building in Zhendong (China); the Oriencoop Office Building (Talca); and Social Housing (Requinoa), all in Chile unless stated otherwise. Mathias Klotz has received numerous awards for sustainable design including 2010 Green Good Design awards for La Roca House and the Nicanor Para Library of the Diego Portales University (Santiago, 2010–11), as well as a 2011 Holcim Award for the same building.

MATHIAS KLOTZ wurde 1965 in Viña del Mar in Chile geboren. Er schloss sein Architekturstudium 1991 an der Pontificia Universidad Católica de Chile ab. Sein Büro gründete er im gleichen Jahr in Santiago. Klotz lehrte an verschiedenen Universitäten Chiles und war Direktor der Architekturfakultät der Universidad Diego Portales in Santiago (2001–03), wo er seit 2004 Dekan ist. Zu seinen neueren Projekten zählen u. a. die Casa Viejo (Santiago, 2001), das Geschäftszentrum Smol (Concepción, 2001), 20 Einfamilienhäuser in La Dehesa (Santiago, 2003), die Fakultät für Medizin an der Universidad Diego Portales (Santiago, 2004), der Umbau des Hauses Cerra San Luis (Santiago, 2004), die Casa Ocho al Cubo (Marbella, Zapallar, 2005), das Haus La Roca (Punta del Este, Uruguay, 2006), das Haus Techos (Nahuel-Huapi-See, Patagonien, Argentinien, 2006–07), das Haus 11 Mujeres (Cachagua, 2007), das Haus Raul (Aculeo, 2007, hier vorgestellt), das Haus Bitran (Cachagua, 2010, ebenfalls hier vorgestellt), die Casa L (Buenos Aires, Argentinien, 2011) sowie die Baubehörde in San Isidro (Buenos Aires, Argentinen, 2011–12). Laufende Projekte sind u. a. die Gebäude H und O in Zhendong (China), das Bürogebäude Oriencoop (Talca) sowie Sozialwohnungen in Requinoa, alle in Chile, sofern nicht anders vermerkt. Für seine nachhaltige Architektur wurde Mathias Klotz mit zahlreichen Preisen ausgezeichnet, darunter 2010 mit dem Preis für Green Good Design für das Haus La Roca und die Bibliothek Nicanor Parra an der Universidad Diego Portales (Santiago, 2010–11) sowie 2011 mit einem Holcim Award für dasselbe Projekt.

MATHIAS KLOTZ, né en 1965 à Viña del Mar au Chili, est architecte diplômé de l'Université catholique du Chili(1991). Il a fondé son agence à Santiago la même année. Il a enseigné dans plusieurs universités chiliennes et a été directeur de l'École d'architecture de l'université Diego Portales à Santiago (2001–03) dont il est doyen depuis 2004. Parmi ses réalisations, la plupart au Chili, figurent : la Casa Viejo (Santiago, 2001) ; l'immeuble Smol (Concepción, 2001) ; 20 maisons unifamilales à La Dehesa (Santiago, 2003) ; la faculté de la Santé de l'Universidad Diego Portales (Santiago, 2004) ; le remodelage de la maison Cerra San Luis (Santiago, 2004) ; la maison Ocho al Cubo (Marbella, Zapallar, 2005) ; la maison Roca (Punta del Este, Uruguay, 2006) ; la maison Techos (lac de Nahuel Huapi, Patagonie, Argentine, 2006–07) ; la maison des 11 Mujeres (Cachagua, Chili, 2007) ; la maison Raul (Aculeo, 2007, publiée ici) ; la maison Bitran (Cachagua, 2010, publiée ici) ; la Casa L (Buenos Aires, Argentine, 2011) et l'immeuble du département de la Construction San Isidro (Buenos Aires, Argentine, 2011–12). Plus récemment, il est l'auteur des immeubles H et O à Zhendong (Chine) ; de l'immeuble de bureaux Oriencoop (Talca) et de logements sociaux (Requinoa). Mathias Klotz a reçu de nombreuses distinctions dans le domaine de la conception durable dont le prix Green Good Design 2010 pour la maison La Roca et la bibliothèque Nicanor Para de l'université Diego Portales (Santiago, 2010–11) ainsi que le prix Holcim 2011 pour ce même projet.

RAUL HOUSE
Aculeo, Chile, 2007

*Area: 180 m². Client: not disclosed
Cost: not disclosed. Collaboration: Magdalena Bernstein*

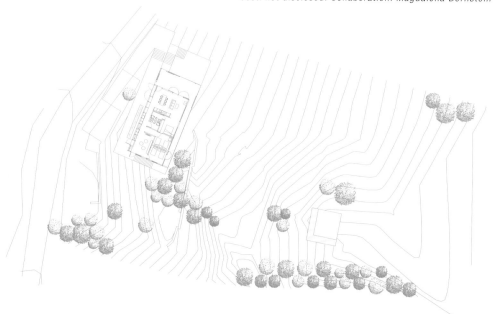

A site plan to the left and, below, a view of the sheltered, exterior terrace of the house.

Links ein Lageplan, unten ein Blick auf die geschützte Außenterrasse des Hauses.

À gauche, un plan du site et ci-dessous, une vue de la terrasse abritée.

Elevation drawings and a photo (above) show the way in which the rectangular volume of the house is perched on a steep slope and is held in place by angled supports.

Aufrisse und ein Foto (oben) veranschaulichen, wie der rechteckige Baukörper auf einem Steilhang sitzt und von schrägen Stützen gehalten wird.

L'élévation et la photographie ci-dessus montrent la façon dont la maison de plan rectangulaire est soutenue par des piliers inclinés et perchée au-dessus d'une pente abrupte.

This weekend house is located on a steep site in the mountains near the Aculeo Lagoon, about 60 kilometers from the Chilean capital. The design involves a continuous white interior space on a single level. White was chosen to increase luminosity inside the house, just as the exterior coloring is dark in order to allow the architecture to "merge" into the landscape. The architect explains: "Since cost was a relevant point that influenced the design and construction process, the challenge was to develop an interesting project only with basic materials and technology. The structure is a combination of concrete pillars for the base, and steel and wood structure for the rest."

Das Wochenendhaus liegt in den Bergen unweit der Lagune Aculeo, rund 60 km von der chilenischen Hauptstadt entfernt, auf einem steilen Hanggrundstück und ist als durchgängiger weißer, eingeschossiger Raum konzipiert. Weiß lässt den Innenraum heller wirken; die Farbgebung des Außenbaus ist nach demselben Prinzip dunkel gewählt und lässt den Bau mit der Landschaft „verschmelzen". Der Architekt erklärt: „Da Kosten ein entscheidendes Kriterium waren und Entwurf und Konstruktionsprozess beeinflussten, bestand die Herausforderung darin, mit einfachen Materialien und Techniken ein interessantes Projekt zu entwickeln. Der Bau ist eine Kombination aus einem Unterbau aus Betonpfeilern und einer Stahl- und Holzkonstruktion für die übrigen Bereiche."

Cette résidence de week-end a été édifiée sur un terrain escarpé dans les montagnes qui entourent le lagon d'Aculeo à 60 km environ de la capitale chilienne. Le projet consiste en un unique volume blanc d'un seul niveau. Si le blanc a été choisi pour rendre l'intérieur plus lumineux, les façades sont de couleur sombre pour mieux se fondre dans le paysage. «Le coût était un problème important qui a influencé les plans et leur réalisation, explique l'architecte. Notre défi était de mettre au point un projet intéressant uniquement à partir de matériaux et de technologies basiques. La structure combine des piliers en béton pour le socle et une construction en bois et acier pour le reste.»

Unpainted wood and colors that range from beige to white mark the interior of the house, whose broad glazing allows in ample natural light.

Unlackiertes Holz und ein Farbspektrum von Beige bis Weiß bestimmen das Interieur. Die großzügige Verglasung lässt reichlich Tageslicht ins Haus.

Le bois naturel et une palette de couleurs qui vont du blanc au beige caractérisent l'intérieur de cette maison dont les vastes baies laissent entrer des flots de lumière.

An elevation drawing shows how the house is supported on its sloped site. Above, the dining area, with the living space (also seen left) and the view from the house in the background.

Ein Aufriss zeigt, wie das Haus im Hang verankert ist. Oben ein Blick in den Ess- und Wohnbereich (auch links im Bild) und auf die Aussicht im Hintergrund.

L'élévation montre les colonnes soutenant la maison. Ci-dessus, le coin des repas, le séjour (également à gauche) et la vue de la maison donnant sur le lagon.

BITRAN HOUSE

Cachagua, Chile, 2010

Area: 350 m². Client: not disclosed
Cost: not disclosed. Collaboration: Baltazar Sanchez

This is another weekend residence, built with concrete, stone, and wood on a steep slope above the beach of Cachagua. Public areas of the house are conceived as a large terrace space with spectacular views. Bedrooms are on the lower level providing more privacy. With more than half the lower volume set below grade, skylights are used to bring natural light into the space. The roof of the house is conceived as a "lookout." The architect explains: "To achieve the atmosphere of outdoor life, in which the boundaries between interior and exterior are diluted, we made a number of sliding elements among which are both large panes of windows and the wall separating the kitchen/dining room."

Ein weiteres Wochenendhaus aus Beton, Stein und Holz liegt an einem steilen Abhang über dem Strand von Cachagua. Die öffentlichen Bereiche wurden als große Terrasse mit spektakulärer Aussicht konzipiert. Die Schlafzimmer der unteren Ebene bieten deutlich mehr Privatsphäre. Da mehr als die Hälfte der unteren Ebenen unter Bodenniveau liegen, lassen Oberlichter Tageslicht in die Räume. Das Dach des Hauses wurde als „Ausguck" konzipiert. Der Architekt erklärt: „Um eine Freiluftatmosphäre zu schaffen, in der die Grenzen zwischen Innen- und Außenraum verschwimmen, planten wir eine Reihe von Schiebeelementen, darunter großflächige Fenster und die Wand zwischen Küche und Essbereich."

Cette maison de week-end en béton, pierre et bois, s'élève sur un terrain en pente raide au-dessus de la plage de Cachagua. Les parties communes de la maison sont conçues comme de vastes terrasses bénéficiant de vues spectaculaires. Les chambres situées au niveau inférieur offrent davantage d'intimité. Comme plus de la moitié du volume est enterré, des verrières zénithales ont été mises en place. Le toit de la maison est un belvédère. «Pour obtenir cette atmosphère de vie en plein air dans laquelle les frontières entre l'intérieur et l'extérieur se dissolvent, explique l'architecte, nous avons dessiné un certain nombre d'éléments coulissants dont de grandes baies et le mur séparant la partie cuisine-salle à manger. »

Built on a sloped site above the beach, the upper level of the house assumes a U-shaped form, with its concrete surfaces wrapping around the living space.

In der oberen Zone des Hauses, das auf einem Hanggrundstück oberhalb des Strands steht, umgeben Betonflächen in der Form eines u den Wohnraum.

La maison est édifiée sur un terrain escarpé dominant une plage, Le niveau supérieur est en forme de U et le séjour est protégé par des écrans de béton.

Seen from the entrance with the
beach below, the house expresses an
obvious lightness highlighted by large
glazed surfaces. Below, an elevation
showing the slope in the setting.

Ein Blick auf das Haus vom Eingang
her mit dem daruntergelegenen
Strand. Die Leichtigkeit des Baus wird
durch die großflächige Verglasung
betont. Unten ein Aufriss des
abschüssigen Grundstücks.

Vue de l'entrée avec la plage en
contrebas, la maison semble d'une
grande légèreté, impression que renforce l'omniprésence de baies vitrées.
Ci-dessous, élévation montrant la
maison dans la pente.

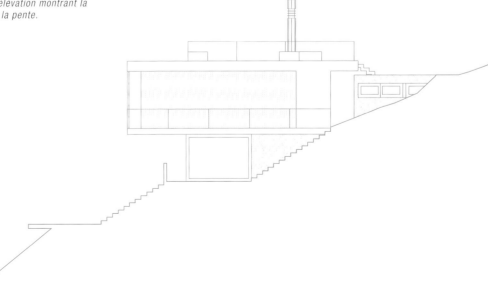

Interior surfaces in wood and stone contrast with the gray concrete tones of the exterior. Below, spectacular views from a bedroom and the terrace.

Die Holz- und Steinflächen des Interieurs kontrastieren mit den Grautönen der Betonfassade. Unten spektakuläre Ausblicke aus einem Schlafzimmer und von der Terrasse.

Le traitement des plans intérieurs en bois ou en pierre contraste avec le béton gris des façades extérieures. Ci-dessous, vue spectaculaire prise d'une des chambres et de la terrasse.

The house has a small pool above the beach and various terraces that are either sheltered by the house itself, or exposed.

Zum Haus gehören ein kleiner Pool über dem Strand sowie mehrere Terrassen, teils geschützt durch das Haus, teils unter freiem Himmel.

La maison possède une petite piscine au-dessus de la plage et diverses terrasses soit protégées, soit ouvertes.

LUSSI + HALTER

Lussi+Halter Partner AG
Neustadt Str. 3
6003 Lucerne
Switzerland

Tel: +41 41 226 16 26
Fax: +41 41 226 16 27
E-mail: info@lussi-halter.ch
Web: www.lussi-halter.ch

THOMAS LUSSI was born in 1961 in Sursee, Switzerland. He obtained his Diploma in Architecture from the ETH (Zurich, 1981–87) and then worked in the offices of S. Gmür (Basel, 1987–90) and E. Bonell, J.-M. Gil (Barcelona (1990–92), before creating his own office in 1992. Starting in 1999 he became a partner in the firm Lussi+Halter in Lucerne. **REMO HALTER** was born in 1964 in Lucerne, Switzerland. He also studied architecture at the ETH (1987–91) before working with Rüssli Architekten (Lucerne, 1991–95). He created his own office in 1995 and has been a partner in Lussi+Halter since 1999. Their recent projects include the Twin Houses in Kastanienbaum (2011, published here); Citybay, a group of 148 apartments, stores, and offices in Lucerne (2011); a 24-apartment complex with stores for the Raiffeisen Bank (Näfels, 2012); and the ongoing SBB Swiss Railways Headquarters (Berne Wankdorf, 2014), all in Switzerland.

THOMAS LUSSI wurde 1961 in Sursee in der Schweiz geboren. Er erlangte sein Architekturdiplom an der ETH Zürich (1981–87) und arbeitete anschließend für S. Gmür (Basel, 1987–90) und E. Bonell, J.-M. Gil (Barcelona, 1990–92), ehe er 1992 sein eigenes Büro gründete. Seit 1999 ist er Partner bei Lussi+Halter in Luzern. **REMO HALTER** wurde 1964 in Luzern in der Schweiz geboren. Auch er studierte Architektur an der ETH Zürich (1987–91) und arbeitete anschließend bei Rüssli Architekten (Luzern, 1991–95). 1995 gründete er sein eigenes Büro, seit 1999 ist er Partner bei Lussi+Halter. Zu ihren jüngeren Projekte zählen die Twin Houses in Kastanienbaum (2011, hier vorgestellt), Citybay, ein Ensemble mit 148 Wohnungen, Geschäften und Büros in Luzern (2011), ein Komplex mit 24 Wohnungen und Geschäften für die Raiffeisen-Bank (Näfels, 2012) sowie die Zentrale für die Schweizerischen Bundesbahnen SBB (Bern-Wankdorf, 2014), alle in der Schweiz.

THOMAS LUSSI, né en 1961 à Sursee (Suisse), est diplômé en architecture de l'ETH (Zurich, 1981–87). Il a travaillé dans les agences de S. Gmür (Bâle, 1987–90) et E. Bonell, J.-M. Gil (Barcelone, 1990–92) avant de fonder son agence en 1992, puis de créer Lussi+Halter à Lucerne en 1999. **REMO HALTER**, né en 1964 à Lucerne (Suisse) a également étudié l'architecture à l'ETH de Zurich (1987–91) et a travaillé chez Rüssli Architekten (Lucerne, 1991–95). Il a fondé sa propre agence en 1995, puis Lussi+Halter en 1999. Parmi leurs projets récents, tous en Suisse : les maisons jumelles de Kastanienbaum (2011, publiées ici) ; Citybay, un ensemble de 148 appartements, commerces et bureaux à Lucerne (2011) ; un immeuble de 24 appartements et commerces pour la Raiffeisen Bank (Näfels, 2012) et le siège des Chemins de fers fédéraux suisses SBB (Berne Wankdorf, 2014).

TWIN HOUSES
Kastanienbaum, Switzerland, 2011

Area: 509 m². Client: not disclosed
Cost: not disclosed. Collaboration: Koepfli Partner (Landscape Architect)

These semidetached houses are located on the shores of the lake of Lucerne. The construction is set in a wooded area "in such a way that only a minimum of the existing terrain is taken for the actual building. From a concrete deck, a ramp ushers you to the building where a concrete overhang defines the veranda area; from there, a wide stairway leads into the forest." A glass façade at ground level further emphasizes the rapport of the architecture with its environment. Terraces on the upper levels and an "introverted inner courtyard" provide ample contact with the open air. Only three basic materials are used for the buildings: black-toned structural concrete visible in the walls and ceilings, a hard redwood from Brazil (Jatobá) for the floors and undersides of the upper terraces, and anthracite-colored woodwork in the kitchens, for example. The architects state: "Timeless architecture reaching beyond any momentary trends or unnecessary gimmicky shapes and forms—these are the aspirations we had in mind when conceiving the Kastanienbaum **TWIN HOUSES**."

Das Doppelhaus liegt am Ufer des Vierwaldstätter Sees und wurde in die waldige Umgebung integriert, „um nur ein Minimum des bestehenden Terrains zu überbauen. Erschlossen wird der Bau über eine erhöhte Terrasse aus Beton sowie eine Rampe. Auf dem auskragenden Gebäudeteil liegt eine Dachterrasse, von hier aus führt eine breite Treppe in den Wald". Die Verglasung der Fassade im Erdgeschoss unterstreicht den Bezug der Architektur zur Umgebung. Loggien und Terrassen in den oberen Etagen und ein „introvertierter Innenhof" bieten reichlich Gelegenheit zum Aufenthalt an der frischen Luft. Für den Bau kamen nur drei Basismaterialien zum Einsatz: schwarzer Sichtbeton für Wände und Decken, rotes Jatobá-Hartholz aus Brasilien für die Böden und die Unterseiten der Terrassen sowie anthrazit gebeizte Holzeinbauten, etwa in den Küchen. Die Architekten erklären: „Zeitlose Architektur, jenseits kurzlebiger Trends oder überflüssiger effekthascherischer Formen – das war es, was uns vorschwebte, als wir die **TWIN HOUSES** in Kastanienbaum entwarfen."

Ces deux maisons semi-détachées sont implantées sur une rive du lac des Quatre-Cantons, dans un site boisé « de telle façon que le minimum de terrain a été utilisé pour la construction. D'une terrasse en béton, une rampe conduit aux maisons où un porte-à-faux en béton définit une zone de véranda ; de là un large escalier mène à la forêt ». Au rez-de-chaussée, la façade vitrée renforce le lien entre l'architecture et son environnement. Les terrasses des niveaux supérieurs et la « cour intérieure introvertie » favorisent le contact avec l'air et la nature. Trois matériaux de base ont été utilisés seulement : un béton structurel noir pour les murs et les plafonds, un bois dur rouge du Brésil (jatoba) pour les sols et les sous-faces des terrasses supérieures et un bois teinté anthracite, entre autres dans les cuisines. « Une architecture intemporelle, au-delà des tendances momentanées ou des formes de gadgets inutiles, telle était notre aspiration lorsque nous avons conçu les **MAISONS JUMELLES** de Kastanienbaum », a précisé l'architecte.

The contrast between black structural concrete employed and the reddish Brazilian wood is striking. Despite its mass, the structure appears to sit lightly on the earth.

Der Kontrast zwischen schwarzem Beton und rötlichem brasilianischem Holz ist beeindruckend. Trotz seiner Masse scheint der Bau ganz leicht auf dem Baugrund zu ruhen.

Le contraste entre le béton structurel noir et le bois du Brésil de couleur rouge est frappant. Malgré sa masse, la maison semble tout juste reposer sur le sol.

The architects refer to the forest
atmosphere that they have retained
all around the Twin Houses. Above, a
suspended concrete stairway and a
covered path.

Die Architekten beziehen sich auf die
Waldatmosphäre, die sie um die Twin
Houses herum erhalten haben. Oben
eine Betontreppe und ein überdachter
Weg.

Les architectes évoquent l'atmosphère de forêt qu'ils ont voulu
conserver autour des maisons
jumelles. Ci-dessus, un escalier suspendu et un passage couvert.

A site plan shows the proximity of numerous trees. Below, a hot tub on the roof of the Twin Houses.

Ein Lageplan zeigt die vielen Bäume in der direkten Nachbarschaft. Unten ein Whirlpool auf dem Dach der Twin Houses.

Le plan du terrain montre la présence de nombreux arbres. Ci-dessous un jacuzzi installé sur le toit des maisons jumelles.

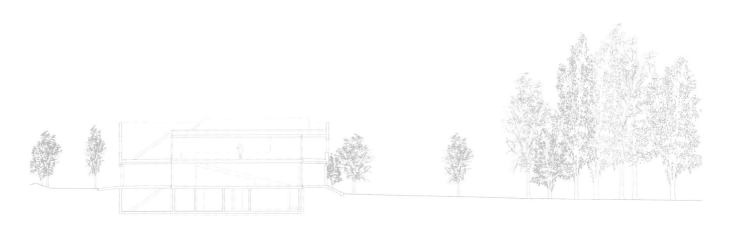

Left page, ramps are used to connect levels in the house—as seen also in the section drawing above. Right, a dining area and, above, a bedroom and terrace with a view of the natural setting.

Rampen verbinden die Ebenen des Hauses (linke Seite), wie auch der Aufriss oben zeigt. Rechts ein Essbereich sowie oben ein Schlafzimmer und eine Loggia mit Blick in die Landschaft.

Page de gauche : les différents niveaux sont connectés par des rampes, comme le montre le dessin de coupe ci-dessus. À droite, un coin repas, et au-dessus, une chambre et une terrasse donnant sur le cadre naturel extérieur.

MADA S.P.A.M.

MADA s.p.a.m.
No. 2, Lane 134, Xinle Road
Xuhui District
Shanghai 200031
China

Tel: +86 21 5404 1166
Fax: +86 21 5404 6646
E-mail: office@madaspam.com
Web: www.madaspam.com

MA QINGYUN graduated from Tsinghua University with a degree in Civil Engineering and Architecture in 1988. He worked briefly in a government historic preservation and urban planning office, before attending the Graduate School of Fine Art at the University of Pennsylvania. He obtained his M.Arch there in 1991. He then worked in the office of KPF in New York (1991–95), before establishing MADA s.p.a.m. (for strategy, planning, architecture, and media) in Shanghai. The firm now also has offices in Xi'an, China, and Pasadena, USA. Since 2006, Ma Qingyun has been the Dean of the School of Architecture at the University of Southern California. The firm's projects include the Ningbo Culture Center (Ningbo, 2000); their own offices in Shanghai (2003–04); Father's House (Xi'an, 2004); Chunshen Floating Street (Shanghai, 2005); Xi'an TV Media Center (2005); and Ningbo Y-Town (Ningbo, 2001–06). More recent work includes the Xi'an Chanba Horticultural Exposition Garden VIP Resort (Xi'an, 2009); Asian Pacific Museum (Pasadena, California, USA, 2009); Glen Oaks Residence (Pasadena, California, USA, 2009–11, published here); and the Luneng International Exchange Center (Beijing, 2013), all in China unless stated otherwise.

MA QINGYUN schloss sein Studium 1988 an der Tsinghua University mit einem Diplom in Bauingenieurwesen und Architektur ab. Er arbeitete zunächst in einem Regierungsbüro für Denkmalschutz und Stadtplanung, ehe er an der University of Pennsylvania ein Studium an der Graduate School of Fine Art aufnahm. Dieses schloss er 1991 mit einem M.Arch. ab. Er arbeitete für KPF in New York (1991–95) und gründete anschließend sein Büro MADA s.p.a.m. (kurz für „strategy, planning, architecture, and media") in Schanghai. Das Büro hat inzwischen Niederlassungen in Xi'an, China, und Pasadena, USA. Seit 2006 ist Ma Qingyun Dekan an der Fakultät für Architektur an der University of Southern California. Zu seinen Projekten zählen das Kulturzentrum Ningbo (Ningbo, 2000), das eigene Büro in Schanghai (2003–04), das Father's House (Xi'an, 2004), Chunshen Floating Street (Schanghai, 2005), das Xi'an TV Media Center (2005) und die Ningbo Y-Town (Ningbo, 2001–06). Jüngere Entwürfe sind der VIP Resort der Gartenausstellung Xi'an Chanba (Xi'an, 2009), das Asian Pacific Museum (Pasadena, Kalifornien, USA, 2009), die Glen Oaks Residence (Pasadena, 2009–11, hier vorgestellt) sowie das Luneng International Exchange Center (Peking, 2013), alle in China, sofern nicht anders vermerkt.

MA QINGYUN est diplômé en ingénierie civile et architecture de l'université de Tsinghua (1988). Il a brièvement travaillé dans une agence gouvernementale de conservation historique et d'urbanisme avant d'étudier à l'École supérieure des beaux-arts de l'université de Pennsylvanie où il a obtenu son diplôme de M.Arch. en 1991. Il a ensuite travaillé pour l'agence KPF à New York (1991–95) avant de créer MADA s.p.a.m. (stratégie, programmation, architecture et médias) à Shanghai. L'agence possède aujourd'hui des bureaux à Xi'An (Chine) et à Pasadena (États-Unis). Depuis 2006, Ma Qingyun est doyen de l'école d'architecture de l'USC (University of Southern California). Parmi les réalisations de l'agence : le Centre culturel de Ningbo (Ningbo, 2001–06), leurs bureaux à Shanghai (2003–04) ; la Father's House (Xi'an, 2004) ; Chunshen Floating Street (Shanghai, 2005) ; le Xi'an TV Media Center (2005) et le Ningbo Y-Town (Ningbo, 2001–06). Plus récemment, elles comprennent : le jardin-exposition d'horticulture et hôtel VIP de Xi'an (Xi'an, 2009) ; l'Asian Pacific Museum (Pasadena, Californie, 2009) ; la résidence Glen Oaks (Pasadena, Californie, 2009–11, publiée ici) et le Centre d'échanges internationaux de Luneng (Pékin, 2013).

GLEN OAKS RESIDENCE

Pasadena, California, USA, 2009–11

Address: 1133 Glen Oaks Boulevard, Pasadena, California 91101, USA
Area: 340 m². Client: Ma Qingyun. Cost: $1.5 million

This project involves an addition to a mid-20th-century Pasadena house. The architect writes: "The addition completely reconfigures and redefines the original home, enhancing its functional capabilities threefold, now to include a family home, office, and gallery. From a minimal, single-story plan, a three-story, semi-public structure emerges: deep purple, organic, and alien. A new identity surfaces to defy the conservative, at times complacent, profile of the neighborhood." With its purple "shotcrete" exterior the structure includes a double-height "public" gallery, kitchen, study, and third-floor dance studio for Ma's wife, Shouning Li. The architect explains that the project represents "the intersection of careful analysis of the needs of the Ma family with the challenges of breaking free from the conventional, mid-century Californian home. Through the utilization of a ramped circulation, the old single-story house is seamlessly fused with the new three-story addition. The expansion allows for aggressive growth in program and function to meet the lifestyle of the family of four."

Das Projekt in Pasadena ist ein Anbau an ein Haus aus der Mitte des 20. Jahrhunderts. Der Architekt schreibt: „Die Erweiterung konfiguriert und definiert den älteren Bau von Grund auf neu und optimiert seine Funktionalität in dreifacher Hinsicht: Sie umfasst das Haus für die Familie, ein Büro und eine Galerie. Über einem minimalistischen eingeschossigen Sockel wächst ein dreistöckiger, halb öffentlicher Bau empor: dunkelviolett, organisch, fremdartig. Eine neuartige Präsenz entsteht, die dem konservativen, mitunter selbstgefälligen Viertel trotzt." Der Bau mit einer violetten Fassade aus Spritzbeton umfasst eine doppelgeschossige „öffentliche" Galerie, Küche und Arbeitszimmer sowie ein Tanzstudio für die Frau des Bauherrn, Shouning Li. Der Architekt nennt das Projekt „die Synthese aus einer genauen Analyse der Bedürfnisse der Familie Ma und der Herausforderung, sich vom konventionellen kalifornischen Eigenheim der 1950er-Jahre zu lösen. Rampen verbinden das alte einstöckige Haus nahtlos mit dem dreistöckigen Neubau. Der Anbau lässt eine offensive Erweiterung von Programm und Funktion zu, die dem Alltag einer vierköpfigen Familie entspricht."

Ce projet est en fait l'extension d'une villa moderne classique du milieu du XXᵉ siècle. « Cette addition reconfigure et redéfinit entièrement la maison d'origine, explique l'architecte, elle améliore ses capacités fonctionnelles qu'elle répartit sur ses trois niveaux comprenant la maison familiale, un bureau et une galerie. À partir d'un plan d'esprit minimaliste développé sur un seul niveau, émerge une construction de deux étages : pourpre, organique et extraterrestre. Une nouvelle identité s'impose qui défie le profil conservateur, parfois suffisant, de ce quartier. » Derrière sa façade en béton projeté de couleur sombre, la nouvelle construction comprend une galerie « publique » double hauteur, une cuisine, un bureau et un studio de danse au deuxième étage pour l'épouse de Ma, Shouning Li. Pour l'architecte, ce projet se trouve « à l'issue d'une analyse approfondie, à l'intersection des besoins de la famille Ma et du défi de vouloir rompre avec le profil conventionnel de la maison californienne des années 1950. Grâce au principe de circulations par rampes, l'ancienne maison de faible hauteur fusionne sans rupture avec son extension de trois niveaux. Cette extension a permis un accroissement massif du programme pour répondre au style de vie d'une famille de quatre personnes. »

The point of juncture between the older residence and the new one is seen on the left page. Above, the "deep purple, organic, and alien" exterior of the new section.

Der Übergang vom Alt- zum Neubau ist auf der linken Seite zu sehen. Oben die „dunkelviolette, organische, fremdartige" Fassade des neuen Teils.

Page de gauche : le point de jonction entre la maison ancienne et la nouvelle. Ci-dessus, la forme « organique et extraterrestre » de la nouvelle partie.

The house is surrounded by trees, rendering its somewhat surprising appearance less evident in the images on this page.

Das Haus ist von Bäumen umgeben, weshalb seine ungewöhnliche Optik auf den Aufnahmen dieser Seite nicht so offensichtlich ist.

La maison est entourée d'arbres, ce qui atténue un peu la surprise que pourrait provoquer sa forme étrange.

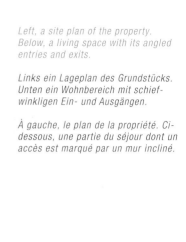

Left, a site plan of the property.
Below, a living space with its angled
entries and exits.

*Links ein Lageplan des Grundstücks.
Unten ein Wohnbereich mit schiefwinkligen Ein- und Ausgängen.*

*À gauche, le plan de la propriété. Ci-
dessous, une partie du séjour dont un
accès est marqué par un mur incliné.*

A dining table is set in the generous living space seen above, with a table at the back where architectural models neighbor the rough rock behind the house. Right, a section drawing.

Ein gedeckter Esstisch im großzügigen Wohnbereich. Im Hintergrund ein Tisch mit Architekturmodellen vor einer Felswand. Rechts ein Querschnitt des Hauses.

Longue table pour les repas dans le généreux espace de séjour. Au fond, autre table sur laquelle sont posées des maquettes d'architecture devant le rocher contre lequel vient buter l'arrière de la maison. À droite, plan de coupe.

Where deep purple reigns on the exterior, the inside is largely white. Its circular openings and angled rectangular windows bring ample natural light into the working spaces seen here.

Während Violett den Außenbau dominiert, ist das Interieur vorwiegend weiß gehalten. Durch Rundfenster und schiefwinklige Fassadenöffnungen fällt großzügig Licht in die hier zu sehenden Arbeitsbereiche.

Si le violet sombre règne à l'extérieur, l'intérieur est essentiellement blanc. Les ouvertures circulaires et les fenêtres obliques laissent pénétrer un généreux éclairage naturel dans les zones de travail.

Relatively traditional furniture seen in the image to the right contrasts sharply with the very modern and high spaces.

Die eher klassischen Möbel rechts im Bild sind ein auffälliger Kontrast zu den sehr modernen hohen Räumen.

Le mobilier assez traditionnel (à droite) contraste fortement avec cet espace contemporain au plafond très élevé.

MÁRIO MARTINS

Mário Martins
Atelier de Arquitectura, Lda
Rua Francisco Xavier Ataíde de Oliveira (Lote 31/32 - Loja P)
8600–775 Lagos
Portugal

Tel: +351 282 76 80 95
Fax: +351 282 78 20 41
E-mail: geral@mariomartins.com
Web: www.mariomartins.com

MÁRIO MARTINS was born in Lagos, Portugal, in 1964. He graduated from the Faculty of Architecture at the Technical University of Lisbon (FA-UTL) in 1988. Martins worked for a year in the office of Manuel Graça Dias + Egas José Vieira, before creating Obliqua Arquitectos in Lagos in 1989 with Vitor Lourenço, with whom he worked on the restoration of historic façades in Lagos. He created the Mário Martins Atelier de Arquitectura in 2000 with Maria José Rio, his business partner and wife. His work, aside from the House in Lagos (2010) and the Colunata House (Luz, Lagos, 2011), both published here, includes the Coco House (Lagos, 2005–07); Varzea House (Aljezur, 2008–10); Fontainhas Houses (Luz, Lagos, 2005–11); and the Malaca House (Sargaçal, Lagos, 2008–11), all in Portugal. In 2011 he published the book *Houses Mário Martins*.

MÁRIO MARTINS wurde 1964 in Lagos, Portugal, geboren. Sein Studium an der Architekturfakultät der Technischen Universität Lissabon (FA-UTL) schloss er 1988 ab. Im Anschluss arbeitete Martins ein Jahr für Manuel Graça Dias + Egas José Vieira, ehe er 1989 in Lagos das Büro Obliqua Arquitectos mit Vitor Lourenço gründete, mit dem er historische Fassaden in Lagos sanierte. 2000 gründete er mit Maria José Rio, seiner Geschäftspartnerin und Frau, das Büro Mário Martins Atelier. Zu seinen Projekten zählen neben dem Haus in Lagos (2010) und dem Haus Colunata (Luz, Lagos, 2011), beide hier vorgestellt, das Haus Coco (Lagos, 2005–07), das Haus Varzea (Aljezur, 2008–10), die Fontainhas-Häuser (Luz, Lagos, 2005–11) sowie das Haus Malaca (Sargaçal, Lagos, 2008–11), alle in Portugal. 2011 erschien sein Buch *Houses Mário Martins*.

MÁRIO MARTINS, né à Lagos (Portugal) en 1964, est diplômé de la faculté d'architecture de l'Université polytechnique de Lisbonne (FA-UTL). Après avoir travaillé un an dans l'agence Manuel Graça Dias + Egas José Vieira, il a créé Obliqua Arquitectos à Lagos en 1989 en association avec Vitor Lourenço (avec lequel il a œuvré à la restauration de façades historiques à Lagos), puis l'agence Mário Martins Atelier de Arquitectura en 2000 avec Maria José Rios, son épouse et associée. Parmi ses réalisations, toutes au Portugal : une maison à Lagos (2010, publiée ici) ; la maison Colunata (Luz, Lagos, 2011, publiée ici) : la maison Coco (Lagos 2005–07) ; la maison Varzea (Aljezur, 2008–10) ; les maisons Fontainhas (Luz, Lagos, 2005–11) et la maison Malaca (Sargaçal, Lagos, 2008–11). En 2011, il a publié l'ouvrage *Houses Mário Martins*.

HOUSE IN LAGOS

Lagos, Portugal, 2010

Area: 205 m². Client: not disclosed
Cost: not disclosed

Located in southern Portugal, this house was designed on a steep and difficult site, offering a broad view of the west coast of the Algarve. Geothermal energy and an integrated "smart home" system permit energy savings. According to the architect: "The main objective was (to create) a house that seemed weightless." Set on a concrete base, the structure "floats" between two terraces and ponds. A roof garden also contributes to the impression of lightness. The public areas—a living room, kitchen, and double-height space—overlook the ponds. Three bedrooms are aligned with a view of the sea, but protected from direct sun and wind.

Das im Süden Portugals gelegene Haus wurde für ein steiles, nicht unproblematisches Hanggrundstück geplant und bietet einen Panoramablick über die West-küste der Algarve. Eine Erdwärmepumpe und ein integriertes intelligentes Haustechniksystem ermöglichen den sparsamen Umgang mit Energie. Der Architekt erklärt: „Es ging vor allem darum, ein scheinbar schwereloses Haus zu entwerfen." Über einem Betonfundament „schwebt" der Bau zwischen zwei Terrassen und Wasserbecken. Auch ein Dachgarten trägt zur visuellen Leichtigkeit bei. Die öffentlichen Bereiche – Wohnzimmer, Küche und ein Raum von doppelter Geschosshöhe – bieten einen Aus-blick auf die Wasserbecken. Drei Schlafzimmer sind zum Meer orientiert, jedoch vor direktem Sonnenlicht und Wind geschützt.

Cette maison située dans le sud du Portugal se dresse sur un terrain escarpé et difficile d'accès, mais qui offre une vue panoramique sur la côte ouest de l'Algarve. « L'objectif principal, explique l'architecte, était [de créer] une maison qui paraisse impondérable. » Reposant sur un socle en béton, la structure « flotte » entre ses deux terrasses et ses bassins. Un jardin sur le toit contribue au sentiment de légèreté. Les parties « publiques » – séjour, cuisine et un volume double hauteur – donnent sur les bassins. Les trois chambres ont vue sur l'océan, mais sont protégées du vent et du soleil direct. Le choix de la géothermie et d'un système de domotique a permis de réaliser des économies d'énergie.

An elevated concrete shell wraps around the interior spaces of the house, providing shade for the ter-races and an unusual form for the residence.

Ein auf einem Sockel ruhendes Beton-band umfängt die Räume des Hauses, spendet Schatten für die Terrassen und gibt dem Bau eine ungewöhnliche Form.

La coque de béton suspendue qui enveloppe le volume intérieur et abrite ses terrasses donne une forme inhabituelle à cette maison.

The long flat form of the house makes it stand out from the trees, as seen above. Right, a pool is seen next to the house that looks out to the ocean.

Der gestreckte Flachbau der Villa hebt sich von den Bäumen ab (oben). Rechts ein Pool neben dem Haus mit Seeblick.

De forme allongée et surbaissée, la structure se détache de son cadre arboré (ci-dessus). À droite, une piscine a été creusée au rez-de-chaussée de la maison, face à l'océan.

The architect orchestrates and composes the lines and openings of the house, contrasting materials and accumulating geometric volumes.

Der Architekt orchestriert und komponiert die Linien und Öffnungen des Hauses, schafft Kontraste mit Materialien und staffelt geometrische Volumen.

L'architecte a orchestré avec soin les axes, les ouvertures et les volumes de la maison et recherché le contraste des matériaux.

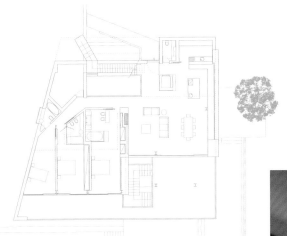

Black and white contrast in the interior spaces (left), which are also seen in the image below. Left, a plan and, above, the living and dining space with its full-height glazing.

In den Bereichen links und unten dominieren Schwarz-Weiß-Kontraste. Links ein Grundriss sowie oben der Wohn- und Essbereich mit raumhoher Verglasung.

Le noir et le blanc viennent en contraste dans les espaces intérieurs (à gauche et en bas). À gauche, un plan de la maison et ci-dessus, le séjour-salle à manger qui se termine par une baie toute hauteur.

COLUNATA HOUSE

Luz, Lagos, Portugal, 2011

Area: 365 m². Client: not disclosed
Cost: not disclosed

This house also faces the sea and seeks to make use of the site to offer the best possible views, but also correct orientation vis-à-vis the sun and wind. Further, the architect sought to create a "gentle" transition from exterior to interior. A group of white columns "free and organically grouped, culminating in a semicircular opening," partially encloses the pool and allows views to the sea. "This results," says the architect, "in the central terrace, the main space of the house, where privacy is felt and where the horizon is predominant." Five bedrooms and a large living room leading to the kitchen are grouped around this central opening. The architect explains: "The house is all in white. It is a southern house, and as such the light is intense. It is this light, with its strong, distinct shadows, that gives color and meaning to the white that covers the building. The strong presence of water and the landscaping surrounding the area accentuate the tranquility of the place."

Auch dieses Haus öffnet sich zum Meer und nutzt das Grundstück für den bestmöglichen Ausblick und die richtige Orientierung im Hinblick auf Sonne und Wind. Außerdem ging es dem Architekten um „sanfte" Übergänge zwischen außen und innen. Eine Gruppe weißer Stützen, „frei und organisch organisiert, wird zu einem offenen Halbrund", umfängt den Pool teilweise und lässt einen Blick aufs Meer zu. „Auf diese Weise entsteht", so der Architekt „eine zentrale Terrasse, Herzstück des Hauses, das Privatsphäre gewährleistet und vom Horizont dominiert wird." Fünf Schlafzimmer und ein großer Wohnraum, der in die Küche übergeht, sind um die zentrale Öffnung gruppiert. Der Architekt erläutert: „Das Haus ist ganz in Weiß gehalten. Es ist ein Haus des Südens, des intensiven Lichts. Dieses Licht mit seinen tiefen, scharfen Schatten gibt dem Weiß des Hauses erst Farbe und Bedeutung. Die starke Präsenz des Wassers und der landschaftlichen Umgebung unterstreichen die Ruhe des Ortes."

Face à l'océan, cette maison a cherché à profiter de son terrain pour offrir à ses occupants des vues spectaculaires tout en bénéficiant de la meilleur orientation possible par rapport au soleil et au vent. L'architecte a par ailleurs cherché à ménager une transition « douce » entre l'extérieur et l'intérieur. Un ensemble de volumes blancs « regroupés de façon libre et organique décrit un profil ouvert semi-circulaire » qui enserre partiellement la piscine et donne sur l'océan… « Ceci détermine la terrasse centrale, principal espace de vie de la maison, lieu intime mais où prédomine néanmoins la vue sur l'horizon. » Les cinq chambres, le vaste séjour et la cuisine sont regroupés autour de cette ouverture centrale. « La maison est entièrement blanche. C'est une maison du sud, et la lumière est intense. Cette lumière qui projette des ombres fortement dessinées confère à cette blancheur immaculée tout son sens. La forte présence de l'eau et l'aménagement paysager alentour renforcent la sérénité de l'endroit », explique l'architecte.

The great arching front of the house faces the ocean and forms a shallow canopy for the terraces. Above, the entrance area.

Die große geschwungene Front ist zum Meer orientiert und bildet ein schmales Vordach über den Terrassen. Oben der Eingangsbereich.

L'immense auvent incurvé de la façade de la maison qui donne sur l'océan protège les terrasses. Ci-dessus, la façade de l'entrée.

Above, the dining area and, right, the kitchen with its generous counter. Black and white are the dominant colors.

Oben der Essbereich und rechts die Küche mit großzügigem Tresen. Schwarz und Weiß bestimmen die Palette.

Ci-dessus, la salle à manger et à droite, la cuisine et son généreux comptoir. Le blanc et le noir sont les couleurs dominantes.

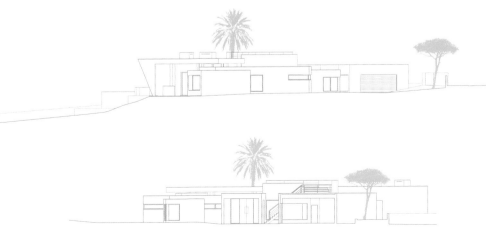

Above, the living area with its view of the ocean and emphasis on black and white contrasts. Right, elevations of the exterior façades.

Oben der Wohnbereich mit Blick aufs Meer und deutlichen Schwarz-Weiß-Kontrasten. Rechts Aufrisse der Fassaden.

Ci-dessus une partie du séjour, également en noir et blanc, et sa vue sur l'océan. À droite, élévations des façades.

MORPHOSIS

Morphosis
3440 Wesley Street
Culver City, CA 90232
USA

Tel: +1 424 258 6200
Fax: +1 424 258 6299
E-mail: studio@morphosis.net
Web: www.morphosis.com

Morphosis principal **THOM MAYNE**, born in Connecticut in 1944, received his B.Arch in 1968 from the University of Southern California, Los Angeles, and his M.Arch degree from Harvard in 1978. He created Morphosis in 1979. He has taught at UCLA, Harvard, Yale, and SCI-Arc, of which he was a founding Board Member. Thom Mayne was the winner of the 2005 Pritzker Prize. Some of the main buildings by Morphosis are the Kate Mantilini Restaurant (Beverly Hills, California, 1986); Cedar's Sinai Comprehensive Cancer Care Center (Beverly Hills, California, 1987); Crawford Residence (Montecito, 1987–92); the Blades Residence (Santa Barbara, California, 1992–97); and International Elementary School (Long Beach, California, 1997–99). More recent work includes the NOAA Satellite Operation Facility in Suitland (Maryland, 2001–05); San Francisco Federal Building (San Francisco, California, 2003–07); 41 Cooper Square (New York, New York, 2006–09); Float House (New Orleans, Louisiana, 2008–09, published here); and the Giant Interactive Group Corporate Headquarters (Shanghai, China, 2006–10). They are working on the Museum of Nature and Science (Dallas, Texas) and the Alexandria Bay Port of Entry (Alexandria Bay, New York), all in the USA unless stated otherwise.

THOM MAYNE, Chef von Morphosis, wurde 1944 in Connecticut geboren. Sein Studium schloss er 1968 mit einem B.Arch. an der University of Southern California (UCLA), Los Angeles, sowie 1978 mit einem M.Arch. in Harvard ab. 1979 gründete er Morphosis. Mayne lehrte an der UCLA, in Harvard, in Yale sowie am SCI-Arc, zu dessen Gründungsmitgliedern er zählt. 2005 wurde Mayne mit dem Pritzker-Preis ausgezeichnet. Ausgewählte Bauten von Morphosis sind u. a. das Kate Mantilini Restaurant (Beverly Hills, Kalifornien, 1986), die Cedar's Sinai Krebsklinik (Beverly Hills, Kalifornien, 1987), die Crawford Residence (Montecito, Kalifornien, 1987–92), die Blades Residence (Santa Barbara, Kalifornien, 1992–97) sowie die Internationale Grundschule in Long Beach (Kalifornien, 1997–99). Jüngere Arbeiten sind u. a. das NOAA-Satellitenzentrum in Suitland (Maryland, 2001–05), das San Francisco Federal Building (2003–07), 41 Cooper Square (New York, 2006–09), Float House (New Orleans, 2008–09, hier vorgestellt) und der Hauptsitz der Giant Interactive Group (Schanghai, 2006–10). Das Büro arbeitet derzeit an einem Museum für Naturkunde (Dallas, Texas) sowie am Hafen Alexandria Bay im Bundesstaat New York, alle in den USA, sofern nicht anders vermerkt.

Responsable de Morphosis, **THOM MAYNE**, né dans le Connecticut en 1944, est diplômé en architecture (B.Arch.) de l'université de Californie du Sud-Los Angeles (1968) et a obtenu son M.Arch. à Harvard (1978). Il a fondé l'agence en 1979. Il a enseigné à l'UCLA, Harvard, Yale et au SCI-Arc dont il est l'un des fondateurs et a reçu le prix Pritzker en 2005. Parmi ses principales réalisations, toutes aux Etats-Unis, sauf mention contraire : le restaurant Kate Mantilini (Beverly Hills, Californie, 1986) ; le Centre anticancéreux de Cedar's Sinai (Beverly Hills, Californie, 1987) ; la résidence Crawford (Montecito, Californie, 1987–92) ; la résidence Blades (Santa Barbara, Californie, 1992–97) et l'École élémentaire internationale (Long Beach, Californie, 1997–99). Plus récemment, il a construit le Centre opérationnel de communication par satellites NOAA (Suitland, Maryland, 2001–05) ; un immeuble fédéral (San Francisco, 2003–07) ; l'immeuble 41 Cooper Square (New York, 2006–09) ; la Float House (New Orleans, Louisiane, 2008–09, publiée ici) et le siège social du Giant Interactive Group (Shanghai, Chine, 2006–10). L'agence travaille actuellement sur un projet de musée de la Nature et de la Science (Dallas, Texas) et le bâtiment de l'Alexandria Bay Port of Entry (Alexandria Bay, New York).

FLOAT HOUSE
New Orleans, Louisiana, USA, 2008–09

Area: 88 m². Client: Make It Right Foundation
Cost: not disclosed

The architects state: "The **FLOAT HOUSE** is a new kind of house: a house that can sustain its own water and power needs; a house that can survive the floodwaters generated by a storm the size of Hurricane Katrina; and, perhaps most importantly, a house that can be manufactured cheaply enough to function as low-income housing." Based on the typology of the local shotgun house, this residence is perched on a raised base containing the mechanical, electrical, and plumbing system. Assembled on site from prefabricated elements, the house can rise up to 3.65 meters on guide posts in case of flooding. It remains anchored to its site with six 13.7-meter-deep concrete piles. Designed to obtain a LEED Platinum rating (certified), the house uses solar panels, rainwater collection, efficient plumbing and insulation systems, and a ground-source heat pump for heating and cooling.

Die Architekten erklären: „Das **FLOAT HOUSE** ist ein neuartiges Haus: ein Haus mit unabhängiger Strom- und Wasserversorgung, ein Haus, das Sturmfluten wie die vom Hurrikan Katrina verursachte sicher überstehen kann, und außerdem – der vielleicht wichtigste Aspekt – ein Haus, das so kostengünstig gebaut werden kann, dass es für den sozialen Wohnungsbau infrage kommt." Es greift den Stil des hier typischen, langen, rechteckigen Hauses auf und steht auf einem Sockel, in dem technische Anlagen, Elektrik und sanitäre Leitungen Platz finden. Das aus Fertigelementen vor Ort zusammengebaute Haus kann bei Überschwemmungen an Führungspfeilern bis zu 3,65 m hoch angehoben werden. Dabei ist es an sechs 13,7 m tiefen Betonpfeilern im Boden verankert. Das Haus wurde mit Solarmodulen, Regenwassernutzung, effizienter Sanitär- und Dämmtechnik sowie mit einer Erdwärmepumpe mit Heiz- und Kühlfunktion ausgestattet und erhielt das LEED-Platin-Zertifikat.

« La **FLOAT HOUSE**, expliquent ses architectes, est un nouveau type de maison : une maison qui peut produire son eau et son énergie, une maison qui peut résister aux inondations provoquées par un événement du type du cyclone Katrina et, plus important encore peut-être, une maison qui peut se fabriquer à coût réduit et être proposée comme logement économique. » S'inspirant de la typologie locale de la maison « shotgun », cette petite résidence repose sur un socle surélevé contenant les systèmes mécaniques, électriques et de plomberie. Assemblée sur place à partir d'éléments préfabriqués, elle peut, en cas d'inondation, s'élever sur des piliers-guides de 3,65 m. Elle reste néanmoins bien ancrée sur son terrain par des pieux de béton de 13,7 m de profondeur. Visant la norme LEED Platinum, elle est équipée de panneaux solaires, d'un système de récupération des eaux de pluie, d'une plomberie et d'une isolation efficaces et d'une pompe à chaleur type puits canadien pour son chauffage et le rafraîchissement de l'air.

The house fits into the general typology of neighboring residences, but takes on a somewhat unexpected appearance with its bright colors and glass canopy.

Das Haus passt sich dem in der Nachbarschaft vorherrschenden Stil an, ist aber mit seinen kräftigen Farben und dem Glasvordach auch eine überraschende Erscheinung.

La maison s'inscrit dans la typologie du voisinage, mais revêt néanmoins une apparence assez inattendue avec ses couleurs vives et son auvent de verre.

The interior of the house is simple with a contrast between wood elements and the overall white and gray color scheme.

Das Interieur des Hauses ist schlicht gehalten. Kontraste entstehen durch die Kombination von Holz mit einer ansonsten grauweißen Palette.

L'intérieur de la maison est aménagé avec simplicité. Le blanc et le gris dominants contrastent avec certains éléments en bois naturel.

Kitchen and bathroom spaces show all of the modernity and intelligence of much more expensive and complex houses. Daylight is present wherever possible.

Küche und Bad sind mit dem modernen Komfort und Anspruch wesentlich teurerer und komplexerer Häuser ausgestattet. Das Tageslicht wird wo immer möglich genutzt.

Le coin cuisine et la salle de bains bénéficient de la modernité et de l'intelligence de maisons plus complexes et certainement plus chères. La lumière naturelle est très présente.

RYUE NISHIZAWA

Office of Ryue Nishizawa
1–5–27 Tatsumi
Koto-ku
Tokyo 135–0053
Japan

Tel: +81 3 5534 0117
Fax: +81 3 5534 1757
E-mail: office@ryuenishizawa.com
Web: www.ryuenishizawa.com

RYUE NISHIZAWA was born in Tokyo in 1966. He graduated from Yokohama National University with an M.Arch in 1990, and joined the office of Kazuyo Sejima & Associates in Tokyo the same year. In 1995, he established SANAA with Kazuyo Sejima, and two years later his own practice, the Office of Ryue Nishizawa. He has worked on all the significant projects of SANAA and has been a Visiting Professor at Yokohama National University (2001–), the University of Singapore (2003), Princeton (2006), and the Harvard GSD (2007). His work outside SANAA includes a Weekend House (Gunma, 1998); the N Museum (Kagawa, 2005); the Moriyama House (Tokyo, 2006); House A (East Japan, 2006); Towada Art Center (Aomori, 2006–08); the Teshima Museum (Teshima, Kagawa, 2009–10); the Garden and House (Tokyo, 2010–11, published here); and the Hiroshi Senju Museum (Karuizawa, Nagano, 2011), all in Japan.

RYUE NISHIZAWA wurde 1966 in Tokio geboren und schloss sein Studium 1990 mit einem M.Arch. an der Nationaluniversität in Yokohama ab. Noch im selben Jahr schloss er sich dem Büro von Kazuyo Sejima & Associates in Tokio an. Gemeinsam mit Kazuyo Sejima gründete er 1995 SANAA, zwei Jahre später sein eigenes Büro Ryue Nishizawa. Er ist an sämtlichen Schlüsselprojekten von SANAA beteiligt und war Gastprofessor an der Nationaluniversität Yokohama (seit 2001), der Universität von Singapur (2003), in Princeton (2006) sowie an der Harvard Graduate School of Design (2007). Zu seinen unabhängigen Projekten zählen ein Wochenendhaus (Gunma, 1998), das Museum N (Kagawa, 2005), das Haus Moriyama (Tokyo, 2006), das Haus A (Ostjapan, 2006), das Towada Art Center (Aomori, 2006–08), das Museum Teshima (Teshima, Kagawa, 2009–10), ein Garten und Haus in Tokio (2010–11, hier vorgestellt) sowie das Museum Hiroshi Senju (Karuizawa, Nagano, 2011), alle in Japan.

RYUE NISHIZAWA, né à Tokyo en 1966, a obtenu son diplôme de M.Arch. à l'Université nationale de Yokohama (1990). Il a commencé à travailler chez Kazuyo Sejima & Associates à Tokyo la même année, avant qu'ils ne fondent ensemble SANAA en 1995 et sa propre agence Office of Ryue Nishizawa deux ans plus tard. Il a été professeur invité à l'Université nationale de Yokohama (2001–), aux universités de Singapour (2003), Princeton (2006) et à la Harvard GSD (2007). Il est intervenu sur tous les grands projets de SANAA. Son œuvre personnelle, entièrement au Japon, comprend une maison de week-end (Gunma, 1998) ; le musée N (Kagawa, 2005) ; la maison Moriyama (Tokyo, 2006) ; la maison A (Japon oriental, 2006) ; le Centre d'art Towada (Aomori, 2006–08) et le Musée d'art de Teshima (île de Teshima, Kagawa, 2009–10) ; le Jardin et maison (Tokyo, 2010–11, publié ici) et le musée Hiroshi Senju (Karuizawa, Nagano, 2011).

GARDEN AND HOUSE
Tokyo, Japan, 2010–11

Area: 66 m². Client: not disclosed. Cost: not disclosed
Collaboration: Teako Nakatsubo, Alan Burden, Hiroki Osanai

Potted plants seem to be a favorite of cutting-edge architects in Japan these days… but greenery fits into the architecture in a natural, generous way.

Topfpflanzen scheinen bei innovativen japanischen Architekten derzeit besonders angesagt zu sein. Dabei fügt sich die Begrünung natürlich und großzügig in die Architektur ein.

De nos jours, la plante en pot est un des accessoires favoris des architectes d'avant-garde au Japon, néanmoins cette verdure réduite s'intègre dans l'architecture de manière naturelle.

Located in a dense urban zone with condominium and office buildings rising above 30 meters in height nearby, this house for two women was built on an 8 x 4-meter site, and includes an office, a common living space, a private room for each, and a guest room. "Suspecting that a building with regular frame walls would result in narrowing the already narrow usable space of the site," states Nishizawa, "I looked for a possibility to create a building with alternative methods. My final decision of structure consisted of a vertical layer of horizontal slabs to create a building without walls. A garden and a room are distributed as a pair on each floor—every room, whether it is the living room, private room or the bathroom, has a garden of its own so that the residents may go outside to feel the breeze, read a book, cool off in the evening, and enjoy an open environment in their daily life." The architect thus determined that a wall-less, transparent building was the best solution for this difficult site.

In einem dicht bebauten urbanen Umfeld mit Eigentumswohnungen und Bürogebäuden, die über 30 m hoch sind, wurde das Haus für zwei Frauen auf einem 8 x 4 m großen Grundstück gebaut. Es umfasst ein Büro, einen gemeinsamen Wohnbereich, ein Zimmer für jede Frau sowie ein Gästezimmer. „Da ein Gebäude mit konventionellen Wänden die ohnehin schmale Nutzfläche des Grundstücks zusätzlich verschmälert hätte", so Nishizawa, „suchte ich nach Möglichkeiten, ein Haus mit anderen Methoden zu bauen. Letztendlich fiel die Wahl auf eine Konstruktion aus vertikal geschichteten horizontalen Geschossplatten, um ein Haus ohne Wände bauen zu können. Auf jeder Ebene wurden ein Garten und ein Zimmer kombiniert – jedes Zimmer, ob Wohnzimmer, Schlafzimmer oder Bad, hat eine eigene Grünzone, sodass die Bewohnerinnen an die frische Luft können, um zu lesen oder abends Abkühlung zu suchen, und im Alltag ein offenes Umfeld genießen können." Der Architekt entschied sich für ein Haus ohne Wände als Ideallösung für ein schwieriges Grundstück.

Située dans un quartier dense dans lequel de nombreux immeubles de logement ou de bureaux se dressent à plus de 20 m de hauteur, cette maison construite pour deux jeunes femmes a été édifiée sur un terrain de 8 x 4 m. Elle comprend un bureau, un séjour commun, deux chambres et une chambre d'amis. «Pensant qu'un immeuble à ossature à murs porteurs réduirait encore l'espace utile déjà limité du terrain, explique Nishizawa, j'ai cherché à concevoir une maison selon des méthodes alternatives. J'ai finalement opté pour une structure présentant une stratification verticale de dalles horizontales afin de créer un bâtiment sans murs. Chaque niveau accueille une pièce et un jardin, et chaque pièce – que ce soit le séjour, les chambres et leur salle de bains – possède son propre jardin afin que les résidentes puissent aller au-dehors pour sentir le vent, lire un livre, se détendre en soirée et profiter au quotidien d'un environnement ouvert. »

A spiral staircase snakes through the space, while curtains provide a certain degree of intimacy in the otherwise very open residence.

Eine Wendeltreppe zieht sich durch den Raum. Vorhänge sorgen für ein Minimum an Privatsphäre in dem ansonsten ausgesprochen offen gehaltenen Haus.

Un escalier en spirale se faufile entre les niveaux tandis que des rideaux offrent un certain degré d'intimité à ce logement par ailleurs très ouvert.

The spiral staircase enlivens the interior and connects the levels. Below, floor plans of each level.

Die Wendeltreppe gibt den Räumen Dynamik und verbindet die Wohnebenen. Unten Etagengrundrisse der einzelnen Stockwerke.

L'escalier en spirale anime l'espace intérieur et relie les différents étages. Ci-dessous, plan de chacun des niveaux.

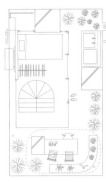
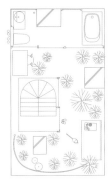

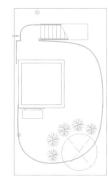

SUSANNE NOBIS

Susanne Nobis
Am Fichtenhain 9
82335 Berg
Germany

Tel: +49 81 51 95 91 87
Fax: +49 81 51 95 91 86
E-mail: info@susannenobis.de

SUSANNE NOBIS was born in Munich, Germany, in 1963. She attended the Architecture Polytechnic of Central London (UK, 1991–92) and obtained her Diploma in Architecture from the University of Applied Sciences (Munich, 1987–92). She received a further Diploma in Architecture from the Technical University of Berlin (1996–99). She worked in the Renzo Piano Building Workshop (Genoa, 1992–93), with Herzog+Partner (Munich, 1994–95), and with Ackermann und Partner (Munich, 1995–96), before creating her own office in 2000. Her work includes House D_Residential (Ulm, 2000–05); House RW (Woerthsee, 2006–08); Architektouren Traveling Exhibition (2008); House H, a residence with an exhibition area (Grossburgwedel, 2007–09); the design of the Ecological Architecture Exhibition (Starnberg, 2009); and Toward Landscape (Lake Starnberg, Berg, 2006–10, published here), all in Germany.

SUSANNE NOBIS wurde 1963 in München geboren. Sie studierte an der Architecture Polytechnic of Central London (GB, 1991–92) und machte ihr Architektur-diplom an der Hochschule für angewandte Wissenschaften München (München, 1987–92). Außerdem erlangte sie ein Architekturdiplom an der Technischen Universität Berlin (1996–99). Sie arbeitete für Renzo Piano Building Workshop (Genua, 1992–93), Herzog+Partner (München, 1994–95) und Ackermann und Partner (München, 1995–96), bevor sie 2000 ihr eigenes Büro gründete. Zu ihren Projekten zählen Haus D_Residential (Ulm, 2000–05), Haus RW (Wörthersee, 2006–08), die Wander-ausstellung Architektouren (2008), Haus H, Wohnhaus mit Galerie (Großburgwedel, 2007–09), die Ausstellungsarchitektur für die Umwelt 2009 Starnberg (Starnberg, 2009) sowie Toward Landscape (Starnberger See, Berg, 2006–10, hier vorgestellt), alle in Deutschland.

SUSANNE NOBIS, née à Munich en 1963, a étudié l'architecture à la Polytechnic of Central London (1991–92) puis a obtenu ses diplômes d'architecture à l'Université des sciences appliquées de Munich (1987–92) et à l'Université technique de Berlin (1996–99). Elle a travaillé pour le Renzo Piano Building Workshop (Gênes, 1992–93), Herzog + Partner (Munich, 1994–95) et Ackermann und Partner (Munich, 1995–96) avant de créer son agence en 2000. Parmi ses réalisations, toutes en Allemagne : la maison D (Ulm, 2000–05) ; la maison RW (Woerthsee, 2006–08) ; l'exposition « Architektouren Traveling » (2008) ; la maison H, résidence et galerie d'exposition (Grossburgwedel, 2007–09) ; une exposition sur l'architecture écologique (Starnberg, 2009) et la maison Toward Landscape (lac de Starnberg, Berg, 2006–10, publiée ici).

TOWARD LANDSCAPE
Lake Starnberg, Berg, Germany, 2006–10

Area: 324 m². Client: not disclosed
Cost: not disclosed

Inspired by the traditional boathouses built along Lake Starnberg near Munich, this project consists in one volume with an open gallery and a two-story "bedroom house." It is the home and place of work of the architect. The two rectangular volumes are slightly lifted off the ground and are connected in the center at ground level. A folded titanium skin is "pulled" over the interior timber structures, with an open, glazed band running through the top of the roofs to provide daylight. Books animate the wall space, but the furnishing of the house remains quite minimal. The two parts of the house have broad glazed façades facing the lake, with terraces raised like the ground level of the structures themselves, allowing the inhabitants to enjoy the beautiful lakeside setting in a house that combines the forms of local tradition with a warm wood interior and modern, metal exterior.

Das Haus, inspiriert von den traditionellen Bootshäusern am Starnberger See bei München, umfasst zwei Baukörper, einen mit offener Galerie, einen zweiten als zweistöckiges „Schlafzimmerhaus". Für die Architektin ist es Wohnhaus und Arbeitsplatz zugleich. Die beiden rechteckigen Volumina sind leicht über dem Boden aufgeständert und im Erdgeschoss mittig miteinander verbunden. Eine Titanblechschicht wurde über die innere Holzkonstruktion „gezogen"; ein bandförmiges Oberlicht verläuft durch den Giebel und lässt Tageslicht einfallen. Bücher beleben die Wände, die Möblierung bleibt eher sparsam. Beide Teile des Hauses öffnen sich mit großzügig verglasten Fassaden zum See. Die Terrassen sind wie das Erdgeschoss selbst leicht erhöht und bieten den Bewohnern Gelegenheit, die reizvolle Lage am See zu genießen. In diesem Haus verbinden sich traditionelle Bauformen mit einem warmen Interieur aus Holz und einem modernen Äußeren aus Metall.

Inspiré des hangars à bateaux traditionnels des rives du lac de Starnberg près de Munich, ce projet consiste en un volume longé d'un passage couvert et d'une « maison de chambres » de deux niveaux. C'est la résidence et le lieu de travail de l'architecte. Les deux volumes rectangulaires sont légèrement surélevés par rapport au sol et se connectent en leur centre au rez-de-chaussée. Une peau de titane pliée a été « tendue » sur les ossatures en bois, un bandeau zénithal central fournissant l'éclairage naturel. Si des livres animent les murs, le mobilier reste assez réduit. Les deux parties de la maison tournées vers le lac possèdent des façades entièrement vitrées et des terrasses dans le prolongement de l'intérieur. Les occupants bénéficient ainsi d'un cadre superbe dans une maison qui associe des formes locales traditionnelles à des aménagements intérieurs chaleureux en bois et à la modernité de ses façades métalliques.

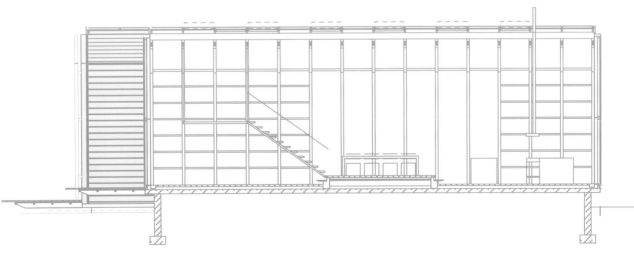

Along the very chic lake edge, near Munich, the architect has created a house and atelier with two shedlike buildings. An elevation shows living space on the mezzanine level reached by a stairway.

In bester Lage am Starnberger See unweit von München baute sich die Architektin Haus und Atelier in zwei scheunenartigen Gebäuden. Ein Aufriss zeigt das Mezzaningeschoss, das über eine Treppe erschlossen wird.

Dans ce quartier élégant en bordure d'un lac près de Munich, l'architecte a créé une maison et un atelier à partir de deux constructions en forme de hangar. L'élévation montre une partie du séjour en mezzanine que l'on atteint par un escalier.

The double-height library space with an elevated platform for the dining room table (left).

Ein Blick in die Bibliothek mit doppelter Raumhöhe. Der Esstisch steht auf einem Podest (links).

L'espace double hauteur de la bibliothèque dans lequel la table des repas a été placée sur une plate-forme (ci-contre).

On the right page, a suspended metal stair and a bridge cross over the library volume and the living space, which opens into the terrace garden.

Auf der rechten Seite eine abgehängte Brücke und Treppe schweben über dem Bibliotheks- und Wohnbereich, der sich zu Terrasse und Garten öffnet.

Page de droite, un escalier métallique suspendu et une passerelle qui traverse le séjour-bibliothèque ouvert sur le jardin.

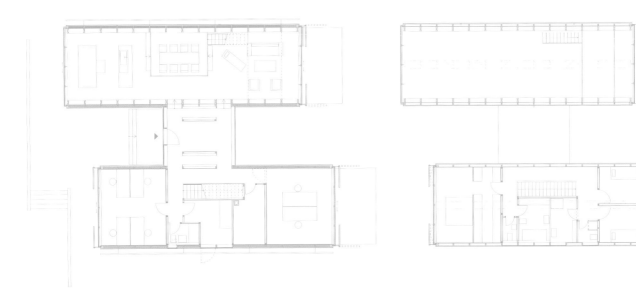

OAB

Office of Architecture in Barcelona (OAB)
C/ Balmes 145 bajos
08008 Barcelona
Spain

Tel: +34 93 238 51 36
Fax: +34 93 416 13 06
E-mail: oab@ferrater.com
Web: www.ferrater.com

Carlos Ferrater Lambarri was born in Barcelona, Spain, in 1944 and received his diploma from the Barcelona ETSA (1971) and his doctorate from the same institution in 1987. He created his current office, **OAB**—Office of Architecture in Barcelona, with Xavier Martí Galí, Lucía Ferrater, and Borja Ferrater, with Núria Ayala as Projects Director, in 2006. Xavier Martí Galí received his diploma from the Barcelona ETSA (1995) and joined the Carlos Ferrater studio as an Associate Architect in 2003. Noted works include House for a Photographer 2 (Ebro Delta, Tarragona, Spain, 2006); Empordà Golf Club (Gualta, Girona, Spain, 2005–07); the Granada Science Park (Granada, Spain, 2008, with Jiménez Brasa Arquitectos); and the Aquileia Tower in Jesolo (Venice, Italy, 2008). Other recent work of OAB includes the Origami House (Vallès Occidental, Barcelona, Spain, 2007–09, published here); an office building in Boulogne-Billancourt (Paris, France, 2009); Holiday Camps in Viladoms (Barcelona, Spain, 2009–10); and a house in Abandoibarra (Bilbao, Spain, 2007–11). Ongoing work includes projects in Turkey, the USA, Morocco, and France. The BF House (Borriol, Castellón de la Plana, 2006–11, also published here) was a joint project of OAB and ADI Arquitectura.

Carlos Ferrater Lambarri wurde 1944 in Barcelona geboren und machte sein Diplom an der ETSA in Barcelona (1971), wo er 1987 auch promovierte. Er gründete 2006 sein heutiges Büro **OAB** – Office of Architecture in Barcelona gemeinsam mit Xavier Martí Galí, Lucía Ferrater und Borja Ferrater sowie Núria Ayala als Projektleiterin. Xavier Martí Galí erlangte sein Diplom 1995 an der ETSA Barcelona und schloss sich dem Studio von Carlos Ferrater 2003 als Partner an. Bekannte Projekte sind etwa das Haus für einen Fotografen 2 (Ebro-Delta, Tarragona, Spanien, 2006), den Empordà Golfclub (Gualta, Girona, Spanien, 2005–07), der Wissenschaftspark Granada (Granada, 2008, mit Jiménez Brasa Arquitectos) und der Aquileia Tower in Jesolo (Venedig, 2008). Weitere jüngere Projekte von OAB sind u. a. das Origami House (Vallès Occidental, Barcelona, 2007–09, hier vorgestellt), ein Bürogebäude Boulogne-Billancourt (Paris, 2009), ein Ferienlager in Viladoms (Barcelona, 2009–10) sowie ein Haus in Abandoibarra (Bilbao, 2007–11). Das Büro arbeitet an laufenden Projekten in der Türkei, den USA, Marokko und Frankreich. Das Haus BF (Borriol, Castellón de la Plana, 2006–11, ebenfalls hier vorgestellt) war ein gemeinsames Projekt von OAB und ADI Arquitectura.

Carlos Ferrater Lambarri, né à Barcelone en 1944, est diplômé de l'École d'architecture de Barcelone (ETSA, 1971) et docteur de la même institution (1987). Il a fondé son agence actuelle, **OAB** (Office of Architecture in Barcelona) avec Xavier Martí Galí, Lucía Ferrater, Borja Ferrater et Núria Ayala, comme directeurs de projets, en 2006. Xavier Martí Galí, diplômé en architecture de l'ETSA (Barcelone, 1995), a rejoint l'agence de Carlos Ferrater comme architecte associé en 2003. Parmi leurs réalisations figurent : la maison pour un photographe 2 (delta de l'Èbre, Tarragone, 2006) ; le club de golf de l'Empordà (Gualta, Girone, 2005–07) ; le parc des Sciences de Grenade (Grenade, 2008, avec Jiménez Brasa Arquitectos) et la tour Aquileia (Jesolo, Venise, 2008). Plus récemment, OAB a réalisé : la maison Origami (Vallès Occidental, Barcelone, 2007–09, publiée ici) ; un immeuble de bureaux à Boulogne-Billancourt (France, 2009) ; des camps de vacances à Viladoms (Barcelone, 2009–10) et une maison à Abandoibarra (Bilbao, 2007–11). La maison BF (Borriol, Castellón de la Plana, 2006–11, publiée ici) est un projet en collaboration de OAB et ADI Arquitectura. D'autres projets sont en cours en Turquie, aux États-Unis, au Maroc et en France.

BF HOUSE

Borriol, Castellón de la Plana, Spain, 2006–11

Area: 1166 m². Client: not disclosed. Cost: not disclosed
Collaboration: project codesigned with Carlos Escura and Carlos Martín (ADI)

This home was built on a steeply sloped, 3000-square-meter site. The architects chose to carefully respect the vegetation on the site, "opting for a prefabricated building system that is deposited on the land practically without touching it, without cutting down trees, and taking advantage of existing terrace/garden areas, which were rebuilt in the damaged areas with the same stone and same techniques." A metal structure facilitated off-site prefabrication, while corrugated sheet metal designed to reduce heat and glare is used for exterior cladding. Photovoltaic panels are used on the roof, and natural ventilation was carefully studied in the design phase. "This is a house with a courtyard," explain the architects, "but with different connotations since each room in the house can be seen from the courtyard's central location, as well as the surrounding landscape, since the courtyard is surrounded on four sides by the house, but is not enclosed by it due to the slope of the plot." The open front area of the house makes the construction system evident, and includes the kitchen, living room, and master bedroom.

Das Haus wurde auf einem steilen, 3000 m² großen Hanggrundstück realisiert. Die Architekten entschieden sich, die Vegetation des Grundstücks zu erhalten, und so fiel die „Entscheidung für ein Fertigbausystem, das praktisch ohne Berührungspunkte auf den Boden aufgesetzt wurde, ohne Bäume fällen zu müssen, und das zugleich weitgehend die bestehenden terrassierten Grünflächen einband, die dort, wo sie schadhaft waren, mit demselben Stein und entsprechenden Techniken rekonstruiert wurden". Eine Metallkonstruktion erleichterte die Vorfertigung, der Außenbau wurde mit Wellblech verschalt, das den Einfluss von Wärme und Licht auf das Haus reduziert. Auf dem Dach wurden Solarmodule installiert, zur natürlichen Belüftung wurden in der Entwurfsphase intensive Studien betrieben. „Dies ist ein Atriumhaus", so die Architekten, „doch nicht im üblichen Sinne, denn hier hat man von einem zentralen Standpunkt im Hof nicht nur einen Blick in sämtliche Räume des Hauses, sondern auch in die Landschaft der Umgebung, da der Hof zwar vom Haus an vier Seiten umfangen wird, jedoch durch das Hanggrundstück nicht verbaut ist." Im offen gehaltenen vorderen Bereich des Hauses wird das Konstruktionssystem sichtbar; hier liegen Küche, Wohnbereich und Hauptschlafzimmer.

Cette maison a été édifiée sur un terrain de 3000 m² en pente abrupte. L'architecte a choisi de respecter la végétation présente sur le site, « optant pour un système constructif de préfabrication, posé sur le terrain sans pratiquement le toucher ni couper d'arbres et utilisant les zones de terrasses/jardins existantes, restaurées dans leurs parties endommagées avec la même pierre et selon les mêmes techniques ». La structure métallique a facilité la préfabrication hors du site et les façades extérieures ont été habillées d'une tôle ondulée métallique pour réduire le gain solaire et l'effet de la lumière. Le toit est équipé de panneaux photovoltaïques et la ventilation naturelle a été prise en compte dès la phase de conception du projet. « C'est une maison à cour, expliquent les architectes, mais avec des connotations différentes puisque chaque pièce de la maison reste visible aussi bien du centre de la cour que du paysage environnant et que la cour est entourée sur ses quatre côtés par la maison sans pour autant être fermée du fait de la forte pente de la parcelle. » La façade ouverte de la maison, derrière laquelle se trouvent le séjour, la cuisine et la chambre principale, permet de comprendre le système constructif.

Although the basic, long, rectangular form of the house is not in itself surprising, the way it is set up on pillars, hovering off the ground, as seen in the drawing and photo on this page, is certainly unexpected.

Auch wenn die gestreckte Rechtecksform des Hauses an sich nicht ungewöhnlich ist, so ist seine Aufständerung und wie es über dem Boden schwebt (Zeichnung und Foto), ohne Zweifel überraschend.

Bien que la forme rectangulaire allongée de la maison ne soit pas une surprise, la façon dont elle est suspendue sur des piliers, comme le montrent la coupe et la photo ci-dessous, crée un effet inattendu.

An interior courtyard formed by the elevated mass of the house allows space for a garden. Vegetation covers the supports for the house.

Der vom aufgeständerten Baukörper umgebene Innenhof bietet Raum für einen Garten. Die Stützen des Hauses sind begrünt.

La cour intérieure formée par les parties surélevées de cette maison offre un espace pour un jardin. La végétation recouvre les supports de la construction.

A staircase rising from the courtyard area to the main, upper section of the house.

Eine Treppe führt vom Innenhof in den darübergelegenen Hauptwohnbereich des Hauses.

Un escalier s'élève de la cour vers la partie supérieure de la maison.

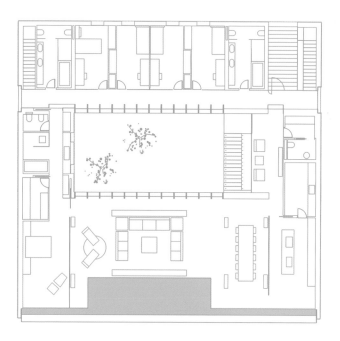

Above, the very sleek kitchen has full-height glazing that offers a view of the verdant landscape. Left, a plan of the house with the courtyard in the upper middle.

Die hochmoderne Küche hat raum-hohe Fenster, durch die der Blick ins grüne Umland fällt. Links ein Grundriss mit dem Innenhof im Zentrum des Hauses.

Ci-dessus, la cuisine très épurée bénéficie d'une baie toute hauteur s'ouvrant sur un paysage verdoyant. À gauche, plan de la maison montrant l'emplacement de la cour-jardin.

The interiors show a refined choice
of materials and lighting effects.
Opaque surfaces alternate with translucent or transparent ones, with color
contrasts highlighting the materials.

Die Interieurs zeichnen sich durch
anspruchsvolle Materialien und Licht-
effekte aus. Geschlossene Flächen
treffen auf durchscheinende oder
transparente Oberflächen. Farbkon-
traste betonen die Materialien.

L'intérieur témoigne d'un choix
raffiné de matériaux et de la
recherche d'effets d'éclairage. Les
plans opaques alternent avec des
parois transparentes ou translucides.
Les contrastes des couleurs mettent
en valeur les matériaux.

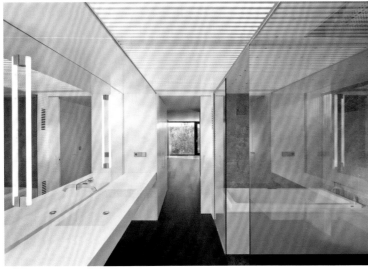

ORIGAMI HOUSE

Vallès Occidental, Barcelona, Spain, 2007–09

Area: 1200 m². Client: not disclosed
Cost: not disclosed. Collaboration: Juan Calvo (Pondio) for the structure

Located in Sant Cugat, next to a forest bordering a golf course, this house is compared by the architects to a "boat anchored in a green sea of grass." An austere plaza gives way to a pool of water in the entrance. Service facilities are hidden on a lower level, and the whole structure has an orthogonal floor plan and an inclined cross section. Four narrow staircases are carefully hidden "like those on a boat." A loft where the client keeps a collection of maps is reached via a folding ladder. The kitchen is compared to a house in itself, "a world opened completely onto the garden and bathed in natural daylight, a systematic laboratory of nutrition, care, cleaning, and work." A collection of cars is stored in a lower-level garage. The architects state: "This is a house and it is the contrary: telluric and anchored at the base, and yet light and floating like a balloon about to leave the ground. It takes us back to the idea of a 'house' as an authentic archetype as understood by Gaston Bachelard and Luis Barragán: with a basement and an attic. With all of its intensity and meaning, this house contains all the symbols. It is a house on pleasant land, all garden, which floats above the grass."

Die Architekten beschreiben das in Sant Cugat an einem Wald am Rand eines Golfplatzes gelegene Haus als „ein Schiff, das in einem grünen Meer aus Gras ankert". Ein strenger Vorplatz führt zu einem Bassin neben dem Eingang. Die Haustechnik verbirgt sich im Untergeschoss. Die Anlage mit rechtwinkligem Grundriss zeigt im Querschnitt zahlreiche Schrägen. Vier schmale Treppen wurden „wie auf einem Schiff" bewusst versteckt. Das Dachgeschoss für die Kartensammlung des Bauherrn wird über eine Klappleiter erschlossen. Die Küche ist ein Haus im Haus, „eine vollständig zum Garten hin geöffnete und lichtdurchflutete Welt, ein strukturiertes Labor der Ernährung, Versorgung, Sauberkeit und Arbeit". Eine Tiefgarage bietet Platz für eine Autosammlung. Die Architekten erklären: Der Bau sei ein Haus und zugleich sein Gegenteil: „Tellurisch, im Boden verankert, dabei leicht wie ein Heißluftballon kurz vor dem Abheben. Eine Rückbesinnung auf den authentischen Archetypus ‚Haus', wie ihn Gaston Bachelard und Luis Barragán verstanden: mit Keller und Speicher. Mit seiner Intensität und Bedeutung vereint dieses Haus all diese Symbole in sich. Ein Haus auf einem reizvollen Grundstück, ganz Garten, das über dem Gras schwebt."

Située à Sant Cugat près d'une forêt et d'un terrain de golf, cette maison est comparée par ses architectes à « un bateau ancré dans une mer de gazon ». L'entrée se signale par une placette austère et un bassin. Les installations de service sont en sous-sol et l'ensemble de la structure suit un plan au sol orthogonal mais marqué en coupe par de nombreuses obliques. Quatre escaliers étroits sont soigneusement dissimulés « comme dans un bateau ». Le client conserve sa collection de cartes dans un grenier accessible par une échelle pliante. La cuisine est presque une maison en soi, « un monde entièrement ouvert sur le jardin et baigné de lumière naturelle, un laboratoire organisé pour la nutrition, les soins, l'entretien et le travail ». Une collection de voitures est parquée dans le garage en sous-sol. « C'est une maison et son contraire, explique les architectes, elle est tellurique, ancrée sur sa base, mais légère et prête à s'envoler comme un ballon. Il nous a fallu revenir à l'idée de "maison", dans le sens de l'archétype exprimé par Gaston Bachelard et Luis Barragán, d'un lieu avec une cave et un grenier. Par son intensité et sa signification, cette maison regroupe tous les symboles. C'est une maison construite sur un terrain agréable, tout en jardin, qui semble flotter au-dessus du gazon. »

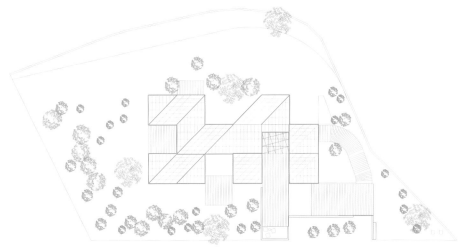

Seen from above, or in the site plan to the left, the house fully lives up to its name, derived from the Japanese art of folding paper.

Auf der Luftaufnahme und dem Lageplan links wird das Haus voll und ganz seinem Namen gerecht, der sich von der japanischen Papierfalttechnik ableitet.

Vue du ciel, ou dans le plan ci-contre, la maison illustre parfaitement son nom qui rappelle l'art japonais du pliage du papier.

The folding effect seen in the aerial
views of the house is visible in this
interior staircase, as well as the outside photo (below).

Die auf der Luftaufnahme erkennbaren Falteffekte zeigen sich auch an
dieser Klapptreppe und der Außenauf-
nahme (unten).

L'effet de pliage aperçu dans les vues
aériennes de la maison se retrouve
dans cet escalier intérieur ou dans la
photo d'extérieur ci-dessous.

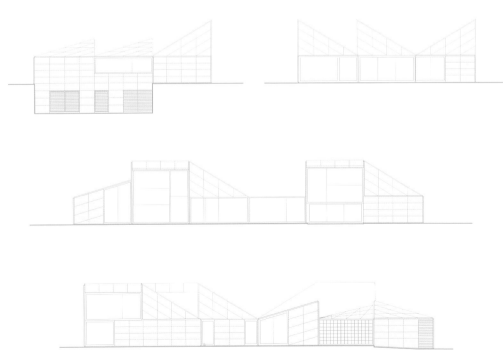

Elevation drawings show the tilted roof surfaces and some of the double-height spaces that can be seen in the photo above.

Aufrisse zeigen die Dachschrägen und einige der doppelgeschossigen Räume, die auf dem Foto oben zu erkennen sind.

Les élévations montrent l'inclinaison des toitures et certains volumes double hauteur que l'on retrouve dans la photo ci-dessus.

As seen in a site plan (left), the house assumes a design made up essentially of rectangles. Sliding glass walls at ground level allow living space to be both inside and outside at once.

Der Lageplan (links) zeigt, dass der Entwurf in erster Linie aus Recht-ecken besteht. Glasschiebetüren im Erdgeschoss sorgen dafür, dass Innen- und Außenraum im Wohnbe-reich fließend ineinander übergehen.

Comme le montre le plan au sol (à gauche), la maison est essentielle-ment composée de rectangles. Au rez-de-chaussée, des panneaux de verre coulissants favorisent l'interpé-nétration mutuelle du dedans et du dehors.

The living space seen on the left
page from the opposite angle. To
the right, the library area.

Der Wohnraum auf der linken Seite
hier aus entgegengesetzter Perspektive. Rechts der Bibliotheksbereich.

Le séjour montré page de gauche,
vu en contre-plan. À droite, la
bibliothèque.

PEZO VON ELLRICHSHAUSEN ARCHITECTS

Pezo Von Ellrichshausen Arquitectos
Nonguen 776
Concepción 4030000
Chile

Tel: +56 41 221 0281
E-mail: info@pezo.cl / Web: www.pezo.cl

Pezo Von Ellrichshausen Architects was founded in Buenos Aires in 2001 by Mauricio Pezo and Sofía Von Ellrichshausen. **MAURICIO PEZO** was born in Chile in 1973 and completed his M.Arch degree at the Catholic University of Chile (Santiago, 1998). He graduated from the University of Bío-Bío (Concepción, 1999). He is a visual artist and director of the Movimiento Artista del Sur (MAS). **SOFÍA VON ELLRICHSHAUSEN** was born in Argentina in 1976. She holds a degree in architecture from the University of Buenos Aires (Buenos Aires, 2002). They teach regularly in Chile and have been Visiting Professors at the University of Texas at Austin, and at Cornell University in New York. They were awarded the Commended Prize at the AR Awards for Emerging Architecture (London, 2005) and the Best Work by Young Architects Prize at the fifth Iberoamerican Architecture Biennial (Montevideo, 2006). Their built work includes XYZ Pavilions (Concepción, 2001); Rivo House (Valdivia, 2003); 120 Doors Pavilion (Concepción, 2003); Poli House (Coliumo, 2005); Wolf House (Andalue, 2006–07); Parr House (Chiguayante, 2008); Fosc House (San Pedro, 2008–09); and several public art projects. Their more recent work includes the Arco (2010) and Cien (2009–11) Houses (both in Concepción, the latter published here); and the Gold Building (Concepción, 2011), all in Chile.

Pezo Von Ellrichshausen Architects wurde 2001 in Buenos Aires von Mauricio Pezo und Sofía Von Ellrichshausen gegründet. **MAURICIO PEZO** wurde 1973 in Chile geboren, erlangte seinen M. Arch. an der Universidad Católica de Chile (Santiago, 1998) und schloss sein Studium an der Universidad del Bío-Bío (Concepción, 1999) ab. **SOFÍA VON ELLRICHSHAUSEN** wurde 1976 in Argentinien geboren. Ihr Architekturstudium schloss sie an der Universität Buenos Aires ab (2002). Beide lehren regelmäßig in Chile und hatten Gastprofessuren an der University of Texas in Austin und der Cornell University in New York. Ausgezeichnet wurde das Team mit dem Empfehlungspreis bei den AR Awards for Emerging Architecture (London, 2005) sowie als bestes Projekt junger Architekten auf der 5. Iberoamerikanischen Architekturbiennale (Montevideo, 2006). Zu ihren realisierten Bauten zählen u. a. die XYZ-Pavillons (Concepción, 2001), das Haus Rivo (Valdivia, 2003), der 120-Türen-Pavillon (Concepción, 2003), das Haus Poli (Coliumo, 2005), das Haus Wolf (Andalue, 2006–07), das Haus Parr (Chiguayante, 2008), das Haus Fosc (San Pedro, 2008–09) sowie verschiedene öffentliche Kunstprojekte. Jüngere Projekte sind das Haus Arco (2010) und das Haus Cien (2009–11; beide in Concepción, Letzteres hier vorgestellt) sowie das Gold-Gebäude (Concepción, 2011), alle in Chile.

L'agence Pezo Von Ellrichshausen Architects a été fondée à Buenos Aires en 2001 par Mauricio Pezo et Sofía von Ellrichshausen. **MAURICIO PEZO**, né au Chili en 1973, a obtenu son diplôme de M.Arch. à l'Université catholique du Chili (Santiago, 1998) et est diplômé de l'université Bío-Bío (Concepción, 1999). Artiste plasticien, il est directeur du Movimiento Artista del Sur (MAS). **SOFÍA VON ELLRICHSHAUSEN**, née en Argentine en 1976, est diplômée en architecture de l'université de Buenos Aires (2002). Ils enseignent régulièrement au Chili et ont été professeurs invités à l'université du Texas à Austin et à l'université Cornell à New York. Ils ont reçu le prix de l'*Architectural Review* pour l'architecture émergente (Londres, 2005) et le prix de la meilleure œuvre de jeunes architectes à la Vᵉ Biennale d'architecture ibéro-américaine (Montevideo, 2006). Parmi leurs réalisations, toutes au Chili : les pavillons XYZ (Concepción, 2001) ; la maison Rivo (Valdivia, 2003) ; le pavillon des 120 portes (Concepción, 2003) ; la maison Poli (Coliumo, 2005) ; la maison Wolf (Andalue, 2006–07) ; la maison Parr (Chiguayante, 2008) ; la maison Fosc (San Pedro, 2008–09) et plusieurs projets artistiques publics. Plus récemment, ils ont réalisé les maisons Arco (2010) et Cien (2009–11), toutes deux à Concepción, la seconde publiée ici, et l'immeuble Gold (Concepción, 2011).

CIEN HOUSE
Concepción, Chile, 2009–11

*Address: Nonguen 776, Concepción, Chile
Area: 430 m². Client: Pezo Von Ellrichshausen
Cost: not disclosed*

A succession of square arches marks this interior living space. Finishings are relatively rough, as might be expected from the outside of the residence.

Das Interieur im Bild ist eine Folge quadratischer Räume. Die Oberflächen wirken vergleichsweise rau, was der Außenbau schon vermuten lässt.

Une enfilade d'arcs carrés rythme le volume du séjour. Les finitions sont laissées relativement brutes, ce qui évoque le traitement des façades.

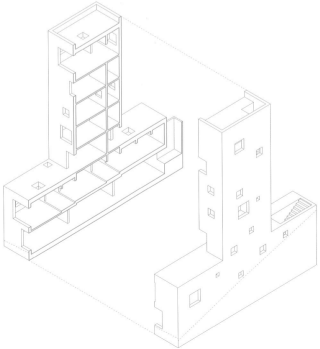

An axonometric drawing shows the "tower" section of the house, as well as its broader base. Above, the kitchen, finished in large wood planks.

Die Axonometrie zeigt nicht nur den „Turm"-Aufbau des Hauses, sondern auch das breitere Sockelgeschoss. Oben die Küche, ausgebaut mit breiten Holzdielen und -bohlen.

Dessin axonométrique montrant la partie « tour » de la maison et sa base. Ci-dessus, la cuisine au sol à larges planches de bois.

This house and office was built by the architects for their own use. They based the design on a series of 12 square modules, one of which concerns the roof. Made of poured concrete, the structure is no less than seven stories high because of the narrow lot it is built on. It is difficult to understand from the exterior what this unusual gray form is intended for, a degree of ambiguity that the architects have often cultivated in their other work. The unusual surface of the structure is made with concrete that has been manually chipped at by workers to expose the large aggregate used. The lowest level of the **CIEN HOUSE** is given over to three studios for art, while the kitchen, living, and dining areas are set on the next floor up. There are bedrooms on the third and fourth floors, with the architects' office above. Wooden stairways offer separate entry to the house and office. Pine was used for cladding, painted gray in the office areas and white in the house. Their own words about the building emphasize its inherent ambiguity: "You reach the studio by facing a mirror that shows in the inside what lies across the street. Entering the tower is a kind of blindness. Here, the cypress turned into steps locks into a continuous spiral that slowly offers the view back while ascending."

Die Architekten bauten das Wohnhaus mit Büro für sich selbst. Der Entwurf basiert auf zwölf quadratischen Modulen, von denen eines das Dach bildet. Der Bau aus gegossenem Beton ist wegen des schmalen Grundstückszuschnitts ganze sieben Stockwerke hoch. Von außen erschließt sich der Zweck des ungewöhnlichen grauen Bauwerks kaum – eine Mehrdeutigkeit, die die Architekten auch bei anderen Projekten bewusst einsetzen. Die ungewöhnliche Betonfassade wurde manuell von Handwerkern bearbeitet, um den groben Zuschlag sichtbar zu machen. Die unterste Ebene des **CIEN HOUSE** ist drei Ateliers vorbehalten, Küche, Wohn- und Essbereich liegen eine Etage höher. Im zweiten und dritten Stock liegen die Schlafzimmer, das Architekturbüro darüber. Über Holztreppen werden Wohnhaus und Büro separat erschlossen. Für die Verkleidung wurde Kiefernholz genutzt, das im Bürobereich grau, im Wohnbereich weiß gestrichen ist. Die Architekten betonen die Mehrdeutigkeit des Baus: „Erreicht man das Atelier, steht man einem Spiegel gegenüber, der nach innen projiziert, was auf der gegenüberliegenden Straßenseite liegt. Beim Betreten des Turms umfängt einen Dunkelheit. Die Treppe aus Zypressenholz setzt sich als Wendeltreppe fort, die beim Aufstieg den Ausblick nach und nach öffnet."

Cette maison et bureau est la résidence des architectes. Le projet repose sur 12 modules carrés, dont l'un est la toiture. En béton coulé sur place, la structure ne comporte pas moins de sept niveaux, ce qu'expliquent les faibles dimensions du terrain. Il est difficile de comprendre de l'extérieur la fonction de cette tour grise, mais ce degré d'ambiguïté est souvent cultivé par les architectes dans leurs réalisations. Les façades sont en béton travaillé à la main pour mettre en valeur la nature de l'agrégat utilisé. La partie inférieure de la **MAISON CIEN** est réservée à trois ateliers, tandis que le séjour, la cuisine et la salle à manger sont aménagés juste au-dessus. Des chambres se situent aux 2e et 3e étages, le bureau des architectes au 4e. Des escaliers en bois donnent un accès séparé à la maison et aux bureaux. Le pin, très présent à l'intérieur, a été peint en gris dans la partie bureau et en blanc dans la partie domestique. L'ambiguïté de l'ensemble s'exprime dans ce commentaire des architectes : « Vous atteignez le studio en faisant face à un miroir qui reflète de l'intérieur ce qui se passe dans la rue. Entrer dans la tour est un peu comme devenir aveugle. Ici les cyprès transformés en marches forment une spirale continue qui vous conduit lentement vers le haut et vous offre, lorsqu'elle tourne, une vision sur l'espace que vous venez de quitter. »

The exterior of the house has something of the feeling of a watchtower, or a fortified structure, but an open window reveals a warmer interior. Right, inside views and an exploded drawing showing each level.

Von außen wirkt das Haus fast wie ein Wachturm oder eine Festung, doch ein offenes Fenster zeigt ein deutlich wärmeres Interieur. Rechts Innenansichten und eine Explosionszeichnung der einzelnen Etagen.

L'extérieur de la maison fait un peu penser à une tour d'observation, ou à un donjon, mais la fenêtre ouverte laisse entrevoir un intérieur plus chaleureux. À droite, vues de l'intérieur et dessin éclaté détaillant chaque niveau.

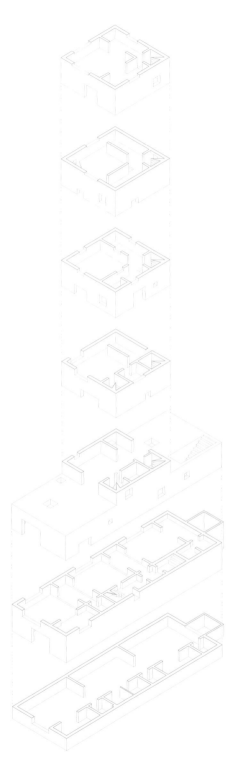

CHARLES PICTET

Charles Pictet Architecte
12A Frank Thomas
1208 Geneva
Switzerland

Tel: +41 22 737 14 14
Fax: +41 22 737 14 00
E-mail: info@pictet-architecte.ch
Web: www.pictet-architecte.ch

CHARLES PICTET was born in 1963. He received his Diploma in Architecture from the École d'Architecture de Genève in 1996. He worked as an intern (1992–93) and as a project architect in the office of Kaus Theo Brenner (Berlin, 1996–97). He completed several projects in collaboration with François Frey between 1998 and 2001. He created his own office in Geneva in 2002. He has taught at the EPFL (Lausanne, 2010, 2011–12). Aside from the Vacation Chalet in Les Diablerets (2007–08, published here), he has completed a house in Frontenex (2006); an orangerie and stables (Vandoeuvres, 2008); an atelier in an agricultural building (Landecy, Geneva, 2010); a building for student housing (Geneva, 2011); and a house in Anières (2011), all in Switzerland. He is currently working on a research center for Genève Internationale (ongoing).

CHARLES PICTET wurde 1963 geboren. Er machte sein Architekturdiplom 1996 an der École d'Architecture de Genève. Er arbeitete als Praktikant (1992–93) und Projektarchitekt bei Klaus Theo Brenner (Berlin, 1996–97). Zwischen 1998 und 2001 realisierte er verschiedene Projekte in Zusammenarbeit mit François Frey. Sein eigenes Büro in Genf gründete er 2002. Er lehrte an der EPFL Lausanne (2010, 2011–12). Neben dem Chalet in Les Diablerets (2007–08, hier vorgestellt) realisierte er ein Haus in Frontenex (2006), eine Orangerie mit Stall in Vandoeuvres (2008), ein Atelier in einem landwirtschaftlichen Gebäude (Landecy, Genf, 2010), ein Studentenwohnheim (Genf, 2011) und ein Haus in Anières (2011), alle in der Schweiz. Aktuell arbeitet er an einem Forschungszentrum für Genève Internationale.

CHARLES PICTET, né en 1963, est diplômé de l'École d'architecture de Genève (1996). Il a été stagiaire (1992–93) puis architecte de projet chez Klaus Theo Brenner (Berlin, 1996–97), puis a réalisé divers projets en collaboration avec François Frey de 1998 à 2001. Il a créé son agence à Genève en 2002. Il a enseigné à l'EPFL à Lausanne (2010, 2011–12). En dehors de son chalet de vacances aux Diablerets (2007–08, publié ici), il a réalisé une maison à Frontenex (2006) ; une orangerie et des écuries (Vandœuvres, 2008) ; un atelier dans un bâtiment agricole (Landecy, Genève, 2010) ; un immeuble de logements pour étudiants (Genève, 2011) et une maison à Anières (2011), le tout en Suisse. Il travaille actuellement sur un projet de centre de recherches pour Genève Internationale.

VACATION CHALET

Les Diablerets, Switzerland, 2007–08

Area: 120 m². Client: not disclosed
Cost: not disclosed. Collaboration: Renaud Pidoux

As is most often the case in Swiss mountain villages, the chalet is designed with a mind to traditional forms, but numerous details, from the windows to the terraces, show that this house is modern.

Das Chalet wurde, wie in vielen schweizerischen Bergdörfern üblich, in Anknüpfung an traditionelle Bauweisen geplant. Dennoch verraten zahlreiche Details wie Fenster und Balkone, wie modern der Bau ist.

Comme souvent dans les villages des montagnes suisses, le chalet respecte les formes traditionnelles, mais de nombreux détails, des fenêtres aux terrasses, montrent qu'il est en fait très moderne.

This wood post-and-beam structure allows for openings around its entire periphery. A concrete tower is placed at the center of the square plan, containing the chimney but also stabilizing the entire structure and connecting all the rooms. The architect insists on the close relation of this design to local construction methods and traditions. The house was the winner of a locally prestigious 2010 Disctinction Romande Award. Astrid Staufer, a member of the jury for the Award, writes: "Contaminated by a contemporary conception of lifestyles, the traditional chalet gives birth here to a new typology, which nonetheless retains familiar images. The complex and engaging atmosphere created inside the building also communicates with the Alpine landscape."

Die Ständerbauweise ermöglichte es, an allen Seiten des Hauses Öffnungen einzubauen. Im Herzen des quadratischen Grundrisses erhebt sich ein turmartiger Betonkern, durch den nicht nur der Kamin verläuft, sondern der zugleich den Bau stabilisiert und alle Räume verbindet. Der Architekt legtbesonderen Wert auf den engen Bezug des Entwurfs zu lokalen Baumethoden und -traditionen. 2010 wurde das Haus mit dem prestigeträchtigen regionalen Preis „Distinction romande d'architecture" ausgezeichnet. Astrid Staufer, Mitglied der Jury, schreibt: „Das traditionelle Chalet, kontaminiert von zeitgenössischen Lifestyle-Konzepten, wird hier zum Anstoß für eine neue Typologie, die vertraute Motive bewahrt. Die facettenreiche, einladende Atmosphäre im Innern schafft auch Bezüge zur alpinen Landschaft."

Contrairement à la tradition, cette construction à poteaux et poutres est percée de fenêtres sur ses quatre façades. Au centre de son plan carré, une tour-noyau en béton contient la cheminée, fait fonction de contreventement de la structure et relie toutes les pièces. L'architecte insiste sur la relation étroite entre ce projet et les méthodes de construction et traditions locales. Ce chalet a remporté le prestigieux prix local de la Distinction romande d'architecture 2010. Astrid Staufer, membre du jury de ce prix a écrit : « Contaminé par une conception contemporaine de l'habiter, le "chalet" traditionnel donne naissance à un nouveau type, dans lequel se nichent les images qui nous sont familières. L'atmosphère à la fois complexe et engageante que dégage l'intérieur du bâtiment se communique aussi au paysage alpin.»

Basically a barnlike form, as seen in the section and elevation drawings below, the structure is situated on a slope. Above, concrete stairs contrast with the wooden structure.

Das Chalet ist, wie Querschnitt und Aufrisse (unten) zeigen, eigentlich wie eine Scheune gebaut und liegt an einem Hang. Die Betontreppe (oben) bildet einen Kontrast zum Holz.

Comme le montrent les coupes et élévations ci-dessous, la structure en forme de grange a été construite en pleine pente. Au-dessus, contraste entre l'escalier en béton et la construction en bois.

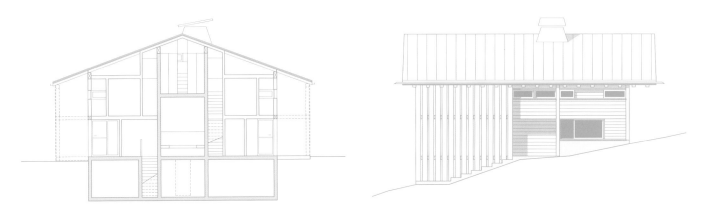

Left, interiors are finished almost entirely in wood, as can be seen in this relatively narrow stairway. Below, plans of the house show a bedroom and play area.

Der Innenausbau erfolgte fast ausschließlich in Holz, wie der Blick in das schmale Treppenhaus zeigt. Die Grundrisse unten zeigen u. a. ein Schlaf- und ein Spielzimmer.

À gauche, les aménagements intérieurs sont presque entièrement en bois, y compris l'habillage de cette cage d'escalier assez étroite. Ci-dessous, plans de la maison montrant une chambre et une salle de jeu.

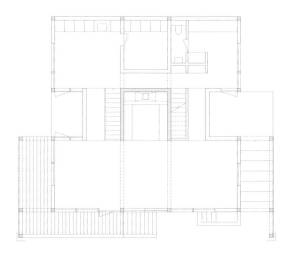

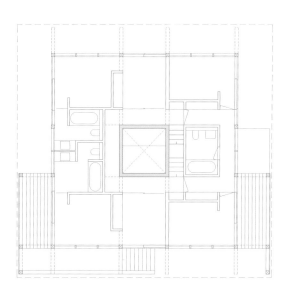

CHRISTIAN POTTGIESSER

Christian Pottgiesser
architecturespossibles
8 Rue Près aux Clercs
75007 Paris
France

Tel: +33 1 56 24 22 28
Fax: +33 9 55 20 22 28
E-mail: info@pottgiesser.fr
Web: www.pottgiesser.fr

CHRISTIAN POTTGIESSER was born in 1965 in Germany. He obtained his degree in architecture (D.P.L.G.) from the École d'Architecture de Paris-Villemin (1991) and a D.E.A. degree in Philosophy from Paris 1, Panthéon Sorbonne (1993). He cofounded the office architecturespossibles in 2005 with Pascale Thomas Pottgiesser. Born in 1962 in Le Havre, **PASCALE THOMAS POTTGIESSER** is an artist who studied at the École des Beaux Arts (graduated 1986) and has collaborated with Christian Pottgiesser since 2002. The name of their office is meant to imply that at the beginning of a project, any form of architecture is possible. Their work includes a temporary garden for the Chaumont Garden Festival (Chaumont, 2006); offices for Pons + Huot (Paris, 2008), winner of a contractworld Award (Best Office Architecture, 2008); and the L House (Yvelines, 2007–11, published here), which won the RIBA 2012 EU Award, all in France.

CHRISTIAN POTTGIESSER wurde 1965 in Deutschland geboren. Sein Architekturdiplom (D.P.L.G.) machte er an der École d'Architecture de Paris-Villemin (1991), es folgte ein Abschluss in Philosophie (D.E.A.) an der Universität Paris 1, Panthéon Sorbonne (1993). Gemeinsam mit Pascale Thomas Pottgiesser gründete er 2005 das Büro architecturespossibles. **PASCALE THOMAS POTTGIESSER**, geboren 1962 in Le Havre, ist Künstlerin, schloss ihr Studium 1986 an der École des Beaux Arts ab und arbeitet seit 2002 mit Christian Pottgiesser zusammen. Wie der Name des Büros vermuten lässt, ist für die Architekten zu Beginn eines neuen Projekts grundsätzlich jede bauliche Form möglich. Zu ihren Projekten zählen ein temporärer Garten für das Gartenfestival in Chaumont (2006), Büros für Pons + Huot (Paris, 2008), ausgezeichnet mit dem contractworld Award für die beste Büroarchitektur (2008), sowie das Haus L (Yvelines, 2007–11, hier vorgestellt), alle in Frankreich.

CHRISTIAN POTTGIESSER, né en 1965 en Allemagne, a obtenu son diplôme d'architecte D.P.L.G de l'École d'architecture de Paris-Villemin (1991) et un D.E.A de philosophie de l'université Paris 1, Panthéon Sorbonne (1993). Il a fondé l'agence architecturespossibles en association avec Pascale Thomas Pottgiesser en 2005. Née en 1962 au Havre, l'artiste **PASCALE THOMAS POTTGIESSER** a étudié à l'École des beaux-arts de Paris (1986) et collabore avec Christian Pottgiesser depuis 2002. Le nom de leur agence signifie qu'au départ d'un projet, toute forme d'architecture reste encore possible. Parmi leurs réalisations, toutes en France : un jardin temporaire pour le Festival des jardins de Chaumont (Chaumont, 2006) ; des bureaux pour Pons + Huot (Paris, 2008) qui ont remporté le prix Contractworld pour la meilleure architecture de bureaux en 2008 et la maison L (Yvelines, 2007–11, publiée ici).

L HOUSE
Yvelines, France, 2007–11

*Area: 616 m². Client: not disclosed
Cost: not disclosed*

Above, a glazed roof offers views of the trees and the surrounding natural setting. The unexpected angles of the window frame are a recurring feature in the house.

Ein Glasdach (oben) ermöglicht den Blick in die Bäume und das natürliche Umfeld. Die ungewöhnlichen Winkel der Fensterrahmen tauchen im gesamten Haus immer wieder auf.

Ci-dessus, une verrière offre une vue sur les arbres et le cadre de verdure. L'originalité du dessin des châssis de fenêtres est récurrente.

Set in a generous (4850 m²) garden, the clients for this house contacted Christian Pottgiesser in 2004 because they had seen his work in a magazine. They wished to add to an existing house, which includes an orangerie that was part of an 18th-century chateau. They imagined a single, high building that would hide views to a neighboring property. The proximity of listed buildings complicated the task, as did local construction rules. Rather than a single structure, the architect finally proposed five small towers—one for each child and another for the parents. Connected at the ground floor to the older building, the form of the base of the house is likened by the architect to that of an amoeba, a "soft" form that is almost 47 meters long. He also refers to a "river of rocks" in which the towers are set. The house won the laureate of the 2012 RIBA European Union Award.

Die Bauherren des auf einem großzügigen, 4850 m² großen Gartengrundstück gelegenen Hauses kontaktierten Christian Pottgiesser 2004, als sie in einer Zeitschrift Entwürfe von ihm gesehen hatten. Sie wünschten die Erweiterung eines älteren Gebäudekomplexes, zu dem auch die Orangerie eines Chateaus aus dem 18. Jahrhundert gehört. Ihre Idee war zunächst ein höherer Einzelbau, der einen Sichtschutz zum benachbarten Grundstück bieten sollte. Doch die Nähe zu denkmalgeschützten Bauten ebenso wie die örtlichen Bauvorschriften verkomplizierten die Planung. Statt eines Einzelbaus entwarf der Architekt schließlich fünf kleine Türme – einen für jedes Kind, einen weiteren für die Eltern. Das mit dem Altbau verbundene Sockelgeschoss vergleicht der Architekt mit einer „Amöbe", einer fast 47 m langen „weichen" Form. Außerdem spricht er von „steinernen Flüssen", in die die Türme eingebettet wurden. Das Haus gewann 2012 den RIBA European Union Award.

Le client de cette maison édifiée au milieu d'un vaste jardin de 4850 m² avait contacté Christian Pottgiesser en 2004 après avoir lu un article sur son travail. Il souhaitait ajouter une extension à l'ancienne orangerie d'un château du XVIIIe siècle et avait imaginé une construction haute qui aurait caché les vues d'une propriété voisine. La proximité de bâtiments classés compliquait la tâche, pour ne pas parler de la règlementation locale. Au lieu d'une construction unique, l'architecte a finalement proposé cinq petites tours – une pour chaque enfant et une pour les parents. La forme de la base de la maison, connectée à l'ancien bâtiment au niveau du sol, est comparée par l'architecte à une amibe, forme « douce » de près de 47 m de long. Il propose également l'image de « rivière de rochers » pour le traitement paysager des alentours immédiats. La maison a remporté le prix RIBA European Union Award 2012.

Volumes that appear to be distinct
are, in fact, connected at the lower
level, as the section drawing repro-
duced here demonstrates.

Die vermeintlich frei stehenden Volumina sind tatsächlich durch ein
Sockelgeschoss verbunden, wie der
hier reproduzierte Querschnitt belegt.

Les volumes qui semblent séparés
sont en fait reliés en partie inférieure,
comme le montre la coupe ci-contre.

Right page, a child plays in an angled window. The shape of the opening itself is asymmetric and unusual because of the design of the frame.

Ein Kind spielt in einem der schiefwinkligen Fenster (rechte Seite). Die Fassadenöffnung ist asymmetrisch und auch wegen der Gestaltung der Fensterrahmen ungewöhnlich.

Page de droite : un enfant joue dans l'embrasure d'une fenêtre curieusement découpée. La forme de l'ouverture elle-même est asymétrique.

Features such as angled windows and light admitted from various sides enliven the otherwise quite mineral interiors.

Besonderheiten wie die schiefwinkligen Fensterrahmen und das von verschiedenen Seiten einfallende Licht beleben die ansonsten eher steinern wirkenden Interieurs.

Les fenêtres inclinées et la lumière provenant de divers axes animent les volumes intérieurs par ailleurs assez minéraux.

A site plan (right) shows the full disposition of the pavilions that make up the complex. Topographic lines reveal the slopes in the land.

Ein Plan (rechts) veranschaulicht die Lage der Pavillons, die den Komplex bilden. Topografische Linien zeigen das Gefälle des Geländes an.

Le plan du site (à droite) montre la disposition des pavillons qui constituent le petit complexe. Les lignes de niveau précisent le profil du terrain.

The hard wall, floor, and ceiling surfaces are tempered by a red surface, some wood, and, above all, light from various sources.

Die Härte der Wand-, Boden- und Deckenflächen wird gemildert durch eine rote Fläche, Holz und vor allem das aus verschiedensten Quellen einfallende Licht.

Le béton des murs, du sol et des plafonds est tempéré par une cloison rouge, quelques touches de bois et, surtout, par la lumière qui vient de diverses sources.

PEDRO REIS

Pedro Reis
Rua da Emenda 30 - CV1
Lisbon 1200–170
Portugal

Tel: +351 21 887 02 75
Fax: +351 21 887 02 75
E-mail: info@pedroreis.pt
Web: www.pedroreis.pt

PEDRO REIS was born in Silves, Portugal, in 1967. He graduated from the Faculty of Architecture of Porto University in 1994 and then worked in the office of Eduardo Souto de Moura. He also worked in New York with Toshiko Mori and later moved to East Timor to coordinate the United Nations reconstruction program and a school design project administered by the World Bank. Pedro Reis established his own practice in Lisbon, in 2003, and since then has been awarded the first prize in several architectural competitions for public and private buildings. He is currently a Professor of Architectural Design at the Department of Architecture of the Universidade Autónoma de Lisboa, and participated in the national representation at the 8th São Paulo International Architecture Biennial in Brazil (2009). His work includes a church (Quelicai, East Timor, 2003); House in Sé (Lisbon, 2003); Santa Catarina Nursery School and Kindergarten (São Tomé and Príncipe, 2009); House in Melides (Grândola, 2010, published here); Fontana House (Lisbon, 2012); House in Carcavelos (Cascais, 2012); and House in Melides II (Grândola, 2013), all in Portugal unless stated otherwise.

PEDRO REIS wurde 1967 in Silves, Portugal, geboren. Er schloss sein Studium 1994 an der Architekturfakultät der Universität Porto ab und arbeitete im Anschluss daran für Eduardo Souto de Moura sowie für Toshiko Mori in New York. Später zog er nach Osttimor, wo er das Wiederaufbauprogramm der UN und ein Schul-projekt für die Weltbank koordinierte. Pedro Reis gründete sein eigenes Büro 2003 in Lissabon und gewann seitdem zahlreiche Architekturwettbewerbe für öffentliche und private Bauten. Derzeit ist er Professor für Entwerfen an der Architekturfakultät der Universidade Autónoma de Lisboa und war einer der portugiesischen Vertreter seines Landes auf der 8. Internationalen Architekturbiennale São Paulo in Brasilien (2009). Zu seinen Projekten zählen eine Kirche (Quelicai, Osttimor, 2003), ein Haus in Sé (Lissabon, 2003), der Kindergarten mit Vorschule Santa Catarina (São Tomé und Príncipe, 2009), das Haus in Melides (Grândola, 2010, hier vorgestellt), das Haus Fontana (Lissabon, 2012), ein Haus in Carcavelos (Cascais, 2012) sowie das Haus in Melides II (Grândola, 2013), alle in Portugal, sofern nicht anders vermerkt.

Né à Silves au Portugal en 1967, **PEDRO REIS** est diplômé de la faculté d'architecture de l'université de Porto (1994). Il a travaillé chez Eduardo Souto de Moura et à New York chez Toshiko Mori. Il a par la suite coordonné le programme de reconstruction des Nations Unies et un projet d'école de la Banque mondiale au Timor oriental. Il a créé son agence à Lisbonne en 2003 et, depuis, a remporté le premier prix de plusieurs concours pour des bâtiments publics ou privés. Il est actuellement professeur de conception architecturale au département d'Architecture de l'Université autonome de Lisbonne et a fait partie de la représentation du Portugal à la VIIIe Biennale internationale d'architecture de São Paulo (2009). Parmi ses réalisations, la plupart au Portugal : une église (Quelicai, Timor oriental, 2003) ; une maison à Sé (Lisbonne, 2003) ; l'école de puériculture et jardin d'enfants Santa Catarina (São Tomé et Principe, 2009) ; une maison à Melides (Grândola, 2010 ; publiée ici) ; la maison Fontana (Lisbonne, 2012) ; une maison à Carcavelos (Cascais, 2012) et la maison à Melides II (Grândola, 2013).

HOUSE IN MELIDES

Melides, Grândola, Portugal, 2010

Area: 344 m². Client: not disclosed
Cost: not disclosed

The façade of the house is in good part designed with full-height glazing. The white shell wraps continuously around these warmer interiors.

Die Fassade des Hauses ist weitgehend geschosshoch verglast. Die weiße Gebäudehülle umgibt die wärmer wirkenden Wohnräume fortlaufend.

La façade de la maison est en grande partie constituée d'une immense baie vitrée, prise dans une coque de béton qui met en valeur le traitement chaleureux de l'intérieur.

Located on the southern Alentejo coast, this is a holiday residence. The client organized an architectural competition between three offices. This winning proposal takes into account the countryside surroundings. Built on top of a hill it appears nonetheless to be protected by the surrounding rugged site. Two overlapping volumes form a cross-like shape. The more exposed upper volume contains what the architect describes as the basic housing space. It has large glazed surfaces, while the more "anchored" lower block clad in earth-colored concrete is meant to give "support and stability" to the house. The kitchen is the crossing point between the two volumes and thus takes on considerable importance in the design. A long pergola encourages the owners to move freely between interior and exterior.

Das Ferienhaus liegt am südlichen Küstenabschnitt des Alentejo. Der Bauherr organisierte einen Entwurfswettbewerb zwischen drei Büros, wobei sich letztendlich der Entwurf durchsetzten konnte, der auch die Landschaft der Umgebung berücksichtigte. Das auf einem Hügel gebaute Haus wirkt durch die felsige Umgebung dennoch geschützt. Zwei einander überschneidende Riegel bilden eine kreuzartige Form. Das obere, exponiertere Volumen bietet Platz für den Hauptwohnbereich, so der Architekt. Hier wurde großflächig verglast, während der untere Riegel, der mit erdfarbenem Beton verputzt wurde, das Haus „erdet" und „Halt und Stabilität" vermittelt. Die Küche befindet sich am Kreuzungspunkt der zwei Riegel, ihr misst der Entwurf entsprechendes Gewicht bei. Eine lange Pergola lädt die Bewohner ein, sich unbeschwert zwischen Innen- und Außenraum zu bewegen.

Cette maison de vacances est située dans le sud de la partie côtière de l'Alentejo. Le client avait organisé un concours d'architecture entre trois agences, que la proposition de Pedro Reis, qui tenait particulièrement en compte l'environnement campagnard, avait remporté. Construite au sommet d'une colline, elle semble néanmoins protégée par le site accidenté. Ses deux volumes se superposent en croix. La partie supérieure, plus exposée et percée de vastes baies contient ce que l'architecte présente comme l'espace domestique principal, tandis que la partie basse, plus ancrée dans le sol, en béton couleur de terre apporte à la maison « soutien et stabilité ». La cuisine, au point de croisement des deux volumes, prend de ce fait une importance considérable dans le projet. Une longue pergola permet aux habitants de se déplacer librement entre l'intérieur et l'extérieur.

The architecture frames a view of a brick surface and a pool, which lead to the forested setting.

Der Bau rahmt die Aussicht auf eine gepflasterte Fläche und einen Pool, die den Blick in die bewaldete Landschaft lenken.

La projection de la toiture cadre une vue de la piscine et de sa bordure en brique orientée vers la forêt.

Above, a general view of the house with the main white volume set at a perpendicular to the lower earth-colored block. Below, a site plan shows the hilly terrain.

Oben das Haus in der Gesamtansicht. Der weiße Riegel ist lotrecht zum daruntergelegenen, erdfarbenen Riegel platziert. Unten ein Lageplan, der die hügelige Topografie zeigt.

Ci-dessus, vue générale de la maison où l'on voit le volume principal posé perpendiculairement sur un bloc inférieur de couleur brique. Ci-dessous, un plan du site montrant le vallonnement du terrain.

The sparsely furnished living area is nearly surrounded by full-height, sliding glass walls. Left, the kitchen with its wooden dining table.

Der minimal möblierte Wohnraum wird fast vollständig von raumhohen Glasschiebewänden umgeben. Links die Küche mit dem Esstisch aus Holz.

Le séjour, très peu meublé est presque entièrement encerclé de parois de verre coulissantes toute hauteur. À gauche, la cuisine et la table des repas, en bois.

Above, plans of the two volumes of the house. Below, the kitchen area is seen to the right of the image, the glass walls fully opened.

Oben Grundrisse der beiden Gebäuderiegel. Unten eine Aufnahme mit der Küche rechts im Bild, die Glasschiebetüren sind weit geöffnet.

Ci-dessus, plans des deux volumes constitutifs de la maison. Ci-dessous, la cuisine avec ses baies vitrées coulissantes totalement ouvertes.

BERNARDO RODRIGUES

Bernardo Rodrigues, arquitecto
Rua do Almada 254, 3 esq 32
4050–032 Porto
Portugal

Tel/Fax: +351 22 205 32 21
E-mail: office@bernardo-rodrigues.com
Web: www.bernardo-rodrigues.com / www.bernardorodriguespress.blogspot.com

Born in 1972 in Ponta Delgada (Azores), **BERNARDO RODRIGUES** obtained a first degree from the Porto School of Architecture (1996), and his M.Arch degree from Columbia University (New York, 1999). He opened his own office in Porto in 2001. He initiated a plan at Harvard in 2006 for sustainable architecture, now used in China, Africa, and the USA. His work includes the Floating Cloud House (Rabo de Peixe, Saint Michael, Azores, 1998); Chapel of the Sky (Ribeira Quente, Saint Michael, Azores, 1999); Flight of Birds House (Saint Michael, Azores, 2006–11, published here); Chapel of Eternal Light (Ponta Garça, Saint Michael, Azores, 2003–); Arch & Orchid Hotel (Xi'an, China, 2009–); Opus Lusa House (Altares, Terceira, Azores, 2009–); Vitreous Babel, 1001 Star Hotel (Luanda, Angola, Africa 2010–); The Myth and the Mountain, a private library (Lousada, Porto, 2011–); the Non-Linear History of Dreams Youth Hotel (Ponta Delgada, Saint Michael, Azores, 2012–); and the House on the Creation of Opacity (Populo, Saint Michael, Azores, 2012–). He is also working on another project called the House on the Theory of Winds (Leiria, 2012–), all in Portugal unless stated otherwise.

BERNARDO RODRIGUES, geboren 1972 in Ponta Delgada (Azoren), erwarb einen ersten Abschluss an der Porto School of Architecture (1996) sowie später einen M. Arch. an der Columbia University (New York, 1999). 2001 gründete er sein eigenes Büro in Porto. 2006 initiierte er in Harvard ein Programm für nachhaltige Architektur, das inzwischen in China, Afrika und den USA Anwendung findet. Zu seinen Projekten zählen das Haus Schwebende Wolke (Rabo de Peixe, Saint Michael, Azoren, 1998), die Kapelle des Himmels (Ribeira Quente, Saint Michael, Azoren, 1999), das Haus Flug der Vögel (Saint Michael, Azoren, 2006–11, hier vorgestellt), die Kapelle des Ewigen Lichts (Ponta Garça, Saint Michael, Azoren, seit 2003), das Hotel Arch & Orchid (Xi'an, China, seit 2009), das Haus Opus Lusa (Altares, Terceira, Azoren, seit 2009), Vitreous Babel, 1001 Star Hotel (Luanda, Angola, seit 2010), Der Mythos und der Berg, eine private Bibliothek (Lousada, Porto, seit 2011), das Jugendhotel Níchtlineare Geschichte der Träume (Ponta Delgada, Saint Michael, Azoren, seit 2012) sowie das Haus über die Schaffung der Undurchsichtigkeit (Populo, Saint Michael, Azoren, seit 2012). Derzeit arbeitet er an einem Haus über die Theorie der Winde (Leiria, seit 2012), alle in Portugal, sofern nicht anders angegeben.

Né en 1972 à Ponta Delgada (Açores), **BERNARDO RODRIGUES** est diplômé de l'École d'architecture de Porto (1995) et titulaire d'un M.Arch. de l'université Columbia (New York, 1999). Il a ouvert son agence à Porto en 2001. En 2006, il a initié à Harvard un programme pour l'architecture durable, utilisé aujourd'hui en Chine, en Afrique et aux États-Unis. Parmi ses réalisations, toutes au Portugal sauf mention contraire : la Maison nuage flottant (Rabo de Peixe, São Miguel, Açores, 1998) ; la chapelle du Ciel (Ribeira Quente, São Miguel, Açores, 1999) ; la Maison vol d'oiseaux (São Miguel, Açores, 2006–11, publiée ici) ; la chapelle de la Lumière éternelle (Ponta Garça, São Miguel, Açores, 2003–) ; l'Arch & Orchid Hotel (Xi'an, Chine, 2009–) ; la maison Opus Lusa (Altares, Terceira, Açores, 2009–) ; le Vitreous Babel, 1001 Star Hotel (Luanda, Angola, 2010–) ; Le mythe et la montagne, bibliothèque privée (Lousada, Porto, Portugal, 2011–) ; l'auberge de jeunesse Histoire non linéaire des rêves (Ponta Delagada, São Miguel, Açores, 2012–) et une Maison sur la création de l'opacité (Populo, São Miguel, Açores, 2012–). Il travaille actuellement sur le projet de la Maison sur la théorie des vents (Leiria, Portugal, 2012–).

FLIGHT OF BIRDS HOUSE

Saint Michael, Azores, Portugal, 2006–11

Area: 360 m². Client: Graça and Pedro Correia. Cost: not disclosed
Collaboration: James Grainger, Nelson Ferreira, Raquel Castaneira

The large red wall acts as a framing and supporting element for the un-usual curved front of the house— seen on the right page in drawings and in the image.

Die große rote Wand hat rahmende und stützende Funktion für die unge-wöhnliche, geschwungene Fassade des Hauses, die oben und auf der rechten Seite auf Zeichnungen zu sehen ist.

Le grand mur rouge est un élément structurel qui soutient et encadre le volume de la façade aux courbes inhabituelles (page de droite et plans).

Located on the northern side of Saint Michael Island in the Azores, this house was designed to protect the residents from dominant winds and frequent rain show-ers with patios and covered courtyards. Glass walls were chosen to offer views of the scenery. The upper floor private area is "more enclosed and protected." The archi-tect explains that despite its unusual appearance, this house "almost follows classical Palladio and Scamozzi central-plan design," with its double-height living room and two lateral wings ending in entrances from the south. Bernardo Rodrigues also says: "The roof offers possibilities of a flight of views over all the island's north shore."

Das Haus liegt im Norden der Azoreninsel São Miguel und wurde so geplant, dass die Bewohner durch überdachte Terrassen und Innenhöfe vor den starken Win-den und häufigen Regenschauern der Insel geschützt sind. Glaswände lenken den Blick in die Landschaft. Die privaten Wohnbereiche im Obergeschoss dagegen wirken „umbauter und geschützter". Dem Architekten zufolge entspricht das Haus – mit doppelgeschossigem Wohnraum und zwei Seitenflügeln mit Südeingang – trotz des ungewöhnlichen Erscheinungsbilds „fast den klassischen Zentralbaugrundrissen Palladios oder Scamozzis". Außerdem betont Bernardo Rodrigues: „Das Dach erschließt zahlreiche Blickachsen über die Nordstrände der Insel hinweg."

Située sur la face nord de l'île de São Miguel aux Açores, cette maison a été conçue en pensant à la protection de ses occupants des vents dominants et des pluies fréquentes par des patios et des cours couvertes. Des murs de verre offrent diverses perspectives sur le paysage. L'étage est « plus fermé, plus protégé ». L'archi-tecte explique que malgré son aspect inhabituel, cette maison, son séjour double hauteur et ses deux ailes latérales se terminant par des entrées orientées au sud « suit presque le concept de plan central de Palladio et de Samozzi… La toiture offre toute une gamme de vues sur la côte nord de l'île ».

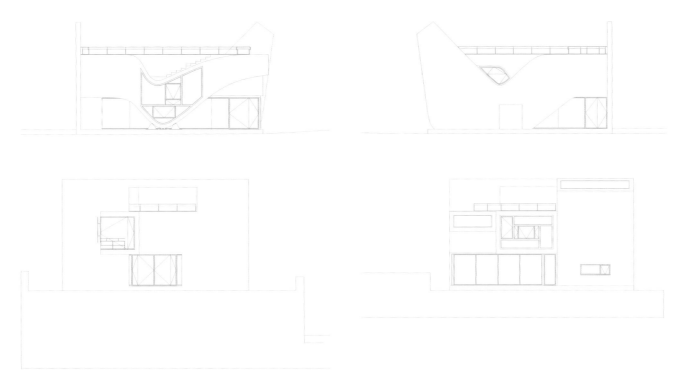

The curved element of the house is used to place a stairway. A reflecting pool lies at the base of the curve.

Im geschwungenen Element des Hauses ist ein Treppenhaus untergebracht. Am Fuß des Bogens befindet sich ein Spiegelbecken.

La partie incurvée de la maison contient l'escalier. Un bassin a été mis en place sous sa courbe.

Details like the curved shelf or seat, seen above, or an apparently rather unprotected roof terrace are quite quirky, in the spirit of the rest of the design.

Details wie die geschwungene Fensternische (oben) oder die offenbar recht ungeschützte Dachterrasse sind so eigenwillig wie der gesamte Entwurf überhaupt.

Divers détails comme le siège incurvé ci-dessus, ou la terrasse en toiture, non sécurisée, paraissent un peu étranges, comme l'ensemble du projet d'ailleurs.

Left page, the exterior curve is echoed in the form of the ceiling. Natural light is admitted both laterally and from above.

Die kurvigen Formen des Außenbaus finden ihr Echo in der Kontur der Decke (linke Seite). Tageslicht fällt von der Seite und von oben ein.

Page de gauche : la courbe vue de l'extérieur se retrouve dans la forme du plafond. L'éclairage naturel provient à la fois des ouvertures latérales et du plafond.

JUNICHI SAMPEI

Junichi Sampei
A.L.X. (Architect Label Xain)
C-type 1–23–1 Kitamagome
Ota-ku
Tokyo 143–0021
Japan

Tel: +81 3 3771 8151
E-mail: sampei@xain.jp
Web: www.xain.jp

JUNICHI SAMPEI was born in Chiba, Japan, in 1968. He received his degree from the Graduate School of the Engineering University (Nippon Institute of Technology, Miyashiro, Saitama, 1995). He worked in the office of the noted architect Shin Takamatsu in Kyoto from 1996 to 1998, and created his own firm A.L.X. in 1999 in Tokyo. His work includes the Shimada House (Shimada, 2003); Ikedayama House (Tokyo, 2004); Myourenji House (Yokohama, 2004); Kamishizu House (Chiba, 2005); T.H.I. (Chiba, 2005); Y.Z.R. (Tokyo, 2006); Sorte (Tokyo, 2008); On the Cherry Blossom House (Toyko, 2008); Dancing Living House (Yokohama, 2008); and House Tokyo (Tokyo, 2010, published here), all in Japan.

JUNICHI SAMPEI wurde 1968 in Chiba, Japan, geboren. Sein Studium schloss er an der Universität für Ingenieurwissenschaften ab (Nippon Institute of Technology, Miyashiro, Saitama, 1995). Von 1996 bis 1998 arbeitete er für den namhaften Architekten Shin Takamatsu in Kioto, 1999 gründete er sein eigenes Büro A.L.X. in Tokio. Zu seinen Projekten zählen das Haus Shimada (Shimada, 2003), das Haus Ikedayama (Tokio, 2004), das Haus Myourenji (Yokohama, 2004), das Haus Kamishizu (Chiba, 2005), T.H.I. (Chiba, 2005), Y.Z.R. (Tokio, 2006), Sorte (Tokio, 2008), das Haus Kirschblüte (Toiko, 2008), das Haus Tanzen Leben (Yokohama, 2008) sowie das Haus Tokio (Tokio, 2010, hier vorgestellt), alle in Japan.

Né à Chiba (Japon) en 1968, **JUNICHI SAMPEI** est diplômé de l'École supérieure de la faculté d'ingénierie de l'Institut nippon de technologie (préfecture de Miyashiro, Saitama, 1995). Il a travaillé dans l'agence de Shin Takamatsu à Kyoto de 1996 à 1998 et créé son agence, A.L.X. en 1999 à Tokyo. Parmi ses réalisations, toutes au Japon : la maison Shimada (Shimada, 2003) ; la maison Ikedayama (Tokyo, 2004) ; la maison Myourenji (Yokohama, 2004) ; la maison Kamishizu (Chiba, 2005) ; l'immeuble de logements T.H.I. (Chiba, 2005) ; l'immeuble de logements Y.Z.R. (Tokyo, 2006) ; l'immeuble de logements Sorte (Tokyo, 2008) ; la Maison cerisier en fleur (Tokyo, 2008) ; la Maison danser et vivre (Yokohama, 2008) et la maison Tokyo (Tokyo, 2010, publiée ici).

HOUSE TOKYO

Tokyo, Japan, 2010

Area: 78 m². Client: not disclosed
Cost: not disclosed

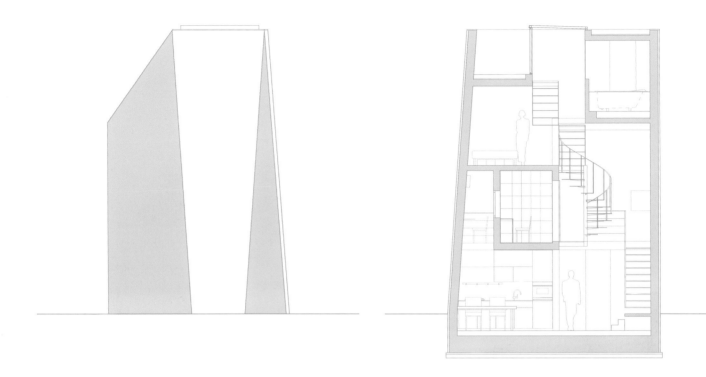

This house was designed for a young family, who compared the work of three different architects before selecting Junichi Sampei. Only 70% of the tiny 44-square-meter street-side site could actually be built on, thus the architect relied on height to give sufficient living space. The living room is located slightly below grade, with a bedroom, bathroom, "hobby space," and space for a child not yet born. Perforated steel covering windows is used to give privacy to the clients while permitting light to come in and allowing some visibility of the exterior from the inside. In fact, the clients wanted to keep some contact with the outside world. Operable windows permit them to hear the sounds of the neighborhood without being overtly visible. The steel surface of the house is thus something like a veil, providing privacy and rendering the building unusual in its folded simplicity. The architect suggests that the name of this project, **HOUSE TOKYO** (as opposed to Tokyo House), is an indication that he is dealing with the typical conditions of tiny construction areas in a generic way.

Die junge Familie, für die das Haus geplant wurde, verglich drei Architekturbüros, bevor sie sich für Junichi Sampei entschied. Nur 70 % des winzigen, 44 m² großen Grundstücks direkt an der Straße konnten bebaut werden, weshalb der Architekt in die Höhe planen musste, um ausreichenden Wohnraum zu schaffen. Der Wohnraum liegt leicht unter Straßenniveau, es gibt ein Schlafzimmer, Badezimmer, eine „Hobbyecke" und ein Kinderzimmer für ein noch nicht geborenes Kind. Lochbleche vor den Fenstern sorgen für Privatsphäre, lassen jedoch Licht herein und erlauben einen gewissen Grad an Ausblick, denn die Auftraggeber legten Wert darauf, etwas Kontakt zur Außenwelt zu wahren. Sie können die Fenster öffnen und die Geräusche der Nachbarschaft hören, ohne selbst gesehen zu werden. Die Stahloberfläche des Hauses wirkt wie ein Schleier, bietet Privatsphäre und gibt dem Bau durch die schlichte Faltung ein ungewöhnliches Profil. Der Architekt versteht den Projektnamen **HAUS TOKIO** (statt Tokio-Haus) als Hinweis darauf, dass er sich hier ganz allgemein mit den typischen Bedingungen derart kleiner Baugrundstücke auseinandersetzt.

Cette maison a été conçue pour un jeune couple qui avait comparé les travaux de trois architectes avant de retenir Junichi Sampei. Seuls 70 % de la petite parcelle de 44 m² étant constructibles, l'architecte a dû jouer sur la hauteur pour obtenir une surface utile suffisante. La maison contient un séjour, en partie en sous-sol, une chambre principale, une salle de bain, « un espace pour hobbies » et une chambre pour un futur enfant. Les ouvertures sont protégées par des panneaux d'acier perforé qui assurent l'intimité tout en permettant le passage de la lumière et en laissant une certaine visibilité vers la rue, les clients voulant conserver le contact avec le monde extérieur. Les fenêtres ouvrables permettent d'entendre les bruits extérieurs sans être vu. La peau d'acier de la façade est une sorte de voile qui assure l'intimité tout en matérialisant la forme inhabituelle de ce projet. Le nom de **MAISON TOKYO**, et non de maison à Tokyo, suggère que l'architecte a voulu aborder le problème typique des minuscules zones de construction de façon générique.

Located on a typical street corner in Tokyo, the house contrasts markedly with neighboring residences, but does respect their scale.

Das an einer typischen Tokioter Straßenecke gelegene Haus kontrastiert auffällig mit den Häusern der Nachbarschaft, orientiert sich jedoch an deren Maßstab.

Implantée à un coin de rue typique de Tokyo, la maison contraste fortement avec ses voisines tout en respectant leur échelle.

Thoroughly unexpected elements like the suspended spiral staircase—seen above, right, and in the plan below—generate spatial surprises inside the house.

Gänzlich unerwartete Elemente wie die schwebende Wendeltreppe – oben, rechts und auf dem Grundriss unten zu sehen – sorgen für räumliche Überraschungen im Haus.

Des éléments inattendus comme l'escalier en spirale suspendu – ci-dessus à droite et dans le plan ci-dessous – provoquent quelques surprises spatiales.

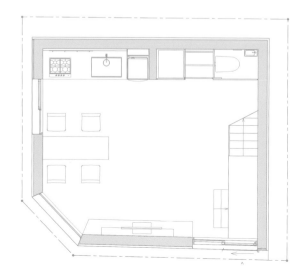

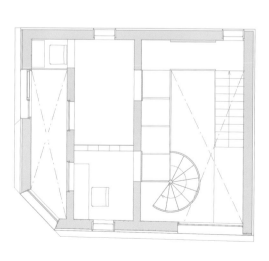

The relative complexity of the interior space is evident in the image above, while living space (below) seems calmer.

Die Komplexität des Interieurs wird auf der Ansicht oben deutlich. Der Wohnbereich (unten) wirkt ruhiger.

La complexité relative de l'espace intérieur est particulièrement nette dans l'image ci-dessus. Le séjour (ci-dessous) paraît plus apaisé.

White metal, glass, and concrete are the only materials in evidence, creating space that may appear to be cold, but it is enlivened by the addition of natural light.

Weiß lackiertes Metall, Glas und Beton sind die einzig sichtbaren Materialien. Solch ein Raum mag kühl wirken, wird jedoch durch das einfallende Tageslicht belebt.

Le métal laqué blanc, le verre et le béton sont les seuls matériaux apparents. L'espace peut sembler froid mais est animé par la présence de la lumière naturelle.

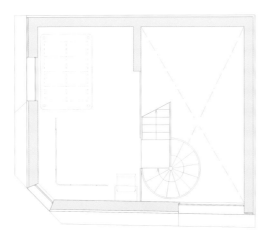

SANAA / KAZUYO SEJIMA + RYUE NISHIZAWA

SANAA / Kazuyo Sejima + Ryue Nishizawa
1–5–27 Tatsumi, Koto-ku, Tokyo 135–0053, Japan
Tel: +81 3 5534 1780 / Fax: +81 3 5534 1757
E-mail: sanaa@sanaa.co.jp / Web: www.sanaa.co.jp

Born in Ibaraki Prefecture, Japan, in 1956, **KAZUYO SEJIMA** received her M.Arch from the Japan Women's University in 1981 and went to work in the office of Toyo Ito the same year. She established Kazuyo Sejima & Associates in Tokyo in 1987. **RYUE NISHIZAWA** was born in Tokyo in 1966, and graduated from the National University in Yokohama in 1990. They began working together in 1990, and created the new firm Kazuyo Sejima + Ryue Nishizawa / SANAA in 1995. In 2010 SANAA was awarded the Pritzker Prize. The built work of Kazuyo Sejima includes the Saishunkan Seiyaku Women's Dormitory (Kumamoto, 1990–91); Pachinko Parlor I (Hitachi, Ibaraki, 1992–93); Pachinko Parlor II (Nakamachi, Ibaraki, 1993); Pachinko Parlor III (Hitachi Ibaraki, 1995); House in a Plum Grove (Tokyo, Japan, 2003); and Inujima Art House Project (1st phase; Okayama, Japan, 2010), all in Japan. The work of SANAA includes the 21st Century Museum of Contemporary Art (Kanazawa, Ishikawa, 2002–04); the Glass Pavilion of the Toledo Museum of Art (Ohio, USA, 2003–06); a theater and cultural center in Almere (the Netherlands, 2004–07); a building for the New Museum of Contemporary Art in New York (New York, USA, 2005–07); the Rolex Learning Center of the EPFL in Lausanne (Switzerland, 2007–09); the Derek Lam Flagship Store (New York, New York, USA, 2008–09); the Serpentine Pavilion (London, UK, 2009); and Shakujii Apartment (Tokyo, Japan, 2009–10, published here). Current work of SANAA includes the new building of the Louvre in Lens (France, 2009–12).

Die 1956 in der Präfektur Ibaraki geborene **KAZUYO SEJIMA** machte 1981 ihren M.Arch. an der Japanischen Frauenuniversität und begann noch im selben Jahr, für Toyo Ito zu arbeiten. 1987 gründete sie in Tokio ihr Büro Kazuyo Sejima and Associates. **RYUE NISHIZAWA** wurde 1966 in Tokio geboren und schloss sein Studium 1990 an der Nationaluniversität in Yokohama ab. Nachdem sie bereits seit 1990 zusammenarbeiteten, gründeten die beiden Architekten 1995 ihr Büro Kazuyo Sejima + Ryue Nishizawa/SANAA. 2010 wurde SANAA mit dem Pritzker-Preis ausgezeichnet. Kazuyo Sejima realisierte u. a. das Frauenwohnheim Saishunkan Seiyaku (Kumamoto, 1990–91), Pachinko Parlor I (Hitachi, Ibaraki, 1992–93), Pachinko Parlor II (Nakamachi, Ibaraki, 1993), Pachinko Parlor III (Hitachi Ibaraki, 1995), Haus in einem Pflaumenhain (Tokio, 2003) und das Inujima-Kunsthaus-Projekt (1. Bauabschnitt, Okayama, Japan, 2010), alle in Japan. Projekte von SANAA sind u. a. das Museum für Kunst des 21. Jahrhunderts (Kanazawa, Ishikawa, Japan, 2002–04), der Glaspavillon am Toledo Museum of Art (Ohio, 2003–06), ein Theater und Kulturzentrum in Almere (Niederlande, 2004–07), ein Gebäude für das New Museum of Contemporary Art in New York (2005–07), das Rolex Learning Center der EPFL in Lausanne (Schweiz, 2007–09), der Derek-Lam-Flagship-Store (New York, 2008–09), der Pavillon für die Serpentine Gallery (London, 2009) sowie das Projekt Shakuji Apartment (Tokio, 2009–10, hier vorgestellt). Zu den aktuellen Projekten von SANAA zählt das neue Gebäude für den Louvre in Lens (Frankreich, 2009–12).

Née dans la préfecture d'Ibaraki (Japon) en 1969, **KAZUYO SEJIMA** a reçu son diplôme de M.Arch. à l'Université féminine du Japon (1981) et a travaillé chez Toyo Ito. Elle a fondé son agence, Kazuyo Sejima & Associates à Tokyo en 1987. **RYUE NISHIZAWA**, né à Tokyo en 1966, est diplômé de l'Université nationale de Yoko-hama (1990). Ils ont commencé à travailler ensemble en 1990 et créé la nouvelle agence, Kazuyo Sejima + Ryue Nishizawa/SANAA en 1995. En 2010, SANAA a reçu le pris Pritzker. L'œuvre de Kazuyo Sejima comprend le dortoir pour femmes Saishunkan Seiyaku (Kumamoto, 1990–91); les Pachinko Parlors I, II et III (Hitachi, Ibaraki, 1992–93, 1993, 1995); la maison dans un verger de pruniers (Tokyo, 2003) et le projet de la maison d'art Inujima (1re phase, Okayama, Japon, 2010), tout au Japon. Les réalisations de SANAA comprennent, entre autres : le Musée de l'art contemporain du XXIe siècle (Kanazawa, Ishikawa, 2002–04); le pavillon de verre du Musée d'art de Toledo (Ohio, 2003–06); un théâtre et centre culturel (Almere, Pays-Bas, 2004–07); le New Museum of Contemporay Art (New York, 2005–07), le Rolex Learning Center de l'EPFL (Lausanne, Suisse, 2007–09); le magasin amiral Derek Lam (New York, 2008–09); le pavillon de la Serpentine (Londres, 2009) et l'appartement Shakujii (Tokyo, 2009–10, publié ici). SANAA travaille actuellement à l'achèvement du Louvre-Lens (France, 2009–12).

SHAKUJII APARTMENT

Tokyo, Japan, 2009–10

Area: 482 m². Client: Mitsuo Motohashi
Cost: not disclosed

This structure contains a total of eight apartments, slightly smaller than the normal Tokyo house. The steel frame is broadly glazed and green areas have been created, offering each inhabitant the type of contact with nature to which Japanese urban residents are sensitive. The complex is designed to fit, in terms of scale and alignments, into an area where row houses are more typical. The architects explain: "Each volume is constructed of a simple column and slab structure ... allowing for slabs to exist on various levels. Rooms expand in plan while living rooms extend (in section), and by half-submerging the space into the ground they are made cozy. This also makes way for covered terraces and parking spaces. Arranging terraces, gardens, parking spaces, and rooms next to one another allows for dense yet bright and well-ventilated spaces. A variety of depths is created along with spaces that blend interior and exterior, extending throughout the complex."

Die Wohnanlage mit acht Wohnungen ist etwas kleiner als das typische Tokioter Haus. Die Stahlrahmenkonstruktion wurde großzügig verglast und einzelne Bereiche begrünt, sodass alle Bewohner Kontakt zur Natur haben, was in japanischen Städten besonders geschätzt wird. Maßstab und Ausrichtung der Anlage ist auf das bauliche Umfeld abgestimmt, in dem Reihenhäuser typisch sind. Die Architekten erklären: „Jedes Haus wurden in einfacher Ständerbauweise errichtet ... so konnten die Geschossplatten auf unterschiedlicher Höhe platziert werden. Die Schlafzimmer breiten sich quer im Grundriss aus, während die Wohnzimmer (im Querschnitt) vertikal orientiert sind und gemütlicher wirken, weil sie zur Hälfte unter Straßenniveau abgesenkt sind. So entsteht außerdem Raum für überdachte Terrassen und Parkplätze. Durch die Reihung von Terrassen, begrünten Bereichen, Stellplätzen und Zimmern ergibt sich eine dichte, aber helle und gut belüftete Raumstruktur. Im gesamten Komplex wurde die Raumtiefe variiert und Bereiche geschaffen, in denen Innen- und Außenraum fließend ineinander übergehen."

Ce projet regroupe huit appartements, de dimensions légèrement plus réduites que celles d'une maison tokyoïte normale. Son ossature en acier est généreusement vitrée et de nombreux petits espaces verts offrent à chaque résidant le type de contact avec la nature auquel les Japonais urbains sont sensibles. Le complexe s'est adapté en termes d'échelle et d'alignements à un quartier où les maisons alignées sont la règle. « Chaque volume, expliquent les architectes, est construit à partir d'une simple colonne et d'une structure en poteaux-dalles... et chaque dalle affirme sa présence à chaque niveau. Les pièces se développent en plan et les séjours (en coupe) verticalement, s'étendent pour moitié confortablement en sous-sol, ce qui permet de dégager des terrasses couvertes et des places de parking. L'implantation des terrasses, des jardins, des parkings et des pièces accolées les unes aux autres permet de créer des espaces denses mais lumineux et bien ventilés. Différentes profondeurs spatiales ont été créées ainsi que des volumes qui fusionnent l'intérieur et l'extérieur et traversent le complexe... »

Though the apartment blocks are rather strictly aligned, with some variations in height, the actual structures are surprisingly open and airy.

Obwohl die einzelnen Blöcke – bei leichten Höhenunterschieden – streng angeordnet wurden, wirken die Bauten erstaunlich offen und luftig.

Si ces petits immeubles d'appartements sont rigoureusement alignés, non sans quelques variations de hauteur, ils restent étonnamment aériens.

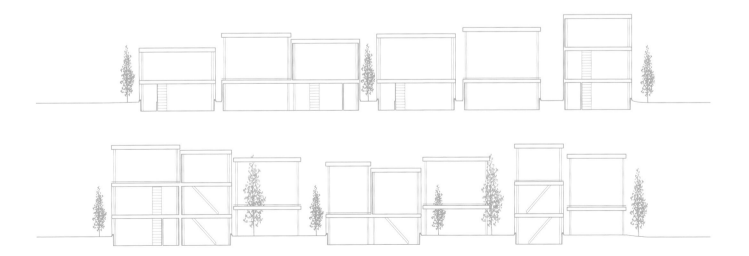

Though Tokyo's climate does not allow for year-round outdoor living, a good deal of space is devoted to these high, open exterior terraces.

Auch wenn das Klima in Tokio das Wohnen im Freien nicht das ganze Jahr über zulässt, wurde den offenen, erhöhten Terrassen viel Raum gegeben.

Bien que le climat tokyoïte ne permette pas de vivre en plein air toute l'année, une importante proportion de la surface a été consacrée à des terrasses extérieures ouvertes.

SHIM-SUTCLIFFE

Shim-Sutcliffe Architects Inc.
441 Queen Street East
Toronto
Ontario M5A 1T5
Canada

Tel: +1 416 368 3892
Fax: +1 416 368 9468
E-mail: info@shimsut.com
Web: www.shimsut.com

BRIGITTE SHIM was born in Kingston, Jamaica, in 1958. She received her B.Arch and her B.E.S. degrees from the University of Waterloo in Ontario, Canada. She worked in the office of Arthur Erickson (1981), and Baird/Sampson in Toronto, before creating her own firm, Brigitte Shim Architect (1988–94). She is a principal and co-founder of Shim-Sutcliffe, created in Toronto in 1994. **HOWARD SUTCLIFFE** was born in Yorkshire, England, in 1958. He also received his B.Arch and his B.E.S. degrees from the University of Waterloo in Ontario. He worked in the offices of Barton Myers (1984–86) and Merrick Architecture until 1993, creating Shim-Sutcliffe with Brigitte Shim the following year. Their recent work includes the Frum African Gallery in the Art Gallery of Ontario (Toronto, 2006–08); Integral House (Toronto, 2005–09, published here); House on Henry's Meadow (Vale Perkins, Quebec, 2007–09, also published here); Fung Loy Kok Institute of Taoism Place of Worship (Markham, 2009–); master plan and bridge for The Narrows for the Mnjikaning Fish Fence Circle (Orillia, 2010–); and the New Polyot Retreat Conference Center, Skolkovo Innovation Center (Russian Federation, 2011–), all in Canada unless stated otherwise.

BRIGITTE SHIM wurde 1958 in Kingston, Jamaica, geboren. Sie machte ihren B.Arch. sowie ihren Bachelor of Environmental Studies an der University of Water-loo in Ontario. Sie arbeitete für Arthur Erickson (1981) und Baird/Sampson in Toronto, bevor sie ihr Büro Brigitte Shim Architect (1988–94) gründete. Sie ist Seniorpartne-rin und Mitbegründerin von Shim-Sutcliffe, gegründet 1994 in Toronto. **HOWARD SUTCLIFFE** wurde 1958 in Yorkshire geboren. Auch er machte seinen B.Arch. und einen Bachelor of Environmental Studies an der University of Waterloo in Ontario. Er arbeitete für Barton Myers (1984–86) und bis 1993 Merrick Architecture und gründete mit Brigitte Shim im darauffolgenden Jahr Shim-Sutcliffe. Zu ihren jüngeren Projekten zählen die Frum Gallery für Afrikanische Kunst in der Art Gallery of Ontario (Toronto, 2006–08), das Integral-Haus (Toronto, 2005–09, hier vorgestellt), das Haus auf Henrys Wiese (Vale Perkins, Quebec, 2007–09, ebenfalls hier vorgestellt), der Andachts-raum am Fung Loy Kok Institute of Taoism (Markham, seit 2009), ein Masterplan und eine Brücke über die Narrows für den Mnjikaning Fish Fence Circle (Orillia, seit 2010) sowie das Neue Polyot-Retreat- und Konferenzzentrum am Innovationszentrum Skolkowo (Russische Föderation, seit 2011), alle in Kanada, sofern nicht anders vermerkt.

BRIGITTE SHIM, née à Kingston en Jamaïque en 1958 a obtenu son B.Arch. et son B.E.S. de l'université de Waterloo (Ontario, Canada). Elle a travaillé chez Arthur Erikson (1981) et Baird/Sampson à Toronto, avant de créer sa propre agence, Brigitte Shim Architect (1988–94). Elle est cofondatrice et dirigeante de l'agence Shim-Sutcliffe fondée à Toronto en 1994. **HOWARD SUTCLIFFE**, né dans le Yorkshire (GB) en 1958, a obtenu ses diplômes de B.Arch. et de B.E.S. de la même université. Il a travaillé chez Barton Myers (1984–86) et Merrick Architecture jusqu'en 1993, avant de créer Shim-Sutcliffe l'année suivante. Parmi leurs réalisations récentes, la plupart au Canada : la galerie d'art africain de la collection Frum au Musée des beaux-arts de l'Ontario (Toronto, 2006–08) ; l'Integral House (Toronto, 2005–09, publiée ici) ; la Maison sur la prairie d'Henry (Vale Perkins, Québec, 2007–09, publiée ici) ; L'Institut du taoïsme et sanctuaire Fung Loy Kok (Markham, 2009–) ; le plan directeur du pont des Détroits pour le Mnjikaning Fish Fence Circle (Orillia, 2010–) et le nouveau Centre de retraite et de conférence de Polyot, Centre d'innovation de Skolkovo (Russie, 2011–).

INTEGRAL HOUSE

Toronto, Canada, 2005–09

Area: 1394 m². Client: James Stewart
Cost: not disclosed. Collaboration: Betsy Williamson, Andrew Hart

This large residence, located in a wooded ravine, includes space for music and performance. The architects write: "Curvilinear, undulating glass walls with syncopated oak fins are used to shape a large gathering space where building and landscape are intertwined. The journey through the house parallels the experience of descending the ravine slope, taking advantage of the sectional qualities of the site and amplifying the journey through the project." The five-story house was designed for James Stewart, the author of widely used textbooks on calculus. He interviewed numerous architects, including Frank Gehry, before selecting Shim-Sutcliffe, asking them to include "curves and performance space" in the design. Aside from his books, Stewart plays violin with a local orchestra. The performance space in his house can seat 150 people. The main living space is one floor below the entry, given the sloped site. Glenn Lowry, Director of New York's Museum of Modern Art (and client of the House on Henry's Meadow, page 372), calls the **INTEGRAL HOUSE** "one of the most important private houses in North America."

Das große Privatanwesen liegt in einer bewaldeten Schlucht und bietet u. a. Raum für Musik und Aufführungen. Die Architekten schreiben: „Kurvenförmige, geschwungene Glasfronten mit synkopisch angeordneten Eichenholz-Lamellen definieren den großen Raum, wo Gebäude und Landschaft ineinandergreifen. Der Weg durchs Haus ist dem Abstieg in die Schlucht nachempfunden; hier werden die Vorzüge des Geländeprofils genutzt, die Reise durch den Bau gewinnt zusätzlich an Faszination." Das fünfgeschossige Haus wurde für James Stewart, Mathematiker und Verfasser zahlreicher weithin genutzter Lehrwerke zur Analysis, gebaut. Stewart sprach mit verschiedenen Architekten, darunter auch Frank Gehry, bevor er Shim-Sutcliffe beauftragte, einen Entwurf zu entwickeln, der „Kurven und einen Aufführungsraum" umfassen sollte, denn der Bauherr ist nicht nur Autor, sondern auch Violinist in einem Orchester. Der Konzertsaal bietet 150 Menschen Platz. Der Hauptwohnbereich liegt, bedingt durch das abschüssige Grundstück, unterhalb der Zugangsebene. Glenn Lowry, Direktor des New Yorker Museum of Modern Art (und Bauherr des Hauses auf Henrys Wiese, Seite 372), nannte das **INTEGRAL-HAUS** „eines der bedeutendsten Privathäuser Nordamerikas".

Cette importante résidence, en bordure d'un ravin boisé, comprend également des pièces pour la musique et des spectacles. « Des murs ondulés, habillés d'ailettes de chêne syncopées mettent en forme un vaste espace de réunion où le bâti et le paysage s'entrecroisent. Le parcours à travers la maison reproduit l'expérience de la descente de la pente du ravin en profitant du profil du terrain », expliquent les architectes. Répartie sur cinq niveaux, cette maison a été construite pour James Stewart, auteur de manuels de mathématiques et violoniste dans un orchestre local. Il s'est entretenu avec de nombreux architectes, dont Frank Gehry, avant de sélectionner Shim et Sutcliffe et leur a demandé de prévoir « des courbes et un espace pour spectacles » dans le projet. Cet espace peut accueillir 150 personnes. La maison étant construite dans une pente, le séjour principal est situé sous l'entrée. Glenn Lowry, directeur du Musée d'art moderne de New York – et commanditaire de la Maison sur la prairie d'Henry, page 372 –, a qualifié l'**INTEGRAL HOUSE** de l'« une des plus importantes résidences privées construites depuis longtemps aux États-Unis ».

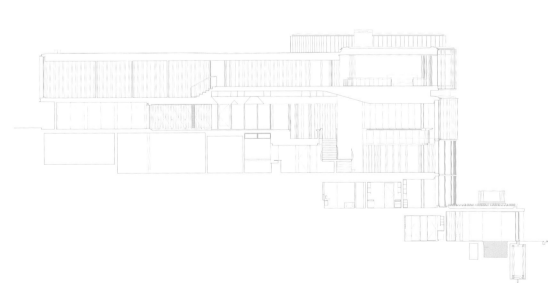

Left page, a covered pool looks into the forest. Above and in the drawing on this page, the complex musicality of the design, highlighted by the use of different materials, is evident.

Ein Pool mit Überdachung (linke Seite) gewährt einen Blick in den Wald. Oben und in der Zeichnung auf dieser Seite wird die komplexe Musikalität des Entwurfs deutlich, die durch den Einsatz verschiedener Materialien betont wird.

Page de gauche : une piscine couverte donne sur la forêt. La photographie ci-dessus et le plan ci-contre témoignent de la musicalité complexe du projet, mise en valeur par le choix des matériaux.

The client asked the architects for curves and, as the plan on this page shows, he got his money's worth. Below, blue glass lines a stairway, contrasting with the otherwise beige or brown tonalities seen in the house.

Le client qui avait demandé à ses architectes de prévoir des courbes a été écouté, comme le montre le plan de cette page. Ci-dessus, un escalier lambrissé de verre bleu qui contraste avec les tonalités beiges et brunes du reste de la maison.

Der Bauherr wünschte sich Kurven und bekam etwas für sein Geld, wie der Grundriss auf dieser Seite belegt. Unten eine Treppe, eingefasst in blaues Glas, ein Kontrast zu den Beige- und Brauntönen, die sonst im Haus zu sehen sind.

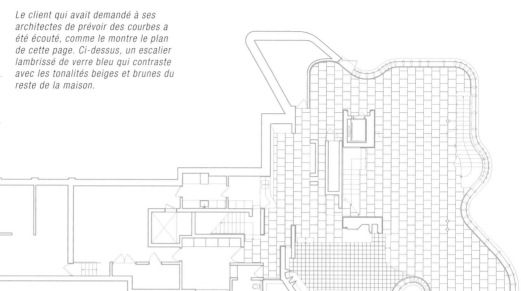

The undulating exterior façade has its logical counterpart in this generous double-height interior space.

Der geschwungene Fassade findet ihr logisches Gegenstück im hier zu sehenden großzügigen, doppelge- schossigen Innenbereich.

La façade extérieure ondulée se retrouve dans ce généreux volume double hauteur.

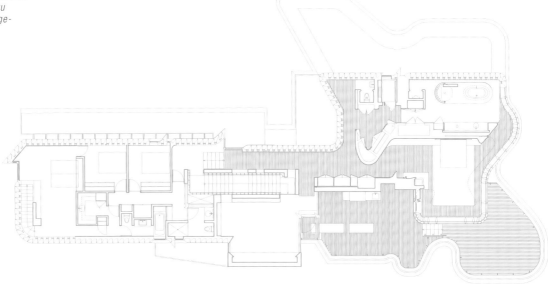

The curved wooden façade allows for a continual view of the natural setting, and of course brings natural light inside. Below, bathroom and bedroom spaces.

Die geschwungene Holzlamellenfassade ermöglicht rundum Ausblicke in die Landschaft und lässt Tageslicht herein. Unten ein Bad und ein Schlafzimmer.

La façade de bois ondulée offre une vue continue sur la nature environnante tout en laissant pénétrer la lumière naturelle. Ci-dessous, une salle de bains et une chambre.

HOUSE ON HENRY'S MEADOW

Vale Perkins, Canada, 2008–09

Area: 266 m². Client: Glenn and Susan Lowry
Cost: not disclosed
Collaboration: Olga Pushkar

The dark coloring of the house allows it to blend into the forest environment, which has been left largely untouched.

Mit seiner eher dunklen Palette fügt sich der Bau harmonisch in die Waldlandschaft, die weitgehend unberührt blieb.

La teinte foncée du bois laisse la maison se fondre encore mieux dans son cadre boisé, laissé en grande partie intact.

A site plan shows the proximity of the house to the lake. Above, an alternation of low stone walls, gravel surfaces, and a pond eases the transition to the forest, which is just beyond.

Ein Lageplan veranschaulicht die Nähe des Hauses zum See. Oben ein Wechselspiel von niedrigen Natursteinmauern, Kies und einem Teich – so entsteht ein fließender Übergang zum Wald direkt hinter dem Haus.

Le plan du site montre la proximité de la maison et du lac. Ci-dessus, l'alternance de murets de pierre, de surfaces en gravier et d'un bassin rend plus fluide la transition vers la forêt, juste derrière.

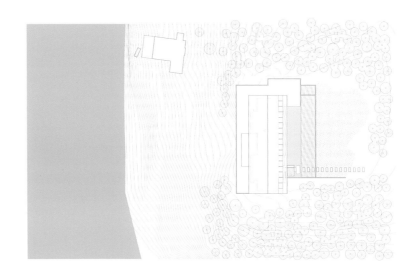

This residence, built for the Director of New York's Museum of Modern Art, is located on the western shore of Lake Memphremagog, near the border between Quebec and Vermont. The house is built on a property with several existing buildings, including a 1920s log cabin that served as a family meeting place for decades. The local tradition of surrounding farms with walls of stacked firewood served as a starting point for the house. Visitors to the house first see a stacked-log wall, and then "a vertical sky-lit slot above wooden light coffers [that] provides deep views through the house and of the stair to the lower level. A clerestory window bringing light to the lower level also allows the seemingly heavy stacked-wood wall to float above the reflecting pool," according to the architects. The north and south elevations are clad in painted wood siding. The main living space is clad with local white pine boards and provides glimpses of Henry's Meadow through the stacked-wood walls on one side and panoramic views of the lake on the other.

Das am Westufer des Lake Memphremagog gelegene Haus unweit der Grenze von Quebec und Vermont entstand für den Direktor des New Yorker Museum of Modern Art. Auf dem Grundstück stehen bereits mehrere ältere Bauten, darunter ein Blockhaus aus den 1920er-Jahren, das der Familie jahrzehntelang als Treffpunkt diente. Ausgangspunkt für den Entwurf war die ländliche Tradition, Kaminholz an den Hauswänden zu stapeln. Besuchern fällt zunächst eine Wand aus gestapeltem Holz ins Auge, erst später „die Treppe zur unteren Ebene und Durchblicke durch das Haus, ermöglicht durch ein vertikales Lichtband über kassettierten Oberlichtern aus Holz. Das Oberlichtfenster, das die untere Ebene mit Tageslicht versorgt, lässt den Eindruck entstehen, die scheinbar massive Kaminholzwand schwebe über dem Spiegelbecken", so die Architekten. Nord- und Südseite haben eine Außenwandverschalung aus gestrichenem Holz. Der Hauptwohnraum wurde mit Brettern aus regionaler Kiefer verkleidet und bietet durch die Kaminholzstapel einen Blick auf Henrys Wiese sowie auf der anderen Seite einen Panoramablick auf den See.

Cette maison construite pour le directeur du Musée d'art moderne de New York, est située sur la côte ouest du lac Memphremagog, près de la frontière entre le Québec et le Vermont. Elle a été édifiée sur un terrain déjà occupé par plusieurs constructions dont une cabane en rondins des années 1920 utilisée par la famille depuis des décennies. Le projet a pris pour point de départ la tradition locale d'empiler le bois de chauffage contre les murs. Les visiteurs se trouvent donc tout d'abord confrontés à un mur de bûches de bois. « Une ouverture verticale étroite offre une perspective à travers la maison et sur l'escalier au niveau inférieur. Un lanterneau filant qui éclaire le niveau inférieur donne l'impression que le mur de bûches flotte au-dessus d'un bassin », expliquent les architectes. Les façades nord et sud sont parées de bardeaux de bois peint. Le séjour principal, habillé de planches de pin clair, offre un coup d'œil sur la prairie d'Henry à travers le mur en bûches de bois d'un côté et des vues panoramiques vers le lac de l'autre.

Using the local practice of stacking wood, the architects have made an entire façade of logs, giving the house a decidedly rural appearance from this angle.

Die Architekten griffen die lokale Tradition auf, Kaminholz vor dem Haus zu stapeln, und gestalteten eine entsprechende Fassade, die dem Bau deutlich rustikalen Charme verleiht.

S'inspirant d'une coutume locale d'entreposage du bois, les architectes ont entièrement habillé de rondins une façade, conférant à ce projet un aspect résolument rural, vu sous cet angle.

The stacked logs are also visible from the interior. Below, a plan of the house, and a dining table with a view on the lake.

Auch von innen sind die gestapelten Scheite zu sehen. Unten ein Grundriss des Hauses und ein Essplatz mit Blick auf den See.

L'empilement des rondins est également visible de l'intérieur. Ci-dessous, un plan de la maison et le coin repas qui donne sur la forêt.

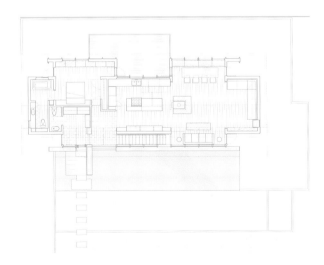

UID ARCHITECTS

UID architects
MORIxhako 2F
3–10–20 Kinosho-cho,
Fukuyama-City
Hiroshima 720–0082
Japan

Tel: +81 84 927 0136
Fax: +81 84 927 0146
E-mail: uid@maeda-inc.jp
Web: www.maeda-inc.jp/uid/

KEISUKE MAEDA was born in 1974 in Hiroshima, Japan, and graduated from the Department of Architecture of Kokushikan University (1999). UID architects was established by Maeda in Hiroshima in 2003. Aside from architecture, the firm specializes in interior design, furniture, exhibition and product design, urban design, planning, consulting, and research. Keisuke Maeda presently lectures at the Hiroshima Institute of Technology. His work includes the Holocaust Education Center (Hiroshima, 2007); House in Tomonoura (Hiroshima, 2008); Art Flow House (Hiroshima, 2008); Rustic House (Fukuyama, 2009); MORI x hako (Hiroshima, 2009); Atelier Bisque Doll (Osaka, 2009); Tumuji + Hako Hosue (Fukuyama, 2010); Nest (Hiroshima, 2010, published here); and the Machi House (Fujuyama, 2011), all in Japan.

KEISUKE MAEDA, geboren 1974 in Hiroshima, schloss sein Studium an der Architekturfakultät der Kokushikan University (1999) ab. 2003 gründete Maeda sein Büro UID architects in Hiroshima. Außer auf Architektur konzentriert sich das Büro auch auf Innenarchitektur, Möbel-, Ausstellungs- und Produktdesign, Stadtplanung, Beratung und Forschung. Gegenwärtig lehrt Keisuke Maeda am Hiroshima Institute of Technology. Zu seinen Arbeiten zählen das Holocaust Education Center (Hiroshima, 2007), ein Haus in Tomonoura (Hiroshima, 2008), das Art Flow House (Hiroshima, 2008), das Rustic House (Fukuyama, 2009), MORI x hako (Hiroshima, 2009), das Atelier Bisque Doll (Osaka, 2009), das Haus Tumuji + Hako (Fukuyama, 2010), das Haus Nest (Hiroshima, 2010, hier vorgestellt) sowie das Haus Machi (Fujuyama, 2011), alle in Japan.

KEISUKE MAEDA est né à Hiroshima en 1974. Diplômé du département d'architecture de l'université de Kokushikan (1999), il a fondé l'agence UID architects à Hiroshima en 2003. En dehors de l'architecture, il s'intéresse également à l'architecture intérieure, le mobilier, les expositions, le design produit, l'urbanisme, le consulting et la recherche. Keisuke Maeda enseigne actuellement à l'Institut de technologie d'Hiroshima. Parmi ses réalisations, toutes au Japon : le Centre d'éducation à l'Holocauste (Hiroshima , 2007) ; une maison à Tomonoura (Hiroshima , 2008) ; la maison Art flow (Hiroshima , 2008) ; la maison Rustic (Fukuyama, 2009) ; MORI x hako (Hiroshima , 2009) ; l'Atelier Bisque Doll (Osaka, 2009) ; la maison Tumuji + Hako (Fukuyama, 2010) ; la maison Nest (Hiroshima, 2010, publiée ici) et la maison Machi (Fujuyama, 2011).

NEST

Onomichi, Hiroshima, Japan, 2010

Area: 121 m². Client: not disclosed
Cost: not disclosed

Seen from the exterior at nightfall, the house seems to be completely open inside, as indeed it is.

Von außen betrachtet wirkt das Haus in der Abenddämmerung innen völlig offen – was tatsächlich der Fall ist.

Dans cette vue prise à la tombée de la nuit, la maison semble entièrement ouverte à l'intérieur, ce qu'elle est en réalité.

This house, located in a forest near a mountain, was designed for a mother and her two daughters. Given the relation of the clients, the architect imagined the metaphor of the nest. "It is like a principle that expands from a nest in a forest, to the forest, then to the earth, and ultimately to the universe," says the architect. Spaces inserted into the ground are compared to "a concrete anthill nest," while the areas above are likened to "a floating wooden nest box composed of things like branches and fallen leaves…" The wood surface of the house is punctured by large openings, some glazed and others open. Aside from this repeated metaphor, the house also offers something that Japanese designers (and their clients) often seek—proximity to nature in its many forms, including light, wind, or the feeling of the forest in this instance.

Das in einem Wald bei einem Berg gelegene Haus wurde für eine Mutter und ihre zwei Töchter geplant. Angeregt durch die Familienkonstellation arbeitete der Architekt mit der Metapher des Nests. „Es ist ein Prinzip, das den Bogen schlägt vom Nest zum Wald, zur Erde und hinaus ins Universum", so der Architekt. Die in den Boden versenkten Zonen vergleicht er mit einem „Ameisenhaufen aus Beton", die oberen Bereiche beschreibt er als „schwebenden Nistkasten aus Ästen und Laub …". Die Holzfassade des Hauses ist mit großen Öffnungen durchsetzt, von denen einige verglast, andere offen sind. Abgesehen von der sich wiederholenden Metapher bietet das Haus etwas, das Architekten (und Bauherren) in Japan oft suchen – die Nähe zur Natur in ihrer vielfältigen Gestalt, zum Licht, zum Wind oder, wie hier, zum Wald.

Construite en forêt dans une région montagneuse, cette maison a été conçue pour sa propriétaire et ses deux filles. Afin de répondre à cette configuration familiale particulière, l'architecte a pensé à la métaphore du nid. « C'est un peu comme un principe qui se développerait du nid en forêt vers la forêt, puis vers la terre et enfin vers l'univers », explique-t-il. Les volumes insérés dans le sol sont ainsi comparés à « une vraie fourmilière », et les parties supérieures à « un nid de bois en suspension, composé de choses comme des branches et des feuilles tombées… » La façade en bois de la maison est rythmée de grands percements, certains laissés ouverts, d'autres vitrés. En dehors de cette métaphore, la maison propose également quelque chose que les architectes japonais (et leurs clients) recherchent souvent, la proximité à la nature sous de multiples formes, dont la lumière, le vent ou, comme ici, le sentiment de la présence de la forêt.

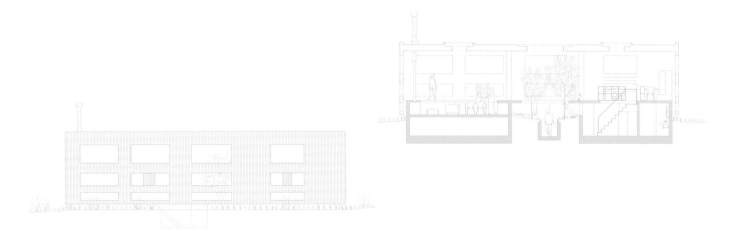

Elevation and section drawings, as well as the interior photo below, show the open interior space with the somewhat surprising tree and rock formation in its midst.

Aufriss und Querschnitte sowie eine Ansicht des Innenraums (unten) zeigen den offenen Innenbereich mit einer überraschenden Baum- und Felsformation in der Mitte.

Les dessins de coupe et d'élévation, ainsi que la photo ci-dessous, montrent le volume intérieur entière-ment ouvert avec, au centre, une étonnante rocaille plantée d'un arbre.

As the plan below and the images on this double page demonstrate, the very heart of the house is given over to a nearly natural setting, with trees growing through the open center.

Wie der Grundriss unten und die Aufnahmen auf dieser Doppelseite zeigen, beherrscht eine fast natürliche Szenerie das Herz des Hauses. Bäume wachsen in der offenen Mitte.

Comme le montrent le plan ci-dessous et les deux photographies, le cœur même de la maison est consacré à une reconstitution de décor naturel planté d'arbres.

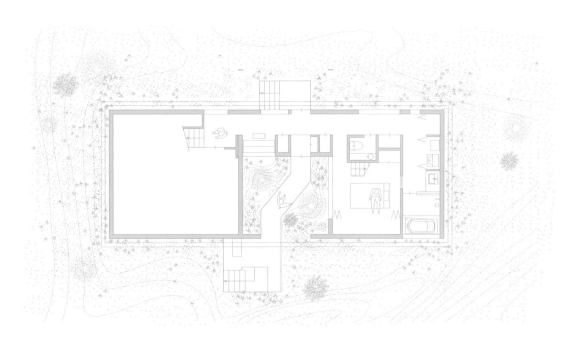

Wood is mixed with concrete for the surface finishes (above). An exploded axonometric drawing shows the relation of the house to the trees. Right, the upper level.

Beim Innenausbau trifft Holz auf Beton (oben). Eine Explosionszeichnung veranschaulicht das Verhältnis der Bäume zum Haus. Rechts die obere Wohnebene.

Le second œuvre associe le bois et le béton (ci-dessus). Un dessin axonométrique éclaté montre la relation entre la maison et son environnement arboré. À droite, l'étage.

Large windows emphasize the open-ness of the house and offer views of the forest. Light comes from above and from the sides.

Große Fenster unterstreichen die Offenheit des Hauses und bieten Aus-blicke in den Wald. Licht fällt von den Seiten und von oben ein.

Les grandes baies augmentent l'impression d'ouverture et offrent des vues sur la forêt. La lumière vient à la fois des côtés et du plafond.

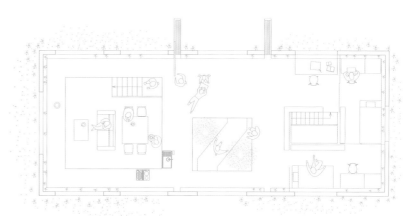

UNSTUDIO

UNStudio
Stadhouderskade 113
1073 AX Amsterdam
The Netherlands

Tel: +31 20 570 20 40
Fax: +31 20 570 20 41
E-mail: info@unstudio.com
Web: www.unstudio.com

BEN VAN BERKEL was born in Utrecht, the Netherlands, in 1957 and studied at the Rietveld Academy in Amsterdam and at the Architectural Association (AA) in London, receiving the AA Diploma with honors in 1987. After working briefly in the office of Santiago Calatrava in 1988, he set up his practice in Amsterdam with Caroline Bos. As well as the Erasmus Bridge in Rotterdam (1996), Van Berkel & Bos Architectural Bureau has built the Karbouw and ACOM (1989–93) office buildings, and the REMU Electricity Station (1989–93), all in Amersfoort. Other works include the Möbius House (Naarden, 1993–98); Het Valkhof Museum (Nijmegen, 1998); and NMR Laboratory (Utrecht, 2000), all in the Netherlands; VilLA NM (Upstate New York, USA, 2000–06); and the Mercedes-Benz Museum (Stuttgart, Germany, 2003–06). More recent work includes the Music Theater (Graz, Austria, 1998–2008); Star Place (Kaohsiung, Taiwan, 2006–08); Burnham Pavilion (Chicago, Illinois, USA, 2009); Haus am Weinberg (Stuttgart, Germany, 2010–11, published here); l'Park City (Suwon, South Korea, 2008–12); Arnhem Station (the Netherlands, 1996–2014); Raffles City (Hangzhou, China, 2008–14); Singapore University of Technology and Design (Singapore, 2010–14); the Dance Palace in St. Petersburg (Russia, 2009–); and Kutaisi Airport (Georgia, 2011–).

BEN VAN BERKEL wurde 1957 in Utrecht geboren und studierte an der Rietveld-Akademie in Amsterdam sowie an der Architectural Association (AA) in London, wo er 1987 das Diplom mit Auszeichnung erhielt. Nach einem kurzen Arbeitseinsatz 1988 bei Santiago Calatrava gründete er mit Caroline Bos sein Büro in Amsterdam. Neben der Erasmusbrücke in Rotterdam (1996) baute das Van Berkel & Bos Architectural Bureau die Büros für Karbouw und ACOM (1989–93) sowie das Kraftwerk REMU (1989–93), alle in Amersfoort. Weitere Projekte sind u. a. das Haus Möbius (Naarden, 1993–98), das Museum Het Valkhof (Nimwegen, 1998) und das Labor NMR (Utrecht, 2000), alle in den Niederlanden, die VilLA NM (bei New York, 2000–06) und das Mercedes-Benz-Museum (Stuttgart, 2003–06). Jüngere Arbeiten sind u. a. ein Musiktheater in Graz (1998–2008), der Star Place (Kaohsiung, Taiwan, 2006–08), der Burnham-Pavillon (Chicago, 2009), das Haus am Weinberg (Stuttgart, 2010–11, hier vorgestellt), l'Park City (Suwon, Südkorea, 2008–12), der Bahnhof Arnhem (Niederlande, 1986–2014), Raffles City (Hangzhou, China, 2008–14), die Hochschule für Technik und Design Singapur (2010–14), der Tanzpalast in St. Petersburg (seit 2009) und der Flughafen Kutaisi (Georgien, seit 2011).

BEN VAN BERKEL, né à Utrecht en 1957 a étudié à l'Académie Rietveld à Amsterdam et à l'Architectural Association (AA) de Londres, dont il est sorti diplômé avec les honneurs (1987). Après avoir brièvement travaillé pour Santiago Calatrava en 1988, il a ouvert son agence à Amsterdam en association avec Caroline Bos. En dehors du pont Erasmus à Rotterdam (1996), l'agence Van Berkel & Bos Architectural Bureau a réalisé les immeubles de bureaux Karbouw et ACOM (1989–93) ; la centrale électrique REMU (1989–93) à Amersfoort. L'agence a également signé la maison Möbius (Naarden, 1993–98) ; le musée Het Valkhof (Nijmegen, 1998) ; le laboratoire NMR (Utrecht, 2000) ; la villa NM (Upstate New York, 2000–06) et le musée Mercedes-Benz (Stuttgart, 2003–06). UNStudio a aussi réalisé une salle de concerts (Graz, Autriche, 1998–2008) ; le centre commercial Star Place (Kaohsiung, Taïwan, 2006–08) ; le pavillon Burnham (Chicago, Illinois, 2009) ; la maison du Weinberg (Stuttgart, 2010–11, publiée ici) ; les immeubles de logements l'Park City (Suwon, Corée-du-Sud, 2008–12) ; la gare d'Arnhem (Pays-Bas, 1986–2014) ; la tour Raffles City (Hangzhou, Chine, 2008–14) ; l'Université de technologie et de design de Singapour (Singapour, 2010–14) ; le Palais de la danse de Saint-Pétersbourg (Russie, 2009–) et l'aéroport de Kutaisi (Géorgie, 2011–).

HAUS AM WEINBERG
Stuttgart, Germany, 2010–11

Area: 618 m². Client: not disclosed
Cost: not disclosed
Collaboration: Astrid Piber, René Wysk, Kirsten Hollmann-Schröter

Seen in this distant view, the house very clearly stands out from the rest of the urban setting that opens at its feet.

Aus der Entfernung hebt sich der Bau deutlich vom städtischen Umfeld ab, der sich zu seinen Füßen ausbreitet.

Vue de loin, la maison se détache clairement du cadre urbain qui s'étend à ses pieds.

Right page, drawings show the different components of the house. The curving roof wraps around the fully glazed interior volume seen in the photograph.

Die Zeichnungen auf der rechten Seite zeigen die einzelnen Komponenten der Hauses. Auf dem Foto umfängt das geschwungene Dach den gläsernen Baukörper.

Page de droite : les dessins montrent les différents éléments constitutifs de la maison. Le toit incurvé enveloppe le volume principal entièrement vitré (photographie de droite).

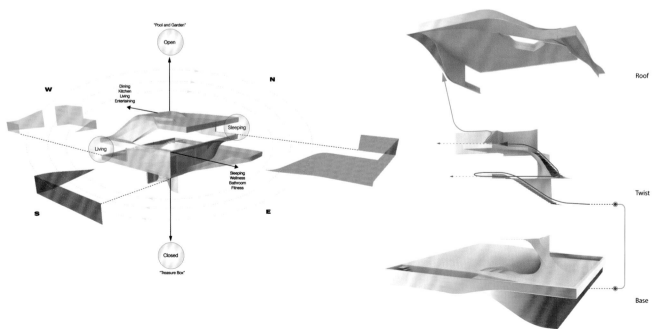

The **HAUS AM WEINBERG** is located at the juncture between rural and urban settings. As the architects explain their design: "The inner circulation, organization of the views, and the program distribution of the house are determined by a single gesture, 'the twist.' In the Haus am Weinberg the central twist element supports the main staircase as it guides and organizes the main flows through the house. The direction of each curve is determined by a set of diagonal movements. Whilst the program distribution follows the path of the sun, each evolution in the twist leads to moments in which views to the outside become an integral experience of the interior." The load-bearing concrete structure was willfully reduced to the minimum. The roof and floor plates are supported by the elevator shaft, two pillars, and a single interior column. All four corners of the structure are glazed and free of columns. A double-height glazed dining area offers views to the northwest, where sliding panes allow the house to be entirely opened. Natural oak flooring, natural stone, and white clay stucco walls are used in the interiors. A darker multipurpose room is located at the core of the house.

Das **HAUS AM WEINBERG** liegt an der Schnittstelle von urbanem und ländlichem Raum. Die Architekten erklären: „Die Wege durchs Haus, die Organisation der Blickachsen und die Verteilung des Programms ergeben sich aus einer einzigen Geste, ‚der Drehung'. Das zentrale Drehelement im Haus am Weinberg manifestiert sich in der Haupttreppe, die die Verkehrswege vorgibt und organisiert. Die Richtung jeder Kurve wird von verschiedenen Diagonalen bestimmt. Während sich die Verteilung der Räume am Sonnenlauf orientiert, erschließt jede neue Drehung Momente, in denen der Blick nach draußen zum integralen Bestandteil des Innenraums wird." Das Betontragwerk wurde bewusst auf ein Minimum reduziert. Dach und Geschossplatten werden vom Aufzugsschacht, zwei Stützen und einer einzelnen Stütze im Innenraum getragen. Alle vier Ecken des Baus sind verglast und stützenfrei. Der hohe verglaste Essbereich bietet Ausblicke nach Nordwesten; hier lässt sich das Haus mit Schiebeelementen vollständig öffnen. Im Haus dominieren Eichenböden, Naturstein und weißer Putz, ein Mehrzweckraum im Herzen des Hauses ist in dunkleren Tönen gehalten.

Cette maison est située à la jonction de la ville et de la campagne. Comme l'expliquent les architectes : « La circulation intérieure, l'organisation des vues et la distribution du programme de la maison sont déterminés par un geste unique, "une torsion". Dans la **MAISON DU WEINBERG**, l'élément central en torsion qui soutient l'escalier principal guide et organise les principaux flux à travers la maison. La direction prise par chaque courbe est déterminée par un ensemble de mouvements en diagonale. Si la distribution du programme suit le déplacement du soleil, chaque évolution de la torsion produit des moments où les vues sur l'extérieur deviennent partie intégrante de la vie dans la maison. » La structure porteuse en béton a été réduite au minimum. Les dalles de sol et de toiture sont soutenues par le puits de l'ascenseur, deux piliers et une colonne interne. Les quatre angles de la maison sont vitrés et libérés de toute colonne. Une salle à manger vitrée double hauteur jouit de vues vers le nord-ouest et de grands panneaux coulissants permettent d'ouvrir entièrement la maison sur le paysage. Les sols en chêne naturel, la pierre et les murs en stuc blanc animent l'intérieur. Une pièce multifonctionnelle forme le noyau de la maison.

Ben van Berkel and UNStudio have long been interested in the continuity of space: here ceilings, walls, and floors appear to flow into each other.

Räumliche Kontinuität ist seit Langem ein Thema für Ben van Berkel und UNStudio. Hier scheinen Decken, Wände und Böden ineinander überzugehen.

Ben van Berkel et UNStudio s'intéressent depuis longtemps à la continuité de l'espace : ici, les plafonds, les murs et les sols semblent former un flux continu.

To the right, the dining area; below, a corner of the kitchen, both with high, glazed walls.

Rechts der Essbereich, unten eine Ecke in der Küche – beide Bereiche sind raumhoch verglast.

À droite, la partie salle à manger et, ci-dessous, un coin de la cuisine, tous deux bénéficiant d'une immense baie vitrée.

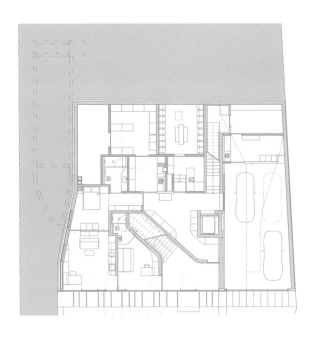

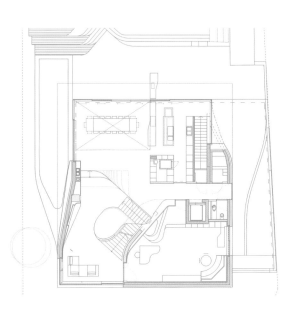

The main stairway flows down and broadens as it descends. Wooden floors contrast with the white walls and ceilings. Plans show the complexity of the interiors.

Die Haupttreppe schwingt sich fließend und breiter werdend nach unten. Holzböden bilden einen Kontrast zu weißen Wänden und Decken. Etagengrundrisse belegen die Komplexität des Raumgefüges.

L'escalier principal, dont la largeur se rétrécit en montant. Les planchers de bois contrastent avec les murs et les plafonds blancs. Les plans montrent la composition complexe de l'intérieur.

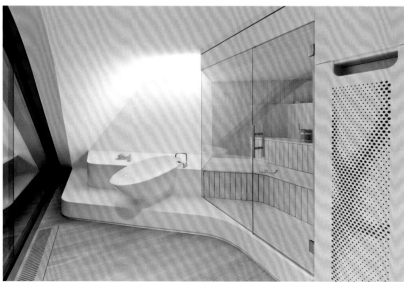

Left, a bathtub with a view, and the curving walls that define the forms of the stairway and make it appear to emerge in the midst of the house like an organic part of the design.

Links eine Wanne mit Aussicht und die geschwungenen Wände, die die Formen der Treppe definieren und dafür sorgen, dass sie scheinbar organisch in der Mitte des Hauses entspringt.

À gauche, une baignoire « avec vue » et le mur incurvé de la cage d'escalier qui semble émerger au milieu de la maison tel un élément organique.

TANIA URVOIS

Tania Urvois
1 Rue du Bois d'Amour
29200 Brest
France

Tel: +33 9 63 64 52 14
Fax: +33 2 98 43 42 23
E-mail: tania@studio-urvois.fr
Web: www.studio-urvois.com

TANIA URVOIS was born in 1974 in Madrid, Spain. She received her B.A. in Environmental Design from the University of Pennsylvania (1993–97), her M.Arch. from the Harvard GSD (1998–2002), and her French architecture degree from the École National Supérieure d'Architecture in Nantes (2007). She worked in the office of Rafael Moneo (Madrid, 1997, 1999), and created her own office Studio Urvois in Brest in 2007. **CLAUDIA URVOIS** received a B.A. in History and Art History from Northwestern University (Chicago, 1998–2002), and a B.A. in Product Design from Central Saint Martins (London, 2002–05). She worked as an interior designer with Studio Urvois (2007–09), before becoming Creative Director of KRT Architecture & Interior Design (Shanghai, 2009–). They have collaborated on Toull Ar Soner (Douarnenez, 2011, published here); a house project (Crozon, 2008–); and a fine foods store in Le Conquet (2011–). Tania Urvois has worked recently on the café of the Domaine de Trévarez (2012) and is presently involved in the construction of an ecological village in Trezmalaouen-Kervel (Plonevez Porzay, 2012–), all in France.

TANIA URVOIS wurde 1974 in Madrid geboren. Sie erlangte ihren B.A. in Environmental Design an der University of Pennsylvania (1993–97), ihren M. Arch. an der Harvard GSD (1998–2002) sowie ein französisches Architekturdiplom an der Ecole Nationale Supérieure d'Architecture in Nantes (2007). Sie arbeitete für Rafael Moneo (Madrid, 1997, 1999) und gründete 2007 ihr Büro Studio Urvois in Brest. **CLAUDIA URVOIS** machte einen B.A. in Geschichte und Kunstgeschichte an der Northwestern University (Chicago, 1998–2002) und einen B.A. in Produktdesign am Central Saint Martins College (London, 2002–05). Sie war zunächst als Innenarchitektin für Studio Urvois (2007–09) tätig, bevor sie Creative Director bei KRT Architecture & Interior Design in Schanghai (seit 2009) wurde. Kollaborationen sind Toull Ar Soner (Douarnenez, 2011, hier vorgestellt), ein Hausprojekt (Crozon, seit 2008) sowie ein Delikatessengeschäft in Le Conquet (seit 2011). Tania Urvois arbeitete unlängst am Café der Domaine de Trévarez (2012) und ist aktuell am Bau eines ökologischen Dorfs in Trezmalaouen-Kervel (Plonevez Porzay, seit 2012) beteiligt, alle in Frankreich.

TANIA URVOIS, née en 1974 à Madrid, a reçu son diplôme de B.A. en conception environnementale de l'université de Pennsylvanie (1993–97) et son M.Arch. de la Harvard GSD (1998–2000) ainsi qu'un diplôme de l'École nationale supérieure d'architecture de Nantes (2007). Elle a travaillé chez Rafael Moneo (Madrid, 1997, 1999) et a ouvert l'agence Studio Urvois à Brest en 2007. **CLAUDIA URVOIS** est diplômée en histoire et histoire de l'art de la Northwestern University (Chicago, 1998–2002) et a reçu un diplôme de B.A. en design produit du Central Saint Martins College (Londres, 2002–05). Elle a travaillé comme architecte d'intérieur au Studio Urvois (2007–09) avant de devenir directrice de la création de KRT Architecture & Interior Design à Shanghai (2009–). Elles ont collaboré sur le projet de la maison Toull Ar Soner (Douarnenez, 2011, publiée ici) ; un projet de maison (Crozon, 2008–) et une épicerie fine au Conquet (2011–). Tania Urvois a récemment travaillé sur le projet du café du Domaine de Trévarez (2012) et participe actuellement à la construction d'un village écologique à Trezmalaouen-Kervel (Plonevez Porzay, 2012–), tous en France.

TOULL AR SONER

Douarnenez, France, 2011

Area: 510 m². Client: SCI Toull Ar Soner
Cost: not disclosed. Collaboration: KRT (Claudia Urvois)

The architect made use of "transparency, reflection, and camouflage" in order to integrate this house into its seashore site while maximizing views of the bay of Douarnenez. The design is made up of a glass pavilion placed on top of a partially buried stone base. The base contains the private areas as well as technical spaces. Seen from the entrance, the glass pavilion seems to sit directly on the earth. It contains a large living area, and a "wooden box" containing the kitchen. Slate is used both in the living area and on the terrace, emphasizing the continuity between exterior and interior. Tania and Claudia Urvois collaborated on the interior design. White surfaces and wood are used in the lower block, while glass, slate, and metal are the main materials in the upper section of the house. The landscaping was done by Erwan Tymen.

Die Architektin nutzte „Transparenz, Spiegeleffekte und Camouflage", um das Haus in sein Umfeld an der Küste einzubinden und zugleich den Blick auf die Bucht von Douarnenez optimal zur Geltung zu bringen. Der Entwurf besteht aus einem Glaspavillon auf einem zum Teil im Boden versenkten Steinsockel. In diesem Sockel sind sowohl die privaten Bereiche als auch die Haustechnik untergebracht. Vom Eingang aus gesehen scheint der Glaspavillon unmittelbar auf der Erde zu stehen. In ihm befindet sich ein großzügiger Wohnbereich sowie eine „Holzbox" mit der Küche. Im Wohnbereich wie auf der Terrasse wurde mit Schiefer gearbeitet, um die Kontinuität zwischen Außen- und Innenraum zu unterstreichen. Die Innenarchitektur entstand in Zusammenarbeit mit Claudia Urvois. Während im unteren Bereich des Hauses weiße Oberflächen und Holz dominieren, sind Glas, Schiefer und Metall die Hauptmaterialien der oberen Zone. Die Landschaftsarchitektur übernahm Erwan Tymen.

L'architecte a eu recours à des principes de « transparence, de reflets et de camouflages » pour intégrer cette maison dans son site côtier tout en optimisant les vues sur la baie de Douarnenez. Le projet se compose d'un pavillon de verre posé sur un socle de pierre en partie enterré, qui contient les parties privées et les installations techniques. Vu de l'entrée, le pavillon de verre semble reposer directement sur le sol. Il regroupe un vaste espace de séjour et une « boîte en bois » contenant la cuisine. L'ardoise au sol et sur la terrasse renforce la continuité entre l'intérieur et l'extérieur. Tania et Claudia Urvois ont collaboré sur les aménagements intérieurs. Dans la partie inférieure, l'accent a été mis sur le bois et des surfaces blanches tandis qu'en partie supérieure, sont privilégiés le verre, l'ardoise et le métal. L'aménagement paysager est dû à Erwan Tymen.

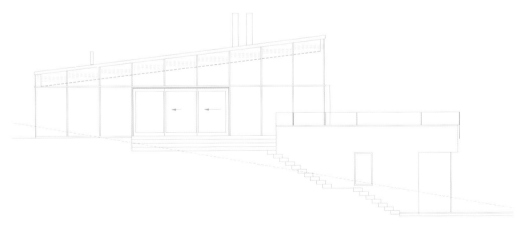

The glazed living space sits above the terraced bedrooms, seen in the image to the left. This page, the dining area and an elevation drawing.

Der verglaste Wohnbereich liegt über den Schlafzimmern mit Terrassenzugang, links im Bild. Auf dieser Seite der Essbereich sowie ein Aufriss.

Le séjour entièrement vitré repose sur une base qui contient les chambres (image de gauche). Ci-dessus, la salle à manger et un dessin d'élévation.

An outdoor dining table on the upper terrace. Right, a site plan and, below, a general view of interior spaces.

Ein Essplatz auf der oberen Terrasse. Rechts ein Lageplan und unten ein Blick in den Innenraum.

Une table pour les repas a été installée sur une des terrasses. À droite, un plan du site et ci-dessous une vue générale de l'intérieur.

The living area rises to double height at the level of the surrounding glass wall. Right, the kitchen with its open view of the exterior.

An den umlaufenden Glasfassaden erreicht der Wohnbereich doppelte Raumhöhe. Rechts die Küche mit unverstelltem Blick nach draußen.

Le séjour bénéficie d'une double hauteur de plafond au niveau de sa façade vitrée. À droite, la cuisine, également ouverte sur l'extérieur.

WERK A

werk A architektur
Lehrterstr.57 / Haus 4
10557 Berlin
Germany

Tel: +49 30 89 73 37 63
Fax: +49 30 89 73 37 64
E-mail: kontakt@werk-a-architektur.de
Web: www.werk-a-architektur.de

GUNTRAM JANKOWSKI was born in Gräfelfing near Munich in 1972. He studied architecture at the Technical University of Berlin (1993–2000). From 1994 to 2002 he did freelance work for several firms such as APP Dominique Perrault (Berlin). He founded werk A in 2003, and was also a partner in Roswag & Jankowski from 2006 to 2009. Since that date he has been the principal of werk A. His work includes Spindler & Klatt, club and restaurant (Berlin-Kreuzberg 2006); Westend Green, a rammed-earth house (Berlin-Westend, 2007); the renovation of the Jahili Fort, museum and visitor center (Al-Ain, Abu Dhabi, UAE, 2008); Lake House (Friedrichswalde, 2010, published here); The Grand, restaurant and bar (Berlin-Mitte, 2012); and the Lake House Studio, studio and workshop building (Friedrichswalde, 2012), all in Germany unless stated otherwise.

GUNTRAM JANKOWSKI wurde 1972 in Gräfelfing bei München geboren. Er studierte Architektur an der Technischen Universität Berlin (1993–2000). Zwischen 1994 und 2002 arbeitete er als freischaffender Architekt u. a. für Büros wie APP Dominique Perrault (Berlin). 2003 folgte die Gründung von werk A, von 2006 bis 2009 war er zudem Partner bei Roswag & Jankowski, seither leitet er eigenverantwortlich werk A. Zu seinen Projekten zählen Spindler & Klatt, Club und Restaurant (Berlin-Kreuzberg 2006), Westend Grün, Einfamilienhaus aus Stampflehm (Berlin-Westend, 2007), Fort Jahili, Sanierung von Museum und Besucherzentrum (Al-Ain, Abu Dhabi, VAE, 2008), Haus am See (Friedrichswalde, 2010, hier vorgestellt), The Grand, Restaurant und Bar (Berlin-Mitte, 2012) sowie ein Atelier- und Werkstattgebäude für das Haus am See (Friedrichswalde, 2012), alle in Deutschland, sofern nicht anders vermerkt.

GUNTRAM JANKOWSKI, né à Gräfelding près de Munich en 1972, a étudié l'architecture à l'Université technique de Berlin (1993–2000). De 1994 à 2002, il a travaillé en free-lance pour diverses agences dont APP Dominique Perrault à Berlin. Il a fondé l'agence werk A en 2003, tout en étant partenaire de l'agence Roswag & Jankowski de 2006 à 2009. Parmi ses réalisations, essentiellement en Allemagne : le club et restaurant Spindler & Klatt (Berlin-Kreuzberg 2006) ; Westend Green, une maison en pisé (Berlin-Westend, 2007) ; la rénovation du fort, musée et centre des visiteurs de Jahili (Al-Ain, Abou Dhabi, EAU, 2008) ; la Maison du lac (Friedrichswalde, 2010, publiée ici) ; le restaurant et bar The Grand (Berlin-Mitte, 2012) et l'atelier de la maison du lac (Friedrichswalde, 2012).

LAKE HOUSE
Friedrichswalde, Germany, 2010

*Area: 48 m². Client: not disclosed
Cost: not disclosed*

Although the materials employed, as for this wooden table, are rough, the broad semicircular window is a modern feature.

Obwohl verschiedene Materialien wie bei dem Holztisch eher rustikal sind, ist das halbrunde Fenster ein modernes Detail.

Bien que les matériaux employés restent traditionnels et bruts, comme par exemple le plateau de cette table, la grande baie semi-circulaire est d'esprit très contemporain.

The village of Friedrichswalde is in the UNESCO Schorfheide-Chorin Biosphere Reserve located in the state of Brandenburg near the Polish border. The town was founded in 1748 by a decree of Frederick II, the king of Prussia. The **LAKE HOUSE** is a prefabricated wooden structure set on the field-stone base of an old barn on a property in the main village street. The house has a rough-sawed larch frame filled with clay bricks. Its large oval windows frame the view of Lake Krummen. The interior surfaces are covered in clay plaster and floor covering is fashioned with recycled panels, tiles, and bricks. A clay-based stove is used for heating.

Die Gemeinde Friedrichswalde liegt in Brandenburg im UNESCO-Biosphärenreservat Schorfheide-Chorin unweit der polnischen Grenze. Die Ortschaft wurde 1748 auf Erlass des Preußenkönigs Friedrich II. gegründet. Das **HAUS AM SEE** ist eine Holzfertigbaukonstruktion und wurde über dem Feldsteinfundament einer alten Scheune auf einem Grundstück an der Dorfstraße errichtet. Das Fachwerk aus sägerauer Lärche wurde mit Tonziegeln ausgemauert. Die ovalen Panoramafenster rahmen den Ausblick auf den Krummensee. Der Innenausbau erfolgte mit Lehmputz, die Böden sind mit alten Fliesen, Paneelen und Ziegeln gestaltet. Geheizt wird mit einem Lehmofen.

Le village de Friedrichswalde, fondé en 1748 par le roi de Prusse Frédéric II, se trouve dans la réserve de la biosphère de Schorfheide-Chorin située dans le land de Brandebourg, près de la frontière polonaise. La **MAISON DU LAC** est une construction préfabriquée en bois posée sur un socle en pierre des champs, qui appartenait à une ancienne grange de la rue principale du village. L'ossature est en bouleau grossièrement débité et le remplissage en briques d'argile. Les grandes fenêtres ovales cadrent des vues sur le lac de Krummen. Les murs intérieurs sont plâtrés et les sol en panneaux de bois recyclé, carrelage et briques. Un poêle en céramique assure le chauffage.

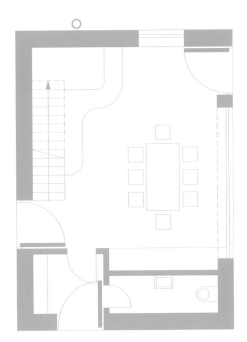
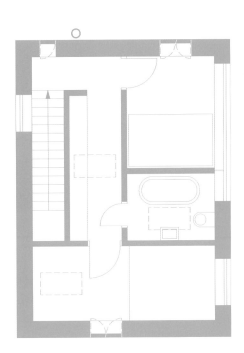

Plans show the strict rectangular configuration of the house. Below, details of the wood cladding and the rounded windows.

Die Grundrisse illustrieren die streng geradlinige Konfiguration des Hauses. Unten Details des Holzverschalung und der Rundfenster.

Le plan montre la configuration strictement orthogonale de la maison. Ci-dessous, détails du bardage extérieur et des fenêtres arrondies.

The round or oval windows make it seem as though interior spaces are entirely open to the exterior. Below, a section drawing with the angled roof visible. Right, the fairly rustic kitchen.

Die runden und ovalen Fenster lassen den Eindruck vollständig offener Räume entstehen. Unten ein Querschnitt, auf dem das Schrägdach zu erkennen ist. Rechts die eher rustikale Küche.

Les fenêtres rondes ou ovales donnent l'impression que les volumes intérieurs sont entièrement ouverts sur l'extérieur. Ci-dessous, un plan de coupe montrant la pente du toit. À droite, la cuisine d'aménagement assez rustique.

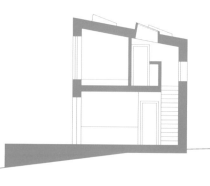

JEAN-MICHEL WILMOTTE

Wilmotte & Associés SA
68 Rue du Faubourg Saint-Antoine
75012 Paris
France

Tel: +33 1 53 02 22 22
Fax: +33 1 43 44 17 11
E-mail: wilmotte@wilmotte.fr
Web: www.wilmotte.com

Born in 1948, a graduate of the Camondo School in Paris, **JEAN-MICHEL WILMOTTE** created his own firm in 1975. Although he is best known for his work in interior design, including numerous galleries of the Louvre (in collaboration with I. M. Pei), Wilmotte joined the Order of Architects in France in 1993. With approximately 200 employees, his office works on industrial and furniture design, such as the lighting fixtures and benches installed on the Champs-Elysées. Wilmotte has completed the Gana Art Center (Seoul, South Korea, 1996–98); a museum for objects given to French President Jacques Chirac in Sarran (France, 2000/2006); the Ullens Center for Contemporary Art (UCCA, Beijing, China, 2006–07); the interior design of the Museum of Islamic Arts (I. M. Pei architect; Doha, Qatar, 2003–08); the Jean-Pierre Raynaud Studio (Barbizon, France, 2009, published here); and the Mandarin Oriental Hotel in Paris (France, 2011). He is completing the interior refurbishment of the Rijksmuseum (Amsterdam, the Netherlands 2012); the new Nice Football Stadium (France, 2010–); and the Arsenal Museum in Kiev (Ukraine, 2010–).

JEAN-MICHEL WILMOTTE, Jahrgang 1948, schloss sein Studium an der Ecole Camondo in Paris ab und gründete 1975 sein eigenes Büro. Obwohl er vor allem für seine innenarchitektonischen Projekte bekannt wurde, darunter die Gestaltung verschiedener Galerien im Louvre (in Zusammenarbeit mit I. M. Pei), ist Wilmotte seit 1993 auch Mitglied der französischen Architektenkammer. Sein Büro beschäftigt rund 200 Mitarbeiter und entwickelt Industrie- und Möbeldesignprojekte, darunter auch die Straßenleuchten und Bänke für die Champs-Elysées. Wilmotte realisierte das Gana Art Center (Seoul, Südkorea, 1996–98), ein Museum in Sarran mit Geschenken, die der französische Präsident Jacques Chirac erhielt (Frankreich, 2000/2006), das Ullens Center for Contemporary Art (UCCA, Peking, 2006–07), die Innenarchitektur des Museums für Islamische Kunst (Architektur von I. M. Pei, Doha, Katar, 2003–08), ein Ateliergebäude für Jean-Pierre Raynaud (Barbizon, Frankreich, 2009, hier vorgestellt) sowie das Mandarin Oriental Hotel in Paris (2011). Vor dem Abschluss stehen derzeit die Sanierung des Reichsmuseums in Amsterdam (2012), das neue Fußballstadion in Nizza (seit 2010) sowie das Arsenal-Museum in Kiew (seit 2010).

Né en 1948, diplômé de l'École Camondo à Paris, **JEAN-MICHEL WILMOTTE** a créé son agence en 1975. Surtout connu au départ pour ses réalisations d'architecture intérieure, dont de nombreuses galeries du Louvre (en collaboration pour I. M. Pei), Wilmotte s'est inscrit à l'Ordre des architectes en 1993. Comptant environ 200 collaborateurs, son agence travaille également sur des projets de design industriel et de mobilier, comme les éclairages et bancs des Champs-Élysées. Parmi ses réalisations : le Centre d'art Gana (Séoul, Corée-du-Sud, 1996–98) ; le musée du président Jacques Chirac (Sarran, France, 2000/2006) ; le Centre d'art contemporain Ullens (UCCA, Pékin, 2006–07) ; l'aménagement intérieur du Musée des arts islamiques (architecte I. M. Pei, Doha, Qatar, 2003–08) ; l'atelier de Jean-Pierre Raynaud (Barbizon, France, 2009, publié ici) et l'hôtel Mandarin oriental (Paris, 2011). Actuellement, il achève la rénovation intérieure du Rijksmuseum (Amsterdam, 2012) ; le nouveau stade de football de Nice (2010–) et le musée de l'Arsenal à Kiev (Ukraine, 2010–).

JEAN-PIERRE RAYNAUD STUDIO

Barbizon, France, 2009

Address: Rue Belle Marie, Barbizon, France
Area: 240 m² (studio); 63 m² (pavilion)
Client: Jean-Pierre Raynaud. Cost: not disclosed

This project is based on an existing Norman-style house called the Clos d'Hortense. The architect removed 1960s extensions to the house and added a large glazed interior space and also developed substantial (475 m²) exterior terraces. A small Nordic-style pavilion that was part of the Norwegian presence at the Universal Exposition of 1889 was rebuilt on the property by a previous owner. Part of the overall composition, the architect suggested painting it black and the artist readily agreed. The landscape design is by Neveux Rouyer. The artist explains: "Barbizon is the first of my studios where nature is conjugated with my own nature, and offers a sort of bridge to the Far East, more particularly with Japan, where flora are more than a living element in a composition, but also part of thought."

Ausgangspunkt für dieses Projekt war ein Altbau im Stil der Normandie, die Clos d'Hortense. Der Architekt ließ Anbauten aus den 1960er-Jahren entfernen und erweiterte das Haus um einen großen Wintergarten und weitläufige Terrassenanlagen (475 m²). Ein kleiner Pavillon im nordischen Stil, ursprünglich Teil des norwegischen Beitrags zur Weltausstellung 1889, war von einem früheren Besitzer auf dem Grundstück rekonstruiert worden und wurde in den Gesamtentwurf integriert; schwarz gestrichen wurde er auf Vorschlag des Architekten, was der Künstler gern aufgriff. Die Landschaftsarchitektur verantwortete Neveux Rouyer. Raynaud erklärt: „Mein Atelier in Barbizon ist das erste meiner Ateliers, in dem die Natur in einen Dialog mit meiner persönlichen Natur tritt; es ist in gewisser Weise ein Brückenschlag nach Fernost, insbesondere Japan, wo die Flora weit mehr als ein lebendiges Element einer Komposition ist, sondern vielmehr Bestandteil des Denkens an sich."

Ce projet s'appuie sur une maison de style normand appelée le Clos d'Hortense. L'architecte a supprimé des extensions datant des années 1960, ajouté un imposant volume vitré et créé de vastes terrasses (475 m²). Un petit pavillon de style scandinave qui avait été celui de la Norvège lors de l'Exposition universelle de 1889 avait été remonté dans la propriété par un propriétaire précédent. Peint en noir à la demande de l'artiste, il fait maintenant partie de la composition d'ensemble. Les aménagements paysagers sont l'œuvre de l'agence Neveux Rouyer. « Barbizon est le premier de mes ateliers dans lequel la nature se conjugue avec ma propre nature et offre une sorte de pont vers l'Extrême-Orient, plus particulièrement vers le Japon, et où la flore est plus qu'un élément vivant d'une composition, mais aussi une part de la réflexion. »

Works by Jean-Pierre Raynaud, such as this large golden pot, are quite present in and around the house. Below, an elevation shows the house to the left and the 1889 pavilion to the right.

Arbeiten von Jean-Pierre Raynaud wie dieser monumentale vergoldete Blumentopf sind überall zu sehen. Ein Aufriss (unten) zeigt links das Haus und rechts den Pavillon von 1889.

Les œuvres de Jean-Pierre Raynaud – comme ce grand pot de fleur doré –, sont assez présentes dans la maison et autour d'elle. Ci-dessous, élévation montrant la maison à gauche et le pavillon de 1889 à droite.

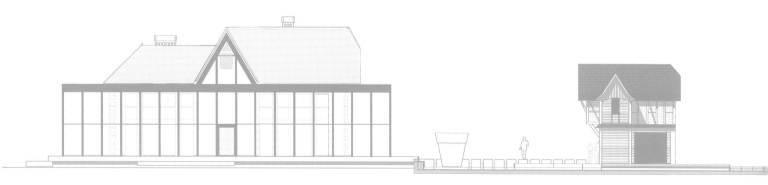

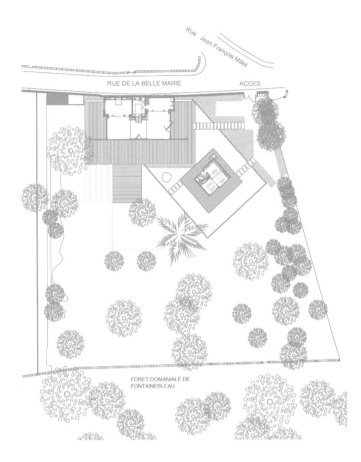

A site plan of the wooded property shows the main house (top) and the smaller pavilion to its right. Below, the main terrace with Raynaud's golden pot.

Ein Lageplan des bewaldeten Grundstücks zeigt das Haupthaus (oben) und den kleineren Pavillon rechts davon. Unten die Hauptterrasse mit Raynauds goldener Topfskulptur.

Le plan de la propriété montre la maison principale (en haut) et le petit pavillon à sa droite. Ci-dessous, la terrasse principale et le pot doré de Raynaud.

Approximately 4000 square meters of the 5183-square-meter property are forested. The main terrace measures 475 square meters and the basin 312 square meters.

Rund 4000 m² des insgesamt 5138 m² großen Grundstücks sind bewaldet. Die Hauptterrasse ist 475 m², der Teich 312 m² groß.

4000 m² environ de cette propriété de 5283 m² sont plantés d'arbres. La terrasse principale mesure 475 m² et le bassin 312 m².

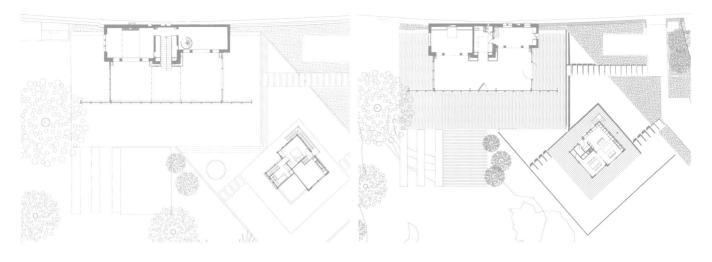

Inside of the main glassed space created by Wilmotte, the artist exhibits works of his own. Above, plans show the two levels of the house and the pavilion.

Im zentralen Glasanbau von Wilmotte präsentiert der Künstler eigene Werke. Etagengrundrisse (oben) zeigen die zwei Ebenen von Haus und Pavillon.

L'artiste présente ses œuvres à l'intérieur du vaste volume vitré imaginé par Wilmotte. Ci-dessus, plans des deux niveaux de la maison et du pavillon.

Jean-Pierre Raynaud has long shown an interest in Asian art as well as his own pieces, which usually call on "ordinary" objects such as pots, flags, or road signs.

Jean-Pierre Raynaud interessiert sich seit Langem für asiatische Kunst. In seinen eigenen Werken greift er in der Regel „alltägliche" Gegenstände auf wie Töpfe, Flaggen oder Straßenschilder.

Jean-Pierre Raynaud s'est longtemps intéressé aux arts de l'Orient. Ses propres pièces s'appuient souvent sur des objets « ordinaires » comme des pots de fleurs, des drapeaux ou des panneaux de signalétique routière.

INDEX OF BUILDINGS, NAMES AND PLACES

INDEX OF BUILDINGS, NAMES AND PLACES

CREDITS